SURVEYORS' LIABILITY
LAW AND PRACTICE

SURVEYORS' LIABILITY
LAW AND PRACTICE

John Virgo MA Oxon, Barrister

and

Ralph Wynne-Griffiths MA Cantab, ACI Arb, Barrister

JORDANS
1998

Published by
Jordan Publishing Limited
21 St Thomas Street, Bristol BS1 6JS

British Library Cataloguing-in-Publication Data
A catalogue record for this book is available from the British Library.

ISBN 0 85308 478 5

Typeset by Mendip Communications Ltd, Frome, Somerset
Printed by MPG Books Ltd, Bodmin, Cornwall

Foreword

In my year as GP Divisional President, I have had the privilege of meeting many surveyors. Most of those hardworking colleagues have shared a concern about the increasingly litigious stance of clients, and the different perceptions about quality and standards of their work.

It is five years since I sat on the Mallinson Working Party which concluded with the publication of the New Red Book. Subsequently, its extensive use by valuers has raised the quality and consistency of valuations considerably, but that is only part of a surveyor's work.

The Red Books by themselves are not enough for client needs; markets and the law move on. Negligence and duty of care provisions therefore need careful understanding by surveyors and lawyers alike, for unfortunately the latter have to become involved as soon as litigation raises its head.

This book has to be recommended for successfully grappling with this huge topic. The two parts dealing with valuation and quantity surveying assist both surveyor in the risk management process and lawyer in understanding the principles of surveying. It is therefore an invaluable work.

Hopefully, students as well as practitioners will find its concise layout and text of great use.

It fills a huge gap in the market and will go a long way in assisting the understanding of all involved with surveyors' liability.

I wish the authors well.

Bruce Duncan BSc FRICS FSVA ACIArb
Cotton Thompson Cole
Wimbledon
February 1998

Preface

This book is intended for surveyors in general practice and for quantity surveyors, but we hope that it will be relevant to surveyors practising in other fields and to their legal advisers. We have divided the task of writing the book between us. John Virgo is responsible for the chapters covering valuations and surveys and Ralph Wynne-Griffiths wrote the chapters on quantity surveying. We have endeavoured to cover the law as it stood at 31 December 1997 but it has been possible, at proof stage, to include some later developments, such as the implementation of Part II of the Housing Grants, Construction and Regeneration Act 1996.

We are extremely grateful to a large number of surveyors and solicitors for their constructive comments, which have been of the greatest help. In particular, we are most grateful to David Anderson FRICS of Mildred Howells for devoting so much of his time and for his encouragement on the chapters dealing with quantity surveying. We would also like to thank Michael Ford of Bond Pearce, Paul Rowe of Wansboroughs and Robert Welfare of Dibb, Lupton Allsop for their helpful comments on the chapters covering valuations and surveys. We would also like to thank our publishers for encouraging us to write the book and for their patience while we struggled to complete it. We are grateful to the Royal Institution of Chartered Surveyors for their kind permission in allowing the reproduction of the materials in the Appendices. Finally, we would both like to thank Bruce Duncan FRICS for his kind Foreword.

We dedicate this book to our wives and children.

John Virgo
Ralph Wynne-Griffiths
Guildhall Chambers
Bristol
February 1998

Contents

Table of Cases

References in the right-hand column are to paragraph numbers.

Table of Statutes

References in the right-hand columns are to paragraph numbers

Table of Statutory Instruments/ EEC Material

References in the right-hand columns are to paragraph numbers.

Table of Professional Guidance etc

References in the right-hand column are to paragraph numbers.

Table of Abbreviations

ACE	The Association of Consulting Engineers
BPF	The British Property Federation
CoWa/F	Form of Agreement for Collateral Warranty for Funding Institutions
CoWa/P&T	Form of Collateral Warranty for Purchasers and Tenants
HBRV	House Buyers' Report and Valuation
HBSV	House Buyers' Survey and Valuation
HSV	Housebuyer Survey and Valuation
ICE	Institute of Civil Engineers
IFC84	JCT Intermediate Form of Building Contract
ISVA	Incorporated Society of Valuers and Auctioneers
JCT	Joint Contracts Tribunal
JCT80	JCT Standard Form of Building Contracts
M & E	Mechanical and Electrical
MW80	JCT Minor Building Works Form of Contract
NJCC	National Joint Consultative Committee for Building
RIBA	Royal Institute of British Architects
RICS	Royal Institution of Chartered Surveyors
RICSIS	Royal Institution of Chartered Surveyors Insurance Services Ltd
SAAMCO	*South Australia Asset Management Corporation* (*v York Montague Ltd* [1996] 3 WLR 87)
SCC	Scheme for Construction Contracts
SMM7	Standard Method of Measurement 7th Edn
SMMIEC	Standard Method of Measurement for Industrial Engineering Construction
SURVIS	Surveyors and Valuers Insurance Services

PART I

THE VALUATION AND SURVEY OF PROPERTY

Chapter 1

MORTGAGE VALUATIONS

RESIDENTIAL PROPERTY

1.1 The typical buyer of a residential property is assisted in his purchase by an advance from a building society or bank. In the case of a building society advance, the lender is obliged to ensure satisfactory arrangements exist for adequately assessing the security for the advance.[1] This includes a duty to obtain and consider a written report on the value of the property in question and upon any factors likely materially to affect its value. The report must be obtained from a person competent to value the property and who is not disqualified under the Building Society Act 1986 from making the report.[2] Although not subject to a similar statutory duty, a bank is unlikely to consider an advance to fund such a purchase without obtaining a similar mortgage valuation report.

1.2 Approximately 90 per cent of applicants for an advance to assist in the purchase of residential property do so without any report other than a mortgage valuation report of the kind referred to in **1.1** being obtained.[3] The valuation is normally prepared by a valuer on a panel of surveyors appointed by the lender for the purpose[4] or by an 'in-house' surveyor employed by the building society.

1.3 Typically, this form of report is commissioned by the lender although ultimately paid for by the prospective borrower either by a direct valuation charge collected by the lender or as part of the mortgage application fee. The report will normally be completed by the valuer on a standard form furnished by the mortgagee with a separate copy being provided to the applicant.

VALUER'S LEGAL RESPONSIBILITY FOR THE REPORT AND VALUATION

1.4 From 1 January 1998, valuations conducted by panel surveyors have been undertaken in accordance with the Model Conditions of Engagement

---

1 Section 13(1) of the Building Society Act 1986 which came into force on 1 January 1987.
2 See s 13(2) of the Act.
3 *Yianni & Anor v Edwin Evans & Sons (a firm)* [1981] 3 All ER 592 at 605.
4 A panel surveyor.

published by the RICS and ISVA[1] where adopted by the parties. It is open to the lender and valuer to agree different terms, although, in most cases, the Model Conditions of Engagement are likely to be the agreed basis of the valuer's retainer. In the case of valuations for lenders, these require the valuer to inspect the proposed security and to report in accordance with the Specification for Residential Mortgage Valuation.[2] The valuer agrees thereby to advise the lender as to the open market value of the property at the date of the inspection along with any factors likely materially to affect its value. The Specification which will be discussed in detail below refers to the extent of the inspection which will be undertaken. A failure to carry out the terms of this engagement with reasonable care and skill will give rise to a breach of contract between the valuer and lender.[3]

1.5 The valuer, having not been commissioned by the borrower to provide the report, owes no similar contractual duty of care to the prospective purchaser. It is, of course, foreseeable that the borrower who is likely in fact to have met the cost of the report will none the less be influenced by the valuer's conclusions in deciding whether to proceed with the purchase. These circumstances led Park J in *Yianni v Edwin Evans & Sons*[4] to conclude that the valuer preparing a mortgage valuation report owed a duty of care in tort to exercise reasonable care and skill in inspecting and reporting upon the proposed security to the borrower.

The facts of this landmark decision deserve attention: the plaintiffs were considering the purchase of a house at its asking price of £15,000 if they could obtain a loan of £12,000 from a building society. They applied to the society for the loan, paying a survey fee for the valuation of the property. The building society instructed the defendants to inspect the house and value it. The society's instructions named the plaintiffs as purchasers, identified the purchase price and the loan required by them. The defendants' representative inspected the house and made a report to the building society in which he stated that the house was adequate security for a loan of £12,000. The building society accepted the report and notified the plaintiffs that it was willing to lend them around £12,000, sending to them a copy of the society's booklet on mortgages which in a paragraph headed 'Valuation' stated that the society did not accept responsibility for the condition of the property offered as security, that it did not warrant that the purchase price was reasonable, that the valuer's report was confidential to the society and for its exclusive use and that if a borrower required a survey of the property for his own information and protection he should instruct an independent surveyor. The plaintiffs accepted the building society's offer without having the house independently surveyed and without ever seeing a copy of the defendants' report. After purchase the plaintiffs discovered cracks in the foundations; the repair cost was estimated at £18,000.

1 See Appendix III.
2 See Appendix III and clause 1 of the Model Conditions attached thereto.
3 Cf clause 1 of the Model Conditions at Appendix III.
4 [1981] 3 All ER 592.

The plaintiffs brought an action against the defendants for damages for negligence. It was alleged that the defendants' statement in their report to the building society that the house was adequate security for a loan of £12,000 meant that the house was worth at least that sum, that that was a negligent statement, that the defendants ought reasonably to have contemplated that the building society would pass on the contents of that statement to the plaintiffs and that the plaintiffs would rely on it and be induced to purchase the house for £15,000 and to mortgage it. The plaintiffs claimed that having done so they had in consequence suffered damage. The defendants admitted negligence but denied owing a duty of care to the borrower. In deciding in the plaintiffs' favour, Park J stated:

> 'It was plainly a house at the lower end of the property market. The applicant for a loan would therefore almost certainly be a person of modest means who, for one reason or another, would not be expected to obtain an independent valuation and who would be certain to rely as the plaintiffs in fact did on the defendants' valuation as communicated to him in the building society's offer. I am sure that the defendants knew that the valuation would be passed on to the plaintiffs and that the defendants knew that the plaintiffs would rely on it when they decided to accept the building society's offer.'[1]

The existence of this duty of care was later confirmed by the House of Lords in *Smith v Eric S Bush*; *Harris v Wyre Forest District Council*.[2] In the former case, a copy of the defendant's valuation report was dispatched to the plaintiffs wrongly stating that no essential repairs were necessary. After purchase, the plaintiffs discovered that the chimneys were in a defective condition and claimed damages from the surveyor. In the latter case, the plaintiffs purchased after a mortgage valuation report had been obtained by their lender. Although they did not see the report, they accepted the mortgage offered. When they came to sell the property three years later, a survey revealed structural defects to the extent that the property was uninhabitable and unsaleable. They brought an action for damages against the surveyor.

In each case, their Lordships concluded it was foreseeable the plaintiffs would be likely to rely on the conclusions of the valuation report; if the report had been negligently prepared (as in each case it had), financial loss would be likely to result to the borrowers and there was a sufficiently proximate relationship between the valuers and prospective purchasers to justify the imposition of a duty of care owed by the one to the other. The lender's recoupment of the valuer's fee from the borrower was regarded as of obvious significance. Lord Griffiths indicated:[3]

> 'The necessary proximity arises from the surveyor's knowledge that the overwhelming probability is that the purchaser will rely on his valuation, the evidence was that surveyors knew that approximately 90 per cent of purchasers did so, and

1 [1981] 3 All ER 592 at 605.
2 [1990] 1 AC 831.
3 [1990] 1 AC 831 at 865.

> the fact that the surveyor only obtains the work because the purchaser is willing to pay his fee.'

In a similar vein, Lord Templeman stated:[1]

> 'The valuer knows that the consideration which he receives derives from the purchaser and is passed on by the mortgagee, and the valuer also knows that the valuation will determine whether or not the purchaser buys the house.'

Yianni was expressly approved.

STANDARD OF CARE

1.6 The standard of care to be expected of the competent mortgage valuer has been summarised in a number of reported decisions.[2] The same standard applies whether the duty being considered is that owed in contract to the lender who has commissioned the report or the buyer who is anticipated to rely upon it. The duty, according to Auld J in *Whalley v Roberts & Roberts*,[3] is: 'to look with the practised eyes of a reasonably competent surveyor for obvious defects that would significantly affect [the] valuation of the property'. In *Smith v Eric S Bush*,[4] Lord Templeman described the duty thus:

> 'The valuer will value the house after taking into consideration major defects which are or ought to be obvious to him in the course of a visual inspection of so much of the exterior and interior of the house as may be accessible to him without undue difficulty.'

The above standard provides for an objective assessment of the surveying valuer's competence so that neither inexperience nor specialist expertise results in the application of a lower or higher (subjective) standard of care. As Graham J said in *Andrew Master Homes Ltd v Cruickshank & Fairweather*:[5]

> 'The degree of knowledge and care to be expected is thus seen to be that degree possessed by a notionally and duly qualified person practising that profession. The test is, therefore, if I may put it that way an objective test referrable to the notional member of the profession and not a subjective test referrable to the particular professional man employed.'

Evidence of the standard of care

1.7 The court will require evidence from a suitably qualified and appropriate expert as to the practices of the ordinary and competent valuer before reaching a decision as to whether a valuation report was negligently prepared.

---

1 [1990] 1 AC 831 at 851.

2 *Roberts v J Hampson & Co* [1989] 2 All ER 504; *Whalley v Roberts & Roberts* [1990] 06 EG 104; *Lloyd v Butler* [1990] 1 EGLR 153; *Smith v Eric S Bush* [1990] 1 AC 831.

3 [1990] 06 EG 104.

4 [1990] 1 AC 831.

5 [1980] RPC 16.

In proving or resisting a claim for professional negligence of a valuer, it will accordingly be important to confine the use of experts addressing that issue to professionals with relevant valuation knowledge, training and experience. Auld J said when dealing with this in *Whalley v Roberts & Roberts*:[1]

> 'In my view it is only the evidence of the surveyors, Mr Dyson and Mr Greenham, that may be of value on this issue. Mr Shore [a civil engineer] and Mr Fairhurst [an architect] however competent they may be in their respective professions, cannot speak with authority on what is to be expected of the ordinarily competent surveyor.'

This was recently confirmed by the decision of the Court of Appeal in *Sansom v Metcalfe Hambleton & Co*,[2] where a finding of negligence against a chartered surveyor at first instance based on the evidence of a structural engineer was overturned. Lord Justice Butler Sloss said:

> 'a court should be slow to find a professionally qualified person guilty of a breach of his duty of skill and care without evidence from those within the same profession as to the standard expected on the facts of the case and the failure of the professionally qualified person to measure up to that standard. While it is not an absolute rule unless it was an obvious case in the absence of the relevant expert the claim would not be proved. As the instant case was not an open and shut case the evidence of the structural engineer was not admissible ... on the issue of the chartered surveyor's negligence.'

1.8 In considering the practices of the ordinary and competent valuer, regard is likely to be had by the profession and the court to the Practice Statements and the Guidance Notes published by the RICS and ISVA. In respect of valuations carried out after 1 January 1998, the relevant materials are found in the RICS Appraisal and Valuation Manual ('the Manual'). This comprises 22 practice statements, compliance with which is mandatory and 18 Guidance Notes (with appendices) which are advisory. Prior to this date, the relevant practice standards were laid down in the Statements of Asset Valuation Practice and Guidance Notes which comprised some 27 statements of practice along with 14 background papers (the so-called 'red book'). This mandatory regime was supplemented by the Manual of Valuation Guidance Notes ('the white book'). These papers offer a useful definition of standard in deciding whether the approach and conclusions of a particular valuation inspection and report have been competently undertaken. Adherence to or departure from the manual and/or the red/white book will not necessarily acquit or convict a valuer of professional negligence. As Sir Michael Ogden QC said in *PK Finans International (UK) Ltd v Andrew Downs & Co Ltd*:[3]

> 'These Guidance Notes are not to be regarded as a statute. I suspect that they are as much for the protection of Surveyors as anything else, in that they set out various recommendations which, if followed, it is hoped will protect the Surveyor from the

1 [1990] 6 EG 104.
2 (1997) *The Times*, 29 December.
3 [1992] 1 EGLR 172.

unpleasantness of being sued. In any event, mere failure to comply with the Guidance Notes does not necessarily constitute negligence.'

In addition, certain building societies provide Guidance Notes of their own to assist the valuer in the completion of its standard form. In practice, these are also treated by the court as equally relevant to issues of professional negligence. Examples of breach of duty are discussed in detail below.

REQUIREMENTS OF THE SPECIFICATION FOR RESIDENTIAL MORTGAGE VALUATIONS

1.9 This document[1] discussed above forms Annex A to Practice Statement 9 of the Manual. The first indicated requirement is that the valuer shall have knowledge and experience in the valuation of residential property in the particular locality where the property to be valued is situated. Where a panel surveyor is appointed, it is likely to be a term of his general retainer that he will only value property within a working radius of typically 20 miles. Where in-house surveyors are employed, depending upon the location of the building society's offices, there may be a greater risk of a valuer having to consider a property outside familiar territory. A good example of this common sense requirement not being followed was the valuer in *Baxter v FW Gapp & Co Ltd*.[2] At first instance, Goddard LJ stated:

'His duty was first of all to use reasonable care in coming to the valuation which he was employed to make and he must be taken to have held himself out as possessing the experience and skill required to value the particular property. If he did not know enough about the property market or the value of the property at the place where the property was situate he ought to have taken steps to inform himself of the values of the properties there or of any circumstances which might affect the property. It would be no defence for instance to say: I made this valuation, but the reason why my valuation has proved inaccurate if it has proved inaccurate is that I was not a person as you know who practised in that locality.'

1.10 Next, the valuer must undertake a reasonably careful visual inspection of so much of the exterior and interior of the property as is accessible to the valuer without undue difficulty. The valuer is not expected to lift carpets, floorboards or even furniture. However, it is to be noted at 3.2 of the Specification:

'If it is suspected that hidden defects exist which could have a material effect on the value of the property the valuer is so to advise and recommend more extensive investigation by the intending borrower prior to entering into a legal commitment to purchase.'

---

1 See Appendix III.
2 [1938] 4 All ER 457.

This accords with the duty imposed by the courts. In *Roberts v J Hampson & Co*,[1] Ian Kennedy J stated:

> 'The position that the law adopts is simple. If a surveyor misses a defect because its signs are hidden, that is a risk that his client must accept. But if there is specific ground for suspicion and the trail of suspicion leads behind furniture or under carpets, the surveyor must take reasonable steps to follow the trail until he has all the information which it is reasonable for him to have before making his valuation.'

An omission to recommend further investigations may be expensive for the valuer so caught out. *In Sneesby v Goldins*,[2] the mortgage valuer failed to notice lack of support where chimney breasts had been removed, being the one obvious sign of shoddy building work. The trial judge held that if that defect had been seen and reported, the purchaser would not have proceeded without commissioning his own survey report which would have revealed a number of other defects. On that basis the purchaser would have been able to negotiate the price with the vendor down and damages were calculated on the basis of its true state with all such further defects.

PARTS TO BE INSPECTED

1.11 Main building – external

(a) Practices vary but many valuers prefer to inspect the exterior of a property first. The condition of the external main building may give an indication as to likely problems within. Hollow or blown rendering may have promoted damp attack internally; blocked or inefficient rainwater goods or roof valleys may have led to timber rot within the roof space. The prudent valuer will note such matters on an external inspection and keep it in mind to check internally whether they have given rise to internal damage to the structure.

(b) Paragraph 2.1 of the Specification lists the following main areas as necessary to a proper external inspection: roof coverings, chimneys, parapets, gutters, walls, windows, doors, pipes, wood or metalwork, paint work, damp proof courses, air bricks and ground levels.

(c) Missed deficiencies in the roof structure accounts for a significant percentage of negligence claims against surveyors. The outward movement of the front and rear walls in *Bigg v Howard Son & Gooch*[3] was indicative of roof spread arising from an inadequate roof design. The defendant was held negligent for failing to identify this particular constellation of symptoms. Similarly, in *Last v Post*,[4] a surveyor who

1 [1988] 2 EGLR 181 at 185.
2 [1995] 2 EGLR 102.
3 [1990] 1 EGLR 173.
4 [1952] 159 EG 240.

missed evidence of roof tile disintegration through efflorescence was found negligent in reporting that the roof was 'soundly constructed'.

(d) In *Smith v Eric S Bush*,[1] it was the omission to notice that chimney breasts had been removed from within the property, leaving the stacks unsupported that led to the finding of liability against the defendant valuer. This is another example of a failure to marry up the internal and external appearances of the premises.

(e) Although a structural survey case, *Kerridge v James Abbot & Partners*[2] is an interesting example of certain exterior defects being observed but not leading to a finding of negligence for failing to warn of their possibly leading to internal dry rot attack of the building fabric: the presence of a valley/parapet gutter, staining of the rafters, holes in the roof and a defective pipe were held not to require such a warning.

(f) The absence or condition of any present damp proof course are important aspects of any inspection for mortgage valuation purposes. The prudent surveyor will also note any evidence of a damp proof course being bridged by external ground levels abutting the property. From such matters the valuer will be able to predict potential damp ingress internally and will need to pay attention to any signs of rotten timbers or dry rot affected areas. Once evidence of dry rot is found even if the attack appears to be dormant the surveyor must 'meticulously examine every bit of wood he [can] sec, to see if there [are] signs of it spreading at all'[3] or at least report what he has found with a sufficient warning of potential risk.

(g) Finally, the condition of the main walls will indicate whether the property is structurally sound. Here it is important to identify the form of construction. In *Peach v Iain G Chalmers & Co*,[4] a valuer was held negligent for valuing a property as if it was made of traditional construction when in reality it was of a 'Dorran' form of build. This entailed construction by means of a series of thin concrete panels bolted together. In the event that these should corrode, repairs would be necessary which would be both extensive and expensive. Most building societies stipulate which forms of non-traditional construction are acceptable for advances so making this a critical part of the valuer's report.

Cracking and patching in the rendering may indicate structural failure in the foundations and a need for underpinning. Scott-Baker J said in *Hipkins v Jack Cotton Partnership*[5] 'these were clues that he should not have missed. These clues led at least to the query that the building was unsound, yet he missed them'.

---

1 [1990] 1 AC 831.
2 [1992] 2 EGLR 162.
3 See *Hardy v Wamsley-Lewis* [1967] 203 EG 1039 per Paull J at 1041.
4 [1992] 2 EGLR 135.
5 [1989] 2 EGLR 157 at 159.

The interpretation of external cracking is a skilled task. The location, width, apparent age and shape/pattern of cracking may suggest a variety of problems: cavity wall tie failure, subsidence, settlement, lintel failure, localised drainage collapse, to name but a few. Where the valuer is unable to diagnose the cause and impact of such matters, he is duty bound to recommend an inspection by another expert (usually an engineer),[1] to indicate the extent of any potential risk and warn the lender/borrower not to proceed until the matter has been fully investigated.[2]

1.12 Main building – internal

(a) Section 2.2 of the Specification defines the principal areas for inspection and contains important exceptions. In particular, furniture and effects are not required to be moved nor floor coverings lifted. Underfloor voids are not inspected. The roof space need only be inspected to the extent visible from the access hatch. As noted above, this does not absolve the surveyor from a duty to 'follow the trail'. As Henry J said in *Fryer v Bunney*:[3]

> '[the surveyor] does not necessarily have to follow up every trail to discover whether there is trouble or the extent of any such trouble. But where such an inspection can reasonably show a potential trouble or the risk of potential trouble, it seems to me it is necessary to alert the purchaser to that risk, because the purchaser will be relying on that valuation form.'

Following a trail of suspicion of damp prompted by any observed defect externally, the valuer will take moisture meter readings at regular intervals internally. A failure to make sufficient use of a protimeter in *Lloyd v Butler*[4] led to a finding of negligence when plumbing leaks which could thereby have been detected were missed.

(b) The 'head and shoulders' roof void inspection appeared in the first edition of the Mortgage Valuations Guidance Notes for Valuers (published in December 1985). *Gibbs v Arnold Son & Hockley*[5] is a good example of the court applying this principle. In that case the valuer was acquitted of negligence for failing to notice cracks in the chimney breast because the judge was not satisfied that these would have been reasonably noticeable from the hatch even with the use of a torch.

Services

1.13 Paragraph 2.3 of the Specification requires the valuer to identify the service media to the property, although it stipulates that 'testing of services is

---

1 See *Jowitt v Woolwich Equitable Building Society* 14 December 1987 (unreported); *Green v Ipswich Borough Council* [1988] 1 EGLR 138.
2 See *Daisley v BS Hall & Co* [1972] 225 EG 1553 at 1555 per Bristow J.
3 [1991] EGLR 155.
4 [1982] 263 EG 158.
5 [1989] 2 EGLR 154.

not undertaken'. In *Strover v Harrington*,[1] the surveyor reported that a property had the benefit of mains drainage, having been thus informed by the vendor. A drains inspection and test report would have identified that the property was in fact served by a septic tank. Sir Nicolas Browne-Wilkinson V-C found the surveyor not to have been negligent for misreporting because it had formed no part of his retainer that a drains test would be performed and it was reasonable to rely upon the information provided by the vendor. The Vice-Chancellor stated:[2]

> 'the likelihood of a Vendor misrepresenting the nature of the drainage must be very remote indeed. Nobody, for example, has referred me to any other case where this has previously happened. In those circumstances, to hold a Surveyor liable for failing simply to qualify the way in which he gives his answer, when he is, in accordance with good practice, relying on information communicated to him which is in the ordinary run of events – indeed the invariable run of events so far as I am aware to have proved to be accurate, would be to be imposing too high a duty.'

The surveyor was also absolved from any criticism that he had failed to qualify the report in respect of the drains by an indication that the statement was a repetition of an unconfirmed assertion by the vendor. It is, however, to be noted that para 3.5 of the Specification requires that, where the valuer relies on information provided by another, this should be indicated in the report together with the source of the information.

Outbuildings, site and neighbouring properties

1.14 Garages and other buildings of substantial permanent construction and structures attached to the property are to be inspected. The presence or absence of a serviceable garage will obviously affect the value.

Generally about the site, the condition of any retaining walls and need of repair to any substantial boundary or access features will need to be considered. Trees close to the dwelling may present a subsidence threat. In *Daisley v BS Hall & Co*,[3] Bristow J said:

> 'A surveyor who finds a house under 10 years old built as close to a row of poplars as High Trees was, where two of those trees had been felled for no apparent reason other than to reduce the risk of root damage, is under a duty to ascertain by effective means the nature of the subsoil whether or not he finds evidence of settlement of the house which may be due to subsoil shrinkage.'

Further, problems apparent with neighbouring properties may indicate a potential for similar defects in the premises being inspected. For example, evidence of subsidence to an adjoining property should put the valuer on enquiry as to whether it is a ground failure specific to that property or whether it is indicative of a generalised problem in the area.

---

1 [1988] 2 WLR 572.
2 [1988] 2 WLR 572 at 582.
3 [1972] 225 EG 1553 at 1555.

The report and valuation

1.15 Sections 3 and 4 of the Specification deal with the form and content of the report along with the valuation. The report will usually be given on a form provided by the lender which should be completed so as to deal with the matters discussed above but otherwise confined strictly to answering questions raised by the lender. Where extensive repair works are needed, this should be reported. If a retention is to be recommended against the cost of such works, the valuer may, in the case of listed buildings or ones of unusual construction, need to recommend a person with appropriate specialist knowledge be asked to advise as to the appropriate works.

The assumptions a valuer will typically be entitled to make in valuing the property are set out in s 4 of the Specification. Of particular note are para 4.1.2 and 4.1.5 which allow the valuer to assume the existence of all necessary planning consents and statutory approvals for the buildings being valued and their use. In *PK Finans International (UK) Ltd v Andrew Downs & Co Ltd*,[1] the valuer stated in his report as follows:

> 'We have made verbal enquiries but have not undertaken any official searches and for the purpose of this valuation we have assumed that full planning consents were obtained for the development of the property as a nursing home, that consents are also in existence for additional nursing home facilities in the stable block and that consent has been given for sheltered housing on plot number 426.'

This was held to be adequate, Sir Michael Ogden QC further stating[2] that as it had been 'conceded that the plaintiffs were negligent in not sending the valuation to their Solicitors, had I found the defendants negligent, I would have assessed contributory negligence at 80 per cent, leaving the percentage of damages to be paid by the defendants as 20 per cent'.

The record of inspection and valuation

1.16 Finally, s 6 of the Specification requires the valuer to make and retain legible notes of the inspection carried out along with a record of comparable transactions and/or valuations considered in valuing the property. Such materials can be of invaluable assistance in defending a claim for professional negligence. The absence of such materials in *Watts v Morrow*[3] proved a considerable handicap to the valuer attempting to resist such a claim.

Units forming part of a larger building or group of related buildings

1.17 Flats and maisonettes comprise units forming part of a larger building. The specification provides that the main duties of inspection apply to a mortgage valuation of such structures. The exterior of the proposed security must be examined along with sufficient of the remainder of the main building to

---

1 [1992] 1 EGLR 172.
2 [1992] 1 EGLR 172 at 174.
3 [1991] 4 All ER 937.

ascertain its general state of repair. As was observed by the court in *Drinnan v CW Ingram & Sons*:[1]

> 'it may be that in the absence of precise instructions to do so a surveyor is not bound to make a meticulous examination of the fabric of a whole tenement but I should be surprised if it is not the normal practice to have regard to anything clearly visible in the structure of the building.'

Plainly the state and condition of the roof will have an impact upon flats below the top floor flat. Cracking to the exterior of the main building may indicate a subsidence problem affecting the security itself. Defects in either area are likely adversely to affect the value of the proposed security itself. The interior of the flat or maisonette must be inspected along with any communal entrance areas and other common parts.

1.18 In valuing a leasehold interest, the valuer is entitled to make certain assumptions, being under no duty to verify these. Principally it will be assumed that the unexpired residue of the lease is 70 years and that it will not be determined save for serious breach of covenant. The valuer will further assume that there are no covenants which are exceptionally onerous to the leaseholder and that other lessees of adjoining premises hold under similar terms. Existence of appropriate insurance arrangements will be taken for granted. Further it will be assumed that in the case of blocks of flats or maisonettes over six dwellings that the properties are all managed by a professional, properly bonded managing agent or otherwise dealt with by the freeholder. For the remainder of the detailed assumptions the valuer may make, attention is invited to s 4.1.12 of the Specification.

THE VALUATION

1.19 In inspecting and reporting for mortgage purposes, the lender and borrower are concerned to obtain an opinion as to the open market value of the property to be secured. This is now defined as:

> '... an opinion of the best price at which the sale of an interest in property would have been completed unconditionally for cash consideration on the date of valuation, assuming (a) a willing seller: (b) that, prior to the date of valuation, there had been a reasonable period (having regard to the nature of the property and the state of the market) for the proper marketing of the interest, for the agreement of the price and terms and for the completion of the sale: (c) that the state of the market, level of values and other circumstances were, on any earlier assumed date or exchange of contracts, the same as on the date of valuation: (d) that no account is taken of any additional bid by a prospective purchaser with a special interest: and (e) that both parties to the transaction had acted knowledgeably, prudently and without compulsion.'[2]

---

1 1967 SLT 205.

2 Practice Statement 4.2.1 of the Manual, effective from 1 May 1996.

The steps which a competent valuer will undertake before reporting an open market figure have been variously described in a number of reported cases.[1] Although not exhaustive, the following comprise the most relevant factors which the valuer will be expected to consider in preparing a report:

(a) the size, condition, tenure and location of the property;
(b) planning permission and permitted user;
(c) the value and use of adjoining and neighbouring premises;
(d) the prices at which similar properties in the same area have sold at the relevant time together with any features peculiar to the property which distinguish it from such comparables;
(e) the state of the property market;
(f) the influence of bank interest rates;
(g) valuations, if any, placed upon the property by other competent valuers in the recent past;
(h) evidence of any recent sale price of the subject property itself.

So far as the latter item is concerned, Phillips J recently expressed the view

> 'a valuation is no more than the opinion of the valuer of the price that the property is likely to realise if sold on the open market . . . where a property has just been sold, the sale price is potentially the most cogent evidence of the open market value of that property'.[2]

1.20 Allowing that valuation is not an exact science, averagely competent valuers may not arrive at precisely the same open market value of the same property. What is expected, however, is that each valuer will be able to report an open market valuation figure within a reasonable margin of error. It was summarised thus by Watkins J in *Singer & Friedlander Ltd v John D Wood & Co*:[3]

> 'The valuation of land by trained, competent and careful professional men is a task which rarely if ever admits of precise conclusion. Often beyond certain well founded facts so many imponderables confront the valuer that he is obliged to proceed on the basis of assumptions. Therefore, he cannot be faulted for achieving a result which does not admit of some degree of error. Thus, two able and experienced men each confronted with the same task, might come to different conclusions without anyone being justified in saying that either of them had lacked competence and reasonable care, still less integrity in doing his work. The permissible margin of error is said . . . to be generally 10 per cent either side of a figure which can be said to be the right figure, ie so I am informed, not a figure which later, with hindsight, proves to be correct but which at the time of valuation is the figure which a competent, careful and experienced valuer arrives at after making all the necessary enquiries and paying proper regard to the then state of the

---

1 *Singer & Friedlander Ltd v John D Wood & Co* [1977] EGD 569; *Mount Banking Corporation Ltd v Brian Cooper & Co* [1992] 2 EGLR 142; *Axa Equity & Law Home Loans Ltd v Hirani Watson* [1994] EGCS 90.

2 *Banque Bruxelles Lambert SA v John D Wood Commercial Ltd* [1994] 2 EGLR 108 at 118.

3 [1997] EGD 569.

> market. In exceptional circumstances the permissible margin:- could be extended to about 15 per cent, or a little more, either way.'

Indeed, more recently in *Private Bank & Trust Co Ltd v S (UK) Ltd*,[1] Rice J accepted evidence that the appropriate margin of error on the facts of that case was 15 per cent either side of a bracket of values. At first blush, this appears to extend the scope for justifying a reported value by substituting consideration of a margin either side of the 'right figure' for a consideration of a margin either side of a range or bracket of values. In practice, however, this is not so because the 'right figure' may not be capable of precise calculation but may itself fall within a narrow band, either side of which proper valuations could be reported. A clear statement of the approach to take to this issue is to be found in *Mount Banking Corporation Limited v Bryan Cooper & Co*[2] where Mr R M Stewart QC said:

> 'The problem that this raises, it seems to me, is: 10 per cent (or whatever margin may be thought appropriate) of what? Applying the Bolam test, the real question, in my judgment, is whether the valuation was that which a competent valuer, using proper skill and care could properly have reached ... The margin of error approach is thus a useful tool for in most straightforward cases it can reasonably be expected ... that competent surveyors acting with proper skill and care and thus acting with all the relevant evidence will come within a moderate bracket of each other. But there is danger in the margin of error approach to which I have alluded ... I do not think it proper to apply it mechanistically in any case so as to say that any valuation outside the consensus of the experts or if they differ outside their average valuation by more than ten per cent is prima facie negligent. Rather ... I think the judge must approach the question first by asking where the proper valuation or bracket of valuation lies. Then if the defendant is more than the permitted margin outside that proper figure, the inference of negligence should be drawn.'

EXCEPTIONS TO THE DUTY OF CARE

Disclaimer

1.21 In spite of the above, much building society literature provided to the applicant for an advance will often contain a notice purporting to disclaim liability on behalf of the reporting valuer to the prospective purchaser for any carelessness in inspecting and valuing the security. Such provisions were considered in *Smith v Eric S Bush*; *Harris v Wyre Forest District Council*.[3] In the former the purchaser signed an application form which included the following:

> 'I understand that the Society is not the agent of the Surveyor or firm of Surveyors and that I am making no agreement with the Surveyor or firm of Surveyors. I understand that neither the Society nor the Surveyor or the firm of Surveyors will warrant, represent or give any assurance to me that the statements, conclusions and

1 [1993] 1 EGLR 144.
2 [1992] 2 EGLR 142 at 145.
3 [1990] 1 AC 831.

opinions expressed or implied in the report and mortgage valuation will be accurate or valid and that the Surveyors' report will be supplied without any acceptance of responsibility on their part to me.'

In *Harris v Wyre Forest District Council* the disclaimer notice stated:

> 'I/we understand ... that the valuation is confidential and is intended solely for the benefit of Wyre Forest District Council in determining what advance, if any, may be made on the security and that no responsibility whatsoever is implied or accepted by the Council for the value or condition of the property by reason of such inspection and report.'

The House determined that it would not be fair or reasonable for the defendants in either case to excuse themselves from liability by reference to these terms, since such notices were unfair and unenforceable having regard to the provisions of the Unfair Contract Terms Act 1977.[1] In referring to the thrust and ambit of this Act, Lord Templeman stated:[2]

> '... The valuer is a professional man who offers his services for reward. He is paid for those services. The valuer knows that 90 per cent of purchasers in fact rely on the mortgage valuation and do not commission their own survey. There is great pressure on a purchaser to rely on the mortgage valuation. Many purchasers cannot afford a second valuation. If a purchaser obtains a second valuation the sale may go off and then both valuation fees will be wasted. Moreover, he knows that mortgagees, such as Building Societies and the Council ... are trustworthy and that they appoint careful and competent valuers and he trusts the professional man so appointed. Finally the valuer knows full well that failure on his part to exercise reasonable skill and care may be disastrous to the purchaser ...'.

It is important to note that their Lordships' views were expressed in respect of dwelling houses of modest value and do not amount to a determination that in all cases disclaimers will be ineffective to excuse liability to third parties relying on a report and valuation provided to the lender.

Expensive properties

1.22 Although their Lordships did not suggest that a duty of care could be excluded in relation to purchases of properties which did not answer the description of 'dwelling houses of modest value', it was accepted that circumstances might arise in relation to very expensive properties which would make it reasonable for the valuer to exclude or limit liability for negligence. Lord Griffiths recognised:[3]

> '... In respect of valuations of quite different types of property for mortgage purposes such as industrial property, large blocks of flats or very expensive houses ... it may well be that the general expectation of the behaviour of the purchaser is quite different. With very large sums of money at stake prudence would seem to demand that the purchaser obtain his own structural survey to guide him in his

---

1 See ss 2(2) and 11 of the Act.
2 [1990] 1 AC 831 at 852.
3 [1990] 1 AC 831 at 859.

purchase and in such circumstances with very much larger sums of money at stake, it may be reasonable for the Surveyors valuing on behalf of those who are providing the finance either to exclude or limit their liability to the purchaser.'

The preservation of a limited degree of liability only in circumstances where the potential value of a successful negligence claim makes professional indemnity cover available only at prohibitive cost was recognised as reasonable. Lord Griffiths continued:[1]

> 'I would not, however, wish it to be thought that I would consider it unreasonable for professional men in all circumstances to seek to exclude or limit their liability for negligence. Sometimes breathtaking sums of money may turn on professional advice against which it would be impossible for the adviser to obtain adequate insurance cover and which would ruin him if he were to be held personally liable. In these circumstances it may indeed be reasonable to give the advice on a basis of no liability or possibly of liability limited to the extent of the adviser's insurance cover.'

These remarks were expressly endorsed by Lord Templeman.[2] A recent application of this analysis is to be found in *Omega Trust Co Ltd and Banque Finindus v Wright Son & Pepper (a firm)*.[3] The court was there concerned with over valuations of three short leasehold interests in small supermarkets in central London. The surveyor provided a valuation of the properties together at £.945 million expressed to be for the sole use of the borrower in applying for a loan to Omega. The report contained a disclaimer providing:

> 'This report shall be for private and confidential use of the clients for whom the report is undertaken and should not be reproduced in whole or in part or relied upon by third parties for any use whatsoever without the express written authority of the surveyors.'

A loan of £350,000 was subsequently made by Omega, which in fact advanced £150,000, the balance of the loan being provided by a second lender, Finindus, to whom the report had been shown. In proceedings brought by the lenders, Omega and Finindus, alleging a negligent over-valuation after the borrower had defaulted and gone into liquidation, the Court of Appeal accepted the valuer's contentions that the disclaimer was effective to negative the existence of any duty of care owed to Finindus. The success of the disclaimer clause from the point of view of the valuers almost certainly reflects the expensive and commercial nature of the premises being valued.[4]

1.23 A further example of such a disclaimer being effectively relied upon to negative liability for breach of duty arose in *Stevenson v Nationwide Building Society*.[5] In that case, an estate agent applied for an advance of £42,750 from the defendant building society to purchase a property at an agreed price of £52,000.

---

1 [1990] 1 AC 831 at 859–860.
2 [1990] 1 AC 831 at 854.
3 [1997] PNLR 424.
4 See further the discussion at paras **2.6** and **3.8**.
5 [1984] 272 EG 663.

The property was constructed over a river, comprising two shops, a maisonette and a flat. The society's valuer inspected the property and reported upon it furnishing a copy of the report to the plaintiff. He valued the property at £57,000 after some recommended work had been performed. The plaintiff was granted the advance sought and purchased the property. A month later part of the floor collapsed owing to structural defects. Although the judge held the valuer had failed to exercise reasonable care and skill, he upheld as reasonable a clause providing that:

> 'No responsibility is implied or accepted by the society or its valuer for either the value or condition of the property by reason of such inspection and report.'

Mr J Wilmers QC sitting as a Deputy High Court Judge held:[1]

> 'Here we have on the one hand a building society which follows what is accepted to be fairly standard practice in importing this term or notice or disclaimer. It does so with a full warning and it offers the applicant a way of circumventing the refusal to accept responsibility by its offer to arrange for a full survey, provided the applicant will pay the extra cost. Since such a survey would involve extra cost I can see nothing unfair in this. Moreover when I bear in mind that the person affected by the disclaimer is someone well familiar with such disclaimers and with the possibility of obtaining a survey and also familiar with the difference between a building society valuation and a survey and their different costs. It seems to me perfectly reasonable to allow the building society in effect to say to him that if he chooses the cheaper alternative he must accept that the society will not be responsible for the content to him.'

It is noteworthy that the decision did not concern a modest property at the lower end of the market nor an inexperienced purchaser. The plaintiff was himself an estate agent familiar with such disclaimers and the range of alternative surveys and valuations available. Further, the property included a commercial element comprising two shops. On its facts, the decision is therefore entirely consistent with the reasoning in *Smith v Eric S Bush; Harris v Wyre Forest District Council.*

Generally, however, attempts to limit or exclude liability by reference to the scope of their Lordships' decisions in *Smith v Eric S Bush*; *Harris v Wyre Forest District Council* have not fared well.

1.24 In *Beaumont v Humberts*,[2] reliance upon Lord Griffiths' exceptional categories of properties in which a purchaser may be expected not to rely on a valuation obtained by the lender for its own purposes failed. In that case the plaintiff purchaser had originally engaged the defendant valuers to carry out a full structural survey (but not a valuation) of the relevant property. Thereafter, the defendants were instructed by the plaintiffs' mortgagees to prepare a valuation for reinstatement purposes. Their retainer had been suggested by the plaintiff in view of their previous involvement with the property. The plaintiff

1 [1984] 272 EG 663 at 671.
2 [1990] 2 EGLR 166.

agreed to pay the further fee for this insurance valuation. At first instance the judge concluded that the defendant could not have been expected to contemplate that the plaintiff would rely upon him to provide an accurate reinstatement figure. On appeal, Taylor and Dillon LLJ found that a duty of care was owed. Taylor LJ accepted:[1]

> 'The present case does not concern a valuation at the lower end of the market. Nor, however, was it in the very expensive category alongside blocks of flats and industrial properties to which Lord Griffiths referred. It is important therefore to look at all the specific circumstances, the probabilities and expectations of the parties.'

Their Lordships noted the fact the purchaser had obtained a structural survey from the defendant on the property at an earlier date; the fact the purchaser was to pay the Bank's valuation fee for the further report and the fact the reinstatement figure would be one at which the bank would require the borrower to insure as persuasive in finding that the requisite proximity existed for a duty of care to arise and that the borrower would be likely to rely on the valuer's reported figure for reinstatement. Had the property fallen fairly and squarely within Lord Griffiths' exceptional categories of properties, the result may have been different.

In *Beaton v Nationwide Building Society*[2] the court considered a disclaimer in the following terms:

> 'No responsibility is implied or accepted by the society or its valuer for either the value or condition of the property by reason of the inspection and report. The society does not undertake to give advice as to the value or condition of the property and accepts no liability for any such advice that may be given. The inspection carried out by the society's valuer was not a structural survey and there may be defects which such a survey would reveal.'

It was contended on behalf of the valuer that it would be fair and reasonable to allow him to rely upon this disclaimer because the house buyers had been advised by their own solicitors to have a full survey, which advice had been rejected and because the estate agents marketing the property had indicated that it had been partially underpinned. These arguments were rejected by the judge who held that, given the high incidents of purchasers of modest dwelling houses simply relying upon the valuation report for mortgage purposes, it was foreseeable that the plaintiffs would be unlikely to take up the solicitor's recommendation for a full survey to be commissioned. It followed the defendants could have anticipated that the borrowers would rely upon the report prepared. Secondly, the estate agents' reference to past underpinning works had not been such as to excite any anxiety in the minds of the plaintiff purchasers so as to make it unreasonable for them to rely upon the defendants' report rather than instituting further professional investigations on their own account.

---

1 [1990] 2 EGLR 166 at 170.
2 [1991] 2 EGLR 145.

Limitation on the extent and purpose of the survey report and valuation

1.25 It is a reflection of the different kinds of survey available that the degree of inspection in valuing a property will differ between, for example, a mortgage valuation and a full structural survey. The Specification for Residential Mortgage Valuation sets out the scope of the inspection relevant to a mortgage valuation which will be provided and warns that 'parts not readily accessible or visible are not inspected and furniture and effects are not moved or floor coverings lifted.'[1] This is not a term excluding liability for missed defects in inaccessible parts, but a statement of the extent of the surveyor's duty undertaken.

Where a limited inspection only has been possible, however, the valuer may be under a duty to warn a lender or purchaser not to proceed with the transaction until inaccessible parts have been examined. In *Heatley v William H Brown Ltd*,[2] the surveyor carrying out the inspection was unable to gain access to the roof voids. This limitation upon the extent of the inspection was noted in the report which otherwise described the property as 'in a reasonable condition for its age'. The roof was in fact in a seriously defective condition and the court held the defendant valuers liable in negligence for omitting to advise the plaintiffs to delay purchase until access to the roof void could be obtained.

Clause 1 of the model conditions of engagement for valuations[3] requires that 'the purpose of the valuation shall be agreed between the client and the valuer'. Clause 3 further allows for agreement to be reached over the basis or bases of a valuation requested, along with any special assumptions relating thereto. Consideration of this aspect of the valuer's engagement may be important in identifying whether a reported value was negligently arrived at or not. There is of course a world of difference between, for example, a valuation for market purposes and an assessment of value for insurance purposes. In *Predeth v Castle Phillips Finance Co Ltd*,[4] the mortgagees instructed the defendant valuer to provide a 'crash sale valuation' of a repossessed bungalow. This instruction was interpreted by the valuer as requiring him to assume a sale even more rapid than a forced sale. The lender thereafter sold the property at a slightly higher figure than that reported. Following a successful claim by the mortgagor against the lender for failing in its duty to obtain the best available price for the property, an action was brought against the valuer alleging negligence in failing to advise on the property's open market value. This claim was rejected by the Court of Appeal on the ground that the valuer had carried out the instructions provided, which did not include the provision of an open market valuation.

---

1 See Appendix III.
2 [1992] 1 EGLR 289.
3 See Appendix III.
4 [1986] 2 EGLR 144.

Contributory negligence

1.26 Section 1 of the Law Reform (Contributory Negligence) Act 1945 provides as follows:

> 'Where any person suffers damage as the result partly of his own fault and partly of the fault of any other person or persons a claim in respect of that damage shall not be defeated by reason of the fault of the person suffering the damage, but the damages recoverable in respect thereof shall be reduced to such extent as the Court thinks just and equitable having regard to the claimant's share in the responsibility for the damage.'

It was argued in *Yianni* that full liability should not attach to the defendant valuer because of the buyers' failure to have an independent survey carried out and their omission to read the literature provided by the building society warning as to the intended limitations upon the liability of the defendant. The Court rejected this argument. Once it is accepted a duty of care exists and that the report, if favourable, will encourage the purchaser to proceed, it is difficult to contemplate that a buyer will ever be found to be contributorily at fault in relying upon the advice of the valuer. As Phillips J in *Banque Bruxelles Lambert SA v Eagle Star Insurance Co Ltd* observed in a related context:[1]

> 'No Court will lightly hold a plaintiff at fault for relying on advice given by a professional adviser who owes a duty of care to the plaintiff.'

The difficulty in successfully criticising a borrower for not commissioning a structural survey apart from the mortgage valuation report is a logical one. As explained above, part of the rationale for imposing liability upon a mortgage valuer to a purchaser of a modest property is that the valuer is aware the house buyer is unlikely to have an independent survey carried out on his own account in any event.[2]

---

1 [1994] 2 EGLR 108 at 139.

2 See *Davies v Idris Parry* [1988] 1 EGLR 147; *Beaton v Nationwide Building Society* [1991] 2 EGLR 145.

Chapter 2

HOMEBUYER SURVEY AND VALUATION

INTRODUCTION

2.1 The Homebuyer Survey and Valuation ('HSV')[1] is the current version of what was originally called the House Buyer's Report and Valuation ('HBRV') and, subsequently, the House Buyer's Survey and Valuation ('HBSV'). The HSV is in a standard format and is designed specifically as a budget service. It is intended only for properties which are conventional in type and construction and in apparently reasonable condition and it focuses on essential matters which have an effect on the value of the property. Unlike a building survey (considered in Chapter 3) it also provides a valuation as an integral part of the service. In each case the survey and valuation is made on a prescribed form which incorporates Standard Conditions and Terms of Engagement. In relation to the HBRV, explanatory notes were published in 1987 and 1990 and Comments and Guidance were published for the HBSV in 1993. These are replaced in the HSV by detailed Practice Notes. Whereas Condition 1 of the 1987 Conditions of Engagement provided that the HBRV was not intended for larger properties, ie houses, bungalows over 185 m sq (external) of floor area, properties over three storeys in height or those built before 1900, Condition 5 of the HSV Standard Terms of Engagement simply provides that the surveyor will be entitled not to proceed with the provision of a HSV report 'if, after arriving at the property, he or she concludes ... that it would be in the typical Client's best interests to be provided with a building survey, plus valuation, rather than the Homebuyer Service'. The background information and advice provided to prospective purchasers by RICS/ISVA states that a building survey is likely to be needed if the property is of unusual construction, dilapidated or has been extensively altered or where a major conversion or renovation is planned. The Homebuyer Service is summarised in a document provided to the client entitled 'Description of the Homebuyer Service'. This new service declares as its objective, the provision of professional advice to assist a client 'to make a reasoned and informed judgment on whether or not to proceed with a purchase, to assess whether or not the property is a reasonable purchase at the agreed price and to be clear what decisions and actions should be taken before contracts are exchanged'. The Service introduces a number of important and defined terms, which the reporting surveyor is exhorted to adopt consistently throughout the text of the HSV. In

1 See Appendix IV, effective from November 1997.

particular, attention is focused upon 'urgent' and 'significant' matters. Urgent matters are defined as 'defects judged to be an actual or developing threat either to the fabric of the building or to personal safety' which it would be advisable to put right as soon after purchase as possible, or even before. Significant matters 'are those which typically in the negotiations over price would be reflected in the amount finally agreed'. Matters which are not considered to be urgent or significant as defined are outside the scope of the HSV and are generally not reported. Urgent and significant matters are to be identified from an inspection comprising 'a general surface examination of those parts of the property which are accessible'. The term 'accessible' is itself defined as follows:

> 'Visible and readily available for examination from ground and floor levels, without risk of causing damage to the property or injury to the surveyor.'

Where necessary, parts of the inspection are made from adjoining public property. The Practice Notes to this provision suggest that inspection may also be made from adjoining private property at the surveyor's discretion.[1]

It is proposed to consider the duties of a surveyor undertaking the HSV as these will now be of most relevance to the practising profession. Where appropriate, comment will, however, also be made upon variations from the earlier HBSV regime.

STANDARD OF CARE

2.2 Clause 2 of the Standard Terms of Engagement provides that the surveyor providing an HSV 'will be a Chartered Surveyor or a Fellow or Associate of the Incorporated Society of Valuers and Auctioneers, who is competent to survey, value and report upon the property which is the subject of these Terms'. The HSV Practice Notes are introduced by Practice Statement 11 which records in PS 11.7 that the surveyor must be in 'possession of sufficient knowledge of the area in which the subject property is situated' and have 'adequate competence in the survey of the sorts of dwelling for which the Service is suitable'. In particular, PS 11.7 states:

> 'The level of expertise required of the surveyor is the same as for a building survey, albeit that the inspections may be more limited – as is the degree of detail and extent of reporting in respect of condition.'

The Practice Notes then set out what are described as the 'HSV Practice Notes (Practice Statements Appendix 12)'. These spell out in detail the duties and the matters which the surveyor should address in carrying out his inspection and completing the HSV form and will be of immense value when the question of liability has to be assessed.

2.3 The level of care to be exercised in carrying out an HBRV was considered in *Cross v David Martin & Mortimer*.[2] The surveyor failed to notice

1 Annex A to Practice Notes, note 6 on B3.
2 [1989] 1 EGLR 154.

a hump in the middle of the lounge, an upstairs door which was sticking and that the loft conversion prejudiced the design of the roof. Having accepted that the duty he owed under the HSV was the same as that owed under a full survey, Phillips J held that:

> 'A house purchaser can properly expect to be informed of any feature of the property that involves uncertainty as to its condition, present or future, even if the Surveyor's opinion as to its significance is reassuring.'

In particular, in respect of the subsidence indicated by the hump, the position may have proved more serious, requiring substantial repairs. In considering the misalignment of the first floor doors, various possible causes were canvassed, one being a degree of movement to the floor because of inadequate support from the partition walls. The judge held that a competent surveyor would have advised the house purchaser of this possibility.

In contrasting this position with the duty of care owed by a mortgage valuer, Auld J stated in *Whalley v Roberts & Roberts:*[1]

> 'The Defendants were not instructed to undertake a structural survey or a survey of the detail called for in the standard form of the Royal Institution of Chartered Surveyors Housebuyer's Report and Valuation inspection. They were instructed to inspect and to provide a mortgage valuation report. It is common ground that this involved them in making a brief and reasonably careful visual inspection to enable them in the terms of the bank report form to provide a valuation and a general guide as to the condition of the property.'

Notwithstanding the extensive Practice Notes and the specific details covered in the HSV, however, it is still debatable whether the standard of service is significantly different from that which a purchaser can expect a mortgage valuer to provide. On this point, the remarks made by Ian Kennedy J in *Roberts v J Hampson & Co*[2] in relation to a mortgage valuation which were expressly approved and adopted by Lord Templeman in *Smith v Eric S Bush*[3] are pertinent:

> 'It is a valuation and not a survey, but any valuation is necessarily governed by condition. The inspection is of necessity a limited one. Both the expert surveyors who gave evidence before me agreed that with a house of this size they would allow about half an hour for their inspection on site. That time does not allow for moving furniture, or lifting carpets, especially when they are nailed down. In my judgment, it must be accepted that where a surveyor undertakes a scheme valuation it is understood that he is making a limited appraisal only. It is, however, an appraisal by a skilled professional man. It is inherent in any standard fee work that some cases will colloquially be winners and others losers from the professional man's point of view. The fact that in an individual case he may have to spend 2 or 3 times as long as he would have expected, or as the fee structure contemplated, is something he must accept. His duty to take reasonable care in providing the valuation remains at the root of his obligation . . . The second aspect of the problem concerns moving furniture and lifting carpets. Here again as it seems to me the

1 [1991] EGLR 164 at 168.
2 [1988] 2 EGLR 181 at 185.
3 [1991] AC 831.

position the law adopts is simple. If a surveyor misses a defect because its signs are hidden, that is a risk that his client must accept. But if there is specific ground for suspicion and the trail of suspicion leads behind furniture or under carpets, the surveyor must take reasonable steps to follow the trail until he has all the information which is reasonable for him to have before making his valuation.'

THE REPORT

2.4 The report form of the current HSV differs from its predecessor. The latter form set out what was to be covered against 45 items arranged under six headings – Information, General Description, External Condition, Internal Condition, Common Parts and Services, and Further Advice and Valuation. The HSV is now arranged under eight headings – Introduction and Overall Opinion, Property and Location, The Building, The Services and Site, Legal and Other Matters, Summary, Valuation, and Common Parts and Services.

With both reports it was, and is, good practice in carrying out an inspection and completing the form of report to make notes on site, including floor sketches annotated with measures, floor coverings, positions of radiators, moisture meter probings, window and door openings and large items of furniture which cannot be moved. Practice Note 2.3 requires the surveyor to give 'reflective thought' to his inspection and observations before formulating conclusions about the property. The practice of dictating the final report on site during the course of the inspection was strongly disapproved by Judge Bowsher QC in *Watts v Morrow*:[1]

> 'The most extraordinary practice adopted by the Defendant was not specifically disapproved by the RICS, but the absence of disapproval was, I suspect due to their failure to realise that some members might adopt this course taken by the Defendant. It is the practice of the Defendant to dictate his survey as he walks around the property during his inspection. He does not dictate notes into a dictating machine. He dictates his survey report into a dictating machine on site. When he returns to the office, he gives the tapes to his Secretary, who types them up and the report is then amended and sent to the client. This was the practice adopted by the Defendant on this occasion so that he had no notes to disclose on discovery of documents. It also led to his report being lengthy and diffuse and to its conclusions being inadequate … Many of the departures from the recommended practice adopted by the Defendant may not have produced important errors but this departure in my judgment was serious. It led to a report which was strong on immediate detail but excessively and I regretfully have to say negligently weak on reflective thought.'

2.5 Let us now look more closely at the eight main headings under which the surveyor provides his report. Being a hybrid form of report, intermediate between a valuation report (considered in the previous chapter) and a building survey (to be considered in the next chapter) much of the analysis relevant to mortgage and building surveys will apply with equal force to the HSV.

1 [1991] 1 EGLR 150 at 153–154.

However, in completing the HSV in respect of the different parts of the property, the surveyor is only required to report either urgent matters requiring action or significant matters which may be relevant to the negotiation of the price. When reporting urgent matters, the surveyor is required to set out the action advised or required to the client. Such advice is to be highlighted by the word 'Action'. Any step so highlighted as requiring 'Action' will then be reproduced in the summary section later on in the report.

Introduction and overall opinion

2.6 The introduction in the new report format highlights Clause 6 of the Standard Terms of Engagement as follows:

> 'Please note that this report is solely for your use and your professional advisers, and no liability to any one else is accepted. Should you not act upon specific, reasonable advice contained in the Report, no responsibility is accepted for the consequences.'

Whilst there is therefore no issue but that the reporting surveyor undertakes a responsibility to the named clients, there must remain a possibility of a liability to third parties who can be shown to be known to be likely to rely upon the report and valuation. It is unlikely, for example, that where an HSV has been commissioned by one of a married couple, the surveyor will not be held to be equally liable to the contracting party's marital partner where it is known that the couple are buying the property to be inspected together. Similarly, in *Miro Properties Ltd v J Trevor & Sons*[1] a married couple, contemplating the purchase of a flat, commissioned a survey report which, it was subsequently contended, had been negligently carried out. It was known to the reporting surveyor that for fiscal reasons the property was to be purchased by an off-shore company which was incorporated for the purchase of the acquisition. Mr Recorder Bernstein QC rejected an argument that the surveyor could not be liable to the company since, inter alia, it had not been incorporated at the date of his retainer. The report was disclosed to the company prior to the acquisition and in those circumstances the judge determined that the surveyors were 'as liable as they would have been if the company had been incorporated immediately before, rather than shortly after, those communications were made'. Likewise, in *Scotlife Home Loans (No 2) Ltd v Gibson MacNeile*[2] a valuation had been provided, as requested, addressed to Scotlife Home Loans (No 1). It was in fact relied upon, however, by a sister company, Scotlife Home Loans (No 2) which made an advance on the strength of the valuation reported. An argument that in those circumstances no liability was owned to Scotlife Home Loans (No 2) was rejected. The valuer knew that the report would be relied upon and was found to have sufficient knowledge of the connection between the two companies to owe a duty of care to Scotlife Home Loans (No 2). More recently, however, the Court of Appeal has upheld the efficacy of a disclaimer notice in negativing any duty of care owed by the surveyor to a third

1 [1989] 1 EGLR 151.
2 [1995] EGCS 106.

party. *Omega Trust Co Ltd and Banque Finindus v Wright Son & Pepper* is discussed elsewhere.[1] The Introduction Section concludes with a statement of the surveyor's overall opinion 'on whether or not this property is a reasonable purchase at the agreed price and on particular features which affect its present value and may affect its future resale'. Although summarising the surveyor's conclusions at the outset, this section of the report will plainly be the last to be completed after the surveyor has given the matter sufficient reflective thought.

Property and location

2.7 Particulars of the property will here be given, addressing its type, form of construction, nature of accommodation and briefly describing any garage/ parking facility and the grounds in which it is set. The surveyor will also comment upon the location of the property dealing with any main features affecting its use/enjoyment. Here will be included physical factors such as a flooding risk, the character of the neighbourhood, sources of inconvenience, eg noise/pollution and any special circumstances (eg is it in a Conservation Area?). The circumstances of the inspection, including the date, weather conditions and limits to the inspection are all important. Deficiencies in the rainwater goods, for example, may be obvious if the inspection is undertaken during heavy rain. Damp may be less obvious at a property during the warmer summer months. The extent of any fitted floor coverings limiting the inspection should also be carefully recorded.

As to the site generally, although leisure facilities are excluded from the duty of inspection, any actual or potential important defects to garages and other outbuildings will need to be reported. In *Allen v Ellis & Co*[2] (a building survey case) the reporting surveyor stated that the garage to the property was of brick build and in satisfactory condition. In fact, it was constructed of breeze-blocks with a brittle, scantily supported and much repaired asbestos sheet roof, at the end of its useful life. The surveyor was found negligent for failing properly to identify and report the true condition of this structure.

The building

2.8 The exterior of the property is to be considered first. Here the main elements to be inspected are similarly stated to those set out under para 2.1 of the Specification for Residential Mortgage Valuations.[3] The analysis considered in Chapter 1 should therefore be borne in mind.

2.9 Any urgent or significant matters should be reported. The chimney stacks and roofs, including any valleys, flashings and soakers will need to be inspected. Chimney stacks will be inspected from ground level only, although the surveyor should have with him a pair of binoculars which may enable a better ground level inspection to be carried out than by relying upon the naked eye alone. Roofs should be inspected from ground level, or from a three-metre

---

1 See para **1.22**.
2 [1991] EGLR 170.
3 See Appendix III and para **1.11**.

ladder, or from any other accessible vantage point. Dormer windows set into the roof often afford a good opportunity for a closer inspection of any flashings and soakers. Flat roofs require particular attention – the limited life and need for proper ventilation being important matters to address, a point emphasised in the Practice Notes. In *Hooberman v Salter Rex*,[1] the defendant's surveyor was found liable for failing properly to appraise the defective constructional detail of a flat-roofed terrace to an upper maisonette of a five-storey Victorian house in North London. Judge Smout QC stated:[2]

> 'I am satisfied that in the state of knowledge in the construction industry and amongst surveyors in 1977 it was generally appreciated that flat roofs were vulnerable, that their construction had to be viewed with caution and that a competent surveyor should have appreciated at that time that they reflected a serious potential danger.'

In that case the surveyor had failed to report that felt up-stands at the walls of the terrace had simply been turned into a groove in the perimeter walls with no zinc or lead wall flashings and no timber angled fillets at the intersection of the perimeter walls and roof decking. As a consequence of these deficiencies, water leaked into part of the property below the terrace.

2.10 In the notes printed in this section of the HSV, attention is specifically drawn to the problems of movement, timber defects and dampness and that if evidence of any of these is found, advice is given on what action should be taken. As with a mortgage valuation inspection, the surveyor should, in considering the main walls, be on the lookout for any indications of structural movement resulting from subsidence, settlement, ground heave, land slip or lack of tying in. Where such matters are noted, the surveyor should be able to give an opinion as to whether any movement is long-standing or recent and, if thought to be continuing, the likely cause of any progressive defect. Where serious, a further specialist report should be recommended.

2.11 Cracking lends itself to ready disguise by, for example, repapering internally and/or filled externally. The surveyor will need to be alert to the possibility of evidence of such defects being concealed by such works. In *Hingorani v Blower*,[3] a property examined by the reporting surveyor was suffering from subsidence so that underpinning works were required. The defendant failed to detect the possibility of structural movement, being taken in by the careful masking works carried out by the vendor. A large crack on the rear elevation had been filled in and internally the premises had been redecorated throughout, thereby covering any signs of internal cracking or tears in old wall coverings. The surveyor was nonetheless found to have been negligent in not seeing through such cosmetic works. The fact of repapering throughout an empty house was identified as a matter which ought to have the surveyor suspicious in itself; further, although the external crack had been filled, the width of the filling was obvious and indicative of a problem.

1 [1985] 1 EGLR 144.
2 [1985] 1 EGLR 144 at 156.
3 (1976) 238 EG 883.

This is an area where any expression of opinion as to the possibility of likely future movement of a structure needs to be carefully given. In *Matto v Rodney Broom Associates*[1] the opinion of an engineer was solicited as to the structural stability of a property. The defendant's engineer reported:

> 'Basically we find that the property is generally structurally stable as discussed. Minor remedial works are recommended in order to secure the continuance of the same. Future movement is considered to be minimal. Should you have any further queries, please do not hesitate to contact us.'

In so advising, the engineer was found by the Court of Appeal not to have gone far enough. Ralph Gibson LJ stated:[2]

> 'The basic skill and experience of the Defendant had not been shown to be lacking. He was caught, I think, in an unfortunate set of circumstances in which he wrote a short report intended to serve his client swiftly and effectively and without a screen of qualifications for his own protection. Nevertheless, his client was entitled to receive a report which dealt adequately with the advice required or a report which expressly stated that it was limited in some particular way. The report, for example, might have added words to the effect that, having regard to the nature of the subsoil and to the nature of the foundations likely to have been constructed for this house, there was a risk of more than minimal movement in the future because such a house can be stable for a number of years and then suddenly move; but that the cost of removing that risk by underpinning would be very large. The Plaintiff would then have been faced with the risk of having his application for a mortgage rejected, but he would have been able to try to negotiate a reduction in the price of the house to a fair value having regard to that risk of future movement as described. In my judgment the Plaintiff was wrongly deprived of that opportunity and I think he is entitled to the agreed sum of damages.'

2.12 Again, the condition of windows, doors and external joinery needs to be considered. Windows should be opened and any rotten sills reported. If double glazing has been installed recently, an enquiry as to the existence of guarantees should be made. Any sticking or jamming of windows or doors may itself afford evidence of structural movement. In *Cross v David Martin & Mortimer*[3] it was the Defendant's departure from this practice of opening and closing doors which resulted in evidence of subsidence being overlooked. One of the first floor doors, for example, was so misaligned as to be unable to be properly closed.

2.13 The main items for internal inspection again generally replicate those indicated in the Specification for Residential Mortgage Valuation Reports.[4] In the case of the roof space, however, the surveyor is expected here to enter the void to carry out an inspection addressing the details of the design and basic construction of the roof. As noted above, the failure to detect roof defects gives rise to a significant number of professional negligence claims and represents the second largest category of claims. In *Parsons v Way and Waller Ltd*[5] the

1 [1994] 2 EGLR 163.
2 [1994] 2 EGLR 163 at 168.
3 [1989] 1 EGLR 154.
4 See Appendix III and para **1.12**.
5 [1952] 159 EG 524.

defendant's surveyor's employee failed to detect roof spread, caused by inadequate tying in of the rafters at their feet. This had led to the roof thrusting against the rear wall and the wall plate being pushed over the head of the brickwork, which was visible within the house.

2.14 Ceilings, walls and floors are to be examined. The slope of the ceilings and floors may, where uneven, indicate internal evidence of settlement/ subsidence or localised compression of rotten floor joists. Such matters will need to be considered, along with any internal shrinkage cracks, tears to applied decorations and the constructional detail of any internal partitions. Cracking along the head of the partition wall at its junction with the ceiling may confirm evidence of a downward deflection in the roof, indicating a structural deficiency. As to the floors, the surveyor need only examine the surface of those not covered, although he is expected to lift where possible any accessible corners of any coverings to identify the nature of the surface beneath. This may also be apparent from any accessible void which has been inspected adjacent to the flooring. Deflections in both solid and suspended floors should be considered with particular care and appropriate warnings given in the report as to the possibility of the same indicating historic or progressive structural movement or any other problem. The surveyor should keep an open mind and approach these issues from a commonsense perspective. As McKenna J said in *Bishop v Watson, Watson and Scoles*,[1] a professional:

> '... who has agreed to make a visual survey is under no obligation to uncover those parts of the building where the flashings or damp proof courses should be found to see if they are there and if they are, whether they are adequate. If he sees anything which would give a reasonably skilled person grounds to suspect that they are missing or inadequate he must draw his client's attention to the matter, but evidence that the building is of cavity construction is not itself ground for suspecting that the safeguards essential to that mode of construction have been omitted or botched.'

2.15 That the court will recognise a limit to the extent of any duty to 'follow the trail' is apparent from *Hacker v Deal* (a building survey case).[2] There, a surveyor of an expensive property in Belgravia did not detect dry rot in the sauna room roof or behind kitchen units. The sauna room roof was capable of being examined in part through a small trapdoor let into the ceiling, which had been overlooked by the surveyor. There was a gap between the kitchen units which could have been looked into using a torch and a mirror. The surveyor was acquitted of any negligence in not making these further inspections. Judge Fawcus QC stated:

> 'Although one is acting as a detective one does not start going into all the little crevices in the hope of finding something unless there is some telltale sign which indicates that it would be advisable to do so.'

Again, as with mortgage valuation inspections, dampness should be investigated. At reasonable and accessible locations, a moisture detecting meter

1 [1973] 224 EG 1881 at 1886.
2 [1991] 2 EGLR 161.

should be used. The surveyor will need to identify the cause of the dampness and where it is found or suspected it is likely to be appropriate for more detailed investigations to be recommended.

2.16 Indeed, where woodworm, dry rot or other timber defects are found or suspected, it is likely to be appropriate to recommend more detailed investigations. In *Oswald v Countrywide Surveyors Ltd*[1] the surveyor in inspecting a farmhouse identified the presence of death-watch beetle, which he referred to in his report as an attack of woodworm. His practice was apparently not to distinguish between these two forms of infestations. He concluded that any infestation was inactive. The vendor had indicated that woodworm treatment had been carried out in the course of renovation works, although the surveyor omitted to inspect the Schedule of Works upon which the guarantee of treatment had been based. The purchaser's evidence was accepted that they would not have proceeded with the purchase if alerted to the possibility of death-watch beetle attack of the timbers without any assurance as to whether it was active or not. Further, the state and condition of internal decorations will be briefly commented upon.

The services and site

2.17 The services benefiting the property should be identified and any obvious defects reported. If the surveyor has any suspicions, a specialist test should be recommended. The surveyor will not carry out a test of services himself and indeed is expected not to turn on services which are turned off, although if not turned on, or any problem is suspected, this should be recorded in the report. In spite of these limitations, however, the surveyor undertaking an HBRV in *Howard v Horne & Sons*[2] was found liable for misreporting that the electrical wiring was in PVC cable when in fact this description applied only to part of the premises. Elsewhere, the wiring was much older and in some respect dangerous. That there was not up-to-date wiring throughout the premises would have been apparent from a more thorough inspection of a number of junction boxes mounted on a board. The judge criticised the surveyor for not making a more detailed inspection of this particular aspect of the electrical installation.

2.18 Finally, the foul and surface water drainage systems should be inspected to the extent of (where possible) lifting covers within the curtilage of the property. The form of drainage in each case (ie cesspits, septic tanks or mains drainage) should be identified and reported. Any obvious deficiencies will lead to a recommendation for a specialist test to be carried out, which is otherwise not included within the inspection duty assumed in an HSV. Further, purchasers will need to be warned to make their own enquiries of the local drainage authority as to the cost and the necessity of emptying any septic tank or cesspit.

---

1 50 Con LR 1, [1994] EGCS 150.
2 [1991] 1 EGLR 272.

Legal and other matters

2.19 First, the tenure will need to be identified, although this may be gathered from an enquiry of the vendor or estate agent's particulars, providing the source of information is identified. The Notes to the 1993 version of the HBSV and the current HSV call specific attention to the need to report the existence of any apparent tenancies. The extent of the valuer's duty in dealing with this aspect of an inspection was considered in *Kingsnorth Finance Co Ltd v Tizard*.[1] In that case, a husband purchased a property using monies partly coming from his wife. Following acquisition he and his wife separated, so that she only occupied the premises on an intermittent basis. The husband applied for a remortgage which necessitated a valuation inspection. The appointed valuer was provided with the prospective lender's standard report form which contained a section entitled 'Occupants'. This contained three questions: Who occupied the property? Are there any tenancies known to you or apparent on inspection? If Yes, please give full details, including rental. The surveyor was advised by the husband applicant that only he, his son and daughter lived at the property and that he and his wife were separated, she living elsewhere nearby. The report was duly completed, the section entitled 'Occupants' being completed by identifying as present at the property the applicant, his son and a daughter only. The second question as to the existence of any tenancies was answered: 'No'. The surveyor did not report that the vendor had told him he was separated from his wife who was nonetheless living nearby. Judge John Finlay QC concluded that, in so reporting, the valuer had not gone far enough. In particular, he stated:[2]

> 'What was [the valuer's] duty? The valuation report is made on a printed form: [the valuer's] duty was to inspect the property for the purpose of completing the form. Had the form contained a section with questions about the marital status of the applicant, his duty would have been to complete it to the best of the information he acquired... In his evidence [the valuer] made it clear that he was suspicious; he was on the lookout for signs of female occupation; not the occupation of a wife, but that of a girlfriend. He found no such signs, but his evidence made it clear that he regarded it as his duty to look for them. He drew the line, however, at opening cupboards and drawers. [The valuer's] understanding of his duty to look for signs of occupation by anyone else accords with mine. That being the scope of his duty, I consider that he should have enlarged on his answer to the question, "Who occupies the property?". The answer that he gave was, "applicant, son and daughter". That was founded in part on his own observations; in part from what Mr Tizard told him. He should in my view have added, either in the "Occupation" or in the "General Observations" section, "applicant states that he is separated from his wife who lives nearby" or something to that effect.'

The surveyor will also be alert to identify apparent and specific items which may have legal implications and which the client should ask his legal advisers to pursue. Examples include compliance with applicable regulations (eg listed building, consent, planning permission for an extension or loft conversion,

1 [1986] 1 WLR 783.
2 [1986] 1 WLR 783 at 791.

liability for drains/sewers and easements). Any guarantees relating to, for example, central heating servicing records and/or damp proofing/fenestration works should be identified. This would also be a convenient point in the report to deal with any non-legal matters, eg the council tax band if known.

Summary

2.20 This is a crucial section of the report, whose principal function is to provide a check list of all the urgent and/or significant matters reported upon in the earlier sections of the report, and to provide advice on how to take any action recommended. The client will need to be advised to forward a copy of the report to his legal advisers. Attention should be drawn to the 'action' paragraph in the report. Any items involving future maintenance requirements should also here be summarised.

Valuation

2.21 In the final section, the valuer will provide his opinion of open market value. This will be subject to standard assumptions and any specifically identified caveats. A reinstatement figure for building insurance purposes will also be provided.

Common parts and services

2.22 These will commonly arise where the property concerned comprises a maisonette or flat held under a leasehold interest. Detailed consideration of the inspection and valuation of such leasehold interest is beyond the scope of this work. It suffices to observe that in considering flats, maisonettes or similar units forming part of a larger building or group of related buildings, the surveyor and valuer will be concerned with the exterior of the accommodation being acquired itself and sufficient of the remainder of the main building within which it is contained in order to ascertain its general state of repair. As Lord Milligan stated in *Drinnan v CW Ingram & Sons*:[1]

> 'It may be that in the absence of precise instructions to do so a surveyor is not bound to make a meticulous examination of the fabric of the whole tenement but I shall be surprised if it is not the normal practice to have regard to anything clearly visible in the structure of the building.'

Common parts will need to be inspected externally and internally to the extent respectively envisaged by the Specification for Residential Mortgage Valuation and HSV Practice Notes. The right to use common services and liability for maintenance is recommended to be addressed by the prospective purchaser to his legal adviser. Detailed valuation assumptions in respect of leasehold interests are set out in the Specification and in the Practice Notes on reporting relating to the HSV.

---

1 (1967) SLT 205 at 208.

Chapter 3

STRUCTURAL SURVEYS

GENERAL CHARACTERISTICS

3.1 The term 'structural survey' was defined by the RICS[1] as 'the inspection of visible, exposed and accessible parts of the fabric of the building under consideration'. This broad description accords with the exposition of His Honour Judge Fox-Andrews in *Summers v Congreve Horner & Co and Independent Insurance Co*[2] who identified four key elements to any structural survey. These are:

(i) the preparation for a visual inspection;
(ii) the visual inspection;
(iii) any valuation of what is seen at the inspection; and
(iv) the written report.

Guidance to surveyors as to what is expected of a competent practitioner undertaking a structural survey was originally to be found in the RICS's Structural Surveys of Residential Property – a Guidance Note.[3] This recorded that chartered surveyors providing such a service were to accept responsibility for assessing their client's needs; determining the extent of the investigations to be made and obtaining instructions from the clients for any additional services required; undertaking the survey of the property to the extent required by the given instructions to establish its true condition and so as to enable the surveyor to report to the client in the detail and style necessary to provide a balanced professional opinion. The surveyor was also expected to agree to comply at all times with any instructions agreed with the client forming part of the terms of any contractual retainer. From 1 October 1996 this note has been superseded by a fresh document published by the RICS in July 1996 entitled Building Surveys of Residential Property – A Guidance Note for Surveyors. This replicates, however, the areas of responsibility which a surveyor is expected to accept in agreeing to perform such a survey summarised above. The guidance note recognises that a member of the public contacting a surveyor about a survey of a residential property is unlikely to have sufficient knowledge to give clear instructions so that advice will need to be given as to the type and extent of survey needed. The surveyor is expected to provide such advice freely, the note

1 Guidance Note on Structural Surveys of Commercial and Industrial Property (1983).
2 [1991] 2 EGLR 139.
3 1st edn 1981; 2nd edn 1985.

emphasising that it is important that the true nature and extent of the obligation being assumed by the surveyor is understood by, and agreed in writing with, the client or his representative. A lack of clarity over instructions resulted in a finding of liability against a surveyor in *Buckland v Watts*.[1] The plaintiff engaged the surveyor to survey a house he was contemplating purchasing and to prepare plans. The defendant, without attempting to clarify the instructions, took them to mean that the plaintiff required a measured survey only. The Court of Appeal found the defendant to have been negligent in failing to undertake an appraisal of the structure and in not discovering defects affecting it. As Salmon LJ said:[2] 'if a prospective purchaser of a house goes to a Chartered Surveyor and says – I want a survey and plans – that ought to convey to any sensible surveyor that what the client wants to know is what is the structural condition of the house and he also wants some plans of the house.'

3.2 At annexe B to the current guidance note is to be found a set of model conditions of engagement which any surveyor would be well advised to adapt as appropriate in agreeing terms of retainer by any client. Where the model conditions of engagement are adopted, the surveyor will agree to 'advise the client by means of a written report as to his opinion of the visible condition and state of repair of the subject property' based on the extent of an inspection, as defined by the conditions. Apart from this strict contractual responsibility, the surveyor will also be subject to a duty to inspect and report with that degree of reasonable care and skill expected of the averagely competent surveyor undertaking such a survey. As Bristow J said in *Daisley v BS Hall & Co*[3] 'the duty of a practitioner of any professional skill which he undertakes to perform ... is to see the things that the average skilled professional in the field would see, draw from what he sees the conclusions that the average skilled professional would draw and take the action that the average skilled professional would take.' In deciding what an averagely competent surveyor would do, the RICS guidance notes are likely to be regarded by the court as evidence of best practice. A departure from the recommended procedures in the notes will not necessarily result in a finding of negligence, but in practice the surveyor will need to provide a good reason to justify an omission to follow the guidance notes. Indeed, the notes recognise that 'it is for each individual surveyor to decide on the appropriate procedure to follow in any professional task.' The omission to have and use a hand mirror was dismissed in *Hacker v Thomas Deal & Co*[4] as not negligent because, although recommended as an item of equipment to be carried by a surveyor performing a structural survey, the court accepted that this was dependent upon the preferences of the individual surveyor. Warning against placing too heavy reliance upon the guidance notes as evidence of the requisite standard of care was given in *PK Finans International (UK) Ltd v Andrew Downs & Co Ltd*[5] where the Deputy Judge

---

1 [1968] 208 EG 969.
2 [1968] 208 EG 969 at 973.
3 [1972] 225 EG 1553.
4 [1991] 2 EGLR 161.
5 [1992] 1 EGL 172.

commented: 'these guidance notes are not to be regarded as a statute ... mere failure to comply with (which) ... constitute negligence.' What is important is whether the practice followed reflects the methods of ordinarily competent surveyors. This calls for a sensible and balanced approach by the court. As Judge Everett QC said in *Leigh v Unsworth*:[1] 'the mere fact that one professional man might suffer from an excessive caution does not mean that another man, exercising his judgment to the best of his skill and ability and taking perhaps a somewhat more optimistic view, is guilty of a departure from the appropriate standard of professional care and skill'.

AGREEING INSTRUCTIONS

3.3 Where the model conditions of engagement are adopted, the surveyor warrants first that he is a chartered surveyor or an incorporated valuer and secondly agrees to advise the client by means of a written report as to his opinion of the visible condition and state of repair of the property, based on an inspection as defined. It is, accordingly, important for the surveyor to agree the ambit of his instructions at the outset. The guidance note provides for pre-inspection agreement to be reached over the extent of the inspection and tests to be carried out. Will it, for example, be confined to the main building or take in outbuildings and grounds? What degree of opening up will be expected in examining structures? Will the surveyor be expected to test the drains, electrical, heating and other installations or engage specialists to investigate such services? Will a valuation be provided? To what extent will the surveyor be required to make enquiries of local and statutory authorities? The surveyor will of course be expected to advise as to the extent of inspection and enquiries likely to be necessary, and once these are agreed with the client the instructions should be confirmed in writing.

PREPARING FOR THE SURVEY

3.4 The guidance note records that the surveyor is to undertake the inspection personally and not delegate his responsibilities to others. He will accordingly need to be physically fit to carry out the inspection and adequately equipped. Recommended equipment is identified to include a torch; claw hammer and bolster; a ladder of sufficient length to give access to hatches and roofs not more than three metres above floor or adjacent ground level; pocket probe for superficial testing of water, joinery, fracture depths, etc; binoculars or telescope; hand mirror; moisture reading meter; screwdriver; measuring rods or tapes; notebook and writing equipment; plumb line and spirit level. More specialist equipment will not normally be part of the stock in trade of the structural surveyor. *Staveley and Glover*[2] mention a number of other items of

1 [1972] 230 EG 501.
2 *Surveying Buildings* (Butterworths, 1983).

equipment which practical experience indicates to be helpful. These are wellington boots, clipboard, extension lead, electric socket adaptors, drain plug, protected lamp holder for lead, spade, tool box and assorted tools and manhole keys. As the guidance note recognises, however, the equipment required will depend to a large extent on the preferences of the individual surveyor and the particular circumstances of the property to be inspected.

On arrival at the property the surveyor should familiarise himself with the district and particularly the character and nature of the property surrounding the building to be inspected. In, for example, a row of terraces, evidence of uniform renewal of any windows to adjoining properties may indicate a common problem of subsidence affecting the whole row of properties including that to be examined. The presence of a row of poplars close to the property being inspected in *Daisley v BS Hall & Co*[1] which had been felled for no apparent reason gave rise to a duty on the part of the surveyor to investigate the nature of the subsoil to assess whether the property was affected by settlement. The surveyor will record the principal design features and extent and nature of the accommodation. Any critical dimensions should be measured. Details of the property should be recorded in the form of site notes.

3.5 In carrying out the inspection the vendor will often be on hand. It is recommended that he be asked questions concerning the history of the property, any replies of significance being noted and reported with an indication of their provenance. Typical enquiries are:

- What is the age of the property and are there original or modification plans available?
- Have there been any structural alterations or additions to the property whilst in the ownership of the vendor (are they aware of any earlier modifications?)
- Have any structural repairs been carried out including timber treatment, underpinning or strengthening? Do guarantees exist?
- Is it known whether the property has ever been flooded?

  Plainly the locality of the property will be relevant in assessing this risk. In *Alliance & Leicester Building Society v J & E Shepherd*[2] a complaint that the surveyor had omitted to warn of the risk of flooding on the property from a nearby river failed for want of proof that no reasonably competent surveyor would have failed to appreciate this particular risk.
- Are there any concealed access hatches to voids under floor spaces? Is there a basement? Such an enquiry may have protected the surveyor in *Conn v Munday*[3] from falling into error. He failed to discover in the course

1 [1972] 225 EG 1553.
2 [1995] GWD11–608.
3 [1955] 166 EG 465.

of the survey woodworm in the cellar of a house. He gave evidence that he was unaware of the existence of the cellar.

- Is there any dispute or claim with neighbours in respect of boundaries, trees, etc. This is of particular importance where there is evidence of a shared access to a property, although to a degree such enquiries overlap with those which the purchaser's solicitor may be expected to make.
- Does the vendor intend to remove any items of equipment which would normally be regarded as fixtures or to leave any items normally removed? Such matters may not only affect the function of the property but will obviously impact upon its value.
- How long has the vendor occupied the premises?

The guidance notes, however, contain an important warning to the effect that the surveyor should not regard the statements made by the vendor as true unless full investigations have been made. This may provide an answer to the elusive question left unresolved in *Oldgate Estates Ltd v Toplis & Harding and Russell.*[1] In that case, part of the criticism of an investment valuation centred upon an omission to verify information given by the vendors as to the rents and outgoings of the premises. The rates had been understated resulting in the dependent valuation being too high. The defendants argued that since the persons providing the information were an accountant and a surveyor it was reasonable to accept their word. Ultimately, this particular issue did not need to be resolved by the court. It is, however, unlikely that the duty to verify information would be regarded by the court as dependent upon the professional status of the vendor.

THE INSPECTION

3.6 It is a matter of preference for the individual surveyor as to the sequence in which a property is inspected. In undertaking a structural survey, however, the surveyor will be expected to open unfixed hatches to roof and floor voids along with screwed-down access hatches to plumbing, concealed boilers, tanks and cavities beneath sanitary fittings. Areas which cannot be seen should be noted with appropriate recommendations for further opening-up. This duty is illustrated by *Hill v Debenham, Tewson & Chinnocks*[2] where a surveyor failed to warn that the roof rafters had failed. The court determined that the defendant ought either to have inspected the otherwise inaccessible roof space by looking through spaces in broken tiling from a ladder or at least warned that the condition of the rafters could not be advised upon because of inadequate access for inspection. The extent of any duty to open up, however, is in part dependent upon whether inspection of accessible parts affords any

1 [1939] 3 All ER 209.
2 [1958] 171 EG 835.

evidence or indication of a defect in a concealed feature of the property. As McKenna J stated in *Bishop v Watson, Watson and Scoles*:[1]

> '[a surveyor] is under no obligation to uncover those parts of the building where the flashings or damp proof courses should be found to see if they are there and, if they are, whether they are adequate. If he sees anything which would give a reasonably skilled person grounds to suspect that they are missing or inadequate he must draw his client's attention to the matter.'

Particular parts

3.7 The guidance note indicates those areas of the property to which particular attention will need to be paid.

(a) The roofs should be inspected as closely as practicable using available equipment and suitable vantage points externally. The interior of the accessible roof voids must be inspected in detail. An omission to inspect roof spaces in *Stewart v HA Brechin & Co*[2] meant that woodworm attack was not identified leading to a finding of negligence liability.

(b) Any uncovered floors should be inspected as far as practicable. In the case of timber floors, sufficient boards should be lifted, where possible, to enable the construction to be identified and the condition checked for any damage due to infestation or dampness. This obligation will particularly arise if other evidence of timber attack has been noted elsewhere in the property. In *Hill v Debenham, Tewson and Chinnock*[3] the court described, the lifting of floorboards when a surveyor is put on enquiry as representing 'the general and proved practice of the profession'.

(c) The effectiveness of ventilation and insulation in preventing condensation liable to damage elements of the structure, together with its effectiveness in limiting heat loss and passage of sound, should be carefully considered and recorded.

(d) Exposed elements of the walls and brickwork to the property merit careful attention internally and externally. Wall foundations, however, need only be exposed where structural defects indicate problems below ground. The failure of the defendant's surveyor in *Hipkins v Jack Cotton Partnership*[4] to notice cracking in the external rendering of a wall resulted in a finding of liability. The defect was indicative of a requirement for underpinning.

(e) The effectiveness and condition of structural timbers in floors, lintels and in supporting the roof should be checked and areas noted where this is not possible. Prudent use of a moisture reading meter is of vital importance. Many materials do not appear or feel damp to touch in spite of high moisture contents. Wood, for example, does not feel damp below a

---

1 [1972] 224 EG 1881.
2 1959 SC 306.
3 [1958] 171 EG 835.
4 [1989] 2 EGLR 157.

moisture content of 30 per cent. Conversely some materials will appear damp at relatively low moisture contents. By way of example, at 3 per cent moisture content most mortar will feel damp and plaster will be very wet. The unaided senses are accordingly not a reliable guide. Joinery near damp areas will need to be carefully considered and reported upon.

(f) Internally hot water installations, boilers, control equipment, etc should be activated where practicable to test physical operation and should be inspected visually for signs of corrosion or leakage. A recommendation may need to be made for an examination by a specialist contractor. In that event, the specialist will owe a duty of care to the individual commissioning the survey. In *Pfeiffer v E & E Installations*,[1] such a contractor was asked to provide a report upon a gas-fired central heating system. The firm was found negligent in failing to use a torch and mirror in examining the heat exchanger, investigation of which would have revealed a crack in this part of the installation.

(g) Drains should be inspected through all accessible manhole covers and subjected to a minimal test by watching the flow through the system. Means of foul and surface water disposal are to be identified and the ownership and effectiveness of equipment or installations checked so that further inspection can be recommended if appropriate.

(h) The guidance note suggests that, subsequent to the inspection, useful enquiry may be made of people with past knowledge of the area. This may identify environmental factors such as flooding and subsidence affecting the district in which the premises are situated.

THE REPORT

3.8 The guidance note describes in general terms the expected content and purpose of the report. First, it should provide a record of the building, its construction and materials, assessed by reference to current recommended standards and to properties of similar style and age. Secondly, it must offer a balanced view of the property giving advice on necessary repairs or modifications required to remedy reported defects and describe further investigation which the surveyor determines necessary if a firm opinion is to be given. The author of the report must accordingly differentiate between factual matters verifiable by observation and his opinion as to the state and condition of the premises where this depends upon making a professional judgment, based on inferences drawn from primary observations. Where repair works are necessary, the surveyor should identify the timescale and warn as to the likely consequences of any failure to implement advised repairs.

---

1 [1991] 1 EGLR 162.

The surveyor may choose to confine those who may rely upon the report to the commissioning addressee only. The guidance note recommends that, in order to reduce the possibility of claims by persons other than the client who rely upon the report, the following clause is inserted:

> 'This report is for the private and confidential use of the client for whom the report is undertaken and should not be reproduced in whole or in part or relied upon by third parties with the exception of [ ] for any use without the express written authority of the surveyor(s).'

Such a clause was considered in *Omega Trust Co Limited and Banque Finindus v Wright Son & Pepper (a firm)*.[1] In that case, a borrower applied to Omega for a £350,000 advance, supported by a valuation of property offered as security prepared by the defendant firm. The valuation report was addressed to Omega, incorporating the clause set out above. In the event, Omega advanced £150,000, the balance being provided by a second lender, Finindus. Following the insolvent liquidation of the borrower, Omega and Finindus brought proceedings against the defendant firm alleging negligence. The claim brought by Finindus was dismissed by the Court of Appeal on the basis that the disclaimer was apt to negative any duty of care being owed by the defendant firm. In holding the existence of the disclaimer fatal to Finindus' claim, Henry LJ stated:

> '[The disclaimer] was clearly entered into to assure clarity, to assure transparency and to assure certainty. The valuer was entitled to do all that could be done to prevent himself having to fight a difficult law suit as to whether he owed a duty to an unknown lender. If his disclaimer had been complied with by either Omega or by the bank, that would have been the position. If his document had been complied with and consent from him had been sought, he could, had he wished, have declined to assume the additional responsibility. It can in certain circumstances be more onerous in fact to face potential claims from two plaintiffs who may be separately represented and in relation to whom there may be two measures of damage appropriate than to face claims from one though that point pales into insignificance beside the point that what he had been deprived of was a position where everything would have been clear and certain and he had, through no fault of his own, a position where he could only rely on the terms of the disclaimer after fighting a difficult law suit in relation to it.'

As to the detailed content of the report, it should recite the client's instructions and the limitations agreed in confirming the terms of engagement, along with any variations found necessary on inspection. The premises must be identified with a general description of the design, principle methods of construction, situation in the road, character of the neighbourhood and other matters relevant to the environment, the topography and character of the immediate district. The surveyor will ensure that each section of the construction or services contained a narrative stating the discovered facts and describing elements which could not be identified with an explanation as to why. This is

---

1 [1997] PNLR 424. See earlier discussion at paras **1.22** and **2.6**.

standard practice. As Judge Carter QC indicated in *Hill v Debenham Tewson and Chinnocks*:[1]

> 'Applying the standard of the profession I entertain no doubt that the practice of the profession is – if you do not look, you must warn.'

Any recommendations for further enquiry or investigation prior to commitment to purchase must be spelt out. Defects and disadvantages of the property should be identified in relation to contemporary standards and those applicable to the period of construction. This may go further than envisaged by the observations in *Fisher v Knowles*[2] where the court stated:

> 'The word – defect – is a word having a number of connotations. Defects may be something which are inherent in the type and age of a building. For example, an Elizabethan cottage is likely to have the defect of having low ceilings, a defect both in the ordinary sense and in the statutory sense. To some people, though, that would be considered to be an enhancement. There are defects of some kind in every home.... it seems that in approaching this matter in the instant case I should have regard to those defects which were of such a nature as a prudent person would have put right and which would have been apparent to the defendant exercising the ordinary skill of an ordinary competent chartered surveyor and taking into account the type and age of the property.'

Where repairs are advised, the cost of such remedial works may be estimated, but the surveyor should be careful to state at some length the reservations and limitations of such advice. If a valuation has been requested, the RICS appraisal and valuation manual should be complied with. In the conclusion to the report the surveyor should pull together the threads of his observations and advice, offering to discuss any points of difficulty arising out of the report. It is recommended that two copies of the report be provided to the client or his representative.

---

1 [1958] 171 EG 835.
2 [1982] 1 EGLR at 154.

Chapter 4

VALUATION METHODOLOGY

INTRODUCTION

4.1 This section, it is hoped, will be of interest and assistance to the legal rather than surveying readership. It is proposed to explain in brief the various methods by which valuers carry out valuations of interests in property. The method adopted will depend upon the instructions given by the client as to the purpose of the valuation and upon the skill in approach of the valuer. Overall, however, it must be borne in mind that there is no individual 'correct' method. This was recognised by Kekewich J in *Love v Mack*:[1]

> 'The law does not say that in any branch of intelligent operation, intelligent skill, there is necessarily one defined path which must be strictly followed, and that if one departs by an inch from that defined path one were necessarily at fault ... there is no absolute rule as regards the proper method of ascertaining the value in this case, and [the valuer] adopted methods which, if they are not perfect, if they are not the best, if they might have been improved upon, still are methods which a man of position, endeavouring to do his duty, might fairly adopt without it being said he was wanting in reasonable care and skill.'

Further, the court, in assessing the competence of a valuation, will primarily be concerned with whether or not the resultant figure reported to the client is one which a competent valuer could have reported – rather than to investigate whether there were errors of approach. This is apparent from *Mount Banking Corporation Ltd v Brian Cooper & Co*[2] where errors in the approach of the valuer were able to be demonstrated but where the reported valuation figure was found to fall within an acceptable bracket of tolerance. The judge indicated:[3]

> 'If the valuation that has been reached cannot be impeached as a total, then, however erroneous the method or its application by which the valuation had been reached, no loss has been sustained, because: it was a proper valuation.'[4]

---

1 [1905] 92 LT 345 at 349.
2 [1992] 2 EGLR 142.
3 [1992] 2 EGLR 142 at 145.
4 Endorsement for this approach is to be found in *Craneheath Securities v York Montague Ltd* [1996] 7 EG 141.

If errors in the adoption and/or implementation of a particular valuation methodology can be demonstrated, however, this is likely to represent a strong indication of a negligently reported final value.[1]

Wording the report

4.2 The way in which a report, however, is worded is crucially important to any consideration of the extent to which the addressee of a valuation is entitled to rely upon it for the purposes of some transaction. In *BFG Bank AG v Brown & Mumford Ltd*[2] the defendant valuers provided a report in relation to the site of a proposed hotel as follows:

> 'There is a high possibility of obtaining consent on this site, even though it may have to be referred to in appeal. Assuming that permission will be obtained for a 100 bedroom hotel ... I am of the opinion that this site may realise in excess of £1 million. Its present value with a reasonably high chance of a successful planning submission should realise between £450,000 and £500,000.'

At the material date the property had a market value in the region of £15,000 to £20,000. Although the defendant did not dispute that the reported valuation was negligent, it sought to contend that the bank which made an advance of £270,000 upon the faith of the report did not in fact rely upon it. The ingenious but flawed argument advanced was that the bank had simply misinterpreted the report. The defendant contended that the report, properly read, was based upon a prospect of planning permission being granted which was remote and not so as to exceed 5 per cent. The bank accordingly, without seeking clarification from the defendant valuer, proceeded to make an advance based upon its own misinterpretation or misreading of the report. This argument was roundly rejected by the Court of Appeal which concluded that the meaning of the letter should be interpreted on the basis of that which an ordinary person to whom the letter was addressed could reasonably have thought was the extent of the risk of planning permission being refused. The valuer could only be excused from liability if he could establish that the interpretation placed by the bank on the letter was an unreasonable one, which it was not. Accordingly, the bank was held properly entitled to have relied upon the report for the purposes of deciding to make the relevant advance.

COMPARATIVE METHOD OF VALUATION

4.3 This is the commonest method of valuation adopted by valuers. The value of a property is ascertained by considering the known contemporaneous values of other similar properties in the locality. In employing this method a value is often attached on a £/m^2 basis. The RICS and ISVA have produced a Code of Measuring Practice so as to ensure uniformity of approach in

---

1 See *Nykredit Mortgage Bank Plc v Edward Erdman Group Ltd* [1996] 2 EG 110.
2 [1997] PNLR 202.

measuring areas. The net internal floor area of a property reflects, of course, only one feature, but the £/m^2 assessment is a useful starting point. The strength of this method depends upon a true comparison of like with like and detailed knowledge by the valuer of the other similar properties (comparables) relied upon. Actual 'sales' are better evidence than other mortgage valuations/ matrimonial valuations/remortgage valuations and/or valuations for rating band purposes. Of particular relevance will be any evidence of recent sales of the subject property. As Phillips J said in *Banque Bruxelles Lambert SA v John D Wood Commercial Ltd*:[1]

> 'Absent ... express instructions (to disregard a recent sale), a valuer who gives an open market valuation without considering the implications of a recent sale in the market of the property being valued is, in my judgment, negligent.'

It was noted earlier[2] that valuation being an art and not a science, it is accepted that surveyors may differ from one another by a margin either side of the 'correct value' or 'bracket of value' without either being incorrect. As Machin QC stated in *McIntyre v Herring Son & Daw*:[3]

> 'The permissible width of the bracket must be a matter to be decided upon the evidence of any particular case.'

With properties on a large housing estate, the acceptable margin of tolerance to allow for differing opinions of valuers will be smaller[4] than where a remote property is being valued with very little in the way of comparables to consider.[5] A rapidly rising market may also justify a greater degree of latitude.[6] It is important, however, that the permissible margin of error is not used as a false disguise for a negligently high valuation. This can inadvertently arise by substituting, for example, 10 per cent of the correct valuation, the figure produced by considering 10 per cent either side of the negligently high valuation.

THE RESIDUAL METHOD

4.4 This is an appropriate method where property has development or redevelopment potential. It is otherwise known as the Hypothetical Development method and is similar to a feasibility study.

In essence, this approach identifies how much a developer can afford to pay for a plot of land. This is itself a function of the amount of money likely to be

1 [1994] 2 EGLR 108.
2 See paras **1.19** to **1.20**.
3 [1988] 1 EGLR 231.
4 5 per cent was suggested in *BNP Mortgages Ltd v Barton Cook & Sams* [1996] 1 EGLR 239.
5 15 per cent was suggested in *BNP Mortgages Ltd v Barton Cook & Sams* supra.
6 15 per cent to 20 per cent was suggested in *Muldoon v Mays of Lillyput Ltd* [1993] 1 EGLR 43.

recovered on a later sale of the developed site ('the gross development value') less the costs of the development itself – including financing the works. The approach is best demonstrated by considering the following table.

5 terraced houses at £200,000 each =			
Gross Development Value	=		£1,000,000
Less			
Costs of development:			
Building costs: 5 houses × 180m^2 @ £500/m^2	=	£450,000	
Professional fees (architects, planners, quantity surveyors) @ 10% of building costs	=	£45,000	
Cost of borrowing half of building costs and professional fees @ 12% = $\frac{12}{100} \times \frac{495,000}{2}$	=	£29,700	
Legal expenses on sale of houses	say	£20,000	
Agent's fees on sale of houses	say	£16,000	
Advertising costs on sale	say	£10,000	
Developer's profit at 15%	say	£150,000	
Total development costs			£720,700
Residual sum			£279,300 (say £.3 million)

Minor adjustments in any of the above data can produce significantly different residual valuations so that the approach is to be regarded with caution in the absence of direct comparative evidence. It was nonetheless accepted in *Nykredit Mortgage bank Plc v Edward Erdman Group Ltd*[1] as capable of being an appropriate method of valuation for mortgage purposes. The factors which a competent valuer will consider in valuing development land were stated by Watkins J in *Singer & Friedlander Ltd v John D Wood & Co.*[2] These were said to include:

'(a) The kind of development of the land to be undertaken.

(b) The existence, if any, of planning permission in outline or in detail as to a part or the whole of the land. And if permission be for the building of houses, the situation and acreage of part of the land excluded from planning permission because, for example, of a tree preservation order, the need for schools and to the lay out of roads and other things. Furthermore, the number of houses permitted or likely to be permitted to be built by the planning authority is a relevant, indeed a vital factor.

(c) The history of the land, including its use, changes of ownership and the most recent buying prices, planning applications and permissions, the implementation or otherwise of existing planning permissions, the reason for the failure, if it be the fact that a planning permission had not been implemented.

---

1 [1996] 1 EGLR 119.
2 [1977] 243 EG 212 at 214–215.

(d) The position of the land in relation to surrounding countryside, villages and towns and places of employment; the quality of access to it, the attractiveness or otherwise of its situation.

(e) The situation obtaining about the provision of services for example, gas, electricity, sewage and other drainage and water.

(f) The presence, if it be so, of any unusual difficulties confronting the development which will tend to increase the cost of it to an extent which affects the value of the land. A visit to the site must surely find a prominent place among physical activities to be undertaken.

(g) The demand in the immediate locality for houses of the kind likely to be built, with special regard to the situation of places of employment and increases to be expected in demand for labour. This will involve, inevitably, acquiring knowledge of other building developments recently finished or still in progress, especially having regard to rate of disposal, density and sale price of the houses disposed of. In this way the existence, if any, of local comparables, a valuable factor, can be discovered.

(h) Consultation with senior officers of the local planning authority is almost always regarded as an indispensable aid, likewise a knowledge of the approval planning policy for the local area; the study of the approved town or county map may prove rewarding.

(i) Whether ascertaining from the client if there have been any previous valuations of the land, and what effect, should be undertaken is probably questionable because the valuer's mind should not be exposed to the possibilities of affectation by the opinion of others.

(j) If he is a man whose usual professional activities do not bring him regularly into locality, or what is more important has never done so, he will obviously need to be especially careful in collecting as much relevant local knowledge as he can, possibly by consulting valuers who work regularly in the area.

(k) The availability of a labour force which can carry out the prospective development.'

The starting point must be, however, to identify with reasonable precision the Gross Development Value which will ultimately determine the residual site value.[1]

THE INVESTMENT METHOD/CAPITALISATION

4.5 This is the method of approach most frequently used to value commercial leasehold property. To understand its operation a grasp of basic terminology is required.

As with all investments, the valuation of any particular interest in property ('the capital value') reflects the returns which prospective investors could

---

1 See *Private Bank & Trust Co Ltd v S (UK) Ltd* [1993] 1 EGLR 144.

obtain by investing their capital elsewhere. The interest rate earned from such an investment is referred to as the 'yield'. The period of time in which the accumulated value of returns will result in the capital value of the investment being recovered is known as 'the pay back period' or 'the year's purchase'. To facilitate easy comparisons, the returns and yields are typically annualised.

Thus, if we assume an investor with £100,000 to spend and two properties – one with a tenant paying an annual rent of £10,000 and one with a tenant paying an annual rent of £20,000 – available to be acquired, the notional investor will have to wait 10 years in the case of the first property and 5 years in the case of the second property to be 'repaid' through the tenant's rent the capital outlay involved in the acquisition. This is equivalent to a 10 per cent and 20 per cent rate of return respectively on the capital sum of £100,000.

These concepts can be reduced to the following formula:

Capital value = annual return × year's purchase

and to obtain the percentage yield

Yield = 100/year's purchase

Let us consider the above by reference to the following table:

1	2	3	4	5
Property	*Net Income*	*Capital Value*	*Years Purchase*	*Percentage Yield*
Factory	£25,000	£250,000	10	10
Shop	£50,000	£550,000	11	9.09
Offices	£75,000	£900,000	12	8.33
Offices	£100,000	£1.3 million	13	7.69

From the above table, it will be apparent that if the purchaser of the first factory with an annual net income flow of £25,000 is prepared to wait 10 years to recover the cost of acquisition (£250,000) this reflects a return on such an investment at the rate of 10 per cent. If he was prepared to wait 20 years to recover the value of his outlay then the percentage yield would be 5 per cent. It will be noted that the lower the yield, the higher the year's purchase and thus the greater the capital value of the premises will be likely to be.

Ascertaining the yearly rent

4.6 The starting point in considering the value of commercial leasehold property, however, is to ascertain the annualised rental value. This involves selecting appropriate units of comparison. If, for example, it is known that a ground floor shop with a frontage of 6m and a depth of 12m has recently been let for an annual rent of £10,000, it is possible to determine the £/m^2 inherent in this letting. Broadly the valuer will proceed as follows:

6m × 12m @ £10,000 pa = 72m^2 @ £10,000
= £138.888/m^2

Armed with the above analysis, the valuer will be in a position to give an opinion as to the value of a similar ground floor shop with (say) a frontage of 5m and a depth of 15.6m. He will conduct the following rent assessment:

5m × 15.6m @ £138.888/m^2 = Estimated rental value
= £10,833 pa (say £11,000 pa)

In the case of shops and similar premises, the frontage is of greater value than the hinter parts of the store which may be used for storage or be less visible to passing trade. With smaller properties, the shop frontage is itself sometimes valued by allocating the annual rent to a £/m^2 shop frontage. This rough and ready approach is of no reliability in the case of more complex units. In such circumstances a more complicated method of approach is employed called 'zoning'.

In this approach the first (usually) 7m of shop front depth attract the highest £/m^2 rent [the 'Zone A rent']. The next 7m depth of floor space is valued at half the rent in terms of Zone A [the 'itza' rent]. This Zone B rent is then again halved in respect of the next (up to) 7m depth of space to create the Zone C rent.

Again, this approach may be best illustrated by considering the worked example set out below:

Analysis of rent of 1 High Street – a shop with a 7m frontage and 18m depth let recently for £16,500 pa.

Zone A = 7m × 7m @ £X/m^2	=	49X
Zone B = 7m × 7m @ $\frac{\text{£X/m}^2}{2}$	=	24.5X
Zone C = 7m × 4m @ $\frac{\text{£X/m2}}{4}$	=	7X
Total rental value £16,500 pa	=	80.5X

X = £204.97

The value/m^2 of Zone A = £204.97 × 49	=	£10,043.53
The value/m^2 of Zone B = £102.48 × 49	=	£5,021.52
The value/m^2 of Zone C = £51.24 × 28	=	£1,434.72
	Total	£16,499.77
	(say	£16,500 pa)

THE CONTRACTOR'S METHOD/SUMMATION METHOD

4.7 This method of approach is relevant to properties which rarely change hands, eg hospitals, schools, libraries and civic buildings where the cost of construction/replacement is the predominant factor. An understanding of this approach is best gathered by considering the following table:

	Cost of site	£1,000,000
Plus	Building cost @ £1,500/m^2 × 450m^2	£675,000
Less	25% obsolescence allowance (based on building cost)	£168,750
		£1,506,250
Less	15% depreciation allowance (based on building cost)	£101,250
	Value of existing property	£1,405,000

In the above table, it will be noted that deductions are made to allow for depreciation of the buildings and obsolescence of design. The precise allowances to be made are difficult to determine and will depend upon the views of individual valuers. The building costs may be assessed from tender figures if available or estimated from tables, eg those published by the RICS Building Cost Information Service. These provide costings on a m^2 basis for different types of structure.

THE MORTGAGE/EQUITY APPROACH

4.8 According to this methodology, the potential purchaser calculates the return required on his own money (his equity) and then deducts this from the income from the property which will leave a balance from which to service interest on money borrowed on mortgage. The maximum price for the property is thus the sum of the investor's own money and what he can afford to borrow. This is an approach rarely used and of little value save as a feasibility study by a potential purchaser. It is again best illustrated by reference to the worked example in the table below:

Total property income		£20,000 pa
Purchaser's capital		£100,000
Return required at 11%		.1
Purchaser's income required		£10,000
Balance available to pay mortgage interest		£10,000 pa
Mortgage obtainable @ 12% pa		
£10,000 = $\frac{MC \times 12}{100}$	MC =	£83,333
	Equity	£100,000
	Plus mortgage	£83,000
Maximum price available for property		£183,333
		(say £180,000)

THE PROFITS METHOD

4.9 By this method, which is also known as the Accounts Method, the estimated rental value which a tenant can afford to pay or a landlord realistically expect to charge may be determined. If, for example, a valuer has to assess the rental value of a public house which in the previous trading year is known to have received gross takings of £250,000 the valuer considering that any incoming tenant would be likely to run the business in a similar way will arrive at the following valuation:

Gross takings			£250,000
Less	Cost of Purchases	£60,000	
	Running expenses	£40,000	
			£100,000
			£150,000
Less	Owner's income from business	£45,000	
	Interest on capital (furniture fittings/ fixtures etc) @ 10% on £50,000	£5,000	
			£50,000
	Divisible balance		£100,000

The valuer may decide it is appropriate to split the divisible balance as to (say) 55 per cent profit to the business, leaving 45 per cent available for payment of rent. The rental value will therefore be estimated at £45,000. In carrying out the above exercise, the valuer will need to have access to any previous books of account. It will also be important to consider whether the business has been run well or badly so that a poor and inefficient trader does not result in an unreasonably low valuation. Similarly, it is possible that the business may have been run by a particularly popular and successful trader whose presence has added to receipts in a way in which it would not be realistic to predict any incoming tenant would immediately replicate.

Valuing fully equipped properties

4.10 Guidance on the approach to valuing fully equipped properties as operational entities (hotels, public houses, other licensed premises, private health care facilities and leisure property) is to be found in Practice Statement 8 of the RICS Appraisal and Valuation Manual revised in June 1996 and effective from 1 August 1996. Generally the competent valuer will be expected to collect the material, such as information as to the income and the outgoings for himself before giving a valuation.[1] Consideration of the broad approach required by the valuer carrying out such a valuation was given by Gibson J in *Corisand Investments Ltd v Druce & Co*:[2]

1 See *Oldgate Estates Ltd v Toplis & Harding and Russell* [1939] 3 All ER 209.
2 [1978] EGD 769 at 781–783.

'I have no doubt after considering the evidence of (the expert witnesses) that in order to discharge the duty of care of an ordinarily competent valuer in valuing property such as this hotel, the valuer must have regard to the following matters of principle and fact:

(i) He must by inspection of the property, and by enquiry, learn enough of the property to be able to start upon the basic method of valuation which he will apply ...

(ii) The purpose of the valuer's work is to determine the price which the property would fetch if offered for sale at the relevant time and in the relevant circumstances ...

(iii) When he has sufficiently informed himself as to the size, nature and condition of the property he can select the various methods of valuation by which he will guide and check his opinion ...

(iv) Hotels are bought and owned to make money by operating them. Accordingly, in estimating what purchasers in the market would pay for a particular hotel, the principle or at least a well known and respected method is to value the hotel as it is as a going concern, including goodwill and contents. The purchaser would calculate what he could expect to earn in the hotel as it stands, or as he could make it operate, and what price it is sensible to pay for the right and opportunity to earn that income. The valuer tries to make the same calculation.

(v) In a valuation for mortgage purposes it is again common ground that the valuer cannot take the open market going concern valuation. The valuer cannot, in short, include in his valuation for this purpose any valuable part of the going concern valuation which would not or might well not be there when the mortgagee attempts to realise his security ....

The essence of this type of valuation is that 'the purchaser (will) calculate what he (can) expect to earn in the hotel as it stands or as he could make it operate and what price it is sensible to pay for the right and opportunity to earn that income. The valuer tries to make the same calculation.'[1]

THE DISCOUNTED CASH FLOW TECHNIQUE

4.11 The investment or capitalisation method discussed above[2] involves a determination of the capital value of the right to receive an income generated by a property or investment at a rate of return fixed in perpetuity. By definition this technique does not allow for variations in the level of receipt of future income. With most investment properties it is likely that the income flow will vary over the length of (for example) a long commercial lease. There will be provision for (usually) upwards-only rent reviews, which may or may not depending upon market conditions at the date of implementation result in increases in the level of rental income. What is therefore required is a method of valuation sensitive to likely future changes so that the present capital value

1 [1978] EGD 769 at 781 to 782.
2 Paragraphs **4.5** to **4.6**.

of an investment can be determined, even though what is being purchased is the right to receive differing levels of future income becoming payable at different future dates. This need is addressed by the discounted cash flow analysis. This approach utilises:

(a) 'the amount of £1 table', ie the amount to which £1 will accumulate if it earns a given rate of compound interest for a given number of years; and

(b) 'the present value of £1 table', ie the sum which needs to be invested at the present time at a given rate of interest in order to accumulate £1 by the end of a given period of time.

Its application is best understood by considering the table set out below:

End of Year	*Particulars*	*Outflow*	*Inflow*	*Net flow + or –*	*PV of £1 @ 12%*	*Net outflow*	*Net inflow*
0	Purchase Price	100,000		–110,000	1	110,000	
	Purchase Costs	10,000					
1	Rent		10,000				
	Repairs	500					
	Insurance	200					
	Management	300		+9,000	0.8928571		8,035.71
2	Rent		10,000				
	Repairs	500					
	Insurance	200					
	Management	300		+9,000	0.7971939		7,174.74
3	Rent		10,000				
	Repairs	2,000					
	Insurance	500					
	Management	500		+7,000	0.7117802		4,982.46
4	Rent		10,000				
	Repairs	200					
	Insurance	500					
	Management	300					
	Sale proceeds		120,000				
	Costs of Sale	5,000		+124,000	0.6355181		78,804.24
						110,000	98,997.15

Net present value = £11,002.85

In the above example we can see that the present value of the premises can be assessed taking into account a prediction as to its future value and making allowances for heavy repairs expenditure in year 3. The analysis is also sensitive to increases in rental income capable of being predicted. Whereas traditional methods cannot reflect the possibility of the future sale of the income-producing asset at an enhanced value, such a calculation is easily incorporated in a discounted cash flow calculation. The discounted cash flow technique is therefore useful in facilitating the estimation of a true return over time, allowing for changes in value and liabilities over the time period.

OVERVIEW

4.12 Rarely will the reporting valuer provide a report which explicitly identifies his reasoning process and/or patently sets out the methodologies employed. The experienced valuer will have a reliable *feel* for the true value of a property. This instinctive approach whilst not amenable to scientific analysis is not to be lightly dismissed. As Gibson J said in *Corisand Investments Ltd v Druce & Co*:[1]

> 'As to the . . . weight to be given by the valuer or by the court to . . . the instinctive or expertise method, this issue is, I think, of more apparent than real importance. It seems to me that all methods of valuation ... are in truth variations of the comparison method, and all, to a greater or lesser extent, proceed by what has been called but inaccurately called the instinctive method. The forming of an instinctive estimate of the value of [a property] must depend upon a valuer deciding that purchasers are likely to pay for this particular [property] so much more or less than other purchasers paid or offered to pay for other [properties] according to what appears to be the relevant differences in size, location and quality etc. That is not an instinctive process – it is the making of an estimate of sale value from experience based upon an indirect and general comparison method. It differs from the direct comparison method in one very important particular – the valuer, if challenged, either does not or cannot produce for scrutiny the comparables upon which he was proceeding in making his estimate. That is no criticism of him – a valuer acting in his profession will at any date have in mind, no doubt, a large amount of information about the market, much of which he could not recall a year later and much of which could not be produced for scrutiny.'

Given the extent to which valuers, however, may now find themselves facing claims by lenders and purchasers/borrowers it is important nonetheless for a detailed record to be kept of the matters taken into account in arriving instinctively at a reported valuation.

1 [1978] EGD 769 at 783–784.

Chapter 5

VALUERS AND RENT REVIEWS

INTRODUCTION

5.1 In practice, valuers become involved in dealing with rent reviews in three distinct capacities: in the capacity of adviser to and negotiator for a landlord or tenant over a review; as an independent expert retained by both landlord and tenant to resolve a review and as an arbitrator appointed by or on behalf of the landlord and tenant to determine the rent due under a lease containing such a provision. In the first case, a duty of care is owed to exercise reasonable care and skill to the retaining client; in the second case, the independent expert valuer owes a duty of care to both landlord and tenant. When acting as arbitrator, however, the valuer is immune from any action in negligence brought against him.[1]

EXPERT OR ARBITRATOR?

5.2 Because of the immunity from suit of an arbitrator, it is important to identify the capacity in which a valuer engaged to fix a rent on behalf of a landlord and tenant has been appointed. The primary account of the different role of experts and arbitrators was given by Lord Esher in *Re Carus-Wilson & Green*[2] as follows:

> 'The intention of the parties was that the [third party] should hold an enquiry in the nature of a judicial enquiry and hear the respective cases of the parties and decide upon the evidence laid before him, (here) the case is one of arbitration ... (but) there are cases in which a person is appointed to ascertain some matter for the purpose of preventing differences from arising – not of settling them when they have arisen – and where the case is not one of arbitration but mere valuation.'

Lord Wheatley identified the following indicia of an arbitration as guidelines in considering whether a person was exercising an arbitral rather than an expert function:

---

1 *Sutcliffe v Thackrah* [1974] AC 727.

2 (1886) 18 QBD 7.

- is there a dispute or difference between the parties which has been formulated in some way or another? Is the dispute or difference to be remitted by the parties to the person appointed to resolve it in such a manner that he is called upon to exercise a judicial function?
- have the parties been provided with the opportunity to present evidence and/or submission in support of their respective claims in the dispute?
- have the parties agreed to accept his decision?[1]

In *Fordgate (Bingley) Ltd v Argyll Stores Ltd*,[2] a tenant challenged the claim of a landlord to have a surveyor appointed as arbitrator to determine the rent due upon a review on the basis that the lease contained a provision only for the appointment of a surveyor as expert. The relevant review clause provided:

> '(3) if the landlord and tenant shall not have agreed the open market rent less than 6 months before the relevant review date, the open market rent shall be determined by a surveyor (hereinafter called the appointed surveyor) to be agreed upon in writing by the landlord and the tenant not less than 4 months before the relevant review date and in default of such agreement to be nominated by the President for the time being of the Royal Institution of Chartered Surveyors upon the application of the landlord ... (4) the determination of the open market rent by the appointed surveyor (which shall be final and binding on the landlord and the tenant without recourse to the provisions for arbitration hereinbefore contained) and the fees of the appointed surveyor shall be borne by the landlord and the tenant in equal shares ....'

The reference to the provisions for arbitration 'hereinbefore contained' was a reference to an earlier clause in the lease which contained three specific references to arbitration. Mr Nicholas Stewart QC held that the above provisions were effective to constitute the appointed surveyor an expert and not an arbitrator:

> '... first ... what I describe as the deliberate non-adoption in [the Rent Review clause] of any express reference to arbitration, by clear contrast with the provisions of clause 5 ... of the lease to which I have referred. Second, the third schedule does not necessarily presuppose a dispute, even though in many instances in practice no doubt that might arise. Third, the nature of the exercise. Of course it could be conducted by, or it could be provided for it to be conducted by, arbitration, but it is an exercise – the determination of rent under a rent review – which is particularly suitable for expert procedures.'

These considerations were found to be compelling. By contrast, in *Palacath Ltd v Flanagan*,[3] the use of the words 'Surveyor', 'determination' and 'final and binding' were regarded as equally consistent with an appointment as arbitrator or expert. After standard review provisions providing for the appointment of a surveyor to determine the rent due, the lease went on to provide:

---

1 *Arenson v Arenson* [1977] AC 405 at 428.
2 [1994] 39 EG 135.
3 [1985] 2 All ER 161.

'for [the purpose of the appointment] the surveyor: (1) will act as an expert and not as an arbitrator (2) will consider any statement of reason of valuation or report submitted to him [by the landlord or the tenant] but will not be in any way limited or fettered thereby (3) will be entitled to rely on his own judgment and opinion (4) will within 2 months after his appointment: give to the landlord and to the tenant written notice of the amount of the rent as determined by him and his determination will be final and binding ....'

In due course the defendant fixed the rent. The plaintiff landlords then brought proceedings in negligence alleging that the surveyor had failed properly to carry out his valuation function. The defendant denied negligence and asserted that on a proper construction of the lease he had been appointed as an arbitrator so that no claim for negligence could be made against him. Mars-Jones J rejected this contention. The key question was whether the defendant was obliged to exercise a judicial function in making his determination. In short, was he to conduct a judicial enquiry by hearing the parties and the evidence of witnesses and to arrive at a decision upon that evidence, or was he entitled to act solely upon his own expert opinion. Given the expressed right for the valuer to rely upon his own judgment and opinion, it was difficult to regard the terms of the appointment as envisaging anything other than an appointment as expert. Indeed, the express stipulation for the defendant to act as an expert and not an arbitrator, although not conclusive, was a strong indicator to be taken into account.

Immunity from collateral suit

5.3 Where the surveyor is acting in an advisory capacity to either the landlord or the tenant and the advice results in a reference to arbitration or resolution of the rent liability by the court, the 'expert' may, in narrow circumstances, also enjoy an immunity from suit. In *Palmer v Durnford Ford*[1] the plaintiff purchaser of a defective lorry tractor unit retained an engineer to prepare a report on the cause of the defects. On the basis of the report, proceedings were taken against the vendor which, in the result, failed. The purchaser then brought proceedings inter alia against the expert complaining that his advice had been negligent and that he had not been sufficiently qualified in any event to provide the advice. The action against the engineer was struck out at first instance as disclosing no reasonable cause of action but reinstated on appeal. In dealing with the immunity attaching to a witness in giving evidence from collateral civil proceedings in negligence, Mr Simon Tuckey QC stated:

'I approached the matter by noting first that experts are usually liable to their clients for advice given in breach of their contractual duty of care and secondly that the immunity is based upon public policy and should therefore only be conferred where it is absolutely necessary to do so. Thus, prima facie the immunity should only be given where to deny it would mean that expert witnesses would be inhibited from giving truthful and fair evidence in Court. Generally I do not think that

1 [1992] 1 QB 483.

liability for failure to give careful evidence to his client should inhibit an expert from giving truthful and fair evidence in Court. Accordingly I do not accept that the immunity can be as wide as that contended for. I can see no good reason why an expert should not be liable for the advice which he gives to his client as to the merits of the claim, particularly if proceedings had not been started and a fortiori as to whether he is qualified to advise at all. Since both these allegations are made in this case I do not think that the decision to strike out the whole of the Statement of Claim can be justified. At least it is not plain and obvious that it should be done. The problem is where to draw the line given that there is immunity for evidence given in Court and it must extend to the preparation of such evidence to avoid the immunity being outflanked and rendered of little use. The problem was considered by the House of Lords in *Saif Ali v Sydney Mitchell & Co* [1980] AC 198 in the analogous but not identical situation of the advocates' immunity from suit for what he does in Court. In that case the House decided that the immunity extended to some pre-trial work but only where the particular work was so intimately connected with the case in Court that it could fairly be said to be a preliminary decision affecting the way that the case was to be conducted when it came to a hearing. I think a similar approach could be adopted in the case of an expert.'

It may be that this decision goes too far. In *Walpole v Partridge & Wilson*[1] the Court of Appeal recognised that whilst in general a professional negligence claim would not be entertained where it involved a collateral attack upon a decision reached in other proceedings, there were a number of exceptions, including where the earlier proceedings had not resulted in a decision on the merits. This may arise because a plaintiff chooses to submit to judgment. This was in fact the position in *Palmer v Durnford Ford* where the plaintiff withdrew his claim at trial. The Court of Appeal in *Walpole* accordingly questioned whether Mr Palmer's claim ought perhaps not to have been struck out as against the engineer.

STANDARD OF CARE

5.4 Whether acting as an independent or advisory expert, the surveyor owes his client or the parties a duty to use the reasonable care and skill of the surveyor of ordinary competence measured by the professional standard of the time.[2] The clearest exposition of the duties of an independent expert was given by Judge Zucker QC in *Zubaida v Hargreaves*:[3]

'I take the relevant principles of law relating to the duties of an independent expert appointed to determine a rent pursuant to the Rent Review provisions in a lease to be well established. They are as follows:-

1 [1994] QB 106.
2 Per Kenneth Jones J in *Belvedere Motors Ltd v King* [1981] 260 EG 813.
3 [1993] 2 EGLR 170 (approved by the Court of Appeal at [1995] 09 EG 320).

1. An independent expert, unlike an arbitrator, does not have immunity from being sued for negligence. He has duties to both parties and is liable in negligence if he causes loss to either of them by failure to take due care or to exercise reasonable professional skill in carrying out his duties.

2. He will not be guilty of negligence if he acted in accordance with the practice of competent professional opinion; and where there is a difference of opinion in the profession if he had acted in accordance with the practice accepted as proper by a substantial number of persons in his profession.

3. The task of valuation rarely admits a precise conclusion. Often there are many imponderables. Experts using care may arrive at different conclusions without anyone being justified in saying that any of them did so through incompetence or lack of care.

4. It is not the task of the court to seek to replace an independent expert's figure with some other figure determined by it, but to determine only whether the independent expert omitted to consider some matter which he ought to have considered, or took into account matters which he ought not to have taken into account, or in some other way failed to adopt the procedure and practice accepted as standard in his profession. If the rent determined by the independent expert in an individual case is significantly outside the bracket which the evidence shows to be acceptable, that may be evidence of negligence on his part.'

The role of the exercise of individual informed judgment by the duly appointed expert was emphasised by Judge Moseley QC in *Wallshire Ltd v Aarons*[1] where he stated:

> '... there was a consensus among the valuers who gave evidence that valuation entails the exercise of judgment. The procedure or thought process of a valuer is to get, first of all, a feel for the right rental and then to cast around for evidence of comparable cases to see whether his feel is right or wrong. He can get that feel for the right rental from his own knowledge or by looking at the comparables themselves. Valuation is not an exact science as the plaintiff's expert vividly put it, he is not a computer. I deduce from that that one does not determine the ITZA by looking at comparables; rather the comparables are of assistance to the valuer in order to enable him to decide whether his feel, his judgment, is right or wrong.'

RICS Guidance Notes

5.5 In 1981, the Royal Institution of Chartered Surveyors published Guidance Notes For Surveyors Acting As Arbitrators Or As Independent Experts. Prior to the sixth edition, earlier versions of this note did not focus specific attention upon the position of experts in rent reviews. The current version of the Guidance Notes (December 1996) is helpful in indicating the materials and method of approach which a competent expert will be likely to adopt. Guidance 2.1.4 reminds the independent expert that his appointment:

---

1 [1989] 02 EG 81.

> 'carries with it a heavy responsibility – a person considered suitable for appointment is approached and asked to confirm: (a) that the subject matter of the dispute falls within the sphere of his own normal professional practice (not merely that of his firm); (b) that he will be able to undertake the task with reasonable expedition; (c) that there is no other reason why he should not accept the appointment; (d) that he complies with any special requirements of the niece; (e) that he is not currently engaged as arbitrator or as independent expert in another case where his duties and functions to the parties would conflict with his duties and functions to the parties in the case; (f) that he has appropriate professional indemnity insurance.'

A surveyor considering accepting such an appointment will do well to establish proper terms of reference before embarking upon the task of determining the rent due. Guidance 4.2.1 encourages the surveyor to agree with the parties terms appropriate to define the extent of the obligations he is undertaking.' It will be usual and useful to hold a preliminary meeting between the parties in order to ascertain the facts giving rise to the need for his appointment and to resolve whether the determination is to take place after oral or written submissions by the landlord and tenant with or without expert assistance, or whether the process is to be one dealt with by the experts unaided in this regard. Guidance 4.3.6 of the sixth edition emphasised the dual function to the expert's approach:

> '... an independent expert has a dual function. In the first place, he must assemble all the information material to a decision on the issue in respect of which he has been appointed. In the second place, he must arrive at a determination upon that material by applying his own professional judgment.'

Once ready to make the determination, 'the independent expert should set it down clearly in writing and make it available to the parties.' Guidance 4.5.1 indicates a framework within which to set out the determination.

BREACH OF DUTY

5.6 Examples of successful actions against expert advisers are few; examples of successful actions against independent experts are even fewer. Any attempt to define the sort of breach for which an expert may be liable would be necessarily incomplete as it is not possible to predict the ingenuity of every future aggrieved party in formulating a criticism or complaint. It is suggested, however, that the following are likely to be matters where any default by the surveyor will lay him open to criticism.

Knowledge of the locality

5.7 Given that a surveyor acting as independent expert will be expected to use his own knowledge and expertise in fixing the rent in addition to considering any materials provided by the landlord or tenant, it will be important that the expert is familiar with the rent paid for comparable properties in the immediate locality of the leased premises. In a successful action against such an expert in *CIL Securities Ltd v Briant Champion Long*[1] Mr John Mowbray QC recorded in his judgment that:

> '[the defendant] was a West End surveyor with little experience of the levels of rents of show rooms in Fonthill Road, which both the expert witnesses and [the defendant] himself agree is unique.'

Whilst the surveyor will, however, be expected to investigate and find out information where his knowledge is lacking or incomplete so that absence of knowledge of the locality does not exclude him from accepting an appointment, it is likely to place an expert at a grave disadvantage.

Interpreting the clause

5.8 The surveyor will be expected to construe the rent review clause properly so as accurately to define the nature of the interest being valued and the assumptions upon which the rent falls to be determined. This will require familiarity with the legal principles underlying the implementation of the rent or price fixing machinery. In *Jenkins v Betham*,[2] the defendant was instructed to value the delapidations of a rectory. The valuation carried out was performed upon an erroneous view of the law, namely that it was required only to deal with the cost of making the premises habitable as opposed to putting them into good and substantial repair. As Jervis CJ said:

> 'the defendants could not be expected to supply minute and accurate knowledge of the law; but we think that under the circumstances they might properly be required to know the general rules applicable to the valuation of ecclesiastical property and the broad distinction which exists between the cases of an incoming and an outgoing tenant and incoming and outgoing incumbent.'

The surveyor must of course maintain his legal knowledge up to date. In *Weedon v Hindwood, Clarke & Esplin*,[3] a valuer was held to be negligent in agreeing a compulsory purchase price with the district valuer based upon a wrong view as to the date upon which the premises were required to be valued.

Extent of the demise

5.9 The extent of the leased premises will be crucial to the determination of the proper rent payable. In *Carreras Ltd v DE&J Levy*,[4] the surveyors retained to assist the plaintiffs in finding suitable office accommodation wrongly indicated that the subject property had a net area of 26,996 sq ft; the correct area was 26,048 sq ft. This miscalculation of floor area was held to be negligent (although the defendant escaped a finding of liability on other grounds).

1 [1993] 2 EGLR 164.
2 [1855] 15 CB 167.
3 [1974] 234 EG 121.
4 [1970] 215 EG 707.

Investigation of comparables

5.10 The surveyor whether acting as expert or in an advisory capacity will be expected to know of and more particularly ascertain evidence of other comparable transactions to support his advice or determination. This duty is explicitly referred to in the guidance notes discussed above. In *CIL Securities Ltd v Briant Champion Long*,[1] the judge stated:

> '[the defendant] was obviously under a duty to inform himself of the current rental values. Finding convincing comparables was the best way of doing that, also of preparing for negotiations with the tenants or their advisers and, if necessary, any arbitration that might come along. I find that [the defendants'] efforts in searching for comparables fell below the required professional standard of care and diligence.'

Giving of proper advice

5.11 In acting in an advisory capacity, the surveyor will often be confronted with the need to decide whether the client's best interests would be served by accepting the other side's proposals for rent or recommending a reference to arbitration or litigation. Whether to settle, continue negotiations or force such a reference will be a difficult and often finely balanced decision. The observations of Anderson J in *Karpenko v Paroian, Currey, Cowin & Houston*[2] in relation to legal advice in favour of settlement apply with equal force to the position of a surveyor advising a client:

> 'in my view, an important element of public policy is involved. It is in the interests of public policy to discourage suits and encourage settlements. The vast majority of suits are settled. It is the almost universal practice among responsible members of the legal profession to pursue settlement until some circumstance or combination of circumstances leads them to conclude that a particular dispute can only be resolved by a trial. I say nothing of the suits which are settled by reason of sloth, or inexperience, or lack of stomach for the fight. They have nothing to do with this case. What is relevant and material to the public interest is that an industrious and competent practitioner should not be unduly inhibited in making a decision to settle a case by the apprehension that some Judge, viewing the matter subsequently, with all the acuity of vision given by hindsight, and from the calm security of the bench, may tell him he should have done otherwise. Through his decision to settle a lawyer brings all his talents and experience both recollected and existing somewhere below the level of the conscious mind, all his knowledge of the law and its processes. Not least he brings to it his hard earned knowledge that the trial of the law suit is costly, time consuming and taxing for everyone involved and attended by a host of contingencies, foreseen and unforeseen. Upon all of this he must decide whether he should take what is available by way of settlement, or press on. I can think of few areas where the difficult question of what constitutes negligence, which gives rise to liability, and what constitutes at worst an error of judgment, which does not, is harder to answer. In my view it would only be in the case of some egregious error:- that negligence would be found.'

---

1 [1993] 2 EGLR 164.

2 [1981] 117 DLR (3d) 383 (Ontario High Court).

None the less, in *CIL Securities Ltd v Briant Champion Long*[1] the court found that the expert advising the landlord in omitting to analyse comparables on both a zoning and an overall basis failed to realise that an arbitrator would have awarded higher rents than those otherwise recommended for acceptance so that negligence was thus established.

Use of appropriate comparables

5.12 The competent surveyor will be expected to know not only of relevant comparable transaction evidence, to find out about and investigate such evidence but to be able to discern what evidence may be properly relied upon and which should be discarded. As Judge Mosley QC said in *Wallshire Ltd v Aarons*:[2]

> 'The exercise in the present case is to enquire as to what is the open market rent of the premises and in discovering what is the open market rent on the premises the best evidence is the decision of the market; that is, open market lettings are the best evidence of what the market's decision is. Second best to that are rent reviews which are negotiated between valuers, because although their aim is to achieve the same end result of deciding what the market rent is, their decision is not tested by the market, their decision, their agreement, is based on their conclusions about what the market would decide. Negotiated settlements therefore can be unreliable because of the possibility of error piled on error. They need as [the plaintiff's expert] says an occasional window of reality provided by open market decisions.'

In *Land Securities Plc v Westminster City Council*,[3] Hoffman J held that evidence of rents determined by an arbitration could not be used as a comparable in other arbitrations. The position would appear to be the same with determinations by the court. The judge indicated:

> 'An arbitration award is an arbitrator's opinion, after hearing the evidence before him of the rent at which the premises could reasonably have been let. The letting is hypothetical, not real. It is therefore not direct evidence of what was happening in the market. It is the arbitrator's opinion of what would have happened [the arbitrator] is no doubt an expert valuer but I do not think he gave his award in that capacity. An arbitrator is obliged to act solely upon the evidence adduced by the parties. [The arbitrator] may, by reason of his expertise, have known about matters which cast doubt upon points which went unchallenged in the arbitration. If he had been acting as an expert he would have been able to take this knowledge into account. As an arbitrator he would not. His position in my judgment was no different from that of a Judge determining the rent of a new lease of premises under the Landlord and Tenant Act 1954. The admissibility of his judgment is evidence of value of the premises in proceedings between different parties cannot depend upon whether he happens to have expertise in valuation.'

---

1 [1993] 2 EGLR 164.
2 [1989] 2 EG 81.
3 [1992] 2 EGLR 15.

The expert or adviser will not, however, be open to criticism for putting forward evidence of transactions which post-date the operative review date. As Staughton J said in *Segama NV v Penny Lee Roy Ltd*:[1]

> 'If rent of comparable premises had been agreed on the day after the relevant date, I cannot see that such an agreement would be of no relevance whatever to what the market rent was at the relevant date itself. If the lapse of time before the agreement becomes greater then, as the arbitrator saw, the evidence will become progressively unreliable as evidence of rental values at the relevant date.'

Overall the important matter will be to ensure that the comparables used are truly appropriate. This may call for refined analysis. In *My Kinda Town Ltd v Castlebrook Properties Ltd*,[2] the rent due in respect of restaurant premises fell to be determined. The evidence comprised evidence of rents paid in respect of other premises in the locality and rents paid in respect of 'destination restaurants' outside the immediate area of the leased premises. It was held entirely appropriate to take into account the latter (higher) rents since the subject property was itself a 'destination restaurant' which would be of interest to other similar tenant proprietors.

Method of valuation

5.13 The expert will be expected to apply a method of valuation appropriate to the rent and premises being reviewed. In *CIL Securities Ltd v Briant Champion Long*[3] the defendant valuer considered the appropriate rent by reference only to the zoning technique.[4] He was rightly criticised by the judge for not also considering the overall rent due on a £/m^2 basis.

Margins of error

5.14 The rent finally determined or recommended will need to be at a level outside a range of potential rents which a competent valuer could have considered appropriate. In *Carreras Ltd v DE&J Levy*,[5] although the defendant surveyor had negligently miscalculated the floor area in respect of which rent would be payable (to the disadvantage of the tenant client), the level of rent ultimately agreed fell within the bracket of market value for the premises in question so that the error was found to have caused no loss. Nominal damages only were awarded.

Acting with reasonable despatch

5.15 In advising a client, the surveyor will be expected to act with reasonable diligence in providing advice and submitting materials on the client's behalf to the arbitrator, lawyers acting in a litigious dispute. In *Rajdev v*

---

1 [1983] 269 EG 322.
2 [1986] 1 EGLR 121.
3 [1993] 2 EGLR 164.
4 See para **4.6**.
5 [1970] 215 EG 707.

Becketts,[1] the surveyor was found to have been negligent in failing to submit representations to an arbitrator on time. Similarly, in *Thomas Miller & Co v Richard Saunders & Partners*,[2] the surveyor was found to have been negligent in failing to ensure that all relevant documentary evidence in his possession was placed before the arbitrator.

DAMAGES

5.16 Negligence in advising upon and/or determining the appropriate rent will be likely to result in a tenant either paying too much for the premises or a landlord receiving too little. The starting point for measuring the loss will therefore be the difference between the proper rent and the rent as agreed or determined. Because any damages will be awarded on a once and for all basis, it will be necessary to discount the sum thus calculated to take into account the fact that the plaintiff will be receiving all of it at once, whereas under the agreed or determined lease terms the rent will continue to be payable for a period of time up until the end of the lease or a further review.

In *Rajdev v Becketts*,[3] the competing rents advanced in negotiations by the landlord and tenant were £7,000 and £4,600 per annum respectively. The arbitrator, to whom the plaintiff's surveyor negligently omitted to make representations, determined a rent of £9,250. In negligence proceedings subsequently brought against the tenant's surveyor, the court found that the proper open market rent at the review date was £7,000 and assessed the difference in value between a lease with a rent of £9,250 and a lease with a rent of £7,000 as £8,100. This approach, however, may only represent the starting point for the assessment of damages. In *Knight v Lawrence*,[4] a mortgagee's receiver negligently omitted to serve trigger notices losing the opportunity for rent reviews of a number of investment properties. The properties subsequently realised less than would have been achieved if the passing rents had been increased. The court held that the landlords were entitled to the extra value which the properties would have realised if the reviews had been carried out. As the Vice-Chancellor said[5] 'the starting point is to try to ascertain what would have been the sale price of the properties if ... the rent reviews had properly taken place. That involves two stages. First, to find out at what level the reviewed rents would properly have been agreed. Secondly, to find out, taking into account the higher rent payable as a result of such review, what increased price would have been obtainable for each of the properties.' In that case, however, the judge went on to indicate that there ought to be an enquiry into how the plaintiff's resulting financial position would have differed if sales at enhanced prices had been capable of being achieved.

1 [1989] 35 EG 107.
2 [1989] 1 EGLR 267.
3 [1989] 2 EGLR 144.
4 [1991] 1 EGLR 143.
5 [1991] 1 EGLR 143 at 147.

It is important in this area to recognise that the court will take a flexible approach so as to ensure, where appropriate, proper compensation is awarded. It may not be sufficient simply to assess damages by difference between the market value of the investment property or leasehold interest with or without the benefit of a particular level of rent. The Court of Appeal has warned that the diminution in value approach 'should not be mechanistically applied in circumstances where it may appear inappropriate'.[1] This flexibility has resulted in a variety of awards in rent review cases involving negligent surveyors and solicitors being made on different footings. An amount equal to the rent lost to a landlord over a rental period was in one case awarded.[2] Damages in another case were assessed by reference to the value of the loss of a chance to a landlord of obtaining a higher rent.[3] Finally, the cost to a tenant company of extracting itself from a disadvantageous underlease was awarded in *County Personnel (Employment Agency) Ltd v Alan R Pulver.*[4]

---

1 *County Personnel (Employment Agency) Ltd v Alan R Pulver* [1987] 1 All ER 289 at 297.
2 *CIL Securities Limited v Briant Champion Long* [1993] 2 EGLR 164.
3 *Corfield v DS Bosher & Co* [1992] 1 EGLR 163.
4 [1987] 1 All ER 289.

Chapter 6

DAMAGES

INTRODUCTION

6.1 The assessment of damages payable by a negligent surveyor/valuer is a complex task. It is convenient to consider the issue from the perspective of three different categories of potential claimant.

PURCHASERS, VENDORS AND MORTGAGE LENDERS

Purchasers

6.2 The guiding principle is that the court will seek to award 'that sum of money which will put the party who has been injured, or who has suffered, in the same position as he would have been in if he had not sustained the wrong for which he is now getting his compensation or reparation'.[1] Applying this principle to the case of a house purchased on the faith of a negligently high valuation, damages will fall to be assessed by reference to 'the difference between the price actually paid for the property on the basis that the advice was good and the price at which it would be bought as it was in fact'.[2] The rationale of this approach was explained in *Philips v Ward*[3] where the plaintiff bought a house at a valuation of £25,000. Because of missed defects, the premises were actually worth £21,000 at the date of acquisition, although the repairs costs were estimated at £7,000. The claim to damages based upon the cost of repairing the property was rejected. Denning LJ stated:[4]

> 'I take it to be clear law that the proper measure of damages is the amount of money which will put the plaintiff into as good a position as if the surveying contract had been properly fulfilled. Now if the defendant had carried out his contract, he would have reported the bad state of the timbers. On receiving that report, the plaintiff either would have refused to have anything to do with the house, in which case he would have suffered no damage, or he would have bought it for a sum which represented its fair value in bad condition, in which case he would pay so much less on that account. The proper measure of damages is therefore the

---

1 Per Lord Blackburn in *Livingstone v Rawyards Coal Co* (1880) 5 App Cas 25 at 39.

2 *Simple Simon Catering Ltd v Binstock Miller & Co* (1973) 228 EG 527 at 529 per Lord Denning MR.

3 [1956] 1 All ER 874.

4 [1956] 1 All ER 874 at 875–876.

difference between the value in its assumed condition and the value in the bad condition which should have been reported to the client. In this action if the plaintiff were to recover from the surveyor £7,000, it would mean that the plaintiff would get for £18,000 (£25,000 paid less £7,000 received) a house and land which were worth £21,000. That cannot be right. The proper amount for him to recover is £4,000.'

This approach was categorically affirmed by the Court of Appeal in *Watts v Morrow*[1] where the cost of repairs to a defective property amounted to £34,000 compared with a difference in value between the reported value/price paid and actual value in defective condition of £15,000. As Bingham LJ stated:[2]

> 'The plaintiffs paid £177,500, the value of the house as it was represented to be. The value of the house in its actual condition was £162,500, a difference of £15,000. The actual cost of repairs was (in rounded up figures) £34,000. If the plaintiffs were to end up with the house and an award of £34,000 damages he would have obtained the house for £143,500. But even if the defendant had properly performed his contract this bargain was never on offer. The effect of the award is to put the plaintiffs not in the same position as if the defendant had properly performed but in a much better one.'

Of course, in assessing retrospectively the true value of the property in its defective condition, it will be necessary to have regard to the likely cost of repairs which the surveyor failed to take into account. As Purchas LJ said in *Steward v Rapley*:[3]

> 'There is no objection to a person who wishes to present a professional assessment of a market value from arriving at that market value by taking a value based on a good state of condition in the house and then deducting from it, either fully or appropriately discounted, the cost of putting it into an acceptable market condition.'

6.3 A recent striking example of the application of the diminution in value principle is *Gardner v Marsh & Parsons*.[4] In that case, surveyors negligently omitted to identify structural deficiencies in a maisonette on the 3rd and 4th floors of a newly converted building which the plaintiffs were considering purchasing on a long lease. On the faith of the defendant's report, they paid £114,000 for the lease. The market value of the interest, taking into account the structural deficiencies of the property amounted to £85,000. However, in negotiations with the landlord following purchase, the defects were remedied at no expense to the plaintiffs. The court, none the less, held that the plaintiff was entitled to recover the difference between the price paid and the true market value of the premises at the date of acquisition. The fact that the repair works had been carried out in any event by the landlord did not detract from

---

1 [1991] 4 All ER 937.
2 [1991] 4 All ER 937 at 959.
3 [1989] 1 EGLR 159 at 161.
4 [1997] 1 WLR 489.

the entitlement to damages. The court held the actions of the landlord were *res inter alios acta* and collateral to the surveyor's negligence.[1]

It follows from the above that, if in spite of a negligent report the purchaser pays the true market price for the property, he will have suffered no loss and will be unable to sustain a claim to anything other than nominal damages.[2] By parity of reasoning, if the purchaser decides to ignore the advice given by the valuer and to buy at a price in excess of the reported value, it is arguable that any damages for negligent over-valuation should be confined to the difference between the reported value and the actual value. This was the approach adopted in *Hardy v Wamsley-Lewis*[3] where the plaintiff paid £4,600 for a house which had been (over) valued by the defendant at £4,300. The true value of the property amounted to £3,500. The court held that the correct measure of damages was £800 (ie £4,300 less £3,500).[4] Given that attention is focused upon the extent to which the plaintiff was induced to overpay for a property, it is usual practice to assess damages as at the date of purchase.[5] Obviously where a purchaser has acquired a property containing unexpected defects, other losses and expenses are likely to arise not only associated with the cost of the immediate repairs. It may be necessary to move out of the premises whilst the repair works are carried out; costs will be likely to be incurred in investigating the extent of any defects and the best method of repair; whilst the remedial works are being undertaken, the premises may be unavailable for habitable or profitable use. Where such matters ought to have been taken into account by the competent valuer had the defects been identified, these losses will fall to be reflected in the true retrospective valuation of the property. In dealing with the cost of alternative accommodation incurred whilst repairs were carried out, Judge Hicks QC said in *Bigg v Howard Son & Gooch*:[6]

> 'If such an award is ever appropriate it is not so when the likely need for and probable cost of vacating the premises during repair, as foreseeable by a purchaser buying at the relevant date with knowledge of the defects, has been taken into account in assessing what price he would have been prepared to pay.'

Such incidental expenses are not, however, always capable of being dealt with in this way. In spite of the diminution in value approach to assessment discussed above, the courts have entertained additional claims to out of pocket expenses – notwithstanding that these represent items of expenditure which, even if known about, would have been unlikely to have formed part of any bargain

---

1 *Treml v Ernest W Gibson & Partners* [1984] 272 EG 68 where the court also held the availability of a grant towards the cost of repairs was irrelevant to the house purchaser's claim to damages for the difference in value between that (negligently) advised and the true value of the property.

2 See *Ford v White & Co* [1964] 2 All ER 755.

3 [1967] 203 EG 1039.

4 Cf *Oswald v Countrywide Surveyors Ltd* [1994] EGCS 150; *Shaw v Halifax (SW) Ltd* [1994] 2 EGLR 95.

5 See *Perry v Sidney Philips & Son* [1982] 3 All ER 705; *Reeves v Thrings & Long* [1993] NPC 159.

6 [1991] EGLR 173 at 175.

capable of being negotiated with the vendor. Such items include the wasted legal costs of purchase,[1] plus the value of a deposit forfeit to the vendor following withdrawal from a purchase upon discovering the deficiencies in the valuation report prior to completion.[2] The costs of resale were allowed in *Hardy v Wamsley-Lewis*.[3] The cost of investigating the defects has been allowed;[4] the cost of temporary repairs may also be recovered,[5] along with the expense of removing/storing furniture whilst repairs are carried out,[6] loss of rent whilst repairs were executed[7] and the loss of use of the home.[8]

Further, where the consequences of the unreported defects include physical inconvenience experienced by the purchasers in attempting to use and occupy the property, a modest award of damages for distress and inconvenience flowing therefrom may be recovered. As Bingham LJ stated in *Watts v Morrow*:[9]

> 'Damages are, in my view, recoverable for physical inconvenience and discomfort caused by the breach and mental suffering directly related to that inconvenience and discomfort. If those effects are foreseeably suffered during the period when defects are repaired I am prepared to accept that they sound in damages even though the cost of the repairs is not recoverable as such.'

The award of £2,000 each to the plaintiffs in *Watts v Morrow* by the trial judge was reduced on appeal to £750 each. Awards typically do not exceed £1,000 although figures in excess of this have been allowed.[10]

Vendors

6.4 Here it is possible for the valuer to under-value or over-value a property being sold. In *Kenney v Hall, Pain and Foster*,[11] the plaintiff relied upon the defendant's over valuation of his property in acquiring and improving two other premises. The cost of this venture greatly exceeded that which the plaintiff would have undertaken had he been properly advised as to the true value of his own home. It was agreed that had a proper value of the plaintiff's property been initially provided, he would have purchased one other house at a cheaper price than that expended in buying two properties. Damages were

---

1 *Buckland v Watts* [1968] 208 EG 969.

2 *Parsons v Way and Waller Ltd* [1952] 159 EG 524.

3 [1967] 203 EG 1039.

4 See *Morgan v Perry* (1973) 229 EG 1737; *Broadoak Properties Ltd v Young & White* [1989] 1 EGLR 263.

5 *Treml v Ernest W Gibson & Partners* [1984] 272 EG 68.

6 *Hill v Debenham Tewson and Chinnocks* [1958] 171 EG 835.

7 *Tremayne v P Mortimer Burroughs & Partners* [1934] 165 EG 232.

8 *Gibbs v Arnold Son & Hockley* [1989] 2 EGLR 154.

9 [1991] 4 All ER 937 at 960.

10 £2,000 each to a husband and wife in *Oswald v Countrywide Surveyors Ltd* [1994] EGCS 150; £1,500 and £3,000 to a husband and wife in *Heatley v William H Brown Ltd* [1992] 1 EGLR 289 and £4,000 to a married couple in *Ezekiel v McDade* [1994] EGCS 194.

11 [1976] 239 EG 355.

therefore assessed by reference to the difference between this hypothetical position and the actual circumstances in which the plaintiff found himself.

Where a property being marketed is sold for less than its true value, damages will simply represent the difference between the price received and the price that ought otherwise to have been secured.[1]

Mortgage lenders

6.5 In the event of default by a borrower, the lender who fails to realise from a disposal of the charged security enough to meet the sums outstanding under the mortgage will naturally investigate whether the advance was originally made upon the faith of a valuation which was negligently high. If advised that the original valuation was excessive, the lender will then usually assert that had the true position been known, either no advance to the defaulting borrower would have been made – or at least a much smaller loan would have been considered. If the lender can establish either of these positions in evidence, an entitlement to damages will arise.[2] Assuming the lender can prove that properly advised he would not have made the loan to the defaulting borrower, the law historically assessed damages by reference to the following formula.

The value of the advance
Plus
Cost to the lender of making the advance
Plus
Costs of repossession and sale
Less
Repossession sale proceeds and the value of any repayments made by the borrower together with interest on the resultant award.[3]

The difficulty with the above approach is that the repossession sale proceeds may turn out to be comparatively very small not only because the original value was overstated but because property values may have fallen in any event between the date of the advance and sale and possession due to market forces unconnected with the inaccuracy of the defendant's reported valuation.

6.6 In *SAAMCO v York Montague*[4] Lord Hoffman recognised that in providing a mortgage valuation of a property, the valuer is simply providing the lender with information as to the proposed security's value against which to decide what if any advance to make; logically damages for any negligent over estimation should therefore be limited so as to reflect the consequences of the advice being inaccurate – rather than to make the valuer liable for all the

---

1 See *Weedon v Hindwood, Clarke and Esplin* (1974) 234 EG 121.

2 The onus of proof in this regard is on the lender, see *Mount Banking Corporation Ltd v Brian Cooper & Co* [1992] 2 EGLR 142.

3 See *Swingcastle Ltd v Alistair Gibson* [1991] 2 WLR 1091.

4 [1996] 3 WLR 87.

consequences of thereafter making a loan based on the reported value. As Lord Hoffman stated:[1]

> 'One therefore compares the loss [the lender] has actually suffered with what his position would have been if he had not entered into the transaction and asks what element of this loss is attributable to the inaccuracy of the information.'

This position is contrasted with that where the accuracy of the valuation is warranted. In the latter situation the measure of loss is the difference between the actual value of the security and the value as warranted. It will be unusual of course for a valuer to warranty the accuracy of his valuation. Normally it will form no part of the valuer's duty to protect the lender against losses due to effects on the value of the security, aside from the accuracy of the reported valuation itself. It is instructive to see how the House approached the broad issue of quantification of losses in the three individual appeals dealt with in *SAAMCO*. In the lead case itself, South Australia Asset Management Corporation made an advance of £11 million against a reported value of £15 million. At first instance, May J found that the true value of the security at the relevant time was £5 million. Following the borrower's default, the property was sold for £2.47 million. Losses were quantified by May J at £9.75 million. Lord Hoffman therefore concluded:[2]

> 'The consequence of the valuation being wrong was that the plaintiffs had £10 million less security than they thought. If they had had this margin, they would havc suffered no loss. The whole loss was therefore within the scope of the defendant's duty.'

In the second appeal, *United Bank of Kuwait Plc v Prudential Property Services Ltd* the lenders advanced £1.75 million on the security of a property valued by the defendants at £2.5 million. The judge at first instance found that the correct value was between £1.8 million and £1.85 million. The security was sold for £950,000. Gage J quantified the lender's loss at £1,309,874. In allowing an appeal against this award, Lord Hoffman expressed the House's view as follows:[3]

> 'In my view the damages should have been limited to the consequences of the valuation being wrong, which were that the lender had £700,000 or £650,000 less security than he thought ... I would therefore allow the appeal and reduce the damages to the difference between the valuation and the correct value.'

Finally, in *Nykredit Mortgage Bank Plc v Edward Erdman Group Ltd*, the lenders advanced £2.45 million on the security of a property valued by the defendants at £3.5 million. The correct value was found by Judge Byrt QC to be £2 million. Losses were quantified at £3,058,555. Again, an appeal was allowed against an award made in this sum. It was appropriate according to Lord Hoffman[4] to:

---

1 [1996] 3 WLR 87 at 97.
2 [1996] 3 WLR 87 at 102.
3 [1996] 3 WLR 87 at 102–103.
4 [1996] 3 WLR 87 at 104.

> 'substitute for the Judge's award of damages a figure equal to the difference between £3.5 million and the true value of the property at the date of the valuation'

ie £2 million. It will be seen that it remains convenient to consider the extent of the lender's losses by reference to the traditional formula to begin with. It is then necessary to consider what extent of those losses in fact fall within the scope of the valuer's assumed duty.

6.7 So far we have looked at the position of the lender who is able to establish that properly advised as to the value of the security, no loan would have been made. It is possible that the most the lender will be able to satisfy the court about is that, had a different (and non-negligent) valuation been reported, a lesser advance would have been made to the same borrower compared with the sum in fact advanced. Indeed, the valuer may wish to attempt to persuade the court of such a scenario. In that case the true measure of damages was said by Stephenson LJ in *London and South of England Building Society v Stone*[1] to be:

> 'the difference between the sum the building society actually advanced on the false valuation, which the surveyor carelessly and unskilfully put on the property, and the sum the building society would have advanced on the true valuation, which a careful and skilful surveyor would have put on it.'

Although Lord Hoffman in *SAAMCO* dismissed as 'quite irrelevant to the scope of the duty of care'[2] the distinction between a lender who may have made no advance or a lesser advance given accurate valuation information about a property, the difference between the two scenarios was recognised as having 'a certain pragmatic truth' when the question of loss computation fell to be considered.

Where the distinction proves relevant to an assessment of damages, the lender will claim in addition to the size of any excess advance, the cost to it of making the additional sum so loaned. The costs of repossession and sale will not in this event be allowed. However, these would have arisen in any event, given the default by the borrower in respect of the loan, to the extent that any lesser sum would have been secured over the subject property. Curiously, however, the courts have required credit to be given for all the repayments made by the borrower prior to default.[3] This seems illogical. The borrower's repayments (if any) serve to discharge his liability both in respect of the loan to the extent it would have been made and the liability for the excess portion of the loan which would not have been made. There is no reason why the defendant should have the benefit of the former element of payment so as to reduce his overall liability in respect of that portion of the loan only made as a result of his negligence.

---

1 [1983] 1 WLR 1242 at 1262.

2 [1995] 2 EGLR 219 at 229.

3 *Corisand v Druce & Co* [1978] 248 EG 315; *Assured Advances Ltd v Ashbee & Co* [1994] EGCS 169.

Finally, three situations subsist in which damages may be recoverable on a more generous basis than that discussed above. First, where the valuer is not only providing advice as to the value of the proposed security but undertakes to advise as to the course of a prospective loan transaction, he may be liable for all the foreseeable consequences which result from the lender pursuing the course of action advised.[1] This will obviously be an unusual scenario. Secondly, a fraudulent valuation may also render the provider liable for all the losses arising as a consequence of entering into the transaction. Thirdly, should the valuer warranty the accuracy of the valuation, he will be liable for any difference between the true value and value as warranted.

ANCILLARY ISSUES

Contributory negligence

6.8 Section 1 of the Law Reform (Contributory Negligence) Act 1945 provides that:

> 'where any person suffers damage as the result partly of his own fault and partly of the fault of any other person or persons a claim in respect of that damage shall not be defeated by reason of the fault of the person suffering the damage, but the damages recoverable in respect thereof shall be reduced to such extent as the court thinks just and equitable having regard to the claimant's share in the responsibility for the damage.'

We considered earlier the opportunity for a valuer to criticise a borrower for relying upon his valuation and not undertaking further investigations and enquiries.[2] Such allegations have in the past been raised with greater success against lenders who proceed on the basis of a valuation report without giving such further careful consideration to the proposed transaction as would be expected from other prudent lenders. The nature of the lender may be important. Building societies are regulated by the Building Societies Commission and expected to observe the Prudential Notes issued by it from time to time. No such regulatory regime governs mortgage lending by secondary banks. The expectations for prudent enquiries apart from the value of the security are therefore higher in relation to building society loans than others. In either case, however, an important factor will be the size of the loan relative to the value of the property. As Wright J stated in *Hit Finance v Lewis & Tucker Ltd*[3] in relation to an advance of £1.54 million against a valuation of £2.2 million:

> 'The cushion apparently provided by the property on the basis of the defendant's valuation was accordingly £660,000. In such circumstances, even if the borrowers turned out to be complete men of straw, the lenders were entitled to regard

1 See per Lord Hoffman in *SAAMCO* [1996] 3 WLR 87 at 97.
2 See para **1.26**.
3 [1993] 2 EGLR 231.

> themselves as being more than adequately covered not merely in respect of the capital sum lent, but also any likely loss of interest and indeed all the costs and expenses likely to be incurred in foreclosing upon and realising the security ... it is very difficult to see how such a lender could properly be characterised as being imprudent.'

This was echoed by Gage J in *United Bank of Kuwait v Prudential Property Services Ltd*:[1]

> 'It seems to me that it is important to bear in mind: that the nature and extent of enquiries required may vary widely and that an important factor will be the margin of safety provided by the security offered.'

In *Platform Home Loans v Oyston Shipways Ltd*[2] Jacobs J at first instance criticised a loan to value ratio of 70 per cent being applied to a loan of £1.05 million where inadequate enquiries were made of the borrower. This, combined with the failure to obtain information from the borrower as to the previous purchase price of the property resulted in a finding of contributory negligence of 20 per cent.

6.9 Apart from the size of the loan, it will be important to consider whether it represents a straightforward advance to be repaid over a number of years (where the quality of the borrower's covenant will be important) or whether it represents short-term bridging finance where repayment is only likely to come from sale or remortgage. In the latter case, it will be difficult to sustain any argument that the lender was at fault in relying primarily on the defendant's valuation.[3] Most lenders have in-house guidelines dealing with the criteria for making an advance and stipulating the enquiries, apart from the investigation of the value of the proposed security, which should be undertaken. It is common for valuers defending a negligence claim to criticise the lender for any departures from its own in-house lending policy. Such an approach was given short shrift by Phillips J in *Banque Bruxelles Lambert SA v Eagle Star Insurance Co*:[4]

> 'the important issue in the case of each transaction is whether it was intrinsically imprudent and I cannot see that it matters whether or not ... [the lender's own guidelines] were breached.'

If the guidelines reflect commonsense, they add nothing. If they represent anything more amounting to a counsel of perfection then any departure from them is not likely to be viewed as unreasonable.

Most successful criticisms have been based upon carelessness in assessing the quality of the borrower's covenant and/or any material throwing doubt upon the reliability of the reported value in terms of the transaction to be based upon it. For example, if the lender were to:

---

1 [1994] 30 EG 103.
2 [1996] 49 EG 112, ChD.
3 See *Britannic Security & Investments Ltd v Hirani Watson* [1995] EGCS 46.
4 [1995] 2 All ER 769 at 829.

> 'Shut his eyes to any obviously unsatisfactory characteristics of the proposed borrower [he] would not be acting prudently [to make] a loan in circumstances where he had substantial reason for suspecting the honesty of the borrower.'[1]

In *Banque Bruxelles Lambert SA v Eagle Star*[2] a finding of 30 per cent contributory negligence was made because of a failure by the lender to seek an explanation as to the wide difference between the purchase price and reported value. The failure to heed a recommendation for planning assumptions in a valuation to be confirmed by the lender's solicitor would have resulted in a finding of 80 per cent contributory negligence in *PK Finans International v Andrew Downs & Co.*[3]

6.10 The extent to which allegations of contributory negligence based upon a failure to undertake prudent investigations into the quality of the borrowers' covenant would be able to be successfully advanced following *SAAMCO* became a moot point. The following argument was advanced by lenders: it is implicit in the wording of s 1 of the Law Reform (Contributory Negligence) Act[4] that the damages capable of being reduced on account of a successful allegation of contributory negligence will be confined to the damages awarded in respect of the relevant damage sustained by the plaintiff. Since, in the light of *SAAMCO*, the *damage* sustained by the lender is confined in essence to the extent to which the margin of security turns out to be less than believed to be, the loss thereby occasioned by the negligent valuation is not a loss which is in any sense affected by a failure to investigate the quality of the borrower's covenant. In a recent decision of Moses J in *Coventry Building Society v William Martin & Partners*[5] the court reasoned as follows:

> '*South Australia* decides that, in a case where there is a duty to provide information the kind of damage the plaintiff can recover is that which is the consequence of the incorrect information. Such a case is to be distinguished from a duty to provide advice. It seems to me to follow, therefore, that it is only such negligence as contributed to the damages which resulted from the negligent valuation which will lead to a reduction. This case affords an illustration of the distinction. If the plaintiff had been negligent in realising the security by, for example, failing to sell it at an appropriate time or at a price which was negligently ascertained, such negligence would have been causative of the kind of damage which it is entitled to recover.'

The nature of the allegations in that case, however, not being directed to the value of the property itself, no deduction on account of contributory negligence was entertained. A similar approach was taken in *Interallianz Finanz AG v Independent Insurance Co Ltd.*[6] In that case, amongst other allegations of contributory negligence was an assertion that a cash deposit covering six

---

1 Per Wright J in *Hit Finance Ltd v Lewis and Tucker* [1993] 2 EGLR 231.
2 [1994] 2 EGLR 108.
3 [1992] 1 EGLR 172.
4 Paragraph **6.8**.
5 [1997] 48 EGLR 159.
6 [1997] EGCS 91.

months' interest ought to have been taken. Thomas J rejected this criticism as irrelevant since as the omission was the result of a negligent assessment of the credit worthiness of the borrower, it was not relevant to the valuation. In other words, the extent of the losses for which the valuer could be made liable within the *SAAMCO* principle would be the same whether or not the cash deposit had been stipulated.

As noted earlier,[1] such a distinction was not recognised by Jacobs J in *Platform Home Loans v Oyston Shipways.*[2] The argument in favour of a limitation on the valuer's ability to contend for a reduction in damages on the grounds of contributory negligence by the lender also failed in *UCB Bank plc v Pinders*[3] and *Barclays Bank v Peter Wardle Associates.*[4] These issues were further ventilated before the Court of Appeal in *Platform Home Loans v Oyston Shipway*[5] when Jacobs J's approach at first instance was considered and upheld. The decisions[6] supporting a contrary view which narrowed the potential scope of application of the contributory negligence defence were also considered and rejected. Morritt LJ held that any negligence of the lender whether in investigating the borrower's covenant or in following up queries relating to the valuation alone were part and parcel of the lender's decision to make an advance and as such were equally relevant to a consideration of the extent to which the lender had caused or contributed to his own losses.

Mitigation

6.11 A plaintiff cannot recover damages in respect of losses which ought reasonably to have been avoided. In *Nyckeln Finance Co Ltd v Stumpbrook Ltd*[7] an unreasonable delay in repossessing and selling the security meant that the property sold for less on the falling market than might otherwise have been achievable by more prompt action. Judge Fawcus QC held the defendant valuer not liable for that part of the loss attributable to this delay. This arose on two grounds: the reduced value of the capital receipts reflected in the late sale of the property and the continuing cost of the outstanding loan to the lender incurred by reason of the delayed action.

Where the borrower has defaulted it will be unlikely that a defendant valuer will be able to demonstrate that the lender is unreasonable in not pursuing the

1 See para **6.8**.
2 [1966] 49 EG 112.
3 [1997] EGCS 179.
4 3 December 1997 (unreported).
5 [1997] EGCS 184.
6 *Interallianz Finanz AG v Independent Insurance Co Ltd* [1997] EGCS 91; *Coventry Building Society v William Martin & Partners* [1997] 48 EGLR 159; *Britannia Building Society v Hallas* [1997] EGCS 117; *Bristol and West Building Society v Fancy & Jackson* [1997] 4 All ER 582; *Britannia Building Society v White & Co*, 13 August 1997 (unreported).
7 [1994] 2 EGLR 143.

borrower on his mortgage covenant. The very fact of default in most cases will make it unlikely that such a pursuit would be worthwhile.[1]

In *Alliance & Leicester Building Society v Wheelers (a firm)*[2] (a solicitors' negligence action) the plaintiff lender had omitted to sell the subject property promptly and in a favourable market. This circumstance did not, however, justify, in the view of the court, any reduction in damages since the most important consequence of the valuation error in over valuing the property was that the lender's security was substantially diminished in value. This loss could not be attributed in any way to the society's negligence and failure to mitigate. This reasoning should now be regarded as unsound in the light of the Court of Appeal's decision in *Platform Home Loans v Oyston*.[3]

MIG policies

6.12 It is common, where the value of the advance exceeds the lender's usual loan-to-value ratio, for the borrower to be required to pay the premium for a mortgage indemnity guarantee. It is sometimes argued by the defendant valuer that the proceeds of any monies recovered under such a policy should enure to his benefit in reducing any damages payable for a negligent valuation *pro tanto*. Although the contention was accepted as arguable in *Alliance & Leicester Building Society v Edgestop*[4] the weight of authority favours the view that the insurance payments are *res inter alios acta*. As Phillips J indicated in *Banque Bruxelles Lambert SA v Eagle Star*:[5]

> '[The principle requires] the court to disregard an indemnity received by the plaintiff from a third party in respect of the loss caused by the defendant. The law disregards the (extraneous) intervention so that the plaintiff remains entitled to recover from the defendant the full amount of the loss or damage initially suffered.'

This is consistent with the insurer's rights to bring proceedings by virtue of the doctrine of subrogation in the name of the lender against the valuer.

INTEREST

6.13 In claiming damages it is important to consider the extent to which interest may also be awarded upon any losses. There are two distinct bases for such an award. First, the claimant may have incurred interest charges, for example in connection with the costs incurred by a lender in obtaining monies from which to make an advance. Alternatively, where losses fall to be compensated in damages, the claimant will have been deprived of the use of the money represented by the entitlement to damages until they are paid. Interest

---

1 See *London and South of England Building Society v Stone* [1983] 1 WLR 1242.
2 23 January 1997 (unreported).
3 [1997] EGCS 184.
4 [1993] 1 WLR 1462.
5 [1994] 2 EGLR 108.

may be awarded to compensate for this loss by the court exercising a statutory discretion under s 35A of the Supreme Court Act 1981.[1]

Claims by purchasers

6.14 In actions involving claims by purchasers, the principles of loss assessment[2] focus attention upon the extent to which a buyer was induced to over-pay for a property on the faith of a negligently high valuation. The excess monies so paid represent the quantum of any entitlement to damages to which interest may be added. It is usual to allow interest to run from the date of completion to the date of judgment. The rate of interest will generally be taken by the court as the rate prescribed from time to time in respect of unsatisfied judgments under the Judgments Act 1858. As Nichols LJ said in *Pinnock v Wilkins & Sons*:[3]

> 'It is, in my view, abundantly clear (if the position were ever in doubt) that there is nothing exceptional in the court using those rates in the exercise of its discretion for my part I see much force in the view that today, where the court is considering what is an appropriate rate of interest under s 35A for a period from the accrual of the course of action up to the date of judgment, a convenient starting point will often be the rate payable on judgment debts from time to time over that period.'

This may be thought to be unduly generous in that the rate prescribed from time to time under the Judgments Act is intended to reflect a degree of compulsion imposed on the debtor to pay. None the less, in practice it is the rate usually applied. The award, however, remains discretionary. In *Morgan v Perry*[4] the court refused to make an award of interest on the grounds that although as a result of the defendant's negligence the plaintiffs had acquired a property which was worthless, they were nonetheless living in it at the date of trial and thus deriving some benefit from it. Indeed, in most cases the plaintiffs would, if properly advised as to the condition of an intended purchase, have simply bought an alternative, defect-free property for the same capital outlay. The value of any investment would thereafter have risen or fallen with the market. It is arguable that where this can be shown to have been the most likely alternative course of events, any award of interest would be inappropriate.

Claims by lenders

6.15 The historical position of lenders, induced to advance monies on the faith of a negligent report, is different. If the lender was cash-rich at the time of the advance (eg building societies) then it will be likely to be able to demonstrate that by entering into the loan transaction it was deprived of the opportunity of otherwise placing its funds on deposit or utilising the monies to make a more satisfactory loan elsewhere. If either of these positions can be

1 In the High Court; and under s 69 of the County Courts Act 1984 in relation to county court actions.

2 See Chapter 7.

3 (1990) *The Times*, 29 January.

4 [1973] 229 EG 1737.

demonstrated in evidence, the loss of earned interest may also be claimed as damages. If the lender itself borrowed monies in order to fund the advance, the interest paid on such initial borrowing may also be recovered. Lenders are sometimes coy about giving discovery of their own borrowing rates/charges and often such losses are left to be assessed by the court which is invited simply to make an award in the form of damages for loss of use of the monies advanced by an award of interest at a commercial rate. As Lord Lowry said in *Swingcastle Ltd v Alistair Gibson*:[1]

> 'In the absence of any evidence as to how the lenders financed the loan or evidence showing how the money, if not lent to the borrowers could have been profitably employed I consider that 12 per cent interest, ... is the proper rate at which to recompense the lenders for being deprived of their [advance].'

6.16 In the case of the lender who has itself borrowed monies to make the advance, any default in recovery is likely to mean that the borrowed monies have not been repaid, so that the extent of the facility continues to grow as unpaid interest is charged to the lender's account. There is no reason in principle why, in that situation, any compensatory award of interest should not be computed on a compound basis.[2] Where, however, repayments have been made from time to time by the borrower, these ought to serve to reduce the sums upon which interest would otherwise fall to be calculated. Somewhat illogically, however, the court does not generally expect the lender to bring the credit into account in this way but allows the total of monies paid simply to be set off against the total claim in respect of the advance and cost of borrowing.[3]

6.17 The approach to a lender's entitlement to interest where a valuer has been successfully sued in negligence has, however, been radically affected by the House of Lords' decision in *Nykredit Mortgage Bank plc v Edward Erdman Ltd*.[4]

As noted earlier,[5] the court is empowered to award simple interest under s 35A(1) of the Supreme Court Act on '... damages in respect of which judgment is given ... for all or any part of the period between the date when the cause of action arose and ... the date of the judgment'. In lender claims the cause of action was held in *First National Commercial Bank plc v Humberts*[6] to first arise when the value of the security and that of the borrower's covenant fell below the value of the sum advanced and outstanding to the lender. This approach has now been endorsed by the House of Lords in the *Nykredit* case.[7] Lord Nicholls began by asking the following question:

---

1 [1991] 2 WLR 1091 at 1103.

2 This appears to have occurred at first instance in *South Australian Asset Management Corporation v York Montague Ltd* [1996] 3 WLR 87.

3 See *Banque Bruxelles Lambert SA v Eagle Star Insurance Co Ltd* [1994] 2 EGLR 108; *Corisand Investments Ltd v Druce & Co* [1978] 248 EG 315.

4 [1997] 1 WLR 1627.

5 See para **6.13**.

6 [1995] 2 All ER 673.

7 [1997] 1 WLR 1627.

'When then does the lender first sustain relevant measurable loss? The first step in answering this question is to identify the relevant measure of loss. It is axiomatic that in assessing the loss caused by the defendant's negligence the basic measure is the comparison between (a) what the plaintiff's position would have been if the defendant had fulfilled his duty of care and (b) the plaintiff's actual position ... Thus typically in the case of a negligent valuation of an intended loan security the basic comparison called for is between (a) the amount of money lent by the plaintiff which he would still have had in the absence of the loan transaction plus interest at a proper rate and (b) the value of the rights acquired, namely the borrower's covenant and the true value of the overvalued property.'

The date upon which such a differential in values can first be identified will be the date on which the cause of action can be held to have accrued not only for Limitation Act purposes but also as the starting date for the computation of a statutory award of interest. The principle, it is anticipated, is easier to state than apply. The House rejected the argument that the cause of action should be treated as arising only at the date of a sale of the security for a sum insufficient to cover the lender's outlay. Lord Nicholls stated:

'Realisation of the security does not create lender's loss, nor does it convert a potential loss into an actual loss. Rather it crystallises the amount of the present loss which hitherto had been open to be aggravated or diminished by movements in the property market.'

The House also rejected an argument that the cause of action should be treated as arising when the lender first became entitled to enforce the security due to the borrower's default because:

'this suggestion involves the proposition that until then ... the lender can never suffer any loss and the lender can never issue his writ whatever the circumstances. That does not seem right ... If the basic comparison shows a loss at an earlier stage why should the lender have to wait until the borrower defaults before issuing his writ against the negligent valuer?'[1]

Whilst a valuer may be able to provide a retrospective range of valuations of the subject property at a variety of dates with a view to assessing the competence of the defendant's opinion as to value which triggered the original advance, putting a figure on the value of the borrower's covenant may prove more difficult in practice. These difficulties were dismissed with what is respectfully suggested to be a degree of unrealism by Lord Nicholls who indicated:

'Ascribing a value to the borrower's covenant should not be unduly troublesome. A comparable exercise regarding lessee's covenants is a routine matter when valuing property. Sometimes the comparison will reveal a loss from the inception of the loan transaction. The borrower may be a company with no assets, its sole business may comprise redeveloping and reselling the property and for repayment the lender may be looking solely to his security. In such a case if the property is worth less than the amount of the loan, relevant and measurable loss will have been sustained at once. In other cases the borrower's covenant may have value and until

1 *Nykredit Mortgage Bank plc v Edward Erdman Ltd* [1997] 1 WLR 1627, per Lord Nicholls at 1633.

> there is default the lender may presently sustain no loss even though the security is worth less than the amount of the loan.'

The analogy with valuing tenants' covenants may be difficult to apply to the worth [sic] of a mortgagor's covenant since whilst there is a market in tenanted investment properties, sales of mortgaged properties with non-defaulting borrowers in residence do not readily arise in practice.

Chapter 7

COURT PRACTICE AND PROCEDURE

INTRODUCTION

7.1 This is not an appropriate place for a detailed account of the practice and procedure of the civil courts. Reference should be made to other works dealing with the subject.[1] It is proposed to give no more than a brief outline of the main steps involved in bringing and defending a claim. Thereafter, three areas of particular relevance to professional negligence actions involving surveyors will be considered.

PRE-TRIAL STEPS

Venue

7.2 Claims arising out of negligent surveys and valuations may be commenced in the county court or High Court. Although the county court has unlimited financial jurisdiction over such claims, it is unusual for anything other than straightforward negligent survey cases to be commenced in that court. Any claim involving complex issues of expert evidence and/or substantial sums of money will be brought in a division of the High Court. As a general matter of practice, the Queen's Bench Division will hear claims brought against valuers by purchasers; the Chancery Division of the High Court and the Mercantile Courts will hear claims against surveyors and valuers brought by mortgage lenders and the Official Referees Court will determine claims by either category of litigant. Given the specialist nature of Official Referees and their familiarity with the principles involved in such actions, it is wise to consider commencing all but straightforward claims of modest value in that court.

Statement of Claim

7.3 In each court, the claimant will begin the proceedings by setting out a summary of his case in the form of a pleading. A precedent Statement of Claim[2] is provided later to which reference may be made for its general form and content. Because of the specialised nature of any such action it is sensible to particularise any complaint of professional negligence with care and the

1 See Odgers, *Principles of Pleading and Practice* (Sweet & Maxwell, 1986).

2 See Appendix I.

assistance of the expert to be retained to advise in connection with the proceedings. Once served with the summary of claim, the defendant has, as a general rule, 14 days in which to serve a defence. Where appropriate this pleading apart from denying liability should raise any defence of limitation or counter allegations of contributory negligence or breach of duty to mitigate to be relied upon against the plaintiff bringing the action. Again, attention is invited to the precedent given later in this work.[1] In the event that either party considers the nature of the case or defence thus pleaded is unclear, it is open to raise a Request for Further and Better Particulars. Where appropriately served, such a request can serve both to elaborate and pin down an opponent's case. Any attempt later to present a materially inconsistent case with that thus particularised may be disallowed by the court or at the very least will cast doubt on the reliability of the nature of the case originally put forward. Properly used, requests for further and better particulars can form an important weapon in the armoury of either litigant.

Discovery

7.4 Once pleadings have been thus exchanged, the next step is discovery. This obliges each party to serve upon the other a list of all relevant documents relating to the matters in question in the action which are or have been in its possession. The test of relevance was given by Brett LJ in *Compagnie Financiere du Pacifique v Peruvian Guano Ltd*:[2]

> 'It seems to me that every document relates to the matters in question in the action, which not only would be evidence upon any issue, but also which it is reasonable to suppose, contains information which may – not which must – either directly or indirectly enable the party requiring [discovery] either to advance his own case or to damage the case of his advocacy. I have put in the words directly or indirectly because as it seems to me, a document can properly be said to contain information which may enable the party requiring [discovery] either to advance his own case or to damage the case of his advocacy, if it is a document which may fairly lead him to a train of enquiry which may have either of these two consequences ... in order to determine whether certain documents are within this description, it is necessary to consider what are the questions in the action: the court must look, not only at the Statement of Claim and the plaintiff's case, but at the Statement of Defence and the defendant's case.'

Once lists of such materials are exchanged, a right to inspect the documents and take photocopies arises. The main ground for withholding discovery of any document is that it contains legal advice given by the client's solicitor or provided in connection with the subject litigation.

In actions brought by purchasers, the following documents are likely to be important: the surveyor's/valuer's site notes; any drafts and workings brought into existence in connection with the preparation of the final, disclosed report; written particulars of any comparables relied upon by the valuer in valuing the

1 See Appendix I.
2 (1882) 11 QBD 55.

property. The purchaser is likely to have fewer relevant materials to disclose, although, subject to any objection to discovery on the ground of legal professional privilege referred to above, the purchase file may contain useful information. Perusal on behalf of the defendant valuer may suggest that the plaintiff purchaser was under pressure to proceed with the transaction in any event, so that he would not have been deterred by any additional warnings about unmentioned defects. Similarly, the file may disclose that the purchaser had been warned by the vendor or his own solicitor about, for example, a subsidence history to the site and/or lack of planning permission or building regulation approval to structures comprised within the property. In cases brought by lenders, similar documents to those described above are likely to be in the possession of the valuer and will need to be disclosed. So far as the lender is concerned, it will need to disclose copies of the borrower's application, any documents dealing with the surveyor/valuer's engagement; records dealing with the approval and making of the loan together with copies of any in-house lending criteria; documents dealing with the history of the borrower's performance under the loan and relating to any repossession and sale of the property.

Witness statements

7.5 Once discovery has taken place, the parties to the action will be expected to prepare and offer for exchange statements from any witnesses of fact to be relied upon. Such statements will need to be exchanged in accordance with the Rules of Court or as otherwise provided for by the court in which the action is progressing. Any departure from a timetable for exchange may result in the court refusing to admit the evidence. The Master of the Rolls indicated in *Beachley Properties Ltd v Edgar*:[1]

> 'Unless there are circumstances which justify the court exercising discretion in favour of the party in default, that discretion will not be exercised and the party will be deprived of the evidence.'

More recently the Court of Appeal has confirmed, however, that in spite of non-compliance with the court's timetable, the overriding consideration must be to ensure justice is done. Accordingly, the court will not simply allow a party to obtain a tactical advantage from a failure to comply with time limits which is capable of being reasonably explained.[2] The Master of the Rolls and the Vice-Chancellor have approved the following guidance with regard to what is expected of litigants in adhering to time-limits laid down by the court. These are:

(a) Time requirements laid down by the Rules and directions given by the court are not merely targets to be attempted; they are rules to be observed.

(b) At the same time the overriding principle is that justice must be done.

1 See *Beachley Property Ltd v Edgar* (1996) *The Times*, 18 July.

2 *The Mortgage Corporation Ltd v Sandoes* [1997] PNLR 263.

(c) Litigants are entitled to have their cases resolved with reasonable expedition. Non-compliance with time-limits can cause prejudice to one or more of the parties to the litigation.

(d) In addition, the vacation or adjournment of the date of trial prejudices other litigants and disrupts the administration of justice.

(e) Extensions of time which involve the vacation or adjournment of trial dates should therefore be granted only as a last resort.

(f) Where time-limits have not been complied with the parties should co-operate in reaching an agreement as to new time-limits which will not involve the date of trial being postponed.

(g) If they reach such an agreement they can ordinarily expect the court to give effect to that agreement at the trial and it is not necessary to make a separate application solely for this purpose.

(h) The court will not look with favour on a party who seeks only to take tactical advantage from the failure of another party to comply with time-limits.

(i) In the absence of an agreement as to a new timetable an application should be made promptly to the court for directions.

(j) In considering whether to grant an extension of time to a party who is in default, the court will look at all the circumstances of the case including the considerations identified here.[1]

Plainly, careful consideration should be given as to the content of any witness statement.

The form and content of witness statements

7.6 The Rules of Court provide for the form and general content of lay witness statements. The statement of the witness should represent his evidence-in-chief and should be treated as if he were giving evidence in the witness box. The evidence should be stated in a clear, straightforward narrative form, using the language of the witness, his ipsissimma verba. For the sake of easy and ready reference, the statement should be divided into consecutively numbered paragraphs, each being confined to a distinct portion of his evidence and following a chronological sequence. The practice direction (civil litigation: case management)[2] states that 'unless otherwise ordered, every witness statement shall stand as the evidence-in-chief of the witness concerned.' Drafting of such statements is accordingly of crucial importance. If the witness statement fails to deal with a material issue in the case, it is likely to expose the deponent to awkward and embarrassing cross-examination. Where factual matters are predictably likely to be hotly disputed, however, the court may depart from the practice direction and require the relevant witness(es) to be

---

1 [1997] PNLR 263 at 284–285.
2 [1995] 1 WLR 262.

taken through their evidence-in-chief by the historically conventional process of questions and answers. As the Court of Appeal recently indicated in *Cole & Others v Kivells (a firm)*:[1]

> 'The practice direction on witness statements should not be inflexibly applied. To the extent that the witness statements reveal that there is no factual dispute, it is sensible that they should stand as evidence-in-chief. It is stated in Volume 1 of the Supreme Court Practice ... that even where directions are given for the pre-trial exchange of witness statements, the trial judge retains a discretion to require a witness to give evidence orally. That discretion is unfettered. In this case it would have been appropriate to ask the judge to exercise his discretion so that the key witnesses .... .could have given their evidence in chief orally on the issues where there was a conflict of fact. That course may have clarified the issues of fact and sharpened focus on the conflicts of evidence to be resolved.'

Broadly, in claims by purchasers and lenders, it will be important to provide evidence as to the 'nuts and bolts' of the purchase/loan transaction; brief evidence from a lay perspective of the problems complained of in the action will be set out along with details of any losses and damage alleged to have been caused by the defendant's want of care. It will be necessary to demonstrate that the surveyor/valuer's report was itself relied upon in entering in to the particular transaction concerned whether of purchase or loan. The court will, however, be likely readily to draw the inference that any representations made or advice given by the surveyor/valuer about the property will have influenced the purchaser/lender in deciding to proceed. As Stephenson LJ said in *JEB Fasteners Ltd v Marks, Bloom & Co*:[2]

> 'As long as a misrepresentation plays a real and substantial part, though not by itself a decisive part, in inducing a plaintiff to act, it is a cause of his loss and he relies on it, no matter how strong or how many other matters which play their part in inducing him to act.'

It will therefore be difficult for a defendant to establish that no liability should attach for any negligent report simply on the grounds that it was immaterial in causing or influencing a plaintiff to proceed with a purchase or loan. Indeed, in certain circumstances the court will be prepared to infer that (for example) a lender relied upon a mortgage valuation report, even in the absence of direct evidence that the report was read and influenced the decision to lend from a lending official who participated in the process of sanctioning the advance.[3] There are, however, rare examples where a defendant has been able to persuade a judge of this position.[4] Where the pleadings disclosed allegations of contributory negligence and breaches of duty to mitigate, these should be made by (where possible) appropriate lay evidence. On the defendant's side, the surveyor/valuer will need to explain the background to his engagement, how

---

1 [1997] TLR 238.

2 [1983] 1 All ER 583 at 589.

3 *Cavendish Funding Ltd v Henry Spencer & Sons Ltd* [1996] PNLR 554.

4 See *Rona v Pearce* [1953] 162 EG 380; *Banque Bruxelles Lambert SA v Eagle Star Insurance Co Ltd* [1995] 2 All ER 769; *Nyckeln Finance Co Ltd v Edward Symmons* [1996] PNLR 245.

the inspection was carried out and the way in which the report came to be drafted. Insofar as claims are often brought long after the date of the inspection and report, many valuers find it difficult to recall any particular property clearly. This emphasises the importance of making and retaining detailed site notes.

Experts

7.7 Without the agreement of both parties or the consent of the court, expert evidence will not be admissible. The preparation and presentation of this important aspect of any case is considered below.

LIMITATION

The six-year time-limit

7.8 Whether commencing a claim or considering how it may be defended, it will be important to investigate whether any action is statute-barred. The Limitation Act 1980 (as amended) provides time-limits within which actions must be commenced. The position depends on whether the action is one for breach of a contractual duty arising under the surveyor/valuer's engagement, or whether the proceedings are brought in simple negligence for breach of a common law duty to exercise reasonable care and skill. Section 6 of the Limitation Act 1980 provides 'an action founded on simple contract shall not be brought after the expiration of six years from the date on which the course of action accrued'. In contract, a cause of action accrues immediately the contract is broken – whether or not the other party to the agreement then suffers loss. In most cases, therefore, any omission to inspect the property with reasonable care and skill will give rise to a breach of contract at that stage, notwithstanding that loss may not be caused to the party commissioning any report until it is later relied upon in deciding to buy premises or advance monies to be secured over them.

Section 2 of the Limitation Act 1980 provides, however, in relation to an action founded on tort that it 'shall not be brought after the expiration of six years from the date on which the cause of action accrued'. In tort, a cause of action does not accrue until the plaintiff suffered anything more than minimal damage.[1] Such damage is likely first to arise when the purchaser exchanges contracts to buy a property in respect of which the valuer has not fully reported.[2] In the case of a mortgage lender, however, it is more difficult to identify the stage at which reliance upon a negligent over-valuation results in damage. In *First National Commercial Bank Plc v Humberts*,[3] an argument was

---

1 See *Pirelli General Cable Works Ltd v Oscar Faber & Partners* [1983] 2 AC 1.

2 See *Felton v Gaskill Osborne & Co* [1993] 2 EGLR 176; *Secretary of State for Environment v Essex Goodman & Suggitt* [1986] 1 WLR 1432; *Horbury v Craig Hall & Rutley* [1991] EGCS 81; *Hamlin v Edwin Evans* [1996] PNLR 398.

3 [1995] 2 All ER 673.

rejected that damage was caused the moment the mortgage monies were advanced. In that case, it was clear the underlying value of the security was more than equal to the value of the advance when first made. It was not until a later date, when the borrower defaulted and the property had reduced in value through market forces, that the lender became financially exposed. The court held that it was not until this state of affairs came about that any loss could be said to have been caused to the lender so as to start the limitation clock ticking. In attempting to ascertain whether or not damage has been caused, a view will need to be taken as to the at times fluctuating values of the underlying security and the extent to which any repayments have been made by the borrower. Whilst it would appear more logical to treat the damage as first occurring when the security is repossessed and sold if the proceeds prove insufficient to meet the sum otherwise secured, this approach was rejected by the House of Lords in *Nykredit Mortgage Bank plc v Edward Erdman Group Ltd*.[1]

The three-year qualification

7.9 The fact that a purchaser or lender suffers a loss as a result of reliance upon a negligent survey and valuation report may not be readily apparent to either party. Indeed, certain missed defects with a property may not become apparent to the lay purchaser until long after its acquisition. To prevent what would otherwise be an unjust application of a rigid limitation rule described above, it is provided in relation to claims in tort that where knowledge of the material facts about the loss and damage does not come about until later, a plaintiff may bring proceedings either within six years from the date of the damage or three years of learning about it (whichever is the later). The 'starting date' for the latter purpose is defined by s 14A of the Limitation Act 1980 as follows:

> 'the earliest date on which the plaintiff or any person in whom a cause of action was vested before him first had both the knowledge required for bringing an action for damages in respect of the relevant damage and a right to bring such an action.'

The knowledge referred to means knowledge both '(a) of the material facts about the damage in respect of which damages are claimed and (b) of the other facts relevant to the current action mentioned in subs (8) below'.[2] The reference to 'material facts about the damage' means such facts as would lead a reasonable person to consider the damage sufficiently serious to justify instituting proceedings. The 'other facts' are:

> '(a) that the damage was attributable in whole or in part to the act or omission which is alleged to constitute negligence and (b) the identity of the defendant and (c) if it is alleged that the act or omission was that of a person other than the defendant, the identity of that person and the additional facts supporting the bringing of an action against the defendant.'[3]

---

1 [1997] 1 WLR 1627; see further para **6.17**.
2 Limitation Act 1980, s 14A(6).
3 Limitation Act 1980, s 14A(8).

Knowledge in this context does not mean 'know for certain and beyond the possibility of contradiction'. It does however mean:

> 'know with sufficient confidence to justify embarking on the preliminaries to the issue of a writ, such as submitting a claim to the proposed defendant, taking legal and other advice and collecting evidence. Suspicion, particularly if it is vague and unsupported will not be enough, but reasonable belief will normally suffice.'[1]

Sometimes it may be difficult from a lay perspective to identify whether or not any perceived damage may be attributable to acts or omissions of the person responsible for the initial survey and/or valuation of the property. It was said by Purchas LJ in *Nash v Eli Lilly & Co*:[2]

> 'A firm belief held by the plaintiff that [the damage complained] was attributable to the act or omission of the defendant, but in respect of which he thought it necessary to obtain reassurance or confirmation from experts ... will not be regarded as knowledge until the result of his enquiries was known to him or, if he delayed in obtaining that confirmation, until the time at which it was reasonable for him to have got it.'

The last qualification reflects an important further provision contained in s 14A(10) of the Act which provides that a person's knowledge includes knowledge which he might reasonably have been expected to acquire:

> '(a) from facts observable or ascertainable by him and (b) from facts ascertainable by him with the hclp of appropriate expert advice which it is reasonable for him to seek.'

If a potential plaintiff omits to obtain expert advice when it ought to have been obtained then he will be treated as having the relevant degree of knowledge for the purposes of the three-year limitation clock starting to tick. In *Finance for Mortgages v Farley*,[3] a mortgage lender which failed, following repossession and sale, to obtain appropriate retrospective valuation evidence until eight months later was treated as if it had obtained such expert advice shortly after the sale, with the result that proceedings commenced later were treated as statute-barred notwithstanding that it was not until the later date the lender had actual knowledge of the excessive nature of the defendant's (original) valuation.

It is important also in this context to appreciate that once the purchaser or lender has knowledge that the defendant's inspection or report was negligently carried out and provided in any respect, the limitation clock will start to tick. It will be irrelevant that the purchaser or lender does not know of each and every potential deficiency in the professional service provided. This is illustrated by *Horbury v Craig Hall & Rutley*[4] where a surveyor had failed to notice that certain chimney breasts had been removed, leaving the flues unsupported. This defect was remedied by the purchaser with the surveyor's co-operation. More

1 See per Lord Donaldson in *Halford v Brookes* [1991] 1 WLR 428 at 443.
2 [1993] 1 WLR 782 at 792.
3 [1996] NPC 19.
4 [1991] EGCS 81.

than three years later, dry rot was discovered which, it was contended, ought to have been detected by the original surveyor/valuer. Proceedings in respect of this further damage failed on the grounds of limitation, Judge Bowsher QC stating that the cause of action against the surveyor was:

> 'one single cause of action, not a bundle of causes of action relating to different defects in the house and different elements of inconvenience as they arise.'[1]

The Limitation Act 1980, however, provides a longstop in s 14B(1) which provides:

> 'an action for damages for negligence, other than one involving personal injuries shall not be brought after the expiration of 15 years from the date or, if more than one, from the last of the dates on which there occurred any act or omission – (a) which is alleged to constitute negligence and (b) to which the damage in respect of which damages are claimed is alleged to be attributable in whole or in part.'

Section 14B(2) makes it plain that this 15 year longstop runs from the defendant's last breach of duty, whether or not the time limits provided for in ss 2 or 14A have expired or even begun.

Exceptions

7.10 The only exceptions to the above rules are to be found in s 32 to the Limitation Act 1980. This provides:

> '(1) ... where in the case of any action for which a period of limitation is prescribed by this Act, either (a) the action is based upon the fraud[2] of the defendant or (b) any fact relevant to the plaintiff's right of action has been deliberately concealed from him by the defendant ... the period of limitation shall not begin to run until the plaintiff has discovered the fraud or concealment ... or could with reasonable diligence had discovered it.'

In the context of valuation and survey reports, however, the fraud exception is unlikely to apply. Concealment of factual matters, however, may arise. In *Westlake v Bracknell District Council*,[3] the defendant firm in preparing a mortgage valuation report negligently omitted to identify serious deficiencies in a concrete floor slab. The purchasers, who soon after moving into the property discovered widening gaps between skirting boards and floors enquired of the defendant firm as to the cause. The plaintiff purchasers were told that the cracks were the result of settlement about which they should not be concerned. When the plaintiffs attempted to sell, some six years later, the true nature of the problem came to light and the property became unmortgageable. Within two years of discovering the true position, the purchasers brought proceedings, to be met in the first instance with a plea that their action was now statute-barred. Relying upon s 32, however, the court held that the reassuring statements made by the defendant's surveyor upon the occasion of

---

1 See to like effect *Hamlin v Edwin Evans* [1996] PNLR 398.

2 Although valuation fraud was the subject of the action in *Alliance & Leicester Building Society v Edgestop Ltd (No 3)* [1994] 2 EGLR 229.

3 [1987] 1 EGLR 161.

his visit subsequent to the plaintiffs' purchase amounted to deliberate concealment of facts relevant to their cause of action. Deliberate concealment was held apt to embrace inter alia 'conduct involving recklessness or turning a blind eye or unconscionable conduct'.

USE OF EXPERTS

The chartered surveyor as expert witness

7.11 The need for and importance of cogent expert evidence in support or contradiction of a negligence claim against a surveyor or valuer cannot be overstated. As Lord Templeman indicated in *Smith v Eric S Bush*:[1]

> 'A valuer will only be liable if other qualified valuers, who cannot be expected to be harsh on their fellow professionals, consider that, taking into consideration the nature of the work for which the valuer is paid and the object of that work, nevertheless he has been guilty of an error which an average valuer, in the same circumstances, would not have made.'

It has been increasingly emphasised by the courts that experts addressing such issues must approach the task uninfluenced by the exigencies of the litigation. As Cazalet J stated in *Re J (A Minor) (Child Abuse: Expert Evidence)*:[2]

> '... expert witnesses are in a privileged position: indeed only experts are permitted to give an opinion in evidence. Outside the legal field the court itself has no expertise and for that reason frequently has to rely on the evidence of experts. Such experts must express only opinions which they genuinely hold and which are not biased in favour of one particular party. Opinions can of course differ and indeed frequently experts who have expressed the objective and honest opinion will differ but such differences are usually within a legitimate area of disagreement. On occasions, and because they are acting on opposing sides, each may give his opinion from different basic facts. This of itself is likely to produce a divergence. The expert should not mislead by omissions. He should consider all the material facts in reaching his conclusions and must not omit to consider the material facts which could detract from his concluded opinion.'

The clearest exposition of the expert's duties in this regard was given by Creswell J in *National Justice Compania Naviera SA v Prudential Assurance Co (The Ikarian Reefer)*[3] where the following points were listed:

> '1. Expert evidence presented to the court should be, and should be seen to be, the independent product of the expert uninfluenced as to formal content by the exigencies of litigation.
>
> 2. An expert witness should provide independent assistance to the court by way of objective unbiased opinion in relation to matters within his expertise an expert witness in the High Court should never assume the role of an advocate.

---

1 [1991] AC 831 at 851.

2 [1990] FCR 193.

3 [1993] 2 EGLR 183.

3. An expert witness should state the facts or assumptions upon which his opinion is based. He should not omit to consider material facts which could detract from his concluded opinion.

4. An expert witness should make it clear when a particular question or issue falls outside his expertise.

5. If an expert's opinion is not properly researched because he considers that insufficient data is available, then this must be stated with an indication that the opinion is no more than a provisional one in cases where an expert witness who has prepared a report could not assert that the report contained the truth, the whole truth and nothing but the truth without some qualification, that qualification should be stated in the report.

6. If, after exchange of reports, an expert witness changes his view on a material matter having regard to the other side's expert's report or for any other reason, such change of view should be communicated (through legal representatives) to the other side without delay and when appropriate for the court.

7. Where expert evidence refers to photographs, plans, calculations, analyses, measurements, survey reports or other similar documents, these must be provided to the opposite party at the same time as the exchange of reports.'

The degree of responsibility thus entrusted to the expert cannot be overstated. The court will seek guidance from such a witness and be likely to rely upon expert expressions of opinion. As Gibson J stated in *Corisand Investments Ltd v Druce & Co*:[1]

> '[The expert valuer] has said – that is my opinion, based upon my experience – the court will not readily conclude, when that is said by a valuer of acknowledged skill and integrity, that he is propounding an opinion which no competent valuer could hold unless there is clear evidence that he has ignored or misunderstood the facts, or that he has failed to apply some principle which a competent valuer ought to apply. The assertion by a valuer of acknowledged skill and experience that in his judgment a property was worth a particular sum on a particular date will again not readily be shown to have been such an opinion as no competent valuer could hold by simple reliance upon the assertion of another valuer, also of acknowledged skill and experience, that in his judgment the proper valuation was a figure so much lower than the first that the first must be regarded as a valuation which no competent valuer could put forward.'

A failure to adhere to the principles set out above will be likely to render any 'expert evidence' inadmissible[2] or so undermine the credibility of the witness that his evidence will be disregarded.[3]

7.12 With effect from 1 March 1997, chartered surveyors acting as expert witnesses will be expected to abide by the RICS' 'Surveyors Acting as Expert

1 [1978] EGD 769 at 784–785.

2 See *Alliance & Leicester Building Society v Edgestop Ltd (No 2)* 28 June 1993 (unreported) ChD.

3 See *Carla Homes (South) Ltd and Others v Alfred McAlpine Homes East Ltd* 1995 CILL 1083, ChD, per Laddie J.

Witnesses: Practice Statement and Guidance Notes'. This applies whenever a chartered surveyor is required to provide expert evidence to a judicial or quasi-judicial body. It is emphasised that 'the primary duty of a surveyor is to the judicial body to whom his evidence is given. The duty is to be truthful as to fact, honest as to opinion and complete as to coverage of relevant matters ... the surveyor's evidence must be independent, objective and unbiased. In particular, it must not be biased towards the party who is responsible for paying him'. Where, after preparing a report, the expert changes his view on a material matter or identifies a material inaccuracy, this must be communicated to his client and the other parties to the dispute. Any written report must include a declaration that it has been prepared in accordance with the requirement of the Practice Statement.

Without-prejudice meetings

7.13 It is the almost invariable practice of the court in surveyor's negligence cases to direct that the expert witnesses of like disciplines on either side of the case meet without prejudice to agree any facts capable of agreement and identify and narrow issues prior to the preparation of their reports. Order 38, Rule 38 of the Rules of the Supreme Court provides:

> 'In any cause or matter the court may, if it thinks fit, direct that there be a meeting 'without prejudice' of such experts within such periods before or after the disclosure of their reports as the court may specify, for the purposes of identifying those parts of their evidence which are in issue.'

Where the action is one relating to the competence of the valuation so that evidence of comparable transactions will be important, the court will also be likely to direct that each expert furnish to his opponent details of any comparables relied upon. Following the without-prejudice meeting, the experts will usually prepare their reports and be directed to meet again with a view to preparing a joint statement of matters that are capable of agreement and those which remain unagreed. Until the joint statement is signed, the contents remain without prejudice and may not be referred to the court. The procedure is governed by the rules of the Supreme Court, the balance of Rule 38 providing:

> 'Where [a without-prejudice meeting] takes place the experts may prepare a joint statement indicating those parts of their evidence on which they are, and those on which they are not, in agreement.'

There is need for great caution here, however, in that, whilst the experts may be happy that they have resolved certain issues between them, the resolution may not be to the liking of the lay client. The latter is not bound by any agreement reached but would for all practical purposes be unable to continue to rely upon an expert whose views were not accepted. Once agreement has been reached and openly assented to in the form of a joint statement, the views expressed to that extent cease to be without prejudice. The position is succinctly summarised by Judge Newey QC in *Richard Roberts Holdings v Douglas Smith Stimson Partnership*:[1]

> 'In my opinion there are no words in Rule 38 which purport to confer upon expert's power to bind anyone. If it did, then since the Rule would not be dealing with procedure, but with substantive rights of persons under the law of agency, it would, I think be ultra vires. The first sentence of the rule and powers of the court to direct without prejudice meetings of experts; it does not confer power to require open meetings. The second sentence does not authorise experts to do anything. It is, I think, no more than a sensible reminder to experts that it may be useful for them to reduce the results of their discussions to writing. There is nothing in the second sentence to state that joint statements should be open. I think it would be quite alien to the role of expert witnesses that they should have an automatic power to bind parties at the conclusion of without prejudice meetings. An expert does not represent a party in the way that a solicitor represents his client; he is principally a witness and his duties are to explain to the court ... technical matters and to give expert opinion evidence. If every Order for a meeting of experts were likely to result either in an agreement disposing of all or part of the case without either party or with legal advisers being consulted, orders for meetings would be likely to be strongly opposed.'

None the less, the initial without-prejudice meeting between the experts usually affords an important watershed in the history of any case. It is the first real opportunity for each side to assess the strengths and weaknesses of the action as a whole.

The expert's report

7.14 The expert's report will in content and format obviously reflect the exigencies of the particular case. That said, in most actions the following main issues will need to be addressed.

- what was the method of approach to inspecting the property and valuing it employed by the defendant surveyor/valuer?
- what was the likely condition of the property at the date of the inspection; which defects if any would have been likely then to have been apparent to a competent surveyor/valuer within the constraints of the type of inspection report being provided?
- what was the 'true value' of the property at the date of the valuation reported?
- given the nature of the property, how easy or difficult was it then to value; what margin of error may be considered appropriate or (of values)?
- in the light of the above, is there material to confirm or refute a contention that the inspection and report provided fell below that which would be expected from the competent surveyor/valuer?

---

1 [1996] Const LJ 70.

Although the last question is the legal issue to be resolved by the court, experts need not be shy of addressing it overtly.[1] In establishing the correct retrospective valuation of the property, whether or not missed defects explain the reported value, it will be necessary to consider evidence of comparables. If the expert has direct, personal knowledge of transactions contemporaneous to the valuation in question his views are likely to carry more weight with the court than the expert who has to rely upon secondhand information. None the less, in an action of this kind it is entirely permissible to produce such secondhand evidence because any valuer is likely to take such material into account in providing an initial valuation of a property and the question for the court is whether in the light of all the information which the competent valuer would have obtained, the reported figure was one which the reasonable valuer could have reported.[2]

Court-appointed experts

7.15 Historically, civil courts enjoyed an inherent jurisdiction to appoint expert witnesses. In *Colls v Home and Colonial Stores Ltd*,[3] Lord MacNaughten said:

> 'I have often wondered why the court does not more frequently avail itself of the powers of calling in a competent adviser to report to the court upon the question. There are plenty of experienced surveyors accustomed to deal with large properties in London who might be trusted to make a perfectly fair and impartial report, subject, of course, to examination in the court if required.'

There are early examples of this power being exercised. In *Kennard v Ashman*,[4] the court was so confused by the contradictory surveying evidence called on behalf of the litigants that the case was adjourned for a report from an independent surveyor nominated by the judge. In practice, however, these examples have been followed rarely.

Under Ord 40 of the Rules of the Supreme Court, however, there is explicit jurisdiction now conferred for the court to appoint an independent expert upon the application of any party. A recent example of the court appointing an expert, in spite of objection, is *Abbey National Mortgages Plc v Key Surveyors Nationwide Ltd*.[5] In that case, the plaintiff lender had made a series of advances over 29 properties, valued by eight different valuers employed by Key Surveyors Nationwide Ltd. The lender sought the appointment of a single court appointed expert to advise upon the retrospective value of the securities. The application was acceded to by the court, the defendants' submissions that they needed 29 separate valuers with knowledge of local market conditions in order

1 See *United Bank of Kuwait v Prudential Property Services* [1995] EGCS 190.
2 See the views expressed in *Abbey National Mortgages v Key Surveyors Nationwide* [1996] 3 All ER 184.
3 [1904] AC 179.
4 [1894] 10 TLR 213.
5 [1995] 2 EGLR 134; confirmed on appeal [1996] 3 All ER 184.

properly to defend the allegations of negligent over-valuation being rejected. The argument was dealt with by Judge Hicks QC as follows:

> 'It is a little difficult to take seriously the argument that only one valuer per property will do from defendants who themselves cover 29 properties with eight valuers, including a Bedford based valuer who reported on a Lowestoft property, a Southampton based valuer who reported on a Weston-super-Mare property, a Manchester based valuer who reported on one in Llanrwst and an Ipswich based valuer who reported on properties in Tilbury and Leigh-on-Sea.'

Further, the court pointed out that under Rule 6 of Order 40 where an expert is appointed by the court, 'no party may call more than one (expert) witness without the leave of the court' which will not be granted save in exceptional circumstances. Judge Hicks QC found nothing exceptional in the circumstances of the case before him and Key Surveyors Nationwide Ltd were accordingly confined to relying upon one expert to defend all of the alleged negligent over valuations.

Chapter 8

DIRECT PROFESSIONAL ACCESS AND INSURANCE MATTERS

INTRODUCTION

8.1 In this chapter, it is proposed to consider the separated but related topics of direct professional access and general insurance considerations applicable to chartered surveyors.

Historically, chartered surveyors and their clients were only able to benefit from the advice and provision of advocacy services by a barrister if he was instructed through a solicitor. Traditionally, the roles of a solicitor and barrister differed, each accepting responsibility to a client for different functions. The solicitor would be involved in the background preparation of a case, the barrister being consulted either on issues of complex law or to conduct particular hearings before a court or tribunal. Nowadays many solicitors have as much (and in some cases more) specialist knowledge as a barrister working in the same field of law. Further, many solicitors now have rights of audience before the higher courts. It was accordingly a welcome extension when in April 1989 the Bar Council announced that chartered surveyors were to be granted direct access to practising barristers. This gave members of the surveying profession and their clients a choice of deciding, where legal services were necessary, whether to engage a solicitor or retain counsel directly, with or without the involvement of a solicitor. A decision to consult a barrister directly, however, necessarily involves the surveyor undertaking much more of the background, preparatory work which historically would have been carried out by a solicitor. There are accordingly important insurance considerations to take into account when electing for direct professional access.

DIRECT PROFESSIONAL ACCESS

Services required

8.2 The RICS has published Guidance Notes to assist Chartered Surveyors in the use of Direct Access to barristers.[1] It is recommended that this document be consulted before deciding whether to elect for direct professional access and

1 Current edition, July 1994.

dispense with the services of a solicitor intermediary. In considering whether to consult a barrister directly, surveyors should determine with their client whether such a step would be appropriate. First, it should be recognised that a barrister offers particular areas of expertise, namely advice on legal matters, drafting, settling and approving legal documents; drafting pleadings, advising on evidence and advocacy at hearings. The usual areas where a surveyor and/or his client may seek advisory assistance will be matters involving any aspect of landlord and tenant law, for example the Landlord and Tenant Act 1954, the Leasehold Reform Act 1967, the Housing and Rent Acts and the Agricultural Holdings legislation. There may be need to obtain a correct legal interpretation of provisions in a lease, such as rent review clauses or conveyances or other documents affecting the use and enjoyment of land. All aspects of planning law, including consideration of whether planning permission is required for a particular development may fall within the barrister's field of practice expertise. The law relating to valuations for statutory purposes, including compensation for compulsory purchase and planning restrictions, rating, taxation and leasehold enfranchisement may similarly benefit from an expert legal appraisal. The instructing surveyor may need guidance upon the interpretation of provisions in building or civil engineering contracts and the validity of actions taken by persons concerned with such contracts, for example notices of or leading up to determination of a contractor's employment. There may be an advantage in seeking an opinion from tax counsel as to the most suitable method by which a land transaction can be structured so as to secure tax advantages. This is by no means an exhaustive list of topics. The potential advantage of direct access to a barrister for advice in any of the above areas is the saving of expense to the lay client which will otherwise arise in having first to discuss the matter with a solicitor.

8.3 Apart from the provision of such advisory services, the chartered surveyor and/or his client may be in need of advocacy services. There remain limitations upon the extent to which a chartered surveyor may instruct counsel directly to conduct hearings. A barrister cannot be briefed by a chartered surveyor to appear in the House of Lords, the Privy Council, the Supreme Court (which includes the High Court and the Court of Appeal), in a County Court, Crown Court or the Employment Appeals Tribunal. Of particular importance in this excluded category is the inability to instruct counsel directly in any High Court matter, which would therefore include any item of Official Referees business. Advocacy services may be solicited directly, however, for appearances in the Lands Tribunal, Agricultural Land Tribunals, and before arbitrators and inquiries dealing with planning, compulsory purchase orders, highways, enforcement notices, local plans and special orders. In addition, a barrister may be retained directly to appear before Rent Assessment Committees and Rent Tribunals and Leasehold Valuation Tribunals.

8.4 If advisory or appropriate advocacy services may be obtained directly, the chartered surveyor will need to consider whether his client's interests would be better served by taking advantage of this facility. It should here be recognised that a solicitor is likely to have very much more experience in preparing instructions to counsel and getting a matter ready for a hearing so that the client may lose the benefit of such experienced assistance in those areas if a solicitor is not involved. The instructing member will need to carry out much of the work which the solicitor would otherwise have performed. If a hearing is to be prepared for, the member will need to be responsible for interviewing any witnesses and obtaining expert witness evidence. If the chartered surveyor is to attempt to act as the expert witness for his own client then it may be very difficult for such a member to be involved properly and dispassionately in the preparation of the papers and other materials needing to be collated to enable an effective case to be presented.

Where direct professional access work is to be undertaken, the member will need to ensure that proper professional indemnity insurance is in place. The insurers will need to be notified and their written acceptance of the risk obtained. Counsel undertaking such work are also required to obtain separate insurance cover from the Bar Mutual Indemnity Fund Ltd. In the case of the surveyor, the insurers will want to know the nature and extent of any proposed direct professional access work. An additional premium will be likely to be required. The member should obtain a clear written indication of the insurer's requirements for the keeping of records relating to such work. The administrative burden in all of this is not to be overlooked. In organising and arranging a hearing, it may well be that the instructing member will in due course have to handle client's money. Witness expenses, arbitrator's fees, counsel's fees and the allocation of compensatory payments received will all need to be properly and efficiently dealt with. None the less, in some cases, it may be to the lay client's advantage for the surveyor to be able to provide such a range of services, including direct professional access to a barrister.

Instructing counsel

8.5 The first practical step in instructing counsel directly, is to identify an appropriate specialist. Certain chambers enjoy a reputation for specialist knowledge in some of the work areas referred to above where chartered surveyors typically are assisted by a lawyer. The Bar Council maintains a list of barristers who accept direct professional access work. Contact with the Bar Council will assist in identifying such practitioners. The clerk to an individual set of chambers will have a detailed understanding of which members of chambers undertake such work and who would be the counsel best able to satisfy the needs of the surveyor and his client. The RICS has included in the Guidance Notes some model terms of engagement which it is recommended should be used in instructing counsel directly. One or two of these model terms merit highlighting. First, the model terms provide that unless otherwise agreed, the barrister will deal with any instructions other than a brief as soon as he reasonably can in the ordinary course of his work. If there is any urgency in the papers being dealt with, that information must be communicated to the barrister or his clerk separately from the instructions themselves. This is important, given that much of the legislation regulating agricultural and business tenancies involve strict time-limits being observed with regard to the service of notices. The importance of recognising the existence of any time limits affecting a lay client's position cannot be over emphasised. Where any such limit may apply, the position must be drawn to the attention of the barrister to be instructed at the outset. The model terms of engagement also provide that the barrister will not be deemed to have accepted instructions until he has had a reasonable opportunity to peruse them and decide whether they are appropriate for direct professional access. The barrister may decide that it is in the best interests of the lay client that he be instructed through a solicitor and will be expected to advise accordingly if that view is taken. In that event the instructing member may either comply with the request or withdraw the instructions. Further, the standard terms provide that, unless otherwise agreed, a barrister accepts a brief for a hearing upon the understanding that he may be unavoidably prevented by a conflicting professional engagement from attending the case. Last minute returns of briefs to other barristers are unsatisfactory. The instructing member may wish to attempt to secure a commitment from counsel of his choice, therefore, to attend a hearing – or at least ensure that the availability of adequate alternative cover exists.

Where a barrister is instructed directly, the instructing member becomes *personally* liable for counsel's fees. The guidance notes indicate that the RICS will consider that any failure by an instructing member to pay a barrister's fee will normally amount to professional misconduct. Care should therefore be taken to ensure appropriate fees are agreed with counsel's clerk from the beginning. Finally the instructing member in the model terms of engagement will agree to maintain a proper collection of all the papers to and from counsel, along with notes of any advice(s) given in conference with the barrister. These are likely to represent requirements of the insurers in any event.

8.6 In preparing papers for advice or a hearing the following practical guidance should be considered. In drafting instructions to counsel to advise, the instructing member should attempt to identify the problem upon which an opinion or advice is sought by a concise and clear recital of facts and background circumstances. The written instructions should have attached copies of all relevant documents, organised by connected subject matter and paginated. Original documents should never be forwarded to counsel. Where any correspondence needs to be included, this should be copied in chronological sequence and paginated. If the instructing member is concerned about any particular statutory or regulatory provision, this should be set out *in extenso* with a full reference to the primary source. The submitted papers will conventionally be enclosed under cover of a 'back sheet', giving the name of the client and the instructing member. The barrister will endorse the back sheet at each separate occasion of his involvement. It is important that this convention is followed as these materials are considered by any taxing master who may be responsible for investigating the reasonableness of fees charged.

Where counsel is being instructed for a hearing, the brief should include a statement of the forum for the hearing, a summary of the client's case and that of the opposing party (as viewed by the instructing member). The evidence to be called should be included in the form of the collected witness statements and expert reports, if any. The instructing member should include any observations of his own as to lines of argument he feels may be important. Where the matter is to progress to a hearing the instructing member will also be responsible for ensuring that the case is ready for trial and in a format acceptable to the court/tribunal. The instructing member will accordingly need to have a good working knowledge of the procedural requirements of the relevant court or tribunal. It is likely that prior to any main hearing the court or tribunal will have given preliminary directions for the service/exchange of lay and expert witness evidence. Directions are likely also to have been given for the mutual exchange of all and any relevant documents. This process of *discovery* is of crucial importance in any case. Knowing what documents are discoverable and those which ought not to be disclosed is by no means straightforward and an instructing member should always seek legal advice upon such matters before disclosing any of his client's documents. It is this sort of detailed preparation for a hearing where a member may regret the absence of the customary services of a solicitor. Counsel is generally unable by reason of the Bar Code of Conduct to interview witnesses himself and/or consult with witnesses directly. The barrister may see the lay client and any expert in conference but must be attended by the instructing member. The chartered surveyor will here consider whether, even with the limited extent to which counsel can give practical help on such matters, the interests of the client may not be better served by retaining a solicitor.

INSURANCE MATTERS

8.7 Prior to April 1996, chartered surveyors obtained professional indemnity insurance cover through RICS Insurance Services Ltd (RICSIS). The latter was a broker, rather than an insurer. Following the demise of RICSIS, the Institution elected to approach the issue of professional indemnity insurance from a new perspective. Rather than pursuing the matter through a broker, the RICS decided on the new concept of endorsing an insurer to provide a bench mark policy together with the quality of service and claims handling that the Institution would expect of other insurers. The endorsed insurer is Archer Underwriting Ltd. Policies are now being provided through a specialist facility called Surveyors and Valuers Insurance Services (SURVIS). SURVIS is a name owned by the Institution and is currently being used under the terms of an agreement between the Institution and Archer Underwriting.

The chartered surveyor's rule book in its current form, effective from 1 January 1997, stipulates at Bye-Law 19(8) that: 'every member shall, in accordance with the regulations, be insured against claims for breach of professional duty as a surveyor.' Regulation 3 stipulates that the minimum limits of indemnity cover are as follows:

(a) £100,000 for each and every claim where the gross income of the firm in the preceding year did not exceed £50,000; or

(b) £250,000 for each and every claim where the gross income of the firm in the preceding year exceeded £50,000 but did not exceed £100,000; or

(c) £500,000 for each and every claim where the gross income of the firm in the preceding year exceeded £100,000.

Regulation 4 imposes limits to the level of uninsured excess. These are up to £5,000 with a limit of indemnity up to £100,000; £7,500 for each and every claim with a limit of indemnity between £100,000 and £250,000; and, in the case of a policy with a limit of indemnity over £250,000, 2.5 per cent of the sums insured or £10,000 for each and every claim, whichever shall be the greater. Regulation 5 stipulates that every member who is a partner or director of a firm offering surveying services to the public shall ensure that any former partner, director or consultant continues to be insured on each and every claim basis against any claim arising from work previously undertaken by such former partner, director or consultant for a period of six years from the date when such individual ceased to be a partner, director or consultant. Where the firm is subsequently dissolved or wound up, each former partner, director or consultant becomes responsible for maintaining his own insurance cover for the relevant period. Likewise, any sole principal who has ceased to practice is required to maintain insurance cover in respect of his previous practice for a period of six years. Having regard to the discussion elsewhere[1] as to limitation periods for the bringing of claims, surveyors are well advised to consider maintaining insurance cover for up to 15 years from the date of the last piece of professional advice given.

Professional indemnity wording

8.8 Regulation 2 of Bye-Law 19(8) requires that: 'members shall insure by means of a policy no less comprehensive than the form of the RICS professional indemnity policy in force at the time when the policy of insurance is taken out'. The SURVIS-approved wording is as follows:

> '1. Civil liability
> To indemnify the insured against any claim or claims first made against them or any of them during the certificate period in respect of any civil liability whatsoever or whensoever arising (including liability for claimant's costs) incurred in the course of any profession or business carried on by the insured. Where a series of such claims arise from a breach of or repeated breaches of a single duty or identical duties owned and arising from a single engagement all claims within that series shall for the purpose of the limit of indemnity … and the excess … under this certificate be treated as a single claim. Provided that any and all such claims arising from a single survey and/or valuation shall for the like purpose be treated as a single claim under this certificate.'

In addition, there is a required provision for fidelity insurance, whereby the insured is to be indemnified 'against their own direct loss or losses which, during the certificate period they shall discover they have sustained by reason of any

1 See paras **7.9–7.10**.

dishonesty or fraud of any past or present partner, director or employee of the firm(s) named in the schedule'. Such cover will only apply where 'such dishonest or fraudulent act(s) are carried out by the person(s) concerned with the manifest intent to cause such loss to the insured or to obtain improper personal gain either for themselves or in collusion with others'. Plainly, indemnity is not afforded to any person committing or condoning such dishonesty or fraud. It is a further condition of availability of such fidelity insurance cover that the annual accounts of the insured have been prepared and/or certified by an independent accountant or auditor. Accountants' fees incurred as a result of such fraud are covered up to £15,000 or such amount as may be agreed by the insurers. Finally, insurance cover must be in place 'to indemnify the insured against reasonable costs and expenses of whatsoever nature incurred by the insured in replacing or restoring documents either the property of or entrusted to or lodged or deposited with the firm(s), having been discovered during the certificate period to have been damaged, lost or mislaid and which after diligent search cannot be found'.

Implicit in the above wording is the notion that the insurers have an obligation to indemnify in the event of a claim being made during the currency of a policy. For this purpose, a claim is made when it is first communicated to the insured. In *Robert Ervin & Burns (a firm) v Stone & Others*,[1] a firm of surveyors and valuers were covered under a claims-made policy of professional indemnity insurance from 15 July 1994 to 14 July 1995. In April 1995, a writ was issued by the Royal Bank of Scotland, claiming damages in respect of an alleged negligent valuation. The insured was not aware of the writ until it was served on 15 August, after the policy had expired. The insured sought a declaration that the insurers were liable under the policy on the basis that the claim was made on the date the writ was issued. This argument was rejected by the Court of Appeal. Staughton LJ held that in the ordinary meaning of the English language 'claims made' indicated communication by the client to be insured of some discontent which would or might result in a remedy being expected from the insured. The SURVIS professional indemnity wording incorporates certain exclusions and operates subject to particular general conditions.

Exclusions and general conditions

8.9 Attention is here drawn to the following particular exclusions: first, the certificate does not extend to losses covered by any other policy of insurance or any claim or circumstance that may give rise to a claim which has been notified to any insurance intermediary or insurer pursuant to any other policy or certificate of insurance attaching prior to the inception of the certificate or disclosed on the completed proposal form, forming the basis of the contract. Secondly, disputes between the insured and any present or former employee are not covered. Thirdly, claims or losses arising out of any trading losses or trading liabilities incurred by any business managed or carried on by the

---

1 16 October 1997 (Unreported).

insured including loss of any client account or business are excluded from cover. Claims or losses arising out of the use of any motor vehicles by the insured in circumstances in which the provisions of the Road Traffic Acts apply and loss and damage arising out of the death or bodily injury or disease of any employee under a contract of service with the firm are not covered. Finally, any claim or loss arising out of a survey/inspection and/or valuation report of real/leasehold property is excluded unless such survey/inspections and/or valuations have been carried out by a fellow or professional associate of the RICS or a fellow or associate of the Incorporated Society of Valuers and Auctioneers, a fellow or associate of the Faculty of Architects and Surveyors or a fellow or associate of the Royal Institute of British Architects or a fellow or associate of the Royal Incorporation of Architects in Scotland. Further, the relevant survey/inspection/valuation must have been provided by such a person who has not less than five years' experience of such work or by any other person delegated by the insured to execute such work as part of their training, subject always to supervision of such work by a person answering the above description or otherwise as agreed in writing with the insurers prior to cover being granted.

As to general conditions, the insured must not admit liability for, or settle any claim, or incur any costs or expenses in connection therewith, without the written consent of the insurers. The latter are entitled at any time to take over and conduct in the name of the insured or the firm(s) the defence or settlement of any such claim. The insured must give the insurers as soon as possible details in writing of any claim or claims made against him and/or of the discovery of any loss which may be the subject of indemnity. In addition, the insured must notify the insurers as soon as possible during the certificate period of any circumstance of which the insured first becomes aware during the certificate period which may give rise to a claim and/or the discovery of a reasonable cause for suspicion of dishonesty or fraud on the part of the present partner, director or employee of the firm(s), whether giving rise to a claim or loss under the certificate or not, and of any threatened or actual proceedings under the Property Misdescriptions Act 1991. If such notice is given, any subsequent claim or discovered loss will be treated as having been made or discovered during the certificate period.

General law

8.10 Contracts of insurance are contracts *uberimae fidei*. As such, apart from an entitlement to deny cover for breach of policy conditions and/or under an exclusion provision, the policy may be avoided as a result of any failure by the insured to disclose material facts affecting the risk. In deciding what matters are material so as to require disclosure, the court will only permit the insurer to avoid liability on the policy where two conditions can be satisfied: first, the matter not disclosed must be of a kind which would influence the prudent insurer in deciding whether to offer insurance cover and at what premium. Secondly, the insurer will have to demonstrate to the court that the undisclosed material would in fact have influenced the decision to insure in the particular case. As Lord Mustill observed in the now leading case on the subject (*Pan Atlantic Insurance Co Ltd v Pine Top Insurance Co*):[1]

> 'True, the inequalities of knowledge between assured and underwriter have led to the creation of a special duty to make accurate disclosure of sufficient facts to restore the balance and remedy the injustice of holding the underwriter to a speculation which he had been unable fairly to assess; but the consideration cannot in logic or justice require courts to go further and declare the contract to be vitiated when the underwriter, having paid no attention to the matter which was not properly stated and disclosed, has suffered no injustice thereby.'

In reality an assured is likely to have 'an uphill task in persuading the court that the withholding or misstatement of circumstances satisfying the test of materiality has made no difference'.[2]

So far as a failure to comply with any condition of the policy is concerned, an interesting example of an attempt to avoid cover is *Summers v Congreve Horner & Co (a firm) and Independent Insurance Co Ltd*.[3] In that case, a claim arose out of an allegedly negligent structural survey carried out by a trainee surveyor. He did not fall within the category of surveyors now falling within para 13(a) and (b) of the standard terms of cover. He was, however, a 'person delegated by the assured to (carry out) such work as part of (his) training subject . . . to . . . supervision of such work by' an appropriately qualified person. In determining whether a policy exclusion applied, the court was accordingly concerned with the degree of supervision necessary to bring the individual within what is now para 13(c). The training took the form of a period of accompanying and observing a partner when conducting surveys, followed by the trainee carrying out inspections under the constant supervision of a partner. Once the firm was satisfied that the trainee was progressing appropriately, he was permitted to undertake surveys of sites, in the course of which a partner would carry out a visit for 30 minutes or so to ensure that there were no difficulties. Once sufficiently confident in the trainee's ability, he was allowed to undertake surveys on his own. A checklist was provided to which the trainee was expected to work and the content of any report was discussed before it was finalised with a partner. The alleged negligent survey occurred during the course of a trainee carrying out an inspection on his own. At first instance the court upheld the insurer's contention that there was insufficient supervision of the trainee to attract cover under the terms of the indemnity policy. On appeal, however, the Court of Appeal was satisfied that the degree of supervision offered was sufficient in all the circumstances.

Where the insurers seek to avoid liability on the grounds of fraud, the court will expect such an allegation to be proved to a very high degree. Such an attempt failed in *BNP Mortgages Ltd v Goadsby & Harding Ltd*[4] where insurers alleged that an excessively high valuation was provided fraudulently as a result of

1 [1994] 3 All ER 581 at 610.
2 [1994] 3 All ER 581 per Lord Mustill at 610.
3 [1992] 2 EGLR 152.
4 [1994] 2 EGLR 169.

collusion with the owner of the property. The trial judge, having witnessed the valuer under cross-examination, concluded:

> 'The fact that [the valuer] cut many corners, eg failing to visit the site, failing to ascertain the sale position of units 3 and 4, the failure to ascertain the then asking prices for the unsold units and the fact that almost contemporaneously he was accurately reflecting the depressed state of the market in [another valuation] are all factors from which a dishonest belief could be determined. Indeed as a paper exercise it may be that I would have made such a finding. But the overwhelming impression I had of him in the witness box was of a man who had no intention of acting dishonestly but who did unfortunately show unusual negligence.'

COSTS

8.11 This is not an appropriate place to discuss the topic of costs orders arising in the course of litigation. In broad terms, a successful party to any litigious dispute will be likely to find that the court orders the unsuccessful party to pay the costs of the action. The matter of costs is raised in the context of direct professional access and insurance considerations because of the potential risk of adverse costs orders being made directly against insurers and/or third party funders of disputes. In *Eastglen Ltd v Grafton & Others*,[1] a firm of surveyors brought proceedings for unpaid fees against a development company. The company went into liquidation. The liquidator thereafter commenced an action on behalf of the company against two of its directors, alleging that they had paid sums of the company's money to themselves. The surveyors, being the biggest single creditor, had a direct interest in the success of the liquidators' action. The directors, who were individuals of modest means, sought an order that the company put up security for the costs of the action. The surveyors, who had previously been underwriting the liquidator's costs, decided not to provide funds to enable security to be given, and in default of security being provided the liquidator's action was struck out. The directors, who had incurred costs of their own, realised that these would plainly not be payable by the liquidator and/or the insolvent company. They accordingly sought an order for costs directly against the surveyors who had encouraged the original action to be brought. By s 51 of the Supreme Court Act 1981 the court have a discretionary power to order such third party funders to meet the costs of an opposing party to the action. In the event, Lindsay J dismissed the application for costs against the surveyors but indicated that the decision as to whether they should be liable for such costs was finely balanced.

A similar risk is run by indemnity and litigation insurers. In *Murphy v Young & Co's Brewery plc*,[2] legal expenses insurers to an unsuccessful plaintiff whose action they had funded were pursued by the successful defendant in the action upon an application for the defendant's costs to be paid by them directly. The

1 [1996] BCC 900.
2 [1997] 1 All ER 518.

plaintiffs at the outcome of the case were unable to meet these costs themselves. The application was refused on the facts, the Court of Appeal laying down some guidelines as to when such an exceptional order for costs against a third party may be appropriate. In particular, Phillips LJ indicated that such an order would be justified where the third party funder habitually took responsibility for underwriting the costs of the unsuccessful party being assisted. An example is the assistance given by trade unions to their members to pursue litigation. Likewise, if the insurer/third party funder had agreed to indemnify the unsuccessful party being assisted against adverse costs orders, this would afford a basis for an order being made directly against such concern. In addition, where the maintenance offered by the third party funder could be described as 'wanton and officious inter-meddling with the disputes of others' a direct order for costs would be likely. In *Pendennis Shipyard Ltd v Margrathea (Pendennis) Ltd (in liquidation)*,[1] professional indemnity insurers who effectively took over the defence of an action in the hope of avoiding their obligation to indemnify the insured were ordered to pay the opposing successful party's costs, notwithstanding the existence of a limit of insurance cover as between the insurers and the insured. It will accordingly be important in any action being defended by insurers for this to be done upon the clear instructions of the surveyor concerned and with a view to protecting his interests rather than the insurers' own in not having to meet a claim.

1 (1997) *The Times*, 27 August.

PART II

QUANTITY SURVEYORS

Chapter 9

THE QUANTITY SURVEYOR'S TERMS OF ENGAGEMENT

INTRODUCTION

9.1 In 1870, the role of a quantity surveyor was judicially described as being that of a person:

> 'whose business consists in taking out in detail the measurements and quantities from plans prepared by an architect for the purpose of enabling builders to calculate the amounts for which they would execute the plans.'[1]

The role now is more accurately described as that of project cost manager. In practice, the work of preparing bills of quantities only occupies a small proportion of a typical quantity surveyor's time: the work may also include the preparation of initial estimates of the cost of proposed works; advising on tenders, negotiating the reduction of tenders and, after a building contract has been awarded, measuring and valuing work and variations; assessing claims for loss and expense and fluctuations; or, in more complex projects, acting as the employer's agent.

9.2 Originally, a quantity surveyor was engaged by the building contractors who were tendering for a particular contract, to analyse the specification and drawings and from them to prepare an itemised list or 'bill' of the quantities of materials required to complete the work. This was then supplied to the contractors who would use it to make their own lump sum tenders. The quantity surveyor would then be paid by the successful bidder. Frequently, the fee was included in the bills supplied to the contractors and included in their tenders, and it would then be paid by the building owner to the successful contractor. Gradually, this practice changed so that the quantity surveyor was directly employed by the building owner. This was attributable to the development of building contracts in which the price was subject to re-measurement, calculated from the as-built quantities, and in which the contractors' bills of quantities were used as a basis for comparison. In order to protect the owners' interests it was essential that there should be no under-statement of the quantities, so it became more appropriate for the quantity surveyor to be engaged directly by the owner, or by the architect on his behalf, to prepare the bills of quantities before they went out to tender.

---

1 *Taylor v Hall* (1870) IR 4 CL 467 at 476 per Morris J.

9.3 There are no restrictions as to who may practise as a quantity surveyor, although only those who have passed the necessary examinations and requirements of the Royal Institution of Chartered Surveyors may describe themselves as 'Chartered Quantity Surveyors'.[1] The Institution of Quantity Surveyors amalgamated with the RICS in 1983. The Quantity Surveyors Division is the second largest division in the RICS with over 29,000 members.[2]

THE QUANTITY SURVEYOR'S DUTIES

9.4 Quantity surveyors are most commonly associated with building work in which they may act for employers as well as being employed or retained by contractors. More recently, some quantity surveyors have specialised in building engineering services. They are able to provide much more effective cost control than has been customary in projects where such services are included in the bills of quantities as prime cost sums, either because service engineers often failed to provide enough information for measurement, or the quantity surveyors were unaccustomed to measuring such work, or where the contractors had preferred to offer quotations on the basis of drawings and specifications only. Quantity surveyors are also employed by civil engineering contractors by whom they are valued for their expertise in analysis, measurement and valuation of work. Civil engineering projects use a different method of measurement – the Civil Engineering Standard Method of Measurement or Method of Measurement for Roads and Bridgeworks – and different conditions of contract – the ICE Conditions. More recently, quantity surveyors have also become involved in heavy and industrial engineering works where they perform the role of cost engineers. The RICS and Association of Cost Engineers have now produced their own Standard Method of Measurement for Industrial Engineering Construction ('SMMIEC'). The discussion in this chapter is primarily concerned with the work of quantity surveyors who are retained to act in relation to building work.

9.5 The work of quantity surveyors includes the provision of the following services:

(a) preliminary cost advice;
(b) cost planning, including investment appraisal, life-cycle costing and value analysis;
(c) procurement and tendering procedures;
(d) contract documentation;
(e) evaluation of tenders;
(f) cash-flow forecasting, financial reporting and interim payments;
(g) final accounting and settlement of contractual disputes;
(h) cost advice during use by client;
(i) project management;

---

1 *RICS v Shepherd* (1947) 149 EG 370.
2 20,363 Fellows and Associates and 8,549 in training (source RICS November 1997).

(j) specialist services.

These duties will be examined in detail in Chapters 11 and 12.

TERMS OF ENGAGEMENT

The RICS forms

9.6 The RICS publish a Client Guide for the Appointment of a Quantity Surveyor which is intended for use in conjunction with the Form of Enquiry and Fee Quotation for Quantity Surveyors and the Form of Agreement, Terms and Conditions. The Form of Enquiry and Fee Quotation provides for various permutations of scale fees, hourly charges or lump sum fees. The scope of work covered specifically relates to the work involved in a construction project and does not include all of the services listed above. The option of a simplified procedure for more straightforward projects or a detailed procedure for more complex, unusual or large scale projects is provided. This specifies the exact range of services required to be performed by the quantity surveyor and defines the services which are to be included within his quoted charges. The RICS Form of Agreement, with the Terms and Conditions for Appointment of Quantity Surveyors, is designed for use with the published fee scales, with or without adjustment, or with other methods of defining services and fees. The fee scales published by RICS provide for a range of different services covering building works, civil engineering works, term contracts, housing schemes for Housing Associations, housing and environment improvement works, fire loss assessment and other insurance-related purposes. The latest current editions of the fee scales were published in July 1988. The fee scales are not mandatory and a quantity surveyor is free to undertake services on any basis that he may wish. The scales do, however, provide a useful basis upon which a quantity surveyor may be engaged or his fees negotiated.

The Form of Agreement

9.7 This expressly incorporates and appends the RICS Terms and Conditions for Appointment and details the fees and services agreed, as set out in the Form of Enquiry and Fee Quotation or other document. It sets out any terms which have been specifically agreed as to payment by instalments and may be executed as a deed or under hand. The client is referred to throughout as 'the Employer'.

The recitals to the Form of Agreement include an undertaking by the quantity surveyor to have and keep in effect professional indemnity insurance in the minimum sum as prescribed by the RICS. The Form expressly refers to Bye-Law 24(9A). This in fact has been replaced by Bye-Law 19(8) and it is advisable that the Form is amended to avoid any confusion on this point. The Regulations made under this bye-law require all members of the RICS who hold themselves out as a principal, partner, director or consultant to any firm offering surveying services to the public to take out insurance by means of a policy which is no less comprehensive than the form of the RICS Professional Indemnity Policy in force at the time it is taken out. The insurance cover must be for a minimum amount varying from £100,000 for each claim up to £500,000 per claim, depending upon the turnover of the firm during the preceding year. Insurance cover must be maintained for six years after the member ceased to practise as a principal, or is no longer a partner, director or consultant of the firm or company, as the case may be.[1]

The Terms and Conditions for Appointment

9.8 These deal firstly with the payment of fees by the client. Clause 1.8 provides that, unless otherwise agreed, the quantity surveyor is entitled to be paid:

(a) at three-monthly intervals for pre-contract services (excluding the preparation of bills of quantities or other tendering documents);

(b) in two-monthly instalments for the preparation of tendering documents with the balance becoming payable upon acceptance of a tender or, if no tender is accepted, three months after their completion; and

(c) for post-contract services at three-monthly intervals.

Interest will be charged on invoices not paid within 28 days.

9.9 Under clause 1.6, the quantity surveyor is obliged on written demand by the client, to provide time-sheets for any work paid by time and receipts or other evidence of payment for any expenses claimed.

Where fees are calculated on a percentage of total construction costs, these are defined so as to include all adjustments in relation to variations, fluctuations, provisional and prime cost sums, contingencies and the cost of materials, labour and services provided by the client and to exclude any claim for loss or damage caused by defects in the work or materials. Unless otherwise specified, the quantity surveyor is entitled to additional payment for work and to reimbursement of any expenses caused by changes in the scope or timing of the works undertaken by the client, or by any delay, defective performance or insolvency of the client, or by any other party involved in the project as well as any contested, or insurance, or tax claims, or other matters specified in the Form of Enquiry and Fee Quotation or otherwise.

Clause 3.1 prohibits the assignment or transfer of all or any part of the agreement by one party without the consent of the other party. The effect of this clause will be considered further in paras **10.7–10.9** below.

Termination and suspension

9.10 Provision is made for the suspension or termination of the agreement by the client giving written notice to the quantity surveyor, at any time.

1 See regs 2(a), 3 and 5 of the Compulsory Professional Indemnity Insurance Regulations 1997.

The quantity surveyor may only suspend performance or terminate the agreement in the following circumstances set out in clause 6 of the agreement. If the client is in breach of the agreement, the quantity surveyor may terminate or suspend performance of the agreement by written notice if this persists for 30 days after a preliminary notice has been given, specifying the breach and requiring it to be remedied on pain of suspension or termination.

9.11 Under clause 6, the quantity surveyor may also suspend performance or terminate the agreement if the client falls into financial difficulties, defined comprehensively to include the following:

(a) the client committing an act of bankruptcy;
(b) the client having an administration or receiving order made against him;
(c) the client making an arrangement with creditors;
(d) distress or execution being levied or threatened on any of his property;
(e) if a judgment against the client remains unsatisfied for more than 14 days; or
(f) if the client is a company, and it enters into liquidation or has a receiver appointed.

The quantity surveyor is also entitled to terminate the contract by notice under clause 6 if the performance of his services has been suspended at his instance for more than 14 days. The quantity surveyor is only permitted to suspend performance following breach by the client or in the case of financial difficulties, so this gives the quantity surveyor the right to terminate the agreement after the sanction of suspension has been invoked. The quantity surveyor may terminate the agreement after his work has been suspended by the client for more than six months after notice requiring an instruction to resume work within 14 days on pain of termination has been given and, if no such instruction is given within 30 days thereafter. This may provide the quantity surveyor with the opportunity to renegotiate his fees with his client after a project has been delayed. Finally, clause 6.6 provides that the agreement will terminate automatically on the death of the quantity surveyor. However, if a partnership is retained as the quantity surveyor under the agreement, each of the partners is joined as a party and it is arguable whether this clause would apply in the event of the death of one of the partners. The death of a partner would dissolve the partnership and it is suggested that, unless specific provision is made to cover this possibility, the agreement with the partnership would be terminated under this clause.

In the event of the suspension or termination of the agreement by either side, the quantity surveyor is entitled to invoice the client for his outstanding fees for all services performed, whether wholly or in part. The quantity surveyor is also entitled to be compensated for all subsequent and consequential losses including disbursements which had been or were properly to be incurred unless the agreement was terminated because of the quantity surveyor's own repudiation or death.

Other terms

9.12 Clause 8 provides that, unless otherwise agreed, the quantity surveyor is to retain copyright in and ownership of all documents prepared by him.

Clause 12.1 provides that the Terms and Conditions for Appointment shall prevail in the event of any discrepancy with the terms of any fee scale appended to the agreement.

Finally, clause 11.1 provides for arbitration and for the arbitrator to be appointed by the President or Vice-President of the Chartered Institute of Arbitrators, in default of agreement.

EXCLUSION AND LIMITATION CLAUSES

9.13 Under clause 9.1, the quantity surveyor is required to perform his duties with reasonable skill, care and diligence but sub-paras (a) and (b) to the clause purport to limit his liability to 'such liability as ought to be covered by the professional indemnity insurance' referred to in the recital to the agreement and to the minimum sum prescribed for such insurance. The form of professional indemnity policy which is now in force is the Professional Indemnity Wording issued by SURVIS, the Surveyors and Valuers Insurance Services, which took over from the RICS Insurance Services Ltd after it was wound up in April 1996. The policy provides indemnity in respect of 'any civil liability whatsoever and whensoever arising ... incurred in the course of any professional business carried on by the Insured'. The wording is clearly intended to cover any claim for breach of the QS's obligations under the agreement.

9.14 However, this provision may have the effect of excluding liability altogether where a claim is brought more than six years after a quantity surveyor has ceased to practise as a principal or partner, director or consultant in a firm or company. In that case, he is no longer obliged under the Compulsory Professional Indemnity Bye-Law and Regulations 1997 to maintain any professional indemnity insurance cover. The quantity surveyor may still be liable in respect of a claim brought after that period has elapsed because the limitation period in respect of a breach of contract, if the agreement is made under seal, is 12 years from the date of the breach of contract and six years from the date on which any damage is caused in the case of negligence. In those circumstances, the effect of clause 9.1(a) will be to exclude all liability in respect of that claim.

9.15 The extent of a quantity surveyor's liability for breach of contract or negligence may exceed the cover which he is obliged to take out under the Regulations and clause 9.1(b) may therefore limit his liability significantly, depending upon the size of the claim and the minimum level of cover. This is determined by the previous year's turnover and not by the extent of the losses which may be foreseeable under the contract.

9.16 The exclusion of liability in clause 9.2 for any loss caused by the act, omission or insolvency of any person other than the quantity surveyor may (at first) seem unobjectionable. But it assumes that the quantity surveyor may never be responsible for the default of another party. To take an example, what if the loss was caused by an architect's interim certificate which was based on an error in an interim valuation which had been prepared by the quantity surveyor? If the contractor then became insolvent before the error was corrected in a subsequent certificate, the quantity surveyor could then be liable for the loss incurred by his client.

The Unfair Contract Terms Act 1977

9.17 The provisions in these clauses are subject to the Unfair Contract Terms Act 1977 which by s 2(2) applies to any contractual term by which the liability of one party for negligence is excluded or limited. Under s 1(1) of the Act 'negligence' is defined as both the breach of any obligation to exercise reasonable skill and care under a contract as well as the breach of a duty to do so at common law. The provisions would also be caught by s 3(2) which applies where one party deals on the other's written terms of business and the other party seeks to restrict or exclude his liability for breach by reference to any of those terms.

The requirement of reasonableness

9.18 Where ss 2 or 3 apply, a term cannot be used to exclude or limit liability 'except in so far as the term ... satisfies the requirement of reasonableness'. This is set out in s 11(1) as being that: 'the term shall have been a fair and reasonable one to be included having regard to the circumstances which were, or ought reasonably to have been, known to or in the contemplation of the parties when the contract was made'. In the case of a term which limits a party's liability to a specific sum of money, the court is directed by s 11(4) to have regard to the resources which that party could expect to be available to him for meeting that liability should it arise, and how far it was open to him to cover himself by insurance.

9.19 Although they are not expressed to be relevant to the question of whether a term caught under ss 2 or 3 meets the requirement of reasonableness, the courts will also have regard to the guidelines set out in Sch 2 to the Act. The factors which are relevant here can be summarised as:

(a) the relative strength of the parties' bargaining positions, taking into account any alternative means by which the customer's requirements might have been met;

(b) whether the customer received an inducement to agree to the term or had an opportunity of contracting without such a term with other parties;

(c) whether the customer knew or ought reasonably to have known of the existence and extent of the term.

It is for the quantity surveyor relying upon any exclusion or limitation of liability under these clauses to prove that it satisfies the requirement of reasonableness and, in the case of the limitation in clause 9.1(b), why adequate insurance could not be obtained. In that case, it is significant that the notes to the Compulsory Professional Indemnity Bye-Law and Regulations urge members to take advice as to whether they need higher levels of cover than the minimum amounts.

Cases on the requirement of reasonableness

9.20 There are now a number of reported cases in which the courts have considered whether the requirement of reasonableness was satisfied where a party sought to exclude his liability or to limit it to a specified sum. The decisions in each of these cases turn upon their facts, and the way in which each judge weighs up the relevant factors in deciding whether a term satisfies the requirement of reasonableness may vary significantly. This process is acknowledged to be fairly subjective and provided the judge takes all of the relevant factors into account, an appeal is not likely to succeed unless the decision was one which no court could reasonably have arrived at. The answer will always depend upon the circumstances before the contract is entered into. The reported cases do at least illustrate the ways in which the courts address this issue and may be of some assistance in considering the application of the requirement of reasonableness test to the facts of a particular case.

9.21 Cases in which the reasonableness of limitation clauses were in issue will be considered first. One case in which such a clause was upheld was *Singer v Tees and Hartlepool Port Authority*[1] in which liability for damage to a cargo being loaded by the defendant was limited to £25,000 per tonne. The case concerned a claim in excess of that limit for damage caused to machinery when the crate it was in collapsed while it was being hoisted into a ship. In that case, the limitation clause was held to be reasonable for a number of reasons. The Port Authority had little or no knowledge of the nature or value of the goods it handled and it did not have any control over the way in which they were packed. In the great majority of cases the value of the cargoes handled did not exceed the limit and the consignor could have opted to contract without a limitation clause at greater expense. It was also held to be significant that the relevant risks were insurable by both of the parties.

In two cases concerning the supply of defective computer software, limitation clauses in the suppliers contracts were held to be unreasonable. In *Salvage Association v CAP Financial Services*,[2] liability for defects was limited to only £25,000. No evidence was adduced to explain or support this financial limit and it was found that the suppliers' directors had already decided that the limit should be raised to £1 million at the time that the contract was made. Apparently the supplier was able to and did insure for liability well over that

1 [1988] 2 Lloyd's Rep 164.
2 [1995] FSR 654.

figure. But the judge found that the customer would not have been able to insure against the risk of loss for a reasonable premium.

Similarly, in *St Alban's City Council v International Computers Ltd*,[1] the court held that a limit of £100,000 for liability for loss caused by the defective performance of the software was unreasonable. No evidence had been adduced to justify that figure. The judge found in applying the tests under s 11(4) that the supplier had ample resources with which to cover the full amount of its liability to its customer. This part of the judgment was not subject to an appeal when the case later went to the Court of Appeal.

In both of these cases, the court was assisted by the observations of Lord Griffiths in *Smith v Bush*[2] as to the matters which should always be considered when applying the requirement of reasonableness. This case concerned an exclusion clause and it has already been discussed in paras **1.5** to **1.6** but it may be helpful to set out here the matters which Lord Griffiths thought should always be considered. These were that, in one-off cases between parties of equal bargaining power, the requirement of reasonableness would be easier to satisfy than in cases where a disclaimer was imposed on a customer who had no opportunity to object, and, in the case of advice, whether it would have been reasonably practicable to obtain advice from an alternative source taking into account the costs and time available and the difficulty of the task for which liability was sought to be excluded. Where a very difficult or dangerous task was undertaken which had a high risk of failure, that might indicate that the exclusion or limitation of liability was reasonable but not where the work should present no difficulty when it was carried out with reasonable skill and care. Finally, Lord Griffiths referred to the question of what were the practical consequences of the finding of reasonableness which involved the size of the potential sums at stake and the ability of the parties concerned to bear the loss, which inevitably led to the question of insurance.

9.22 In applying these considerations to each of the exclusion and limitation provisions in clauses 9.1 and 9.2, the most striking feature is that the quantity surveyor has or can easily procure indemnity insurance against the risks which may arise, but it may be much more difficult for the client, whatever his means, to do so. In every case, it will be for the quantity surveyor to prove that the relevant term satisfies the requirement of reasonableness. This will in turn depend on the circumstances of the parties and their state of knowledge at the time that they contract, having regard to the guidelines provided in the Act and the observations made in *Smith v Bush* referred to above.

The Unfair Terms in Consumer Contracts Regulations

9.23 In the case of an agreement made with a client who is dealing as a consumer, the terms of the agreement will also now be subject to the provisions of the Unfair Terms in Consumer Contracts Regulations 1994, SI 1994/3159.

1 [1995] FSR 686.
2 [1990] 1 AC 831 at 858.

The Regulations were introduced with effect from July 1995 in order to implement EEC Council Directive 93/13/EEC on Unfair Terms in Consumer Contracts. A 'consumer' is defined for the purpose of these Regulations as an individual who in making the contract 'is acting for purposes which are outside his business'. So the Regulations may be relevant whenever a quantity surveyor is engaged by an individual who is not a property developer. The Regulations apply to terms which have not been individually negotiated in contracts made between a consumer and a supplier of services or seller of goods who do so in the course of a business.

The scope of the Regulations is wider than the Unfair Contract Terms Act in a number of respects. Terms which have not been 'individually negotiated' include those which have been drafted in advance where the consumer has not been able to influence their substance. Even where terms have been individually negotiated, the Regulations may apply to the remainder of the contract if an overall assessment of the contract indicates that it is a pre-formulated contract. The onus is on the supplier or seller to show that a term was individually negotiated with the consumer.

The Regulations apply to any terms which are unfair, and not just to exclusion or limitation clauses. The fairness of terms which define the subject matter of the contract, or concern the adequacy of the price or remuneration as against the goods or services supplied do not have to be assessed, providing they are expressed in clear and intelligible language. An unfair term is defined as any term which 'contrary to the requirement of good faith causes an imbalance in the parties' rights and obligations under the contract to the detriment of the consumer'. In order to assess the unfairness of a term, the court will take the nature of the goods or services concerned into account and refer to all of the circumstances in which the contract was made, all other terms of the contract and any other contract upon which it is dependent.

9.24 In order to assess the good faith of a term, criteria are provided in Sch 2 to the Regulations. The court is required to have regard to the strength of the parties' bargaining positions, whether the consumer had an inducement to agree to the term, whether the goods or services were supplied to the consumer's special order, and, finally, whether the supplier or seller 'has dealt fairly and equitably' with the consumer. However, a useful indication of the terms which may be regarded as unfair is provided in Sch 3 to the Regulations. This lists a variety of different forms of exclusion and exemption clauses as well as other terms which are too one-sided in favour of the seller or supplier. A term which is unfair is not binding on the consumer but this will not affect the validity of the contract if it is capable of 'continuing in existence' without the unfair term.

It is difficult to foresee how these vague and circular directions will be applied in practice by the courts. It is possible that the introduction of these Regulations will mark the advent of a more interventionist approach to consumer contracts. Until a body of case law has developed, it is difficult to predict how far the requirement of good faith will be applied to contracts for professional services.

However, one requirement should always be observed in drafting contracts for such services with consumers. Regulation 6 provides that any written terms should be written in clear and intelligible language and that, in the event of any doubt, the term must be interpreted in the way which is most favourable to the consumer.

SCALE FEES

9.25 The RICS publish the following scales of charges for quantity surveying services:

Scale No 36
Inclusive scale of professional charges for quantity surveying services for building works (29 July 1988).

Scale No 37
Itemised scale of professional charges for quantity surveying services for building works (29 July 1988).

Scale No 38
Itemised scale of professional charges for quantity surveying services for civil engineering works (29 July 1988).

Scale No 39
Scale of professional charges for quantity surveying services for term contracts (29 July 1988).

Scale No 40
Scale of professional charges for quantity surveying services in connection with housing schemes for local authorities (1 February 1983).

Scale No 44
Scale of professional charges for quantity surveying services in connection with improvements to existing housing and environmental improvement works (1 February 1973).

Scale No 45
Scale of professional charges for quantity surveying services in connection with Housing Schemes (1 January 1982).

Scale No 46
Scale of professional charges for quantity surveying services in connection with loss assessment of damage to buildings from fire, etc (29 July 1988).

Scale No 47
Scale of professional charges for the assessment of replacement costs of buildings for insurance, current cost accounting and other purposes (29 July 1988).

9.26 The scales include some or all of the following features:

(a) a percentage fee which is determined by reference to the complexity and the total final account value of the work, including all nominated subcontractors and suppliers;

(b) an additional percentage fee on the total value of air conditioning, heating, ventilating and electrical services, if these are covered in the services provided by the quantity surveyor;

(c) an additional percentage fee on the value of works of alteration and repair or redecoration and associated minor repairs;

(d) provision for the adjustment of fees in the case of substantial variations to the works, or excessive amounts of abortive work, or exceptional delays caused by any reason outside the quantity surveyor's control;

(e) provision for the application of time charges, in the case of additional work which is not normally necessary, for which the quantity surveyor is specifically instructed by the client, such as in the case of the premature termination of the building contract before its completion, liquidation of the contractor, fire damage, arbitration and litigation in relation to contractors' claims;

(f) the definition of the hourly charges payable for services carried out by a member of the quantity surveyor's staff;

(g) provision for the payment of fees in instalments, in some cases the first instalment becoming due upon acceptance of a contractor's tender, calculated on the value of the tender;

(h) fees charged being exclusive of travelling and other expenses and the costs of reproducing Bills of Quantities and other documents, unless otherwise agreed.

Incorporation of scale fees

9.27 Unless the application of a scale fee is expressly agreed, a surveyor may not be entitled to charge on this basis unless he can show that his client knew that such a charge would be applied. This may be easier where the client has previous experience of engaging the surveyor or other surveyors on these terms or knowledge of such a practice. Otherwise, a scale fee can be claimed only if the surveyor can show that there is, in the circumstances, a well-established and well-known custom that such fees will be applied. Historically the courts have been reluctant to accept evidence of such a custom although this attitude appears to have changed in more recent cases.[1]

9.28 An example of a case where there was no evidence of custom or prior knowledge on the part of the client is *Gilbert & Partners v Knight*.[2] The surveyor had agreed to act for a lump sum fee in respect of alterations being

1 See paras **9.41** and **9.42** below.
2 (1968) 112 SJ 155 (CA).

made to the client's property, which he estimated would cost £600. The client subsequently increased the amount of the building work so that the final cost was over £2,000. The surveyor sought to recover an additional fee based on a scale without having warned the client that there would be any increase in the fee he would charge. It was held that, having agreed to do the work for a fixed sum, the surveyor could not then ignore that contract by seeking to claim more on the basis of a *quantum meruit*. His claim for further fees failed.

9.29 The terms of Scales Nos 36 and 37 will now be considered in more detail. Scale No 36 purports to be inclusive. The following services are expressly included:

> '(a) Budget estimating, cost planning and advice on tendering procedures and contract arrangements.
>
> (b) Preparing tendering documents for main contract and specialist subcontracts; examining tenders received and reporting thereon or negotiating tenders and pricing with a selected contractor and/or subcontractors.
>
> (c) Preparing recommendations for interim payments on account of the contractor; preparing periodic assessments of anticipated final cost and reporting thereon; measuring work and adjusting variations in accordance with the terms of the contract and preparing final account, pricing same and agreeing totals with the contractor.
>
> (d) Providing a reasonable number of copies of bills of quantities and other documents; normal travelling and other expenses.'

9.30 The inclusive scale is divided into three categories:

Category A: relatively complex works and/or works with little or no repetition. Examples include cinemas, petrol stations, churches and colleges. In this category, the minimum fee is £3,380 plus 6 per cent from £50,000 up to £150,000 and the maximum is £189,380 on contracts worth £6 million plus 2.4 per cent on the balance over £6 million.

Category B: less complex works and/or works with some element of repetition. Examples include community and shopping centres, hotels and self-contained flats and maisonettes. In this category, the minimum fee is £3,260 plus 5.8 per cent of the value from £50,000 up to £150,000 and the maximum £164,010 on contracts worth £6 million plus 2 per cent on the balance over £6 million.

Category C: simple works and/or works with a substantial amount of repetition. Examples are factories, multi-storey car parks, warehouses and workshops. The minimum fee is £2,750 plus 4.9 per cent of the value from £50,000 up to £150,000 and the maximum £139,200 on contracts worth £6 million plus 1.6 per cent of the balance over £6 million.

The fees are calculated on the final account value including all nominated subcontractor and supplier's accounts and the value of any work which is separately let but which would normally be included in the building contract. Additional fees are charged for quantity surveyor services on air-conditioning, heating, ventilation and electrical services of at least 5 per cent of their value. On works, or sections of work, which are mainly works of alteration and repair, an additional charge of 1 per cent is made. On works of redecoration and associated minor repairs an additional charge of 1.5 per cent is made.

9.31 In the event of substantial variations or abortive work, the quantity surveyor is not bound by the above percentages and he is entitled to seek an adjustment to his fees. Time charges may be levied in respect of abnormal additional work arising in circumstances such as premature termination, liquidation, arbitration and litigation.

9.32 Scale 36 also provides for payment of fees by instalments in the absence of agreement to the contrary. But if the scale is appended to the RICS Form of Agreement, the terms of clause 1.8 will prevail.[1] The scale provides for payment of one half of the fee calculated on the amount of the accepted tender and for payment of the balance to be made by instalments between the date of the first certificate and one month after certification of the final account. If no tender is accepted, one half of the fee shall be paid three months after the preparation of the tender documents, based on the value of the lowest bona fide tender. In that event, it would seem that no further fees are payable to the quantity surveyor. In the case of the project being abandoned at any other stage, the proportion of the fee to be paid is to be left to be negotiated between the parties.

By contrast, Scale No 37 breaks down the fees according to the particular stages, so that the client can opt to pay separately for whichever service he wishes. However, the same categories are used as in the inclusive scale for different types of work. The scale provides for different fees depending upon whether the contract is based on bills of quantities, or bills of approximate quantities, or schedules of prices, or it is a prime cost contract.

9.33 For the first type of contract, separate percentage fees are payable in respect of the preparation of the bills of quantities, examining and reporting on tenders, cost planning services, negotiating tenders and post-contract services. Two alternative bases of fees are provided for post-contract services. The client can choose between a fee for all such services or for the fees to be split between valuations for interim certificates, preparing accounts of variations and cost-monitoring services. Similar divisions of fees are adopted for contracts based on approximate quantities in respect of the percentage fees.

For contracts based on schedules of prices and for prime cost contracts, the percentage fees are calculated only on the value of the works and the fees are divided more simply between pre- and post-contract services. In all cases, additional fees are charged on the value of air-conditioning, heating, ventilating and electrical services, and on alteration and redecoration works as under Scale No 36.

1 See para **9.8**.

CONTRACTS OUTSIDE THE RICS FORMS AND SCALES

9.34 A quantity surveyor is free to contract on such terms and in such form as he may agree with his client. Frequently the contract may take the form of an exchange of letters or of a formal letter of engagement. The fees payable may be calculated in relation to the total value of the works by way of percentage or as a fixed sum, in which case any work or expenses which are to be covered should be specified, or he may simply charge for his time on an hourly basis. This may be more economical in the case of a client for whom a variety of partial or different services are provided, which would not fall within the scheme of scale charges or be covered by a lump sum. In the case of time charges, it is recommended that provision should be made for the regular submission and payment of accounts and for the hours worked and expenses incurred to be specified and properly recorded by the quantity surveyor, as provided in clause 1.6 of the RICS Form of Agreement.

9.35 The charging of 'success fees' or contingency fees has been the subject of several recent cases in which clients have sought to avoid liability on the grounds that these were contrary to public policy. The charging of fees on this basis may arise in respect of post-contract services for contractors in which quantity surveyors have frequently taken on the role of 'claims consultants'. However, in reported cases, the point has been raised in a different context.

In *Pickering v Sogex Services*[1] the surveyors agreed to act in the negotiation of a rating assessment in return for a fee equal to the annual value of any reduction they were able to agree, instead of charging a scale fee. The clients claimed that the agreement was unenforceable on the ground that as the compromise had to be recorded by the Valuation Court, it constituted champerty, or the wrongful maintenance of litigation. This defence failed on the grounds that the Valuation Court was not a court of law and because the negotiation and formal recording of the agreement by the District Valuation Court did not constitute litigation.

A similar defence was raised in *Picton Jones v Arcadia Developments*[2] where the surveyors sought to recover 'success fees' for obtaining gaming permits and planning permission for amusement arcades on two sites. In one case this had involved appearing at a public enquiry after planning permission had been refused. The court held that champerty only applied to litigation and that the planning and gaming permit applications could not be described as litigation. Nor was the court impressed with the argument that such a fee could not be recovered because charging a contingency fee was then contrary to the professional rules of the RICS. Under Rule 24(6), a member was forbidden from acting in any judicial or quasi-judicial proceedings on the basis that his fee would be dependant upon the outcome. This rule was deleted in March 1986.

---

1 [1982] 20 BLR 66.
2 [1989] 1 EGLR 43.

9.36 But the rule against champerty will make any agreement to pay a contingency fee in relation to any litigation or arbitration proceedings unenforceable. Nor will the client be able to recover such a fee as part of the costs awarded against the losing party. Indeed, the court may order an adviser acting on a contingency fee to pay the costs of the other side if it is successful, on the grounds that they had thereby funded the action. This was recently demonstrated in *McFarlane v EE Caledonia*[1] where the plaintiff had brought an action for damages for personal injury with the assistance of Quantum Claims Compensation Specialists Ltd who agreed to act on the basis that they would only charge him a fee if his claim was successful. The court held that the fact that Quantum did not accept any liability for the other side's costs also made its agreement with Mr McFarlane illegal, quite apart from element of the champerty which was admitted.

IMPLIED TERMS

9.37 Where no express terms are agreed, implied terms may apply. These may arise in law or through custom or in order to make the contract effective. It is proposed to deal first with terms that may be implied by law.

In the case of contracts for construction work which does not relate to work on dwellings in which the client lives or intends to live, Part II of the Housing Grants, Construction and Regeneration Act 1996 ('the Act') will apply (subject to certain exclusions set out at para **14.13**) when it is brought into force, which is anticipated to be in April or May 1998. The Act will bring a number of changes to construction law generally. It proposed now to summarise those changes and to consider how they will affect contracts made with quantity surveyors.

9.38 The Act imposes certain contractual rights which, if they are not contained in the express terms of a contract or, in the case of stage payments, subsequently agreed, will be incorporated in the form set out in the Scheme for Construction Contracts ('the SCC').[2] The contractual rights can be summarised as follows:

(a) the right to refer any dispute to adjudication under s 108 which allows a party at any time to refer any dispute arising under the contract to an adjudicator who will then make a decision within a tight timetable which can only be subsequently varied by arbitration, litigation or agreement, and which may result in an entitlement to immediate payment;

(b) the entitlement to stage payments under s 109 which provides for the right to payment by instalments, stage payments or other periodic payments unless it is specified in the contract that the work will take or it is agreed that the work is estimated to take less than 45 days;

---

1 [1995] 1 WLR 366.

2 See the Schedule to the Scheme for Construction Contracts (England and Wales) Regulations 1988. The text is based on the draft Regulations which were laid before Parliament on 18 December 1997.

(c) dates for payment under s 110. Every contract will have to specify when payments will become due and payable and that notice will be given no later than five days after payment is due of the amount which has been or will be paid and how it is calculated;

(d) under s 111, withholding payment of any sum after it becomes due and payable will not be permitted unless prior written notice has been given of the amount and grounds for doing so;

(e) the right to suspend performance for non-payment under s 112 which allows for suspension on giving at least 7 days' notice after a sum has become due and payable and no proper withholding notice has been given, in accordance with s 111;

(f) the prohibition of provisions making payment conditional upon receiving payment from a third party ('pay when paid' clauses) under s 113, the only exception being where the third or other party from whom payment is to be provided becomes insolvent.

It is anticipated that the terms of the RICS Forms of Agreement and fee scales will be revised to ensure that they comply with the above requirements. In particular, none of these forms of contract make any provision for the adjudication of disputes, which is potentially the most far reaching of the reforms introduced by the Act. The present form of Agreement and Terms and Conditions for Appointment appear to cover the other statutory requirements adequately except for those in (d) and (f) above. The requirement for a withholding notice will be of particular significance. The client's failure to give such a notice will facilitate the recovery of outstanding fees by serving a statutory demand, without having to issue proceedings. In the event that grounds are given for disputing payment, these can be disposed of promptly by reference to an adjudicator.

Compulsory adjudication

9.39 Section 108 imposes the following basic requirements in relation to the adjudication of disputes which will have to covered by the express terms of the contract failing which the adjudication provisions of the SCC will apply:

(a) the right of either party to give notice of the intention to refer a dispute at any time;

(b) the provision of a timetable with the object of securing the appointment of an adjudicator and the referral of the dispute to him within seven days of such notice being given;

(c) to require the adjudicator to reach a decision within 28 days of referral or such longer period as is agreed by the parties after the dispute has been referred;

(d) to allow the adjudicator to extend the period of 28 days by up to 14 days, with the consent of the party by whom it was referred;

(e) to impose a duty on the adjudicator to act impartially; and

(f) to enable the adjudicator to take the initiative in ascertaining the facts and the law.

Further consideration will be given to the duties of the adjudicator in Chapter 14.

The Supply of Goods and Services Act 1982

9.40 In cases where the quantity surveyor is engaged in relation to work on a house or flat in which the client is living or intends to live, the provisions of Part II of the 1996 Act will not apply. In relation to all contracts for the provision of a quantity surveyor's services, Part II of the Supply of Goods and Services Act 1982 will continue to apply. This imposes implied terms as to the standard and time for performance and the consideration due for services provided in the course of a business.

Section 13 of the 1982 Act imposes an implied term that the supplier of a service will carry it out with reasonable care and skill. Unless the time for performance is fixed, or to be determined by the terms of the contract or by the course of dealing between the parties, a term will be implied under s 14(1) that the service will be carried out within a reasonable time. If the consideration for a service is not so fixed or determined, there will be an implied term under s 15 that the client will pay a reasonable charge. What is a reasonable charge is a question of fact.[1]

Implication of fee scales

9.41 Two recent cases suggest that the court may have regard to the professional fee scales where no fee has been expressly agreed, in order to determine what is reasonable for the service provided. In *Wilkie v Scottish Aviation*,[2] a chartered surveyor was retained as a valuer, adviser and witness in relation to the arbitration of a claim for compensation for compulsory purchase. The surveyor claimed a fee based on the current RICS scale, calculated on the value of the compensation that was awarded, on the grounds that payment on this basis had been implied as a matter of custom. The client challenged the claim by taking the procedural point that it did not amount to a proper claim in law. The surveyor had not kept any detailed record of the work he had done because he had expected to be paid by reference to the scale fee. The surveyor did not make an alternative claim for *quantum meruit* so the only issue before the court was whether the surveyor was entitled to base his claim on the allegation that it was an implied term of the contract that the scale fee should be paid.

The court held that, in the absence of an express agreement governing his remuneration, the surveyor would be entitled to be paid on the scale fee rate if

1 Section 15(2).
2 1956 SC 198.

he could prove that 'such a custom was reasonable, certain and notorious'. For that purpose it was not necessary to show that the client had known of the custom. It would be sufficient if the custom was well recognised, so that it ought to have been known by both the parties. Even if this was shown, the court would not be bound to apply it unless it considered that the application of the scale to the facts of the case produced a reasonable result. The court also indicated that the professional scale fees would still be relevant in considering what was a reasonable fee, in relation to a claim for *quantum meruit*, if it was shown to be the basis on which the profession operated. There is no report of what happened when the case proceeded to trial.

9.42 In *Graham & Baldwin v Taylor, Son & Davis*,[1] a claim for fees was made by an architect who had been engaged by a surveyor in respect of the design of a development. The architect had claimed for the scale fee based on the estimated cost of the works. The court held that the issue was not whether the RIBA scale had been incorporated into the contract but what sum was payable on a *quantum meruit*. It was held that the RIBA scale was evidence of what surveyors generally considered reasonable because it had been reproduced in the RICS scale and it would be taken into account in assessing the sum due. In determining the amount of the fee that should be paid the following factors were found to be relevant:

(a) the architect had achieved the result for which he had been engaged, which was the grant of outline planning permission for the construction of a building, in accordance with the client's requirements;

(b) the high qualifications and experience of the architect;

(c) the architectural merits of the scheme that he had devised;

(d) the size and value of the building, because of its relationship to the scale fee;

(e) the fact that the surveyors would earn substantial fees estimated at £30,000 from the project.

In the event, the architect recovered less than half of the scale fee.

9.43 In *Kelly and Partners v Northshore Development*,[2] quantity surveyors had been engaged by the developer's architects to draw up bills of quantities, prepare interim certificates and to adjust variations. The dispute arose over the interpretation of the terms agreed for the adjustment of variations which were '2.5 per cent on the value of measured additions and 1.5 per cent on the value of omissions excluding the value of omissions where the exercise of professional skill is not required'. The construction work had been subject to so many variations that the additions could not be isolated from the work which had been included in the building contract originally and all of the work had had to be remeasured. The contract price of the work had been £46,000 and the total

1 (1965) 109 SJ 793.
2 (1963) 5 WIR 379.

cost was over £68,000. The quantity surveyors contended that they were entitled to claim the percentage fee for additions on all of the work on the grounds that it must be treated as a 'measured addition' and the value of the original estimate should be treated as a 'measured omission' for which no charge was made, as the exercise of professional skill was not involved. Alternatively they claimed a *quantum meruit* fee on the whole of the work. At trial they only recovered a fee for additions on the difference of over £22,000 between the original and final contract sums.

The Court of Appeal in Jamaica held (by a majority) that the contractual term could not be applied because the additions could not be isolated from the rest of the work. It was held that the parties had not contemplated that the variations would be so extensive as to require the complete remeasurement of the work and that the quantity surveyors were entitled to recover a fee of 2 per cent of the total value on a *quantum meruit* basis.

TERMINATION

9.44 The parties' rights to terminate and to make any payment or compensation thereafter are expressly covered in the RICS Form of Appointment. The client may terminate the agreement on making appropriate payment having regard to the work stage that has been reached.

9.45 The position at common law can be illustrated by the case of *Edwin Hill & Partners v Leakcliffe Properties*.[1] The plaintiff surveyors had been retained by the developer of a site to provide architectural services and it was agreed that they would be paid a fee of 10 per cent of the total cost of the work (including the fees of the quantity surveyors and engineers). The issue was whether the developer had wrongfully terminated the contract when the financiers required the plaintiffs to be replaced by a better known firm of architects.

The court held that where there was a simple agreement for the employment of an architect or surveyor for a particular project and nothing was said or agreed as to termination, the client could not lawfully terminate the contract before its performance had been completed. In those circumstances, the architect or surveyor would be entitled to claim reasonable remuneration for the work he had already done and damages for the fees he was prevented from earning until the work was finished. On these points, the court followed obita dicta made by the Court of Appeal to this effect in an earlier case, *Thomas v Hammersmith Borough Council*,[2] and refused to hold that such a contract was subject to an implied term that entitled the client to terminate it at will.

9.46 In the absence of express provision, the remedies available in the case of the wrongful termination of the contract are to claim payment of the fees

1 [1984] 29 BLR 43.
2 [1938] 3 All ER 201 at 208 and 211.

which have already been earned and damages for the loss of profits on the fees that the surveyor could expect to earn on the remainder of the project. These would be calculated on the gross fees, less the expenses which would be incurred in earning them. Alternatively, the surveyor may treat the contract as at an end and sue in *quantum meruit* for the value of the work he has performed.

But the contract may provide differently for the consequences of termination. The point arose in the case of *Du Bosky v Shearwater Property Holdings*[1] in which the question was whether a quantity surveyor whose appointment had been terminated was entitled to any further fees. The agreement had provided for payment of a lump sum for the quantity surveyor's services in respect of a proposed development and for payment by instalments. The client could terminate the contract at any time without cause when the quantity surveyor would be entitled to payment of all sums which he had earned. The quantity surveyor claimed for additional payment on a *quantum meruit* basis and the question which had to be decided was whether the quantity surveyor was entitled to any more than the instalments which had already been paid. The Official Referee found that the contractual term was unambiguous and that it provided only that the instalments which had become due should be payable and that the quantity surveyor had no right to any further payment in respect of the lump sum fee which had been agreed. This decision was upheld in the Court of Appeal.[2]

1 [1991] 54 BLR 71.
2 (1992) 61 BLR 64.

Chapter 10

ASSIGNMENT, NOVATION AND COLLATERAL WARRANTIES

INTRODUCTION

10.1 It is proposed in this chapter to deal first with the different ways in which rights and duties under the contract by which a surveyor is retained may be transferred to other parties. The obligations arising in relation to sub-contracts and collateral warranties will then be considered.

ASSIGNMENT

10.2 It is necessary to distinguish between: (i) the rights; and (ii) the obligations arising under a contract. In practice, the parties to a contract will each have rights and obligations and distinguishing between them is not always straightforward. In order to explain the legal principles behind the distinction, the party who under the contract has rights to transfer will be described as the 'creditor' and the party who is under an obligation will be described as the 'debtor'.

10.3 The rights under a contract may, subject to the matters considered below, be transferred to another party without the consent or knowledge of the debtor. But a debtor cannot validly transfer his obligations under a contract to another without the creditor's agreement. In that case, a new contract is usually substituted in its place. This process is described as novation and it is treated separately below. The transfer of a party's rights under a contract is described as assignment.

Under s 136 of the Law of Property Act 1925, rights under a contract can be transferred to a third party ('the assignee') by a written assignment signed by the creditor ('the assignor'). Written notice of that assignment must be given to the debtor. The debtor then becomes obliged to render performance to the assignee, who then becomes the 'creditor'.

The assignment of a party's rights under the contract in this way is known as a legal assignment. If no notice is given of the assignment to the debtor, the assignee may still enforce the contract but he may be required to join the assignor in order to do so.[1] In that case, the assignment is known as an equitable assignment.

The term 'equitable assignment' is also used to describe arrangements by which only part of the rights under a contract are assigned or where the assignment is not 'absolute' and is made by way of a charge. In that case, no valid notice of assignment can be served on the debtor.

10.4 The above principles apply only to rights which are capable of being assigned. The contract may prohibit assignment without the other party's consent, as in the case of the RICS Form of Appointment, Terms and Conditions. In that case an assignment will not be binding on the debtor. A clause of this type was upheld in the case of *Linden Gardens Trust Ltd v Lenesta Sludge Disposals Ltd*.[2] In that case, the vendors of properties on which building work had been carried out purported to assign the benefit of the building contracts to the purchasers. The building contracts were in the 1963 JCT standard form (July 1975 revision). Clause 17(1) of the contracts provided that 'the employer shall not without the written consent of the contractor assign the contract'. Clause 4.1 of the RICS Form of Appointment goes further in forbidding the assignment or transfer of any part of the agreement without the consent of the other party.

The assignment of claims for the purpose of litigation may be contrary to public policy. To be valid such assignments may only properly be made if they are ancillary to the transfer of a right or interest in property or if there are proper commercial grounds, such as in the case of a creditor who has a financial interest in the claim or an assignment to a factor who has discounted the debt or to an insurer who paid a loss and who would otherwise be subrogated to that claim. The assignment of a 'bare' right to litigate is otherwise invalid and unenforceable.

Rights under personal contracts are not assignable. These are contracts in which the contractual right involves personal skill or judgment on the part of the creditor. The benefit of a contract is only assignable 'in cases where it can make no difference to the person on whom the obligation lies to which of two persons he is to discharge it'.[3] This has to be determined objectively and not by the debtor's preference for one contracting party over another.[4]

NOVATION

10.5 A contractual obligation cannot be validly transferred without the consent of the party to whom it is owed. The consent may be express or it may be inferred from the creditor's conduct. In that case it is usually necessary to

---

1 See *Weddell v Pearce and Major* [1988] Ch 1.

2 [1994] 1 AC 85.

3 *Tolhurst v Associated Portland Cement Manufacturers (1900) Ltd* [1902] 2 KB 660 at 668.

4 See the judgment of Staughton LJ in *Linden Gardens Trust Ltd v Lenesta Sludge Disposals* (1992) 57 BLR 57 at 77 and 78.

prove that the creditor has accepted performance of the contract by another party in the place of the original party. The effect of such an arrangement is that the obligations owed by the original party are replaced by the obligations owed by the new party. In effect a new contract is made under which the creditor accepts the new debtor in the place of the old debtor.

10.6 This point was raised recently in a case involving surveyors in which the client sought to avoid liability by contending that its obligation to pay the surveyors had been taken over by another company: *Kinney & Green v Johns.*[1] The court held as a matter of law that before there can be any novation all three parties must have the intention to contract for the debtor to be substituted and to agree to release the original debtor from liability. The Court was prepared to accept that no particular form of words was necessary and that substitution and release may be inferred where the creditor's conduct is sufficiently clear and unambiguous. Reference was made to the case of *Re European Assurance Society (Miller's case)*[2] in which the insured had been requested to cease paying premiums to one insurance company and to instead pay them to another insurer. The insured had done so and it was held that this constituted a valid novation by which the obligations of the original insurer were released and were substituted by those of the new insurer.

In the *Kinney* case the surveyors had been asked to and did apply for payment to the company with whom novation was alleged. But it was held that the fact that the surveyors had hoped and expected to be paid by the new company was quite different from saying that they ever released their original client or that they agreed to look solely to the other company for payment. The judge accepted the surveyors' evidence that they had always regarded the defendant as their client.

TRANSFERS OF RIGHTS AND LIABILITIES

10.7 When a surveyor's rights or obligations have been transferred, the question frequently arises as to what effect this may have on his liability to the original client or to the new client, assuming that his obligations have been validly assigned. The issues which arise are:

(a) the extent of any defences available to a debtor against an assignee;

(b) the extent of a debtor's liability to the assignor and to the assignee.

The assignee takes the benefit of the rights assigned to him subject to any defences or set-offs that the debtor had against the assignor up to the time at which notice of assignment was given. This may include cross-claims for debts due from the assignor under other contracts as well as claims relating to the contract itself. Thereafter the debtor may only raise claims relating to the

1 [1985] 2 EGLR 46.
2 [1877] 3 ChD 391.

contract, such for breach of contract, and set off debts which are closely connected to that contract against any claim brought by the assignee. In either case, the amount of any set-off or cross-claim may not exceed the value of the right assigned. The debtor must sue the assignor for the excess.

10.8 It may be helpful to illustrate this with an example. If a client (assuming that he is permitted to do so) assigns the benefit of his contract with a quantity surveyor, a claim brought for breach of that contract by the assignee would be subject to the following defences or set offs:

(a) any fees due under that contract and any other contracts with the client which were outstanding at the time that notice of the assignment was received;

(b) any fees under that contract which became due after the notice was received; and

(c) claims for damages for breach of that contract whenever the breach was committed.

The quantity surveyor would not be able to set off any claim that he might have for fees under any other contract with the client which became due after notice of assignment was received unless there was a close connection between the contracts.

10.9 The extent of a debtor's liability after assignment may give rise to great difficulties. For example, a building owner may assign the benefit of his contract with a quantity surveyor in respect of the construction of, or works to, the building. If a defect is subsequently discovered by the new owner, what is the extent of the surveyor's liability? Is he entitled to say that the assignor has suffered no loss, since, because he has been able to sell his interest in the property for the full price, no damages may be awarded against him if the assignee subsequently sues him for the cost of repair ?

This question was considered both by the Court of Appeal and by the House of Lords in the *Linden Gardens* case. In the Court of Appeal, Staughton LJ expressed the view that the assignee should be able to recover the same amount of damages as the assignor would have done but for the assignment,[1] a view with which the other members of the court agreed. But this view is not strictly binding because both the Court of Appeal (by a majority) and the House of Lords held that the assignments were not binding on the contractors because they were prohibited by Clause 17 of the building contracts. However, the House of Lords in a Scottish case, *GUS Property Management v Littlewoods Mail Order Store*,[2] had decided that an assignee could recover substantial damages for the cost of repairs caused by a tort committed before the property had been transferred to the assignee.

1 (1992) 57 BLR 57 at 84 to 94.
2 [1982] SLT 533.

In the *Linden Gardens* case, the House of Lords had to consider the converse point which was whether the assignor could recover for the loss caused by the breach of the building contract which occurred after he transferred his interest in the property to the assignee. As the assignee was unable to sue because the assignment was not binding on the contractor, the only party who could sue the contractor for breach of contract was the assignor. It was held that a building contractor could not avoid liability for breach of contract on the grounds that the contracting party no longer had an interest in the property which was the subject of the work and, thus, had not suffered any loss. The reason was that the contract concerned a large development which it could be foreseen would be occupied and possibly purchased by third parties and not by the contracting party itself. It could also be foreseen that those third parties could suffer substantial loss as the result of a breach of the building contract. But the building contractor had specified in the contract that it could not without their consent be enforced by any other parties. It was held to be appropriate in those circumstances to treat the parties as having contracted on the basis that the employer would be able to recover damages for the loss caused to third parties who would not have any right to enforce the contract themselves.

SUBCONTRACTING

10.10 This is a method by which one party to a contract can arrange for his obligations to be performed by another who is not a party to the contract. Although this is not likely to arise in the case of a surveyor who is engaged to provide professional services,[1] it may be helpful to set out the circumstances in which this is permissible.

10.11 The point is illustrated by the case of *Southway Group v Wolff & Wolff*.[2] The issue was whether the vendors of a warehouse, which under the sale contract was to be refurbished by them prior to the sale being completed, were able to assign the benefit of that contract. The purchasers contended that it was essential that the refurbishment work was carried out by the assignor and that they were entitled to rescind the contract when the assignee purported to carry out the work on the assignor's behalf. The issue was therefore whether the assignor was permitted to arrange for another party – the assignee of the benefit of its contract with the purchaser – to perform its obligations under that contract. It was held that on the evidence it was clear that the vendor and the purchaser had left the details of the refurbishment works to be discussed and agreed between them. The contract contained only a bare outline specification of the work which the vendor was to carry out. The vendor was therefore free to carry out the works in whatever manner he saw fit as long as they fell within the terms of the specification. It was held that this could have been left to the

1 One of the authors is aware that valuers may sometimes 'subcontract' valuations 'off patch' to another branch or firm and then countersign the report for lenders.

2 [1991] 57 BLR 33.

discretion of the vendor only because of the purchaser's confidence that the vendor would carry them out in accordance with his wishes. The court held that the vendor was not entitled to arrange for his obligations under the contract to be performed by someone else. Lord Justice Parker commented that:

> 'a building contract is one which of itself suggests that there is at least some inference of selection, the more particularly when the works to be carried out are extensive and ill defined. One would not expect, for example, that anyone would contract with a builder to build at a fixed price a four bedroomed house of brick construction and with wooden windows unless that person had trust and confidence in that builder either from general reputation or recommendation or personal experience and had in addition confidence that the builder would co-operate in arriving at the details.'

10.12 The question whether a contract for services requires personal performance by the party who provides them depends upon the common intention of the parties, as inferred from the nature of the services, the other terms of the contract and all the circumstances of the case. It is submitted that the subcontracting of all but the most basic functions performed by a surveyor would usually be contrary to the terms of his contract. Indeed a contract for the provision of professional services must usually constitute an example of a contract in which personal performance of the professional engaged is essential to the proper performance of the contract.

COLLATERAL WARRANTIES

10.13 By this term, it is intended to refer to agreements under which a surveyor (or another consultant concerned with the design or construction of a building) promises to a person other than his client to carry out his duties properly. Before examining this subject in detail, it may be helpful to explain the background which has led to the requirement that professional advisers retained in relation to building work should give such warranties.

10.14 Prior to 1987, the position of a professional consultant acting in relation to the design and inspection of the construction or works to a building was that he could be held liable in tort for negligence to compensate not only his client but subsequent owners and occupiers of the building for damage caused by defects for which he was responsible. The position was changed by two decisions in the House of Lords which have reduced the scope of tortious liability considerably. As these decisions are of general importance, they are examined in detail below.

10.15 The first of these was *D & F Estates v Church Commissioners*.[1] A claim was brought in negligence against building contractors for the cost of repairing defects to work which had been carried out for the previous owners of a flat. The defects concerned plasterwork which had fallen down and which

---

1 [1989] AC 177.

then had to be replaced. No damage was caused by this defect to any other part of the building (except for dirtying the carpets which could be cleaned). The House of Lords held that the basis of the builder's liability in tort was causing personal injury or damage to other property by his careless work. Where careless work had created a danger of injury or damage to other property, a claim in negligence could only be brought for the cost of averting that danger. A claim could not be made for the cost of repairing a defect which had not caused personal injury or damage to other property or the danger of such injury or damage being caused. Such a claim was for economic loss and irrecoverable, so that if a defect in a building was discovered before it caused such damage or injury, no claim could be made by the subsequent owner against the builder for the cost of repairing or replacing it in tort. It was held that the claim for the cost of replacing the defective plaster constituted economic loss which could not be recovered against the builder by a claim in negligence. However the House of Lords left open the question of how such a rule should be applied to what were described as 'complex structures' such as a building. In that case the building could be treated as a single indivisible unit or, alternatively, the defect in one part of the structure which caused damage to another could be treated as damage to other property for the purpose of the rule and form the basis of a claim in negligence.

10.16 In *Murphy v Brentwood District Council*,[1] a local authority was sued in negligence for approving plans which caused a property to be built with defective foundations, which had caused extensive damage to the walls and the pipework. A committee of seven Law Lords held that the earlier case of *Anns v Merton London Borough Council*,[2] was wrongly decided and should be departed from and that the local authority was not liable for the damage which had not caused any danger to the health and safety of the occupants of the property. In the *Anns* case, the House of Lords had held that the owners of properties suffering from subsidence caused by the inadequate foundations which had been laid when the local authority had negligently failed to inspect them properly, could recover damages for the cost of remedying the defect. The House of Lords held in *Murphy* that when a defect became apparent before any personal injury or damage was caused, the loss suffered by the owner of the building was purely economic loss. In principle, the owner of a building could only recover such loss under the principle of *Hedley Byrne & Co v Heller & Partners*[3] where he had relied upon the professional skill or advice of an architect or engineer and where the loss was caused by his negligent design or advice. The speeches of the Law Lords emphasised the importance of the Defective Premises Act 1972 which had been passed to address this problem.

Different views were expressed by the House of Lords about the application of the complex structure theory to defects in a building. Generally, its application was disapproved because in reality the structural elements in a building formed

1 [1991] 1 AC 398.
2 [1978] AC 728.
3 [1964] AC 465.

an indivisible unit of which the different parts were essentially interdependent. However where one part inflicted positive damage, such as by an explosion, on the structure in which it was incorporated, a claim could be made for the damage caused to the other parts of the structure. Another possible application of the complex structure theory was when one part of the structure was supplied by a different contractor.

10.17 This possibility was explored in *Jacobs v Moreton & Partners*.[1] A firm of consulting civil and structural engineers had been retained to advise on a scheme of remedial works to repair cracking in a property which had been caused by ground movement and to prevent further cracking. They recommended that the original foundations should be replaced by a piled raft foundation. The engineers specified and approved the design of the piling and supervised the construction of the new foundation. The property was subsequently purchased by the plaintiffs who sought to claim damages for negligence against the engineers when the new foundations failed to prevent further damage being caused by ground movement. They alleged that the only practical way of remedying the faults was to demolish and rebuild the property.

The judge (Mr Recorder Jackson QC) concluded that the complex structure theory was part of English law but that its application was strictly limited and it was more accurately described as an exception to the general principle that defects in a building should be characterised as economic loss suffered by the building owner and not therefore recoverable in tort. He found that the following considerations were relevant to deciding whether the exception applied:

(a) whether the item in question was constructed by someone other than the main contractor responsible for the main building works;

(b) whether the item has retained its separate identity, eg a central heating boiler, or merged with the remainder of the building, such as a wall;

(c) whether the item positively inflicts damage on the building or simply fails to fulfil its function, causing damage to occur;

(d) whether the item was constructed at a different time from the rest of the property.

The judge found that the complex structure exception did apply to the facts in that case as the new foundation had been designed and constructed by persons who had no responsibility for the rest of the house, it was constructed later than the rest of the property, it had not entirely merged and it had inflicted positive harm to the rest of the property because the original damage could no longer be repaired by underpinning.

10.18 The effect of the two cases of *D & F* (see **10.15**) and *Murphy* (see **10.16**) has been to reduce the liability of professional designers and supervisors

---

1 [1994] 72 BLR 92.

of building works to third parties in respect of any loss caused by defects in the building works which were caused by their negligence. Apart from the complex structure exception, the consultants' liability in negligence only arises where they have assumed responsibility for their work or advice to a party or class of persons. Usually this will apply only to the consultants' clients.

10.19 With the reduction of the scope of liability in negligence to third parties at common law, only the statutory duty under the Defective Premises Act 1972 remains to provide them with a remedy where any construction or conversion work to any dwelling is not sufficient to ensure that it is fit for habitation. The duty is set out in s 1 of the Act in the following terms:

> '(1) A person taking on work for or in connection with the provision of a dwelling (whether the dwelling is provided by the erection or by the conversion or enlargement of a building) owes a duty-
>
> (a) if the dwelling is provided to the order of any person, to that person; and
>
> (b) without prejudice to paragraph (a) above, to every person who acquires an interest (whether legal or equitable) in the dwelling;
>
> to see that the work which he takes on is done in a workmanlike or, as the case may be, a professional manner, with proper materials and so that as regards that work the dwelling will be fit for habitation when completed.'

The duty imposed by s 1 embraces anyone who takes on work in connection with the provision of a dwelling. But it does not apply where the work only concerns the repair or improvement of a dwelling, unless, in the case of repairs, these are carried out in order to rectify work he has already done by a person for, or in connection with, the provision of the dwelling. The duty is owed to any owner or occupier of the dwelling but the limitation period runs for six years from the completion of the building work or of any such repairs and not from the time that defects are discovered or cause damage.

10.20 With the reduction of the tortious liability of consultants in negligence to subsequent owners and occupiers of buildings, the need has grown for collateral warranties by which contractual duties are created for the benefit of the purchasers and tenants as well as the financiers of building developments. Standard forms of collateral warranty have been published which have been vetted by the professional indemnity insurers. As the forms are intended for use by all of the consultants involved in the design and supervision of the construction of or works to a building, the term 'consultant' will be used below. A consultant's insurers will have to be informed of any amendments that are proposed to be made to any of these forms before such a warranty is entered into.

The Form of Collateral Warranty to Purchasers and Tenants

10.21 It is proposed to deal first with the form of Collateral Warranty for Purchasers and Tenants, (CoWa/P&T), issued jointly by the British Property Federation, the Association of Consulting Engineers, the Royal Incorporation of Architects in Scotland, the Royal Institute of British Architects and the Royal Institution of Chartered Surveyors. The current version of this form is the second edition, published in 1993. This form is intended for use where the consultants have been engaged by a developer in the construction of a building which is intended to be sold or let to a number of different purchasers or tenants. The purpose is to confer on the purchasers or tenants and their assignees the benefit of the duties owed by the consultant under his contract with the developer.

It is essential therefore that the terms of the consultant's engagement with his client are agreed and set out in writing before any such warranty is issued. The warranty may be executed under hand when the limitation period will be six years from the date of any breach, or under seal, when the limitation period will be 12 years. The latter period may be appropriate if the consultant's appointment by his client is under seal but not if it was made under hand. The consultant will be expected to provide the warranty to all of those purchasing or letting premises within the development and the names of each such purchaser or tenant and details of the unit or premises within the development which they are to purchase or rent will be required to complete the forms. The warranty provides for consideration for the promises given by using the formula that the consultant acknowledges receipt of £1 from the purchaser or tenant. This is essential for its validity if executed under hand. The main features of the CoWa/P&T form are summarised below.

10.22 The extent of the duties owed to the purchaser or tenant are defined in clause 1. The consultant (throughout referred to as 'the Firm') warrants that he has and will continue to exercise the standard of skill and care stipulated under his contract with the developer (throughout referred to as 'the Client'). In the case of a quantity surveyor engaged under the RICS Form of Appointment, the obligation will be 'to exercise reasonable skill, care and diligence'. But the liability of the consultant is expressly qualified and limited in the following ways:

(a) the consultant is to be liable only for the reasonable costs of repair, renewal or reinstatement incurred by the purchaser or tenant or for which they are or become liable directly or by way of contribution and not for any other consequential or economic loss. Cover for any further liability may require the consultant to obtain additional insurance. A suggestion is made in the notes to the form for an alternative provision for such liability to be included if required but only up to a specified sum in respect of any one occurrence in order to mirror the limit of the consultant's own professional indemnity cover;

(b) the warranty is intended to be given on the basis that similar undertakings will be given by the other consultants involved in the development. The consultant's liability is limited to the extent which would be just and equitable having regard to the extent of his responsibility, on the basis that the other consultants, identified in the form, have themselves entered into similar warranties and have each paid their share in respect of their responsibility for any loss for which the consultant was found to be liable. The consultant's liability is diluted in this way whether or not the other consultants identified in the form have actually given such an undertaking or satisfied their own contribution towards the loss claimed;

(c) the consultant is entitled to rely upon the same limitations and defences against any claim made under the warranty as would have been available to him if the claim had been brought by his client under the terms of his appointment. For example, the consultant would be entitled to set off any unpaid fees owed by his client which accrued after the warranty was given against a claim brought by a purchaser or tenant;

(d) finally, the liability of the consultant is not to be affected if the purchaser or tenant appoints someone else to carry out any independent enquiry into any matter. For example, a surveyor is appointed to inspect the premises prior to its purchase or acquisition.

10.23 Provision is made in clause 2 in respect of the use of deleterious materials. The consultant warrants that he has and will exercise reasonable skill and care to see that such materials are not specified for use in the construction unless authorised by the client. The clause lists high alumina cement in structural elements, wood wool slabs in permanent formwork to concrete, calcium chloride in admixtures for use in reinforced concrete, asbestos products and aggregates for concrete or reinforced concrete which do not comply with British Standards and any other materials as may be specified. This duty is expressly made without prejudice to the consultant's overriding obligation under clause 1 to exercise proper skill and care in discharging his duties under his appointment. For example, to exercise skill and care in his inspections to ensure that such materials are not used in the construction. It is intended that this provision will be deleted in the case of a warranty given by a quantity surveyor.

10.24 The consultant expressly acknowledges in clause 4 that the client has paid all fees due and owing under his appointment up to the time that the warranty is given. This may provide the consultant with an opportunity to demand payment of any fees which are outstanding before he agrees to give the warranty. No provision is made as to what is to happen if any of the fees are disputed at the time that the warranty is given.

A licence is granted to the purchaser or tenant to copy and use any drawings, specifications or other documents or information produced by the consultant for any purpose related to the premises provided that all fees due under his appointment have been paid. The licence does not include the reproduction of any designs for the extension of the building. The purchaser or tenant has no authority to give the consultant any instruction or direction under his appointment.

10.25 One of the most important provisions is set out in clause 6 which obliges the consultant to maintain professional indemnity insurance up to a level and for a period which are to be specified, providing that this is available 'at commercially reasonable rates' (whatever that may mean), and the consultant is obliged to inform the purchaser or tenant immediately if insurance ceases to be available at such rates. This will be of little comfort to the purchaser or tenant or their assignee if the reason for this is the consultant's poor claims record.

10.26 Provision is made in clause 7 to allow the consultant to limit the number of times that the benefit of his warranty can be assigned without his consent. This may be of limited practical significance if the warranty is made under hand where the limitation period will only be six years. Express provision is made in clause 9 to exclude any proceedings being brought outside the limitation period which is to start from the date of practical completion, although the consultant's contractual duties under his appointment with his client may continue for much longer. For example, in the case of an architect, this will be until the issue of the final certificate under the building contract or even later.

10.27 Any limitation of the consultant's contractual liabilities under the collateral warranty will not affect his liability for breach of statutory duty under s 1 of the Defective Premises Act 1972. As set out above, the duty is owed by anyone taking on work for, or in connection with, the provision of a dwelling to anyone acquiring an interest in the dwelling. The duty is to see that the work he takes on is done in a professional manner, with proper materials and so that, as regards that work, the dwelling will be fit for habitation when completed. This duty continues for six years after the completion of the building work or from the date on which he carries out any repairs to that work.

The Form of Agreement for Collateral Warranty for Funding Institutions

10.28 The terms of the Form of Agreement for Collateral Warranty for Funding Institutions (CoWa/F), now in its third edition (published in 1992) and also issued by the BPF, ACE, RIBA and RICS, go much further than the CoWa/P&T. This form is only appropriate where a warranty is to be given to a company providing finance for a proposed development and the consultants have been engaged by the developer referred to as 'the Client'. It is not appropriate where the consultants have been appointed by the contractor in a design and build contract.

The warranty is executed by the consultant and the client either under hand or as a deed. The same formula is used to provide consideration from the funder but no consideration is provided in relation to the promise given by the client. It contains similar provisions to CoWa/P&T in relation to the content and extent of the obligations which are to be owed by the consultant except that his liability to the funder is not limited to the reasonable costs of repair, renewal or reinstatement. The consultant's liability is unlimited but it is subject to the qualification that it shall be no more than what would be just and equitable having regard to the responsibility of the other consultants identified in the form, assuming that they had entered into similar obligations and that they had discharged their obligations to contribute to such loss. The consultant is entitled in any proceedings brought by the funder to rely upon the same limitations and defences as would apply if the claim had been brought by the client.

10.29 The status of the funder is the same as that of the purchaser or tenant under the CoWa/P&T form in that it has no authority to direct or instruct the consultant. It may copy and use the consultant's drawings and specifications, etc provided that all fees due from the client under the appointment have been paid. The consultant is obliged to keep insurance up to a specified level provided that it is available at commercially reasonable rates. The consultant acknowledges in clause 4 that his fees have been paid by the client up to the date on which the warranty was given and that the funder has no liability for such fees unless it takes over the consultant's appointment. But in two cases the funder may, on giving written notice to the consultant, step into the client's shoes and require the consultant to accept its instructions or those of its appointee to the exclusion of the client. The first is if the finance agreement between the funder and the client is terminated. For this purpose a notice given to that effect by the funder is to be treated as conclusive by the consultant. The second is in the event that the consultant becomes entitled to terminate his appointment or to treat it as repudiated or to suspend its performance. In that case the consultant must give the funder no less than 21 days' notice in advance of exercising any right to terminate or suspend. The funder may then give written notice within that period to require the consultant to accept the instructions of the funder or its appointee. The client acknowledges by clause 10 that the consultant will not be in breach of its appointment if the funder takes over the appointment in this way but there seems to be no consideration for this promise. Nor is there any provision requiring the client to be served with a copy of the funder's notice to the consultant or to ensure that the client does not issue instructions after the funder takes over the appointment. The consultant may continue to receive instructions from the client after the funder has taken over, for example where its right to do so is contested by the client.

10.30 Upon service of the funder's notice, the consultant's appointment is then effectively novated with the funder taking over the position of the client under the consultant's appointment. The consultant then has to accept the instructions of the funder or its appointee to the exclusion of the client. The funder becomes responsible for any fees then due (except for any fees outstanding at the time that the warranty was given) or which thereafter accrue under the appointment. The appointment of the consultant continues with the funder notwithstanding his right to terminate or suspend its performance because of his client's default. The consultant becomes liable to the funder or its appointee instead of the client under the appointment. But there is nothing to prevent the consultant from seeking payment of his fees from the client as there is no provision releasing the client from his liabilities under the appointment.

10.31 It has been suggested that the notice given by the funder to step into the client's shoes may not be valid unless the notice recites the provisions set out in clause 7.[1] This requires the funder to accept liability for outstanding fees and expenses (save those incurred before the warranty was given) as a condition of any notice by which the funder steps into the client's shoes. The recital of this condition is recommended to avoid a challenge to the notice on these grounds. Doubts have also been raised as to how far the terms of the form are effective to establish rights and liabilities between the consultant and the funder's appointee.

The difficulty arises because the appointee is not a party to the warranty at the outset and it is not possible for a party to be a party to a contract in the absence of agreement between the parties. Nor does it appear that the appointee is intended to be the funder's agent because it is provided that the funder will guarantee the payment of fees by the appointee. If the appointee was the funder's agent, this provision would be unnecessary because the funder would be the principal and under a primary liability for the consultant's fees. What the warranty does establish is a contract between the consultant and the funder under which the consultant agrees to obey the funder's appointee if the funder decides to take over from the client. It does not provide for a contract between the consultant and the appointee.

A further technical difficulty will arise if the warranty and/or the appointment is made under deed because a deed cannot be varied except by a variation contained in a further deed. The warranty does not provide for a variation such as the appointment of an appointee to be made in this way.

10.32 Clause 11 of the form provides that the funder may assign the warranty by way of absolute legal assignment to another company providing finance for the development without the consent of the client or consultant. But this would not affect the liability of the client for the consultant's fees or the liability of the funder, if it took over the appointment, as these liabilities could not be transferred to another party without the consultant's consent. Another point arises as to how far the obligations of the consultant are assignable. If the performance of the contract by the consultant involves the personal skill and judgment of the client, for instance, where decisions have to be made over matters of design, there is authority to suggest that the right to the performance of such an obligation cannot be validly transferred by assignment.[2] The efficacy of the provision for assignment by the funder may therefore be limited in practice.

Provision is also made in clause 13 of the form for no proceedings for breach of the appointment to be brought against the consultant after the expiry of a period to be specified after practical completion. However, the clause refers to the practical completion of 'the Premises' which are not defined in the form which also refers to 'the Development' which is defined. Again, there is no consideration for this promise in so far as it concerns the client nor does it cover

---

1 See Cornes and Winward, *Collateral Warranties* (Blackwell Science UK, 1990) at para 9.53 discussing a similar point which arose under the first edition of CoWa/F.

2 See para **10.4** and cf para **10.11**.

any claim which could be brought in tort. The consultant is not so constrained, for instance in respect of any fees which might accrue after that stage has been reached.

RESIDUAL DUTIES AND LIABILITIES

10.33 This is intended to refer to the consultant's duties and liabilities to his original client which may continue to exist after the assignment of the benefit of his obligations under his appointment or the giving of any collateral warranty to a third party. An assignment does not affect the content of the duties owed by a consultant to his client whether these arise in contract or in tort. In the *Linden Garden* case the House of Lords considered the ways in which the original client could enforce the contract for the benefit of the assignees. On the particular facts of that case, they were able to find that the assignor was entitled to recover for the loss caused to an assignee although the assignment had not been effective against the contractor. It is suggested that the assignment of the benefit of a contract will not transfer the benefit of any tortious duties owed by the professional consultant to his client unless this is specified in the assignment. It follows that the client may still have the right to bring a claim for the loss caused by the consultant's negligence which he has incurred although the right to enforce a similar obligation under the contract may have been validly assigned to someone else.

The difficulties which may arise under the collateral warranty agreement set out in CoWa/F illustrate the problems which exist when there is no complete novation of the contract between the consultant and the client and those stepping into a client's shoes. In addition to the tortious duty of care which the consultant may continue to owe to his client, his appointment may be subject to a dispute between the client and the funder of the project and conversely, the consultant may be able to sue both for arrears of his fees.

It is open to the parties to regulate the consultant's duties and liabilities by making express provision in the assignment, novation or collateral warranty. However in the absence of any express provision to the contrary, it is suggested that the consultant's duty to exercise reasonable skill and care in carrying out his duties for his client continues with the possible consequences that different limitation periods and measures of loss may apply and that actions in respect of any breach of his duties may be brought by different parties.

Finally, it may be helpful to illustrate some of the points made above by reference to a practical example. Where a design and build contract is used, the employer may engage the design team including an architect, a structural engineer, a quantity surveyor and other consultants, before initial tenders are invited from contractors. The architect may have applied for and obtained planning permission for the development and have drafted the employer's requirements. The contractor may be required to continue to retain the members of the design team after the contract is let. In those circumstances, it is frequently the case that the quantity surveyor is asked to stay on with the employer to act as his agent under the design and build contract, while the architect and the other consultants are then engaged by the contractor. This then raises the question of what are the duties then owed by the architect to the employer.

10.34 If the contract between the architect and the employer is assigned to the contractor, then the employer will still be liable for any fees due because only the benefit of the contract can be assigned. If the architect's contract is novated with the contractor then both the employer and the architect will be discharged from any further liability under the original contract. But the architect will, it would seem, remain liable to the employer in tort in relation to the work he carried out before novation. But what if the architect subsequently commits a negligent error in his design or supervision of the work?

This point has arisen in one reported case decided in South Africa, *Lillicrap, Wassenaar and Partners v Pilkington Brothers*.[1] In that case, engineers who had initially been engaged by the employer but were subsequently engaged as subcontractors were found not to owe a duty of care to the employer. There appear to be no other recent reported cases on this point. It is suggested by the editors of *Keating on Building Contracts*[2] that a consultant engaged by a design and build contractor might be liable to the employer if there was sufficient evidence to show that the consultant had assumed such a responsibility and the employer had relied on him. But it is not difficult to envisage circumstances in which there may be a conflict between the interests of the employer and those of the contractor where the imposition of a tortious duty of care to the employer would make the proper performance of his contract with the contractor difficult or impossible. The existence of such a duty of care would cut across the liabilities for design assumed by the contractor under the contract. It is therefore uncertain whether a duty of care in tort does exist in these circumstances. The most practical solution that can be adopted is to require the architect and other members of the design team who are employed by the contractor to execute collateral warranties in favour of the employer.

1 [1985] 1 SALR 475 and (partially) (1984) 1 Const LJ 211.
2 May, A, *Keating on Building Contracts* (Sweet & Maxwell, 1995), p 195.

Chapter 11

THE QUANTITY SURVEYOR'S DUTIES: PRE-CONTRACT

INTRODUCTION

11.1 It is most helpful to consider the quantity surveyor's duties and responsibilities in relation to a building project under three headings: duties prior to the letting of the contract; duties arising in the course of the contract and other services which a quantity surveyor is or may be required to provide. This chapter considers in detail the various obligations and duties which may arise in the normal course of a quantity surveyor's engagement prior to the letting of a construction contract. Duties arising in the course of a contract and in other circumstances are looked at in Chapter 12.

COST ESTIMATES

11.2 This topic covers one of the most important functions that a quantity surveyor can fulfil and which he is especially well qualified to perform by reason of his knowledge, training and experience. Depending upon the stage at which he is engaged, a quantity surveyor may be instructed to provide preliminary advice on the cost of a scheme, to set a realistic cost budget for a project or to advise generally or more specifically on the cost implications of the design and standards of construction to be used or of possible alternatives. It is not proposed here to go into the different methods and systems that a quantity surveyor may use to calculate or estimate costs but to set out and explain the legal duties and liabilities which may arise as decided in the reported cases. Some of these concern architects and engineers as well as surveyors where similar principles apply.

11.3 One of the earliest cases in which the duty of a surveyor giving an estimate of the cost of construction works was considered is *Moneypenny v Hartland*[1] in which the plaintiff claimed his fees for his work as an architect and engineer in respect of the design and construction of a new road and bridge outside Tewkesbury. The plaintiff had been dismissed after the costs had grossly exceeded the estimates that he had given for the costs of constructing the road and bridge. Expert evidence was given on behalf of the defendants to

1 (1826) 2 Car & P 378.

the effect that the road could not be made for less than three times the sum stated in the plaintiff's estimate. The costs of constructing the bridge had exceeded the plaintiff's estimate because the foundations were partly laid in clay and piles had to be used. Expert evidence was also given by the great road builder Thomas Telford as to the duty of the architect or engineer to investigate the soil conditions for himself.

The significance of the case is that it laid down certain principles as to whether fees could be recovered for professional work where it had been performed negligently and as to the liability of a surveyor for his estimates. On the first point, it was held that the fee could be recovered unless the negligence or want of skill had rendered the work useless to the client. The plaintiff's plans had been partly used by Telford, who had replaced him. But the jury were directed that he was not allowed to recover if his estimate had been made without exercising proper care. The point was made succinctly by Best CJ:

> 'But if a surveyor delivers in an estimate, greatly below the sum at which a work can be done, and thereby induces a private person to undertake what he would not otherwise do; then I think he is not entitled to recover; and this doctrine is precisely applicable to public works. There are many in this metropolis which would never have been undertaken at all, had it not been for the absurd estimates of surveyors.'

11.4 In another 19th-century authority, a claim was made by architects and surveyors for payment for their work in preparing plans and estimates and drawing up quantities for the construction of a school, after they had been dismissed when the tenders exceeded their estimate. Their entitlement to claim fees was held to depend upon whether it was an express condition of their contract that the costs would not exceed their estimate for the cost of the work or alternatively whether there was an implied term that the work should be capable of being done for a sum reasonably close to the estimated cost.[1] The plaintiffs' position in that case can be distinguished from that of a quantity surveyor who is asked to advise on the costs of a project because he is not then responsible for specifying and designing the work so that it can be carried out within the estimated cost.

11.5 Where the architect (or surveyor) has been paid for services from which the client does not derive any benefit because of the underestimate, the fees may be recovered as damages. In the case of *Pratt v St Albert School District*,[2] an architect failed to recover his outstanding fees for work on a school building project which was abandoned after the tenders received had exceeded his estimates, and his clients recovered the fees he had been paid as damages because they had derived no benefit from his work.

11.6 In the more recent case of *Nye Saunders v Bristow*,[3] a claim was made by an architect for fees due for his work on plans and drawings which were made after the client had decided to proceed with the reconstruction of a

---

1 *Nelson v Spooner* (1861) 2 F & F 613.
2 (1969) 5 DLR (3d) 451.
3 (1987) 37 BLR 92.

property in reliance upon an approximate estimate he had given. This proved to be wholly inadequate because it had made no provision for the effect of inflation (the annual rate was then in double figures and peaked at 35 per cent) on the building costs until the work had been finished or for contingencies. The client had told the architect that only £250,000 was available. The architect consulted a quantity surveyor and sent the client the schedule of costs which the quantity surveyor had prepared which totalled £238,000. The architect did not warn the client that no allowance had been made for inflation although it was found by the judge that the architect knew that an estimate for the total eventual cost was required. The client terminated the architect's employment when the estimated costs rose to £440,000 – after allowing for inflation – only seven months after the initial estimate was given.

The client successfully defended the architect's claim on the grounds that the estimate was negligent in not making any allowance for inflation and for not warning him that this was the case and that the fees would not have been incurred had he been properly advised of the likely costs of the work. In particular, the judge found, having heard evidence from four architects on the matter, that it was not proper practice for architects at that time to give no warning as to inflation when providing an approximate estimate of the cost of building works. The trial judge's findings of negligence were upheld by the Court of Appeal.

11.7 A similar point arose in the unreported case of *Aubrey Jacobus and Partners v Gerrard*,[1] a judgment of His Honour Judge Stabb QC given in June 1991. In that case the architects had also provided an estimate with the assistance of quantity surveyors in June 1979 of £365,000 for building a house with a swimming pool. The lowest tender received was approximately £417,000. Since this tender assumed a 'fluctuating' contract, the ultimate cost would have been much higher. The client did not proceed with the project and contended that the estimate was negligently given on the basis that it should have represented the ultimate cost and taken account of cost increases over the period until the completion of the works. This argument was rejected by the judge who stated:

> 'In my judgment the quantity surveyor's duty is to estimate the cost at current rates but to make it plain that the estimate is given on that basis and that increased costs are excluded. If then he is asked to estimate the extent of the likely increases, he can do it with such qualifications as he wishes to add, but I do not consider that he is under a duty to volunteer it.'

11.8 A similar result was achieved in an earlier Canadian case, *Savage v Board of School Trustees of School District No 60 (Alberni)*[2] in which an architect had underestimated the costs of building a new school, partly because no proper allowance had been made for inflation. His estimate was $110,000

---

1 See *Jackson & Powell on Professional Negligence* 4th edn (Sweet & Maxwell, 1977), p 200 footnote 19.

2 (1951) 3 DLR 39.

and the lowest tender was $157,800. After reducing the size of the school by 40 per cent the lowest tender was still $132,900. The court held that the architect's estimate should be reasonably near the ultimate cost and if it was not, it was for him to show how it arose and that it was not his fault.

11.9 These cases all demonstrate the need for a quantity surveyor (or architect) to clearly indicate the extent to which an estimate may be liable to variation and to bring to his client's attention all of the factors which may influence or affect the estimate in the ultimate result. However, the approach of the court in *Savage v Board of School Trustees* to the issue of negligence would not be followed by the English courts. In the recent case of *Copthorne Hotels v Arup Associates*,[1] the clients sought to recover damages against quantity surveyors on the grounds that they had negligently under-estimated the cost of piling work required for the construction. Their estimate was £425,000 and the eventual cost was £975,000. His Honour Judge Hicks QC refused to hold that the estimate was negligent simply because of the wide gap between the estimate and the eventual cost:

> 'The gap was indeed enormous. It astonished and appalled the parties at the time, and it astonishes me. I do not see, however, how that alone can carry the plaintiff home. There is no plea or argument that the maxim *res ipsa loquitur* applies. Culpable under-estimation is of course one obvious explanation of such a discrepancy, but far from the only one. The successful tender was not the lowest. The contractor may have over-specified from excessive caution, or to obtain a greater profit, or to suit the drilling equipment available, or for some other reason. Market conditions may have changed or have been subject to some distortion outside the knowledge and foresight of a reasonably competent professional adviser.'[2]

11.10 In order to prove that an underestimate was negligent, it will therefore be necessary to establish why it was exceeded and whether this was for reasons which should have been predicted or for which some warning or qualification should have been given. One recent case in which a claim for professional negligence against a firm of architects succeeded was *Gable House v The Halpern Partnership*.[3] The clients asked their architects to produce a preliminary cost plan and elemental specification in respect of the proposed demolition and rebuilding of office premises which included an estimate of the total usable office space that would be obtained. It was held that the architects knew that this would affect the clients' decision whether to proceed with the redevelopment or alternatively to refurbish the existing building or to re-sell it because it would form the basis for the calculation of the value of the new building. The architects estimated that the total usable office space would be 33,928 square feet. It transpired that the correct figure was only 31,769 square feet, about 6.3 per cent less than the estimate. The overestimate had been caused by the architects' failure to allow for the space which would be taken up

---

1 (1996) 12 Const LJ 402.
2 (1996) 12 Const LJ 402 at 415.
3 [1995] CILL 1072.

by structural work and by the lettable areas being inaccurately scaled from the architects' drawings. It was held that a note stating 'all areas approximate' was not sufficient to warn the clients of the uncertainties which applied to that estimate and that the architects had failed to warn the clients that the quantity surveyors' calculation of 'usable office space' was not the same as the 'net lettable area' or as to the effect of a change to the specification after which it was found that they would have been able to predict that the amount of net lettable area would be 2,000 square feet less than the usable office space.

The finding that the architects had negligently overstated the usable office area led to a consideration of the loss which had been caused by the clients' reliance upon the estimate in deciding to proceed with the reconstruction. The judge held that if the clients had been properly advised they would not have decided to proceed with the redevelopment and would instead have resold the property. The judgment did not deal with the assessment of damages for which the clients claimed £32.5 million. It is apparent now, following the decision of the House of Lords in the *SAAMCO*[1] case, that the maximum recoverable loss would be the difference between the value of the property with the estimated letting area and its value with its actual potential letting area.

11.11 It is rare for a client to recover damages for construction costs which exceed a negligent estimate because usually he thereby obtains a property of greater value for which he would have to give credit in calculating his loss. One case in which the clients did recover substantial damages for a cost overrun was *Newfoundland Capital Corporation v Mettam.*[2] It was held that the architect had undertaken to the clients that the costs of refurbishing a property would not exceed $225,000 and that he had failed to discuss the cost of variations or increases in costs with the client. The clients called evidence from a valuer to show that the additional work had not actually increased the value of the property in order to show that they had suffered a loss. The architect was held to be liable for the cost overrun on work that he had instructed should be done.

11.12 If the client has already committed himself to a project before an estimate is given, he will not be able to show he has suffered any loss if he succeeds in proving that the estimate was negligent. One of the clients' claims in the *Copthorne Hotel* case failed on this ground. It was alleged that the quantity surveyors had been negligent and had breached the contract in that a cost plan for £11.186 million was inadequate and that it should have been for £13.474 million. The cost plan had been given after the client had entered into the contract for the construction of the hotel and it was not contended that they could or would have sought to withdraw or that they would have otherwise acted differently if the cost plan had given the higher figure.

11.13 Under the tortious measure of loss, the clients would not be entitled to recover any damages unless they could show that their position would have been different if they had received the correct advice. To circumvent this

1 [1997] AC 191.
2 Nova Scotia Supreme Court 1986 22 *Construction Law Cases* 45.

finding, the clients argued that they should still be entitled to recover damages on the basis that the cost plan effectively constituted a warranty that the costs would not exceed the total indicated. The judge held that the distinction between the two measures of damage had not been changed or elided by the decision of the House of Lords in *SAAMCO* and cited the following passage from the speech of Lord Hoffman:

> 'The measure of damages in an action for breach of duty to take care to provide accurate information must also be distinguished from the measure of damages for breach of a warranty that the information is accurate. In the case of breach of duty of care, the measure of damages is the loss attributable to the inaccuracy of the information which the plaintiff has suffered by reason of having entered into the transaction on the assumption that the information was correct. One therefore compares the loss he has actually suffered with what his position would have been if he had not entered into the transaction and asks what element of this loss is attributable to the inaccuracy of the information. In the case of a warranty, one compares the plaintiff's position as a result of entering into the transaction with what it would have been if the information had been accurate. Both measures are concerned with the consequences of the inaccuracy of the information, but the tort measure is the extent to which the plaintiff is worse off because the information was wrong whereas the warranty measure is the extent to which he would have been better off if the information had been right.'[1]

For those reasons, the judge held that the claim in tort in respect of the alleged under estimate of costs in the cost plan failed. But he indicated that in contract the plaintiffs would have been entitled to nominal damages on proof of breach for reasons he did not elaborate. Presumably this was because on the facts found they could not show that they had suffered any loss as the result of the quantity surveyor's failure to exercise proper skill and care in preparing the cost plan.

PROCUREMENT

11.14 There are a wide variety of different methods of contracting and forms of contract available. The quantity surveyor can provide essential advice to the client on the most appropriate means of undertaking the work and the most suitable form of contract. The most important factors for the client will usually be time, cost and quality of the work and, above all, the distribution of risk. These should usually determine the appropriate means and form of contract. Prior to the letting of a contract, the quantity surveyor may also be asked to assess the viability of the project; to recommend an organisational structure for the development of the project; to advise on the appointment of various consultants and contractors and to select the methods for their appointment and to manage and co-ordinate the information and work of the different parties. This section considers the choice of method and form of contract.

1 [1997] AC 191 at 216D–F.

11.15 The most important choices for the client are:

(a) whether the contract should be for a fixed price or whether payment should be by measurement or reimbursement. By fixed price contract, it is intended to mean a contract for a specific project or item of work in which the price is fixed in advance and is not subject to any alteration except in the case of a variation. The expression 'lump sum' contract is also used to describe such a contract but in order to avoid confusion only the term 'fixed price contract' will be used below;

(b) whether to engage consultants or to leave the design and construction of the project to the contractor;

(c) whether to select the contractor by competition or negotiation;

Payment

11.16 The main categories of priced contracts are:

(a) fixed price contracts;

(b) measured or bill of quantities contracts;

(c) schedule contracts;

(d) mixed contracts.

Fixed price

11.17 A fixed price contract is typically one in which a price is given for carrying out and completing the work described in drawings and/or a specification. The contractor undertakes to perform all that may be required to achieve the result indicated in those documents and is responsible for all ancillary and contingent expenditure. This is the method which is most appropriate for straightforward or small projects. Each contractor measures his work from the drawings and specification and prices it to produce a lump sum. Because each contractor may measure the work differently, this method may not allow for a fair or accurate comparison of tender sums. As each contractor has to estimate the quantity of work for himself, this may be wasteful of their resources. As the contractor has to take the risk of being responsible for his measurements, he may tend to overprice to compensate for possible errors and to cover the costs of abortive estimates. These contracts may include schedules of prices or schedules of rates which are used only to value variations or interim payments.

11.18 For building work, the following Standard Forms of Contract issued by the Joint Contracts Tribunal can be used for this type of contract:

(a) the JCT 1980 Form of Contract Without Quantities published in the Local Authorities and Private editions. The current version includes all of the amendments issued up to Amendment 17 published in 1997;

(b) the JCT Intermediate Form of Building Contract can also be used if the contractor is invited to tender for the work shown in the contract drawings and specification;

(c) the JCT Agreement for Minor Building Works. The current version of this form includes the amendments issued up to Amendment MW10 issued in 1996.

Measured/bills of quantities contracts

11.19 In measured or bills of quantities contracts the contract documents in addition to the drawings and specification include bills of quantities. The total price paid for the work is determined by measuring the total 'as built' quantities when the work is completed. This is done by applying the rates set out in the bills of quantity which have been priced by the contractor which are commonly grossed up with 'preliminary' or general items. The contract provides that the tendered prices are only for the quantities stipulated in the bills and that the ultimate contract price is recalculated in light of the final as built quantities of work. In practice, this is unlikely to occur unless errors are found in the bills of quantities or an item of work is uncertain or it is difficult to accurately predict the quantities.

The most important feature of a measured contract compared to a fixed price contract is that it only transfers to the client the risk of the final quantities being greater than those estimated or likely when the contract was let. On the other hand, the client will enjoy the advantage of a reduction in the total price if the final quantities are less. Differences between the final and the anticipated quantities will arise either because the amount of work is unpredictable or because of an initial mistake in calculating the quantities required for the work. However, under the JCT Form and ICE forms of contract, such discrepancies, when they are found, are treated as if they were variations and the contractor may consequently be entitled to be paid proportionately more where the quantities exceed those stated in the bills.[1]

Schedule contracts

11.20 Schedule contracts may be necessary where the precise work is not known at the time of contracting so that drawings and a specification cannot be prepared. Instead, schedules or lists of likely items are priced. No estimate can be made in this form of contract of the total cost of the work and in the absence of any specified quantities, it will be necessary for all of the work to be measured upon completion.

---

1 See clause 2.2.2.2 of the JCT Standard Form of Contract 1980 and clause 55(2) of the ICE Form of Contract 6th edn 1991.

Mixed contracts

11.21 Contracts may include a combination of fixed price items and measured quantities. For example, a fixed price contract may include items for which it may not be possible to accurately predict the quantities, so that provisional sums or approximate quantities are included.

The JCT Standard Form of Contract With Approximate Quantities (published in Local Authority and Private editions) is intended for use where the works have been substantially designed but not completely detailed so that the quantities of work have to be completely remeasured on completion.

COST PLUS

11.22 In cost-reimbursable contracts the client pays for the costs of construction plus an addition to cover the contractor's profit. This may be a straight percentage added to the cost or a fixed or variable fee. In this type of contract, there is no tender or possible final total cost although the additional fee may be subject to competition by tender or negotiation. This type of contract is therefore only suitable for use in special circumstances, such as emergency works, where time does not allow for the traditional process or where the character or scope of the works cannot be determined in advance, where new technology is being used and where there is a special relationship between the contractor and the client.

11.23 Where such a contract is to be used the incentives for speed and economy are greatly reduced or removed. This can partly be redressed by fixing a target cost and or by adjusting of the fee in the event of the cost being exceeded. This form of contract has to be most carefully drafted to protect the client's interests and it should include the following provisions:

(a) detailed schedules defining what is and what is to be included as cost;

(b) the elimination of all discount and profit elements from the contractor's cost items;

(c) the control of the selection and payment of subcontractors;

(d) the adjustment of the target figure as the result of any changes affecting the extent of the work or external factors affecting the costs.

11.24 A Standard Form of Prime Cost Contract is published by the JCT for building work. This is the 1992 edition and in its current form incorporates amendments up to Amendment 4, issued in July 1996. It envisages that some indication of the work to be carried out will be provided in a specification although the actual work will be instructed by the architect and may be subject to alteration. The contract provides for either a percentage or fixed fee to be paid to the contractor in addition to the construction costs which are referred to as the 'Prime Cost' as well as any loss and expense incurred by the contractor because of disruption for which the employer is responsible, such as late instructions, the postponement of work, or delay caused by the work carried out by others employed directly by the employer. The contractor is expected to tender for the fee based on the estimate of the total Prime Cost which is prepared by the client's quantity surveyor. The contractor's fee is subject to adjustment if the nature and scope of the work is altered by the architect's instructions and also, in the case of a fixed fee, if the actual Prime Cost exceeds or is less than the total estimated Prime Cost.

11.25 Expenditure under the contract is controlled by a comprehensive definition of the Prime Cost for which the contractor is entitled to be reimbursed and by providing that the letting of work to domestic subcontractors is subject to the architect's consent and allowing for the nomination of subcontractors. The definition of Prime Cost does not include any loss and expense payable to the contractor. The contract also requires the contractor to carry out the works as economically as possible and not to employ more people on site than are reasonably required to carry out and complete the work. These obligations are policed by the architect who may, having given the requisite notice, instruct the quantity surveyor to disallow any costs arising from the contractor's breach of these obligations.

The definition of Prime Cost: excludes any discounts received by the contractor from subcontractors or suppliers other than those from nominated subcontractors or suppliers; requires the keeping of records, measurements and accounts; allows for a lump sum to be paid in respect of any part of the construction work and defines what is recoverable in respect of labour, management, goods and materials and plant, consumable stores and services and sundry expenses provided or incurred by the contractor and for the subcontracted work.

11.26 The use of a cost reimbursable contract may reflect a lack of planning by the client or his consultants and may in those circumstances lead to disaster. The client should also be advised that with the removal of practically all of the pricing risks, a lower percentage or fee is appropriate to cover the contractor's profit than would be necessary in a priced contract. Finally, in order to ensure that the client is adequately protected, the use of such a contract will require much more detailed and day-to-day administration of the contract by his professional consultants to check the contractor's claims for payment and to supervise and record the delivery of materials and the use of labour on site. On a major project, a permanent site and administrative staff will be required.

DESIGN AND BUILD

11.27 The use of design and build contracts has become much more common in recent years. The greatest advantage of this type of contract for the client is that it places all of the risks on one pair of shoulders. The most important feature of this type of contract is the provision of the design by the contractor. It is now well established that where a client relies upon a contractor for the design, his responsibility will be to produce a work which is suitable for its required purpose. This point is illustrated by the case of *Greaves & Co v Baynham Meikle*.[1] This involved a 'package deal' under which the contractor undertook to supply a warehouse which was to be used for the storage of barrels of oil. The floors were not strong enough to take the weight of the stacker trucks which were used to move the barrels and began to crack. The contractor sued the engineer who they had engaged to design the floors. The case turned on the distinction between the duty owed by a professional man to exercise reasonable skill and care and the term which was found to be implied that the design should be suitable for its intended purpose and structurally sound. The engineers were found to have breached that term as well as their professional duty of care.

11.28 In order to safeguard the client, it is suggested that a design and build contract should include the provision of a warranty by the contractor that the building will be suitable for its intended purpose and this should continue for a substantial period of time and be backed by some form of security such as a surety or guarantee. In order to safeguard the contractor's position, he should have the right to refuse to accept any variations which may compromise the suitability of the structure and to make any variation which may be necessary to ensure its safety and suitability, subject to financial and other safeguards to avoid abuse and the client's or his representative's agreement. The contract should identify any parts of the work which are to be excluded from the contractor's obligation of suitability, and the status and rights of any consultants appointed by the client to supervise any of the work.

11.29 The disadvantages of a design and build type of contract are that variations may be more limited or expensive than under a traditional form of contract. It is also more difficult to compare the prices of different tenders for work on this basis because it may not be clear whether the type and quality of the proposed designs are the same. The NJCC however issued a Code of Procedure for Selective Tendering for Design and Build in 1995. This sets out a number of points which will be relevant to a quantity surveyor advising a client on this method of contracting and is considered further below.

11.30 Several standard forms of contract have been issued for contracts of this type. For building work, where the contractor is to design only part of the work, a Contractor's Designed Portion Supplement 1981 edition for modifying the Standard Form of Building Contract With Quantities 1980 Edition has been issued. Alternatively the provisions for Performance Specified Work in clause 42 of the Standard Form of Building Contract 1980 Edition (introduced by Amendment 12 in 1993) may be used. The Joint Contracts Tribunal have issued the JCT Standard Form of Building Contract with Contractor's Design 1981 Edition where the contractor is to be responsible for the design of all of the work. This has been subject to periodic amendments and in its current form incorporates Amendment 10 issued in July 1996. For engineering work, the Institute of Civil Engineers have produced the ICE

1 [1975] 1 WLR 1095.

Design and Construct Conditions of Contract 1992 Edition. The current version of this form incorporates Amendment CCSJC/GN/March 1995. For building and civil engineering work for Government Departments there is the Government's GC/Works/1 Ed 3 Design and Build Version of contract.

In both the JCT and ICE forms of design and build contract, provision is made for the client to stipulate what is to be included by the contractor. This is referred to as 'the Employer's Requirements' and the contractor sets out how these are to be met in 'the Contractor's Proposals' or, in the case of the ICE Form, 'the Contractor's Submission'. Under the JCT form of contract, the Contractor prepares a Contract Sum Analysis which is used for the valuation of variations. In the event of any inconsistencies in the Employer's Requirements, the Contractor's Proposals are to prevail, but in that case any changes which are necessary are deemed to be variations for which the contractor may be entitled to additional payment. Under both forms of contract, the contractor's responsibility for design is to 'exercise all reasonable skill and diligence' rather than to ensure that the building or works are suitable for their intended purpose.[1] In the JCT Contractor's Designed Portion the contractor is deemed to have the same liability as an architect would have to his employer for any defects in his design.[2]

11.31 The NJCC Code of Procedure for Selective Tendering for Design and Build 1995 states that the following steps are prerequisites for a project to be carried out successfully under design and build procedures:

(a) the appointment of an appropriately qualified and experienced agent and professional consultants. The latter may be able to advise on the adequacy and standards of the design proposed by the contractor and a quantity surveyor may advise the client in respect of the costing and valuation of any variations;

(b) the standard form of contract should be used unamended. It has already been noted that this would reduce the contractor's responsibility for design to that of a professional consultant rather than making him responsible for the suitability of the design;

(c) the employer's wishes should be clearly formulated and set out in the Employer's Requirements by the time tenders are invited. This is crucial to avoid costly variations after the contract has been made.

The Code recommends that very careful consideration needs to be given as to whether design and build is appropriate having regard to the novelty and complexity of the design requirements. It also notes that this method will not be appropriate where the client's architect has gone beyond the detailed design stage or where prolonged negotiations will be required with planning authorities or others before work can proceed. In practice the client can go as far as he likes with his own consultants, as this form of contract can be quite

---

1 See clause 2.5.1 of the JCT form and clause 8(2)(a) of the ICE form.

2 Clause 2.7.1.

elastic. It also suggests that clients should obtain professional help with the preparation of the Employer's Requirements, making a preliminary appraisal of the contractors' capabilities so as to make up a short list and to appraise the tenders and enable the client to make an informed choice.

The Code also contains useful advice on organising the design responsibilities of the clients' own consultants and the contract. It suggests that the client's own design team may be transferred to the successful tenderer's organisation. This should only be done with great care to ensure that there are no gaps between the liability of the client's consultants and the contractor. The design team can only serve one client at a time, so their retainer should be terminated before the agreements are entered into with the successful tenderer.

MANAGEMENT CONTRACTS

11.32 These involve the contractor managing the construction of the work in return for a fee. Each trade required for the project is tendered for separately by subcontractors (referred to as 'works subcontractors'), either on the basis of measured quantities or a lump sum. This may allow the contractor to become involved in the early stages of the design of a project and because the fee is not based on the value of the actual construction work, the client may be able to obtain the lowest possible price for each trade and for the work as a whole.

11.33 For building work which is to be carried out under this form of contract, the JCT have issued a Standard Form of Management Contract 1987 Edition and a Standard Works Contract between the management contractor and the various works contractors together with a Standard Agreement between the employer and a works contractor. The current version of the Form of Management Contract incorporates Amendment 2 issued in April 1989. This form envisages that the client will appoint an architect and/or contract administrator and a quantity surveyor as the 'professional team' for the design and specification of the work. This is not a lump sum contract but as an indication of the price that the employer will pay, exclusive of the fee payable to the management contractor, the quantity surveyor prepares a Contract Cost Plan which has to be agreed by the client and the management contractor before building work proceeds. This will be the principal cost control document used throughout the design and construction. The consecutive receipt of tenders will enable the management contractor to maintain the Contract Cost Plan by re-detailing later packages if this is judged necessary in the light of the tenders received for earlier packages of work.

11.34 The costs actually incurred by the management contractor in carrying out the work are described as the Prime Cost and this is the amount actually paid by the client under interim certificates issued by the architect or contract administrator. The task of the quantity surveyor is to monitor the Prime Cost against the Contract Cost Plan. The fee paid to the management contractor may be a lump sum or calculated as a percentage of the Contract Cost Plan

Total. The Prime Cost payable by the client comprises the sums due to the works contractors and the amounts expended by the management contractor on site staff and facilities, all as certified by the architect (or contract administrator). The contract provides for the management contractor to provide his services in two parts during the pre-construction and construction periods and the management fee is split accordingly. During the first period the management contractor is to advise on the Cost Plan, methods of construction, on design and procurement programmes and to prepare initial works programmes and lists of tenders for Works Contracts, on long delivery materials, use of layouts and standard of workmanship and materials. The client has the power to terminate the contract with the management contractor before proceeding with the Construction stage.

11.35 Where a works contractor has undertaken the design of the work which it is to carry out under its contract with the management contractor, the client may obtain a direct warranty in respect of that design by entering into the form of Employer/Works Contractor Agreement. The works contractor will then be directly responsible to the Employer for any defects in the design of its work.

11.36 The Practice Note issued by the JCT on this form of contract[1] states that this 'Management Contract as written is a deliberately "low risk" contract.' It suggests that it may be suitable where there is a need for early completion, the project is fairly large or its requirements are complex and entail or might entail changing the employer's requirements during the building period, and where the employer while requiring early completion wants the maximum possible competition in respect of the price of the building works. It indicates that the Works Contracts will account for between 80 per cent and 90 per cent of the total cost, so that competition will influence a high proportion of the price paid by the client.

11.37 An alternative form of management contract is 'construction management' in which the individual trade contractors contract direct with the client who appoints a construction manager. He may in turn appoint the design team who are usually on contract with the client. The construction manager is then responsible for the overall control of the design team and of the trade contractors throughout the design and construction stages of the contract.

11.38 'Project management' involves the appointment of a professional adviser who then appoints the appropriate design consultants and select the contractor to carry out the work. This method may be appropriate for large buildings and engineering projects. The project manager is responsible for organising and coordinating the design and construction programme which may be carried out using any of the traditional or other methods of contracting. This method can be compared to 'project coordination' where the client

---

1 JCT Practice Note MC/1 published in December 1987.

retains a consultant to coordinate the work of the other consultants and the contractor who are each engaged separately by the client.

11.39 Another form of management contract is known as 'design and manage' which could also be described as 'design and risk'. In this case the client appoints a design manager who has full responsibility over both the design and construction stages. The design manager appoints and contracts with the quantity surveyor and other consultants and takes on the role of the main contractor by engaging all of the subcontractors and suppliers.

CONTRACTOR SELECTION

11.40 A single contractor may be invited to tender for the proposed work, in which case the contract will be negotiated, or the work may be put out to tender. Interviews with possible contractors and their management teams may assist in the selection of a list of contractors to whom the invitations to tender may be sent. In order to obtain a price by competitive tender, an invitation to tender has to be prepared which contains all the documentation necessary to produce an offer which if accepted will conclude a binding contract. This will usually include drawings, a specification and the conditions of contract and a document to obtain information in order to price variations, such as a schedule of rates or bills of quantities if the contract is to be a measured contract. The object of the invitation to tender is to secure an offer in reply from the tendering contractors which leaves nothing for further agreement. Otherwise the client's bargaining position will be weakened in any subsequent negotiations that may be required. This is achieved by requiring that the tenders are to be irrevocable for a specified period of time after they are submitted.

11.41 Codes of Procedure for Single Stage and Two Stage Selective Tendering are published by the National Joint Consultative Committee for Building. The provisions of the Codes issued in January 1996 will be considered here and in paras **11.63** to **11.65** below. Both Codes contemplate that tenders will be invited from a selected list of tenderers. The Code for Two Stage Selective Tendering is intended where it is desired to secure the involvement of the main contractor before the work has been fully designed.

11.42 The Code for Single Stage Selective Tendering recommends that a shortlist of suitable contractors is drawn up. Because of the cost of preparing tenders, it recommends that the list should not contain more than six names. Where the preparation of the tender involves extensive quantification, specification, specialisation or calculation, the Code recommends that the list should not contain more than four names. It is suggested that in selecting the short list the following factors should be considered:

(a) the firm's financial standing and record;

(b) whether it has had recent experience of building at the required rate over a comparable completion period;

(c) its general experience, skill and reputation in the area in question;

(d) the adequacy of the technical and management structure of the firm for the work involved;

(e) its competence and resources in respect of statutory health and safety requirements;

(f) its approach to quality assurance systems; and

(g) whether it will have adequate capacity at the relevant time.

The tendering procedure recommended by the Code is for a preliminary enquiry to be sent out containing sufficient details of the proposed work, contract conditions and period to enable the contractors to decide whether they will tender. This should state whether or not tenderers are to be given the opportunity to revise their tender if any errors are found in their priced bills. Under the Code, two alternative procedures are to apply in the case of pricing errors in priced bills. The tenderer is either to be given the opportunity to confirm or withdraw his tender or, alternatively, to confirm or to amend it to correct genuine errors. It is suggested that a period of between 4 and 6 weeks is allowed between sending out the preliminary enquiry and the despatch of the tendering documents. On the completion of this stage the final shortlist of contractors is selected. A recommended form of invitation to tender is appended. The Code recommends that qualified tenders should not be considered unless they are also accompanied by an unqualified tender. If only a qualified tender is submitted, the Code recommends that the tenderer should be given the opportunity to withdraw the qualifications and, if he does not do so, that the tender should be rejected if the qualifications give him an unfair advantage over the other tenderers. It is suggested that the invitation to tender should simply state that tenders will not be considered if they do not comply with the tender documents. Otherwise the admission of qualified tenders will undermine the fairness of the competition. A minimum of 20 working days should be allowed for the preparation of tenders. Any errors spotted in the tender documents should be notified by the contractor not less than 10 days before tenders are due. Tenders received after the stipulated time should not be admitted to the competition.

11.43 The Code for Two Stage Selective Tendering sets out similar recommendations for the first stage in which a contractor is selected and a level of pricing is established for subsequent negotiation. During the second stage, the bills of quantities and other design information are completed so that a contract price can be produced on the rates indicated and agreed with the selected contractor. Provision should be made for the possibility that no contract is entered into and for payment of any disbursements and any work done before the second stage is completed. If no agreement is reached, the second stage may recommence with the next lowest tenderer or the fresh tenders invited for the first stage.

THE CHOICE OF CONTRACTING METHOD AND FORM OF CONTRACT

11.44 It is possible to analyse the different forms of contract by reference to:

(a) the risk to the client;

(b) degree of client control;

(c) the amount of effort required to control the contractor;

(d) the amount of information required at tender stage;

(e) the amount of information required to control the costs.

A fixed price contract stands at one end of the spectrum as it involves the least risk to the client. It is easiest for the client to control, needing the least information and minimum effort, but it requires the most detailed information to be available at tender stage. At the other end of the spectrum is the cost plus type of contract with the maximum risk to the owner, being the hardest to control and requiring the greatest amount of information. Between these two ends of the spectrum, moving from the lump sum towards the cost plus, stand the other measurement and cost reimbursement types of contract. The quantity surveyor advising his client must explain the different degrees of risk and control involved in these different types of contract.

11.45 Advice on the most appropriate type and form of contract will depend on the client's wishes and the circumstances in each case. The most relevant factors will usually be some or all of the following:

(a) The size of the project. For small projects the more complex forms of contractual arrangement will not be cost effective.

(b) The client's own preferences based on previous experience.

(c) The overall cost. Open tendering will usually produce the most competitive price. It is believed that negotiated tendering may add about 5 per cent to 10 per cent to the price.

(d) Design. The best design will usually be obtained from someone who is independent of the contractor. Even where a design and build contract is adopted, the design should (ideally) be carried out by those who have the relevant expertise and who are independent from the commercial aspects of the construction. In practice this is highly unlikely to happen.

(e) Quality. The quality of any construction is attributable to the design and specification, and to the supervision and capabilities of the contractor. This may be prejudiced by the use of fast track methods of procurement or if there is a lack of competent supervision.

(f) Organisation. This can be facilitated by the use of a design and build type of contract with a single line of responsibility. However, with the traditional form of procurement the responsibilities of the consultants, the contractor and subcontractors are well known and established.

(g) Market. The most appropriate selection process may vary according to the conditions of the market.

(h) The division of risk between the client and the contractor.

PREPARING BILLS OF QUANTITIES AND SCHEDULES OF WORK

The definition of bills of quantities

11.46 Bills of quantities continue to be used for over 50 per cent of the value of building contracts which are let using firm or approximate quantities. They contain a measurement of the work involved in a project which is taken off the drawings and specification produced by an architect or engineer. For building work, the items are divided according to the trades into different bills. For example, there may be different bills for groundworks, concrete work, brickwork, roofing and joinery etc. In the case of engineering works the bills are usually divided between the different sections of work. In both cases, the bills always include general or preliminary bills. In a building contract these are intended to cover items such as site mobilisation, the hire of huts and scaffolding, insurance and other items which are applicable to all of the trades as well as a tabulation of all of the clauses of the building contract[1] and this may be helpful in order to show, for example, any deletions and amendments. These are described as preliminary items.

11.47 Typically, each page of a bill is divided into columns. The quantity and a description of each item of work are listed in columns on the left-hand side of each page of the bills; in the columns on the right-hand side space is provided for the contractor to insert his price for each item and the total price for the quantity set out in the bill. Although the bills are intended to represent the quantity of work shown in the drawings, the nature of the work cannot usually be understood without referring to the specification. For the purpose of preparing the specification, the National Building Specification may be used. This provides a large library of specification clauses. It is published in three different versions: the Standard version, an abridged Intermediate version and a Minor Works version. In contracts made under the JCT Standard Form of Contract With Quantities in which the bills of quantities form part of the contract, the specification is not a contract document, so this has to be reproduced in the bills by preambles and in the description of each item of work. In bills for civil engineering contracts, the specification is usually part of

---

1 This continues to be required under SMM7 Rule A20.

the contract and items frequently refer back to this document for a description of each item. The amounts charged for each item are collected into a summary for each bill and these summaries are then collected into a grand summary for the whole of the work.

The definition of schedule of rates

11.48 This term may refer to three different types of document. In a fixed price contract, such a schedule may be prepared in order to value any variations made in the course of the work. Where the full extent of the work cannot be defined or estimated when a contract is let, such a document may be used to price the items which are expected to be required in the work and to measure the work when it is completed. Finally, such a document may be used where the contract is subject to a provision for fluctuation of the price in order to set out the prices of materials and labour rates so that the contract price can be adjusted if any of these change during the course of the contract.

The purpose of bills of quantities

11.49 Originally these were developed in order to assist contractors tendering for a lump sum contract and the quantity surveyor would be paid by the successful contractor. Tendering remains the primary purpose of bills of quantities although they are now usually prepared by the quantity surveyor on behalf of the client. They are used by contractors to indicate as accurately as possible the amount and nature of work which is to be carried out under the contract and by the client's consultants to provide a detailed break down of the contract sum for the purpose of comparing tenders. In addition, they may be used in practice by a quantity surveyor, acting for the employer or contractor, for:

(a) valuations for interim payments;

(b) valuation of variations;

(c) ordering materials (if a contractor does so, this is at his risk because he is only bound by the specification and drawings);

(d) cost analysis for future approximate estimating;

(e) final accounts;

(f) quality by reference to the trade preamble clauses;

(h) cost information.

In measured contracts the bills of quantity represent a precise measure of the quantity of work which is to be carried out for the contract price, which will be adjusted in the cases explained above once the works are complete and the actual as-built quantities are known, irrespective of any variations. They will also be used to value variations to the contract, subject to the architect's power to allow for increases to such rates. In the JCT Forms of Contract With

Quantities, the bills will also contain the specification of the work which is to be carried out.

The preparation of bills of quantities

11.50 The quantity surveyor will require the drawings and specification from the architect in order to prepare the bills. He will then take off the quantities from the drawings and incorporate the specification, as appropriate, into the different bills. It is not proposed here to deal with the methods which may be used to take off the quantities.

11.51 In order accurately to describe each item of work in the bills some standard means of description is required. In the JCT Forms of Contract, the Standard Methods of Measurement are expressly incorporated into the contract. The JCT Standard Form of Contract With Quantities 1980 edition provides that the priced bills of quantities (referred to as the 'Contract Bills') are included as part of the contract documents and in clause 2.2.2.1 that 'unless otherwise specifically stated therein in respect of any specified item or items, [they] are to have been prepared in accordance with the Standard Method Of Measurement of Building Works, 7th edition, published by The Royal Institution of Chartered Surveyors and the Building Employers Federation.'

As noted in para **11.19** above, under clause 2.2.2.2 of that contract, any departure from the method of preparation referred to in clause 2.2.2.1 or any error in description or in quantity or omission of items shall be corrected by treating the difference as a variation. So any departure from the Standard Method of Measurement in preparing the bills unless specifically referred to may entitle the contractor to seek additional payment as a variation.

SMM7

11.52 This acronym is used to refer to the Standard Method of Measurement 7th Edition. The Standard provides a uniform basis for measuring quantity but not quality. The general rules in SMM7 state that it 'embodies the essentials of good practice'. This will be relevant to the issue of liability considered below. It may be helpful to set out some of the general rules which apply under SMM7. A full consideration of the detailed rules of SMM7 is outside the scope of this book.

11.53 General Rule 1.1 provides that 'Bills of quantities shall fully describe and accurately represent the quantity and quality of the works to be carried out'. Failure to describe an item and the quality required may therefore entitle the contractor to have the failure corrected and the correction treated as a variation. However, SMM7 makes no detailed provision as to the quality of work to be included in the bills of quantities.

11.54 General Rule 4.6 states that:

> 'Unless otherwise specifically stated in a bill of quantities, the following shall be deemed to be included with all items:

(a) Labour and all costs in connection therewith.

(b) Materials, goods and all costs in connection therewith.

(c) Assembling, fitting and fixing materials and goods in position.

(d) Plant and all costs in connection therewith.

(e) Waste of materials.

(f) Square cutting.

(g) Establishment charges, overhead charges and profit.'

The charges referred to in sub-clause (g) are not necessarily the contractor's actual costs in relation to these items but can be considered as a levy which is applied to the total of items (a) to (f) at a rate which will reimburse the likely outlay for establishment costs (ie the contractor's operating base) and overhead costs (his off-site management). For commercial reasons, the charges may be more or less than the actual costs. The same points apply to the profit allowed under (g). Although such matters are deemed to have been included in the price given for each item of work, they will normally in practice be included in the Preliminaries Section of the Bills, often as a single sum.

11.55 General Rule 9.1 allows the use of composite items where they involve work which is to be manufactured off site. In that case, the price is deemed to include the costs of breaking down for transport and installation and subsequent re-assembly. Otherwise, General Rule 4.2 prohibits the aggregation of a number of measured items which are required to be measured separately under SMM7.

11.56 Where the drawn or specification information required by SMM7 for the measurement of work is not available, General Rule 10.2 provides that it shall be given as a Provisional Sum and identified as 'defined' or 'undefined work'. 'Defined work' is work which is not completely designed but for which information is provided as to its nature and construction, where a statement is given of how and where it is to be fixed to the building and of any other work which is to be fixed thereto and quantities are given which indicate its scope and extent and any specific limitations are identified. Where such information cannot be given in whole or in part, the work is deemed to be 'undefined work'. In the case of 'defined work' the contractor is deemed to have made due allowance in programming, planning and pricing preliminaries. He is not deemed to have made any such allowances where a Provisional Sum is given for 'undefined work'.

SMM7 does not include a definition of a PC (Prime Cost) Sum although this is the subject of clauses 35.1 and 36.1 of the Standard Form of Contract.

Liability

11.57 A quantity surveyor is obliged to exercise proper skill and care in preparing bills of quantities. The failure by a quantity surveyor to follow the rules set out in SMM7 would appear to constitute a breach of this duty.

However, some doubt must remain as to the consequences under the building contract when an item of work which should under SMM7 have been separately shown and identified in the bills, is subject to a claim by the contractor for a correction and consequent variation under clause 2.2.2.2. The doubt arises because the contract does not provide how such a correction is to be corrected or valued. Take, for example, an item which is ancillary to a process specified in the bills, such as the erection of the formwork required to construct fair faced concrete. One approach would be to treat the price stated for the item as including the cost of the ancillary processes required to construct it. This is the approach advocated by the learned author of *Hudson's Building and Engineering Contracts*.[1] If that is correct then the price stated for that item, which must clearly involve the ancillary process, should be adjusted downwards and the missing item added with a figure for the balance. If the correct interpretation is that an additional sum should be added for the missing item on top of the priced item, then the contractor obtains a windfall because the quoted price will have included the missing item. The contractor could make such a claim as soon as the contract was made. If he does not spot the error until later then he will almost certainly have allowed for the missing item in his price. This is the orthodox approach that is usually adopted by quantity surveyors.

A similar difficulty will arise if the bills fail to include an ancillary process which is a contingent item – ie shuttering, planking and strutting – for which the contractor is entitled to payment whether or not it is required. In that case, the contractor may have included an allowance for that contingency in the price given for the item that was stated. If so, the effect of correcting this error should be to reduce that rate unless the contingent item is actually required. Logically, additional payment could only be claimed if that item was actually required.

11.58 There are no reported cases in which a quantity surveyor has been sued, where his client is the building owner, for failing to include an item in the bills. One possible explanation for this is that if the item had been included the client would probably have paid a higher price and there may be little or no difference between that price and the extra sum he may be required to pay under the contract. It is suggested that this explanation is too simplistic. It cannot apply where the omission causes the client to lose a grant or subsidy for the cost of the omitted item. Such a loss did occur in one case[2] in which the quantity surveyor engaged by a housing association had failed to include an item for insulation in spite of this being shown in the architect's drawing. The contractor claimed an additional sum for this item which the housing corporation refused to pay because it was not included in the original application. There was little doubt that this item would have been approved if it had been included and on that basis liability was admitted by the quantity surveyor's insurers.

---

1 Wallace, IND, *Hudson Building and Engineering Contracts*, 11th edn (Sweet & Maxwell, 1994), pp 976–984.

2 Unreported. The details are stated in *Caveat Surveyor II* (RICS Insurance Services Ltd, 1989), p 42.

11.59 The addition of items as variations where they have in error been omitted by the quantity surveyor may be more expensive than if they had been included and had been tendered for initially. This point was recognised in *Turner Page Music v Torres Design Associates*[1] in which a claim was made for defective design. It was held that the defendant firm of architects had negligently failed to make sufficient provision for fire exits in the redevelopment of the Shepherds Bush Empire cinema. It was found that the price of the necessary additional work was higher than it would have been if it been included originally and that the owner was entitled to damages for the additional cost. On the evidence, it was found that the increase was one-third more than if the work had been included in the original contract price and the owners were awarded damages for one quarter of the total cost of the additional works. A similar finding could be made where a quantity surveyor omits to include an item in the bills of quantities for which the contractor is entitled to additional payment as a variation. The contractor may be awarded more than he would have received if the item had been included. Even where a rate for the item is included in the bills, the contractor may be able to recover more than the specified rate under the provisions for valuation of variations if he is able to show that it is executed under different conditions, or if the quantities are significantly different.[2]

11.60 Where a quantity surveyor is acting for a contractor tendering for a lump sum contract, there can be little doubt that his client will suffer if an item of work is omitted which should have been included or the price given is not correctly shown in his tender. In one case in New Zealand,[3] a firm of quantity surveyors were engaged to take out schedules of quantities for a contract without bills (ie a fixed price contract) and failed to include for erecting a fence on the boundary line of a school which was absolutely necessary. They were held to be negligent as it was held that there were clear terms in the specification and that although the plan was not as informative as it might have been, a reasonably careful surveyor would have been put on inquiry and checked the position. Substantial damages were awarded against them.

ADVISING ON AND NEGOTIATING REDUCTIONS IN TENDERS

Assessing tenders

11.61 The employer is not usually bound to accept the lowest or any tender. But if he had no intention of letting the contract to one of the contractors who was invited to tender, he may be liable to pay damages for any expenses that

---

1 [1997] CILL 1263.

2 See clause 13.5.1.2 of the JCT Standard Form of Contract.

3 *Marriott & Haxton v Pillar* [1960] a decision of the Supreme Court reported in the *Builder* on 25 November. The case is summarised in Smellie *Building Contracts and Practice in New Zealand* (Butterworths, Wellington, 1979) p 407.

were incurred. In the case of a bona fide invitation to tender, the employer may be under an implied duty to consider a conforming tender together with other conforming tenders and failure to do so may constitute a breach of contract. This point arose recently in *Blackpool & Fylde Aero Club v Blackpool Borough Council.*[1] The council had invited tenders for the grant of a concession for pleasure flights at Blackpool Airport which had been held by the plaintiffs. They posted their tender by hand before the expiry of the deadline for the submission of tenders. But the council's officers failed to clear their post box, the plaintiffs' tender was not considered and the council accepted a tender higher than that which had been submitted by the plaintiffs. They brought a claim for damages for breach of contract or negligence. The court held that the express request for tenders gave rise to an implied contractual obligation to consider the tenders which were received. The invitation to tender was held to constitute an offer to consider any tenders which were submitted in time in accordance with the tender's conditions and this was accepted by the plaintiffs submitting a conforming tender before the deadline. On these grounds the plaintiffs succeeded in proving breach of contract and negligence. The judge's decision was upheld by the Court of Appeal.

11.62 This case was considered in *Fairclough Building v Port Talbot Borough Council.*[2] This involved a two-stage tendering process for the construction of a new civic centre for which Fairclough had been short-listed and invited to tender. Fairclough's construction director was married to the council's principal architect who was to assess the tenders. Fairclough brought proceedings for breach of contract after it was removed from the selected list of tenderers having already submitted its stage 1 tender. It was held that the council had to choose between removing Fairclough or their principal architect and in the circumstances it was reasonable to have done the former. It was held that a tenderer was always at risk of having his tender rejected, either on its intrinsic merits or on the ground of some disqualifying factor personal to the tenderer.

11.63 The NJCC Code for Single Stage Selective Tendering recommends that only the lowest tenderer should be required to submit priced bills as soon as possible (in any event within four working days) and that all but the lowest three tenderers should be informed immediately that their tenders have been unsuccessful. To safeguard the employer's interests the second and third lowest tenderers should be told that, although their bids were not the most favourable, they may be approached again. The quantity surveyor's task is then to check the priced bills for any arithmetical errors. As the contractor will be bound by any errors that are not spotted before his tender is accepted, it has been suggested that the quantity surveyor may be liable to the contractor for failing to spot errors in his priced bills[3] but there is no direct authority to support this. In

1 [1990] 1 WLR 1195.
2 [1992] 62 BLR 82.
3 *Emden's Construction Law* vol 2 (Butterworths, 1994), division A para 1383.

Dutton v Louth Corporation,[1] it was held that an employer was under a moral duty to draw the contractor's attention to a pricing error which he spotted before the contract was made. If such an error is not brought to the contractor's attention and the error operates in the employer's favour, the contractor may be able to seek rectification of the contract on the grounds that it would in those circumstances be inequitable for the employer to rely on the contract price. An error spotted by the quantity surveyor acting for the employer and not communicated to the contractor may thereby rebound on the quantity surveyor who may then be liable to his client.

11.64 Under the Code, the quantity surveyor should report any errors detected in the computation of the tender to the architect who will determine what action should be taken under whichever of the two alternative procedures applies. Under the first alternative, the tenderer should be given details of the errors which have been detected and given an opportunity to confirm or withdraw his offer. If the tenderer confirms his offer, an endorsement should be added to the priced bill indicating the rates or prices which are to be considered as reduced or increased in the same proportion as the corrected total of priced items exceeds or falls short of such items. Under the second alternative the tenderer should be given the opportunity to confirm his offer or to amend it to correct genuine errors. If he chooses to amend his offer and the revised tender is no longer the lowest, the offer of the next lowest tenderer should be examined. If he does choose to amend his tender figure, he should be allowed to insert the correct details in his original tender or to confirm the alterations in a letter. If he does not, the bills should be endorsed appropriately. If no errors are found in the lowest tender, or the contractor confirms that his price remains the lowest tender after any errors have been corrected, the Code provides that it should be recommended to the client for acceptance.

Negotiating reductions

11.65 Where the tender exceeds the client's budget, reductions may be agreed by adjustments being made to the specification or quantity of work. Any changes should be fully documented, by preparing bills of reduction incorporating the revisions. These will set out all the additions and omissions, at the rates set in the priced bills or at the rates agreed in respect of any additional items. The tender price will be revised accordingly. If these negotiations fail, they should proceed with the next lowest tenderer and if those negotiations fail, with the third lowest tenderer. If all the negotiations fail then fresh tenders may have to be sought.

PREPARATION OF CONTRACT DOCUMENTS

11.66 The task of preparing the contracts for execution by the client and the contractor or other parties is often left to the quantity surveyor. Careful

---

1 [1955] 116 EG 128.

consideration must be given to what documents and drawings are to be included as contract documents and the completion of the appendix and any amendments to the standard forms of contract. Some of the pitfalls are illustrated by the case of *Temloc v Errill Properties*[1] in which '£nil' had been inserted in the space for the amount of liquidated and ascertained damages in the Appendix to a JCT 80 contract. It was held that by making that entry the parties had indicated that no damages were to be payable for delay by the contractor rather than that the contractor would be liable for the actual damage which the employer proved to have been so caused.

11.67 When preparing a JCT Standard Form of Contract the documents and drawings to be incorporated as the contract documents should be clearly identified and listed in the recital and copies should be attached, marked and initialled by those signing the contract. There are certain formalities which must be observed if the contract is to be executed as a deed, which increases the applicable limitation period to 12 years from the date that a breach of contract is committed. The contract must be signed by the parties in the presence of a witness who attests the signature by also signing below the signature made by the contracting party. An individual can execute a contract as a deed by signing or making his mark. A seal is no longer required but the parties must indicate by describing the document as a deed or signing it as such that it is intended to be a deed. Companies and corporations have to execute a deed by attaching their seal although a company incorporated under the Companies Act 1985 may validly execute a deed by two directors or the secretary and director signing on its behalf. Contracts which are not deeds may be executed by a director or any other person authorised to do so on its behalf.

1 [1988] 39 BLR 30.

Chapter 12

THE QUANTITY SURVEYOR'S DUTIES: POST-CONTRACT

INTRODUCTION

12.1 After the client has entered into a contract with the contractor the quantity surveyor may have a dual role to perform. Until the contract was let the quantity surveyor's duties were exclusively owed to his client. The quantity surveyor may now have functions to perform under the terms of the building contract in which he is named. Although the quantity surveyor is not a party to that contract he is bound under his contract of engagement with his client to discharge those functions properly in accordance with its terms. In carrying out these functions, it may be necessary at times for the quantity surveyor to act fairly and impartially and duties may arise to the contractor. The first part of this chapter examines three of those functions in detail: the valuation of interim and final accounts, the valuation of variations and the assessment of claims for loss and expense as well as the continuing duty to monitor and report on costs as required by his client. The second part of the chapter considers the possible liability of the quantity surveyor to third parties such as the contractor and subcontractors and, finally, the other functions commonly performed by a quantity surveyor outside the course of a building contract.

THE STATUS OF THE QUANTITY SURVEYOR UNDER THE JCT FORM OF BUILDING CONTRACT

12.2 Before looking at the quantity surveyor's functions in detail, it may be helpful to consider his status under the JCT Standard Form of Building Contract (1980 Edn) which will be referred to below as 'JCT 80'. This was addressed in the case of *John Laing Construction Ltd v County and District Properties Ltd.*[1] The point arose in the context of the 1963 JCT Form of Contract under which there was a dispute over the application of the fluctuation clause 31D(3). This provided that the quantity surveyor and the contractor might agree what 'shall be deemed for all the purposes of this contract to be the net amount payable to or allowable by the contractor in respect of the occurrence of any event listed in sub-clause (1) of this condition.'

1 [1982] 23 BLR 1.

The arbitrator, His Honour Edgar Fay QC had found that this gave the quantity surveyor authority to waive non-compliance by the contractor with the provision requiring proper notice of the events giving rise to the application of the provisions for fluctuations.

On appeal from the arbitrator on a case stated, Webster J held that the provision did not give the quantity surveyor such authority. He came to this conclusion having considered the position of the quantity surveyor under the conditions of the contract generally. Although his observations on the general effect of the JCT conditions are not strictly binding, they are of considerable weight, particularly as this is the only reported case in which the position and status of the quantity surveyor under that contract has been judicially considered. It is therefore appropriate to quote from the judgment at some length:[1]

> 'He is identified in Article 4 of the Articles of Agreement; by clause 11(4) he is given the express duty of measuring and valuing variations; by clause 11(6) he is given the duty of ascertaining loss and expense involved in a variation if so instructed by the architect; and by clause 24(1) he is given a similar duty in respect of loss and expense caused by a disturbance of the works, etc.
>
> These provisions, together with the implication that he will probably have prepared the bills of quantity referred to in the recital to the articles of agreement, lead me to the conclusion that, save for the fact that if he prepares the bills he will have specified the quality of the works, his functions and authority under the contract are confined to measuring and quantifying and that the contract gives him authority, at least in certain instances, to decide quantum, but that it does not in any instance give him authority to determine any liability, or liability to make any payment or allowance, unless such authority is given to him by clause 31D(3); and, as I have already said, in my view that sub-clause, taken on its own, is not to be construed as giving him any such authority.
>
> . . .
>
> [Counsel for Laings] lays weight upon what he describes as the 'importance' of the quantity surveyor under the contract. As to that, I have no doubt whatever that the quantity surveyor plays an important part; but that fact (if it be a fact properly so called and not simply a matter of comment) cannot in my view have any significance for the purpose of construing this sub-clause. Counsel also stressed and sought to rely upon the words 'for all the purposes of this contract'; but in my view that phrase is material not to the construction of the words in question but only to their effect. Finally, he sought to gain assistance from the provisions of clause 11(4) that
>
>> "... The valuation of variations ... unless otherwise agreed shall be made in accordance with the following rules."
>
> The word "agreed", he submitted, means "agreed by or with the quantity surveyor". I reject that submission. In my view, the word "agreed" can only mean "agreed between the parties", although it may well be that, on the facts of a particular case, the quantity surveyor is given by the employer authority to make such an agreement.'

1 [1982] 23 BLR 1 at 14.

INTERIM VALUATIONS

12.3 Clause 30.1.2 of JCT 80 provides:

> 'Interim valuations shall be made by the quantity surveyor whenever the architect/the contract administrator considers them to be necessary for the purpose of ascertaining the amount to be stated as due in an Interim Certificate.'

A similar provision is made by clause 4.2 of the JCT Intermediate Form of Building Contract which will be referred to below as 'IFC 84'. A distinction has to be drawn between the interim valuation made by the quantity surveyor and the interim certificate which is issued by the architect. The interim valuation is in effect only a recommendation. It is for the architect to decide what should be certified for payment. In practice, the quantity surveyor is usually instructed to prepare valuations before each interim certificate is issued. Where the contract price is subject to adjustment for fluctuations under clauses 37–40 of JCT 80, interim valuations by the quantity surveyor are required before each interim certificate is issued. Interim certificates are usually issued monthly until practical completion and thereafter at not less than monthly intervals when further sums are ascertained to be due to the contractor and upon the expiry of the defects liability period or the Certificate of Completion of Making Good Defects (whichever is the later). Under clause 30.2 of JCT 80 and clause 4.2 of IFC 84, the valuation should be carried out so as to state the value not more than seven days before the date of the issue of the interim certificate.

The valuation of work for interim certificates

12.4 It is suggested in *Emden's Construction Law*[1] that the value of the work should be considered in terms of its value to the employer and not the cost to the contractor because the employer is effectively making payments on account of the contract price to the contractor. The value should be determined by the proportion the work done bears to the contract sum. It is also suggested in *Emden*[2] that the contract bills (ie the bills of quantities which have been priced by the contractor) are the most convenient means of valuing the work done for the purpose of interim valuations.

12.5 The next question is what work should to be taken into consideration. In practice a quantity surveyor is likely to value the work in accordance with the contract bills and SMM 7. For example, temporary formwork used to construct cast concrete has to be separately measured and valued under SMM 7 even though it does not confer any value to the employer. It could be hired by the contractor. It does not seem appropriate to include temporary items if the criterion for interim valuation is the value of the work to the employer rather than the cost to the contractor. The interim valuation should include any adjustments which are appropriate in respect of variations. The work may also

1 (Butterworths, 1994), vol 2, division A para 3007.

2 Op cit at paras 3010–3015.

involve the incurring of fees and charges for which the contractor is entitled to payment under the terms of the contract.

12.6 Clause 30.2.1.1 of JCT 80 expressly provides that an interim certificate should include the total value of the work properly executed by the contractor. Work which is not properly executed should not be included in the interim certificate. In *Sutcliffe v Chippendale & Edmondson*,[1] the architects had included defective work in two interim certificates which were paid and the employer was unable to recover the remedial costs from the contractor when it became insolvent. The employer sued the architects and succeeded in recovering damages for the value of the work which had been over-certified. His Honour Judge Stabb QC heard expert evidence from five experienced architects and quantity surveyors who differed as to what was the correct practice. He found that the strict approach of not including any work which was defective or unsatisfactory was correct since the inclusion of such work could expose the employer to the risk of the contractor's subsequent insolvency. He commented that it was for the architect to inform the quantity surveyor of any work which was not properly executed before he carried out his valuation.

12.7 A similar approach was adopted by the Court of Appeal in *Townsend v Stone Toms*.[2] The case concerned a claim brought by the employers against the architects and the contractor in respect of defects in the rebuilding of a farmhouse. The architects had issued an interim certificate which included items which they knew were defective and which had not been rectified. It was suggested that they were entitled to issue such a certificate because they thought that the remedial costs would be covered by the retention money held by the employer. A majority of the Court of Appeal held that the architects were negligent in certifying work for payment which they knew was defective. Lord Justice Oliver rejected the argument that the architects were entitled to look to the retention money to cover the defects in the work certified:

> 'The whole purpose of certification is to protect the client from paying to the builder more than the proper value of the work done, less proper retentions, before it is due. If the architect deliberately over-certifies work which he knows has not been done properly, this seems to me to be a clear breach of his contractual duty, and whether the certification is described as 'negligent' or as 'deliberate' is immaterial. If, after certification and payment, Laings had gone out of business, leaving the work unrectified, I cannot see how the defendants could possibly have had any answer to a claim for damages – although, of course, retention moneys would be taken into account as a matter of quantum.'

Lord Justice Purchas considered the purpose of interim certificates further:

> 'The purpose in this context of the issue of interim certificates provided for in clause 27 [of the JCT Form of Prime Cost Contract similar in this respect to clause 30.2 of JCT 80] is two-fold. They protect the builder by ensuring that he is promptly

---

1 [1971] 18 BLR 149. This case went up to the House of Lords on a different point under the name of *Sutcliffe v Thakrah* [1974] AC 727.

2 [1984] 27 BLR 26.

paid, subject to retention money for, *inter alia*, the cost of work properly executed and goods and materials properly brought on site. At the same time they protect the building owner from being asked to pay for work which has not been properly executed, or for goods and materials prematurely brought onto site, or insecurely stored there.'

12.8 Returning to the quantity surveyor's task in preparing an interim valuation, it is clearly for the architect to instruct the quantity surveyor as to what work has not been properly executed. Equally, if the quantity surveyor spots unsatisfactory or defective work when on site, it would seem that he would be bound to report this to the architect for his decision. Clause 30.2 provides that in addition to the total value of the work properly executed by the contractor, the valuation for an interim payment shall include the following items on which retention will be deducted:

(a) the total value of materials and goods on site, as long as they are reasonably, properly and not prematurely delivered and are adequately protected. When these are included in an interim certificate, they become the employer's property although they remain at the contractor's risk.

(b) the value of goods and materials which are off site, for example pre-fabricated items, subject to the requirements that they are ready to be fixed and are distinctly marked and the contractor proving that he owns and has insurance cover for them.

(c) sums due to nominated subcontractors and the contractor's profit thereon.

12.9 Clause 30.2 of JCT 80 provides for the following items to be included in the interim valuations for which no retention is deducted:

(a) various reimbursable fees and expenses;
(b) any ascertained loss and expense;
(c) final payments to nominated subcontractors;
(d) any sums due for fluctuations;
(e) loss and expense and other charges and expenses for which the nominated subcontractor is entitled to be reimbursed.

At the time that an interim certificate is issued, the quantity surveyor may be instructed under clause 30.5.2.1 of JCT 80 to prepare a statement of the retentions deducted from the sum due to the contractor and nominated subcontractors. Before dealing with final valuations, it is appropriate to consider the treatment of variations and claims for loss and expense.

VARIATIONS

Entitlement

12.10 A variation is defined by clause 13.1 of JCT 80 as an alteration or modification of the design, quality or quantity of the works, as well as any changes made to the limitations or restrictions to the use of or access to all or part of the site, to working space and working hours or as to the order in which work is to be carried out or completed. In the latter case, the contractor has the right to object to an instruction to that effect from the architect and if the objection is reasonable, the contractor will not be obliged to comply with it. It is suggested that an objection would only be considered reasonable if it would make the performance of the work impossible or unduly onerous.[1] A variation is defined in identical terms by clause 3.6 of IFC 84. Variations under the terms of JCT 80 and IFC 84 may be instructed by the architect in advance or sanctioned by him retrospectively. Variations may also be deemed to occur when any error or omission or any departure from the stipulated method of measurement in the contract bills is corrected under clause 2.2.2.2 or where a divergence is found between the statutory requirements and the contract bills or drawings or architect's instructions and in other cases where adjustment is required under JCT 80.

The function of the quantity surveyor

12.11 Clause 13.4.1 provides that all variations and all work executed in accordance with the architect's instructions for the expenditure of provisional sums *shall* be valued by the quantity surveyor whose name appears in the articles of agreement. Unless the employer and the contractor otherwise agree, it is solely the responsibility of the quantity surveyor to determine the price to be paid or allowed in respect of a variation. The architect has no authority to determine or influence the quantity surveyor's determination in any way. Neither the architect or the quantity surveyor has authority to accept a quotation from the contractor in respect of work which is to be carried out as a variation. The clause provides that the quantity surveyor is to value the work in accordance with the provisions of clause 13.5 unless otherwise agreed by the employer and the contractor. Once an instruction has been given by the architect for a variation the quantity surveyor will be required to value all of its effects up to the point that it becomes necessary for the contractor to claim for its effect on the regular progress of the work under clause 26.

The quantity surveyor is also responsible for measuring variations made under nominated subcontracts but in practice such variations are likely to be valued by other consultants, such as the M & E engineer in the case of subcontracts for mechanical and electrical services. However, not every architect's instruction will constitute a variation. The quantity surveyor must satisfy himself by enquiring of the architect whether an instruction does contain a variation as defined by the contract conditions. If it does not, then the quantity surveyor must consider whether it entitles the contractor to claim an adjustment to the contract price under any other conditions.

1 See Powell-Smith and Sims, *Building Contract Claims* 2nd edn (Blackwell, 1988) at p 94.

Valuation

12.12 There are various different ways in which a variation can be valued. The simplest method is to agree a fixed lump sum (ie an all inclusive price) in advance. The JCT Forms of Contract permit the parties to make such ad hoc agreements: see the provisos to clause 13.4.1.1 of JCT 80 and clause 3.7 of IFC 84 which allow such an agreement to be made before the contractor complies with an architect's instruction. Clause 13A of JCT 80 now provides for variations to be valued by the contractor being invited to provide a quotation. The quotation must include any amount which might otherwise be due for loss and expense and for any disruption caused to the progress of the work. The problem with a lump sum price is that it may not be very competitive. On the other hand, the contractor takes the risk of any unforeseen incidental costs and expenses. It may be advantageous for a client to agree a price in advance in the following circumstances:

(a) where he has to have a fixed cost before the variation is made;
(b) where the rules of valuation will produce an unrealistically high figure;
(c) where the contractor is being asked to perform work which is not a variation as defined;
(d) where there are no rates for the work in the contract documents.

Another consideration is certainty. The valuation of a variation under the rules may be subject to arbitration whereas a separate agreement accepting a quotation for the proposed variation will not be.

Alternatively, the contractor may wish to be paid on a cost reimbursement basis, but this is likely to be more expensive because of the difficulty of monitoring the contractor's costs and ensuring that he works efficiently. Ideally, the price for variations should be calculated by using the rates on which the original contract price was based so that the client has the benefit – so far as possible – of the original bargain. However, this method will not be in the client's best interests if the relevant rate is uncompetitive, either because it has been 'loaded' by the contractor or simply because of an error in pricing. This point can and does frequently cut both ways causing a loss to the contractor. If this method is to work it is essential that the rates in the tender are checked before it is accepted to spot any such errors or unbalanced rates. Although this is the starting point in JCT 80 and in the rules for the valuation of variations under IFC 84 and in the JCT Minor Building Works Form of Contract (which will be referred to below as 'MW 80') when no other agreement is made, it may be impossible to keep the cost within these bounds for the reasons that will be considered below.

The rules of valuation

12.13 Clause 13.4.1.1 of JCT 80 provides that the quantity surveyor is to value all variations and instructions as to the expenditure of provisional sums. Clause 3.7 of IFC 84 is in similar terms. If a quantity surveyor is named in MW80 – in addition to the architect/supervising officer – then he will in practice be responsible for the valuation of variations, although amendment to the form of contract will be required to give him the requisite authority. The rules for the valuation of variations under JCT 80 do not apply to variations under nominated subcontracts or to provisional sums for which the contractor has tendered under clause 35.2. In those cases, variations are to be valued in accordance with the terms of the subcontract or the rates in the contractor's tender and not those in the contract bills. Nor do the rules apply where a price has been agreed as explained above.

The rules for the valuation of variations under JCT 80

12.14 Under JCT 80 With Quantities, three rules apply to the valuation of variations which are capable of measurement. The first is set out in clause 13.5.1.1 as follows:

> 'Where the work is of similar character to, or is executed under similar conditions as, and does not significantly change the quantity of work set out in the Contract Bills the rates and prices for the work so set out shall determine the valuation.'

The terms of this rule give rise to the following questions. First, does 'similar character' mean work which is identical or work which is of like nature? If it means the former, how is the identical work to be identified? If it means the latter, how is the like work with which the variation is compared to be identified? It has been suggested that the rule should be interpreted so that it covers work which would fall within the same description in the contract bills.[1] Other commentators have suggested that 'similar character' must mean that the verbal description of the item is identical in every respect to that of an item in the contract bills.[2] On the other hand, it has been argued that if the rule meant that the work had to be identical, then it could not apply to any variations which by definition are different from the work contemplated by the items in the bills read with the contract drawings.[3]

12.15 The next question is what is meant by 'similar conditions'. It has been suggested[4] that this must mean the conditions indicated by, or to be inferred from, the way in which the work in the contract bills would be carried out. For example, it is relatively easy to identify changes to conditions such as floor levels, working space and outside working where it can be deduced from the contract bills and drawings how the priced work was to be executed. It has been suggested that this aspect can only refer to conditions which are expressly stated in or can be deduced from the contract bills and drawings because it is not otherwise possible to assume the conditions in which the priced work would be carried out. It has also been suggested that the conditions must also include the time at which the varied work is to be carried out in relation to other contract work. In a contract without provision for fluctuations, the fact that

---

1 See Hibberd *Variations in Construction Contracts* (Collins, 1986) at p 105.
2 Powell-Smith and Sims on *Building Contract Claims* 2nd edn (Blackwell, 1988) at p 103.
3 See Hibberd *Variations in Construction Contracts* (1986) at p 105.
4 *Variations in Construction Contracts* (1986) at p 107.

varied work is being carried out later than other similar work in the contract bills must be taken into account.

12.16 The third aspect under this rule is a 'change in quantity'. To stay within the contract rates the varied work must not significantly change the quantity. The question of what is a significant change must be a matter for the judgment of the quantity surveyor. One approach is to assess the amount of the difference in quantity by reference to the cost. But the test under the rule is whether there has been a significant change in the quantity rather than simply in the cost. In practice, it may be very difficult to isolate a difference in quantity from the character or conditions in which the work is carried out. In the absence of any difference in the character and conditions, a significant difference in quantity must refer to a change which affects the means by which the work is carried out.

12.17 One difference between the practice and the strict legal interpretation of this rule is where there is a change to the dimensions of an item which is not then strictly within 13.5.1.1 because it is not work set out in the contract bills. However, in practice it is common to calculate a pro rata rate by using similar but not identical rates in the bills. The quantity surveyor may be reluctant to value such an item under clause 13.5.1.3 of JCT 80 which applies where the varied work is not of similar character and which requires a fair rate to be applied which is not necessarily based on the prices in the bills.

12.18 The second rule of valuation under JCT 80 is expressed in clause 13.5.1.2:

> 'where the work is of similar character to work set out in the Contract Bills but is not executed under similar conditions thereto and/or significantly changes the quantity thereof, the rates and prices for the work so set out shall be the basis for determining the valuation and the valuation shall include a fair allowance for such difference in conditions and/or quantity.'

This rule first requires the rate in the bills to be identified to which a fair allowance has to be made, either upwards or downwards depending on the effect of the change in the conditions and/or quantity. There are three possible ways to calculate the fair allowance:

(a) calculate the difference between the average or market price of the item to be valued and the item in the bills; or

(b) calculate the difference between the average or market price of the item to be valued and the average or market price of the item appearing in the bills; or

(c) calculate the difference between the price of the bill item and the price that the contractor would have given if the varied item had appeared in the original bills.

The approach in (a) is the basis most favoured by the contractor as it allows him to escape from the contract rate. But the purpose of a 'fair allowance' is to adjust the contract rate in a way that is fair in the context of the bargain as set out in the contract rates. Assuming that the bill rate is not a bad rate, then the fairest allowance, as between the contractor and the employer, must be that calculated on the basis in (c). A 'fair allowance' is to be distinguished from a 'fair rate', which may have nothing to do with the contract rates.

12.19 Finally, clause 13.5.1.3 provides that where work is not of similar character, irrespective of the conditions and quantity, it should be valued at 'fair rates and prices'. This could mean that the work is to be valued without regard to the contract rates but at current market prices. However, in practice it seems that the value is calculated on the basis of what it would have been priced for if it had been included in the tender.

Omissions

12.20 Clause 13.5.2 of JCT 80 provides that where work is omitted it is to be valued at the bill rates. But what if the omission changes the conditions under which the remaining work is to be done? In that case, either clause 13.5.1.2 applies – which provides for a fair allowance to be made where there is a difference in conditions and/or quantity – or possibly clause 13.5.6 which allows a fair valuation to be made where 'the valuation of any work or liabilities directly associated with a variation cannot reasonably be effected ... by the application of clauses 13.5.1 to .5'.

Other rules of valuation

12.21 Any valuation of a variation which can be valued by measurement must:

(a) be measured in accordance with the same principles as those governing the Contract Bills ie SMM 7 unless otherwise stated in the bills;

(b) be subject to any percentage or lump sum adjustments in the contract bills. Percentage or lump sum adjustments may be inserted in the final summary or at the end of a section of work or trade bill. A breakdown of any lump sum adjustments so as to indicate what work they refer to should be obtained before the contract is entered into. If not, clause 13.5.3.2 of JCT 80 appears to require the adjustment to be made to the whole of the work which is impractical. If there is no breakdown, the adjustment should only be made to the section of work or trade to which it applies or if it is a general adjustment, it will have to be applied to the whole of the priced building work;

(c) include an allowance as appropriate for addition or reduction of preliminary items as defined in SMM7 s A except where the valuation relates to an instruction of a provisional sum for defined work.[1] Again without a

1 See General Rules 10.1 to 10.6 of SMM7. Under General Rule 10.4 the contractor is deemed to have allowed for all preliminaries in respect of provisional sums for defined work.

proper breakdown of the preliminaries with details of all of the prices, the quantity surveyor will not be able to make an accurate assessment of the adjustment required to the preliminaries in respect of a particular variation. For example, a time based preliminary item such as scaffolding may be irrelevant to a variation made to the depth of the foundations. A variation may involve preliminary items which were not included in the original tender. Provided the preliminaries are as defined in SMM 7 there is nothing to prevent an allowance being made for such items. But it should be noted that in making a valuation under clause 13.5 no allowance is to be made for any effect on the regular progress of the works or for any direct loss and/or expense which would be recoverable under other conditions of the contract. This seems to make the adjustment of preliminary items under clause 13.5 rather academic.

Dayworks

12.22 Clause 13.5.4 of JCT 80 provides that where additional or substituted work 'cannot properly be valued by measurement' it shall be valued by using dayworks. The first issue is what is meant by the requirement that the work cannot properly be valued by measurement for all work can be measured by time. But this is not an appropriate method of measurement under SMM7 which (subject to express provision to the contrary) is to apply to the measurement of variations. It is therefore in those circumstances that this clause must apply. The dayworks are to be valued in accordance with the 'Definition of the Prime Cost of Daywork' issued by RICS and Building Employers Confederation or, if appropriate, the definition of prime cost issued in respect of a specialist trade together with the percentage additions set out in the relevant Contract Bills.

12.23 Payment for dayworks is subject to the proviso that vouchers specifying the daily time spent, the workmen's names and the plant and materials used are delivered by the end of the week following that in which the work was carried out. Non-compliance with this proviso may prevent the contractor recovering payment at dayworks rates, but it cannot relieve the employer from his overriding obligation to pay for the work which has been authorised and carried out on his behalf. As no other clause provides for the valuation of the work, it is suggested that the contractor would in those circumstances be entitled to payment of a reasonable sum, not exceeding what he would have received on the dayworks rate.

12.24 One practical difficulty if the work is vouched for as required by clause 13.5.4.2 is policing the amount of time that the contractor takes in carrying out work on a dayworks basis. This provision appears to be impractical, for how can the architect or his representative accurately check vouchers for the work carried out on a Monday when they do not have to be submitted until the Friday of the following week? The most practical way to ensure that records are checked contemporaneously is to require the contractor to give advance notice to the architect of his intention to keep daywork records for a particular item of work. It is suggested that the contractor would be under an implied obligation to work efficiently and that he should not be entitled to recover payment for excessive time spent on dayworks. But without a high degree of supervision, it is impossible to protect the employer completely in those circumstances.

Effect on other work

12.25 A variation may affect the way in which other work is to be performed under the contract. Provision is made for this in clause 13.5.5 which requires an adjustment to be made to the value of such work as if it was also a variation if the variation 'substantially changes the conditions under which any other work is executed'. This requirement inevitably leads to debate about whether the conditions are changed or remain similar and as to the extent to which conditions are changed by a variation.

Fair value

12.26 A fair value has to be made under clause 13.5.7 of JCT 80 in two sets of circumstances. The first is where the variation involves no additional or substituted work, eg where the access to the site or working hours are changed. The second is where the valuation of the work or liabilities directly associated with a variation cannot be made under the preceding sub-clauses of clause 13.5. In both cases, the scope of what is to be assessed is narrowed by the exclusion of the effect on the regular progress of the works or any loss and expense for which the contractor will be reimbursed under any other provisions in the contract. The effect of this is to limit the claim for fair value to items such as:

(a) the need for preliminary items not covered by SMM7;
(b) transport costs of materials where special journeys are necessary;
(c) re-stocking cost of ordered materials which are no longer required;
(d) costs of removing materials which have been delivered and are no longer required;
(e) management costs incurred because of the particular requirements of the varied work; and
(e) special costs connected to the purchase of a product.

12.27 Clause 30.6 expressly provides for the contractor's right to be present 'where it is necessary to measure work for the purpose of the valuation.' The quantity surveyor has to give the contractor the opportunity to make his own measurements and to take notes whenever such measurement is required. However, the quantity surveyor's obligation is only to give the contractor the opportunity of being present. If the contractor is awkward and unco-operative, there is nothing to stop the quantity surveyor from proceeding unilaterally with the measurement of varied work.

12.28 The JCT 80 Without Quantities Form of Contract contains a number of differences. The first is that variations are valued on a different basis: either from a specification or schedules of work which have been prepared by the architect and priced by the contractor before the contract was made; or a contract sum analysis and a schedule of rates on which the contract sum is based provided by the contractor. In clause 13.5 of this form of contract they are referred to as the 'Contract Documents'. None of these documents may be as comprehensive as priced bills of quantities. For example, they may contain composite items making the measurement of variations under SMM7 impossible. Ideally, they should contain as few composite items as possible.

12.29 The second significant difference is in relation to preliminaries. There is no express provision for allowance to be made for percentage or lump sum adjustments. It is assumed that the rates in the Contract Documents are fully inclusive. But provision is made for any addition or reduction of preliminary items of the type referred to in s A of SMM 7.

The rules of valuation under IFC 84

12.30 The rules are in effect a rather more simplified version of those under JCT 80. It is apparent from clause 3.7 that the agreement of a price between the contractor and the employer is the preferred option. Otherwise the main difference is that the variations are to be valued on the basis of either a priced specification, priced contract bills, contract sum analysis or schedule of rates depending on the option taken by the parties. The first rule of valuation is set out in clause 3.7.3:

> 'for work of a similar character to that set out in the priced document the valuation shall be consistent with the relevant values therein making due allowance for any change in the conditions under which work is carried out and/or significant change in the quantity of work so set out.'

Different words are used compared to JCT 80. For instance, the clause uses the term 'due allowance' instead of 'fair allowance'. There are also changes in the words used in clause 3.7.4 which provides that a 'fair valuation' shall be made where there is no work of similar character or the valuation cannot reasonably be made by using the prices in the priced document. The use of the terms 'due allowance' and 'fair valuation' suggest that a similar distinction is to be drawn as between 'a fair allowance' and 'a fair rate' in clause 13.5 of JCT 80. But it is possible that the term 'a fair valuation' used in clause 3.7.4 might mean something different to 'a fair rate'; for why else would different words have been used. But the terms used in IFC 84 have to be construed in the context of that agreement alone. In practice, the quantity surveyor is likely – as under the JCT 80 – to decide a fair rate by calculating the rates which would have been used in the tender rather than current market rates.

12.31 The other apparent difference is that when it is appropriate for variations to be valued on a dayworks basis, there is no express provision requiring the contractor to provide the information to the quantity surveyor as he has to under JCT 80. In order to remove any possible difficulty this may cause, it is suggested that the form is amended to require the contractor to provide such details promptly to the quantity surveyor. Indeed, it may be difficult for the quantity surveyor to assess whether dayworks will produce a fair valuation unless he has had the opportunity of checking that the records really show the time spent and plant and materials used.

Valuation of variations under MW 80

12.32 The rules of valuation in MW 80 are the most flexible. It states that variations 'shall be valued by the architect/supervising officer on a fair and reasonable basis using, where relevant, prices in the priced specification/ schedule or schedule of rates'. It also gives the architect/supervising officer the power to agree a price with the contractor instead of making such a valuation. This may be appropriate where there are no comparable rates or prices in those documents. In this respect an architect/supervising officer is given far wider powers in valuing or negotiating a price than his counterparts under the IFC 84 or JCT 80 forms. However the architect/supervising officer should ensure that he actually has his client's authority before doing so.

Expenditure of provisional sums

12.33 The rules of valuation under JCT 80, IFC 84 and MW 80 apply equally to provisional sums, although in practice these are often the subject of a fixed price agreement made in advance, based on the subcontractor or the contractor's quotation.

LOSS AND EXPENSE

12.34 Under clause 26 of JCT 80, it is for the architect to decide whether the contractor is entitled to claim loss and expense because the regular progress of the works has been disrupted by one of the causes listed under clause 26.2. The quantity surveyor's task, if instructed by the architect, is to ascertain the amount of loss and expense which is or has been incurred by the contractor. Although the architect may do this himself, in practice, the quantity surveyor is frequently instructed to deal with claims for loss and expense. It is the quantity surveyor's task to ascertain, ie to be certain of the loss and expense that the contractor claims to have incurred. Before dealing with the quantity surveyor's approach, it may be helpful to set out the legal principles which govern this type of claim.

12.35 The leading case is *FG Minter v Welsh Health Technical Services Organisation*[1] in which the Court of Appeal considered the legal basis of a loss and expense claim. The issue was whether the contractor and nominated subcontractors, who had successfully claimed loss and expense under the contract, were also entitled to claim for interest and, if so, from which date. The question turned on the meaning to be given to the words 'direct loss and/or expense' under clauses 11(6) and 24(1)(a) of the 1963 Edition of the JCT

---

1 [1980] 13 BLR 1.

Standard Form of Building Contract. The interest claimed was the interest incurred by the contractor when he had to borrow or use his own money to pay for the loss and expense for which he was entitled to be reimbursed.

The Court of Appeal held that the interest incurred on the money borrowed and spent on loss and expense was recoverable as part of the direct loss and expense incurred because of the employer's default. It was held that 'direct loss and/or expense' was the same as the damage which was recoverable for breach of contract under the first head in *Hadley v Baxendale*.[1] That is 'direct damage which flows naturally from the breach without any intervening cause and independently of special circumstances'. However, interest was only recovered for the period between the loss and expense being incurred and the date on which the contractor made an application for reimbursement. This finding was based on the interpretation of the 1963 form of contract which referred to an application being made when loss and expense had been incurred. This provision was altered when JCT 80 was drafted so that an application for loss and expense made under clause 26 will apply both to what has already been incurred and subsequent losses.

12.36 Loss and expense is commonly claimed under the following heads:

(a) additional site overheads or 'prelims' incurred because of a prolongation of the works;
(b) increased cost of labour and materials;
(c) plant;
(d) loss of productivity or uneconomic working caused by changes in the programme of work and the need to reduce delay;
(e) loss of profits;
(f) head office overheads incurred because of the increased commitment of time and resources;
(g) financing charges on the additional costs incurred because of a variation or disruption.

Increased preliminaries

12.37 Claims for increased preliminaries are frequently calculated on the basis of the costs set out in the contract bills which are time based and which are then multiplied by the period of delay. There are (at least) two factual difficulties about this approach in that the preliminary rates are based on the contractor's estimate and not on his actual costs and because some or all of the preliminaries may not actually be incurred during the prolongation of the contract. The view of some quantity surveyors is that this can only be calculated by examining the contractor's cost records. Difficulties may also arise in identifying the time based elements in the contractor's preliminaries. For example, the costs of providing supervision may be governed more by the volume of work than the time taken to complete it. Staff may be itinerant

1 [1854] 9 Ex 341.

between several sites. It may be necessary to consider the terms of engagement of individual members of staff to see whether a claim for the cost of their time is justified and how that cost is calculated. Items such as the costs of insurance or bonds may not be time based at all but relate to the volume of the contractor's turnover. Nevertheless the claim for increased preliminaries is usually the least controversial head of claim, providing that liability for the delay is established. The proof and calculation of the other heads of claim usually gives rise to greater difficulties.

Inflation

12.38 Claims for increased costs are often calculated on the increased cost of the resources used during the period of delay. The correct way to calculate such costs is to compare the pattern of expenditure incurred during the whole of the contract, including the delay, with what the expenditure would have been had there been no such delay.

Plant

12.39 There are two ways in which this type of claim can be calculated: value or cost. The first may be appropriate where the contractor has not been able to use his plant profitably because of delay caused to the works. In the latter case the cost may be based on the cost of hiring the plant, if this is necessary, or the cost of depreciation. The distinction was recently considered by His Honour Judge Humphrey Lloyd QC in *Alfred McAlpine Homes North Ltd v Property and Land Contractors Ltd.*[1] In the arbitration of a contractor's claim for loss and expense, although it had actually been owned by the contractor the arbitrator had awarded the cost of hiring the plant relying on the RICS Schedule of Basic Plant Charges, which make no distinction as to whether the plant is hired or owned by the contractor.

The court held that 'Clause 26 of JCT 80 requires the architect or quantity surveyor (or arbitrator) to ascertain what was the actual direct loss or expense and not a notional or hypothetical amount, using the method adopted by the arbitrator.' Hire charges would have been recoverable if there had been a finding that the contractor could have hired out the plant or had been obliged to hire it in.

> 'Where plant is owned by the contractor which would not have been hired or which was not able to be hired out the ascertainment of loss and expense must be on the basis of the true cost to the contractor and must not be hypothetical or notional amounts. An ascertainment needs to take account of the substantiated cost of capital and depreciation but will (or may) not include elements which are included in hire rates and which are calculated, for example, on the basis ... [that] the plant will be remunerative for only some of [the] time and at other times will be off hire. Hire rates are usually higher for that reason alone and also, because the rates are overall rates and therefore include elements which may not be incurred by a

1 [1995] 76 BLR 59.

contractor owning the plant ... [on] hire, their application over a period of any consequence will almost certainly produce figures higher than the true loss or expense incurred by the contractor whose own plant is tied up for the same period.'[1]

Head office overheads

12.40 Two types of claim are recognised under this head where there is a prolongation of the contract period. The first is for what have been described as 'unabsorbed overheads'. This refers to the fixed running expenses of the contractor's business which he expects to recover by earning a margin of gross profit on his turnover. The logic behind this type of claim is that the contractor is not able to reduce the fixed overheads by employing his resources to generate turnover on other contracts because of the uncertain nature of the delay caused to the completion to the works and thus he suffers a shortfall because of the consequent reduction to his turnover. This type of claim is to be distinguished from the claim for the recovery of increased overheads because of a prolongation or disruption to the contract and the contractor allocating more overhead expenditure to the work than he contemplated when the contract was made. In the latter case the authorities show the loss has to proved and no assistance can be derived from the use of formulae or assumptions as to the expenditure of overheads.

The Hudson formula

12.41 There are various ways to calculate the claim for 'unabsorbed overheads'. The first and most simple method is to use the 'Hudson' formula. This is defined by the percentage included in the contract sum for head office overheads and profits. The sum produced is then divided by the number of weeks allowed for the completion of the work under the contract and the rate per week is then multiplied by the period of delay. There are a number of drawbacks to this method of calculation:

(a) proving that the contract sum was based on the inclusion of the percentage claimed for head office overheads and profits;

(b) showing that such a percentage could have been recovered if there had been no delays;

(c) by taking a percentage of the contract price, the amount of overheads and profits claimed may be overstated. To avoid duplication, the percentage contained in the contract price for overheads should be deleted ie H/O + P % in Contract Sum × (Contract sum – H/O + P %) divided by contract period and then multiplied by the period of delay;

(d) adjustment is necessary to allow for the recovery of overheads and profit on any additional sums paid for variations. As stated the formula assumes that there is no change in the contract price;

---

1 [1995] 76 BLR 59 at 93.

(e) the formula also ignores the point that the contractor must take reasonable steps to mitigate his loss by deploying his resources elsewhere during a period of delay.

The Emden formula

12.42 Alternatively, there is the 'Emden' formula. This takes the head office percentage by dividing the whole of the total overhead costs of the contractor's organisation by the total turnover. That percentage is applied to the contract sum which is then divided by the contract period. The weekly figure is then applied to the period of delay.

The Eichleay formula

12.43 Another similar approach is to apply what is known as the 'Eichleay' formula. This assumes that the contractor is entitled to recover a proportion of the total overheads incurred by his organisation as a whole over the actual contract period. The proportion is fixed by the ratio that the value of the contract bears to the contractor's total turnover during the same period. The figure is divided by the contract period to produce a daily or weekly rate which is then applied to the period of delay. It assumes that the contractor's contracts are all priced on the same basis and that they all perform equally well in producing sufficient gross profits to cover the overheads. No allowance is made for possible changes in market conditions.

The application of formulae

12.44 All of the formulae calculate the overheads on a time basis and do not make any allowance for the additional commitment of managerial staff caused by disruption to a contract as opposed to delay. The use of one or other of the above formulae have received a mixed reception from the courts. In *Tate & Lyle v GLC*,[1] the issue was whether the plaintiffs were entitled to recover damages for managerial time spent dealing with the effects of the defendants' negligence. This was claimed as a percentage of the costs claimed for additional dredging work which had been necessitated by the defendants' negligence. There was no evidence to show exactly how much time was spent dealing with the work. The judge accepted that managerial time had been spent in dealing with the remedial works and held that the loss of such time was recoverable in principle but refused to allow the claim without specific evidence of the amount of time that was involved:

> 'I have no doubt that the expenditure of managerial time in remedying an actionable wrong done to a trading concern can properly form the subject matter of a head of special damage. In a case such as this it would be wholly unrealistic to assume that no such additional managerial time was in fact expended. I would also accept that it must be extremely difficult to quantify. But modern office arrangements permit of the recording of time spent by managerial staff on

---

1 [1982] 1 WLR 149 (later reversed on other grounds by the House of Lords).

particular projects. I do not believe that it would have been impossible for the plaintiffs in this case to have kept some record to show the extent to which their trading routine was disturbed by the necessity for continual dredging sessions. In the absence of any evidence about the extent to which this occurred the only suggestion ... is that I should follow Admiralty practice and award a percentage on the total damages.... While I am satisfied that this head of damage can properly be claimed, I am not prepared to advance into an area of pure speculation when it comes to quantum.'[1]

The *Tate & Lyle* case demonstrates that the formulae are inappropriate to use in the case of a disruption as opposed to a prolongation type of claim. In such a case the additional management time must be proved by reference to the contractor's internal records of the time spent by its staff. In the recent case of *Babcock Energy Limited v Lodge Sturtevant Limited*[2] in which a claim for the loss of managerial time was made in an action for breach of contract, the trial judge was prepared to accept what he described as 'very general' evidence to the effect that the staff whose time had been recorded against the project in question would have been fully and gainfully employed elsewhere.

12.45 The Emden formula was used in *J F Finnegan v Sheffield City Council*[3] where the issue was whether it should be applied to the whole of the contractor's costs of which two-thirds was made up of subcontractors or only those relating to his own directly employed workforce. The application of the formula as a method of calculating the contractor's loss was not in issue. The judge found that the percentage allowed in the contract for overheads and profits was 5 per cent on a 25-week contract and that the overheads expenditure over the overrun period of 34.5 weeks was not funded by the percentage allowed in the contract. He held that the overheads related to both direct and subcontracted labour and that the contractor was entitled to claim for the loss of overheads on the whole of the contract cost on the basis of the overhead and profit percentage based on a fair annual average, multiplied by the contract sum and the period of the delay in weeks, divided by the contract period.

12.46 In the *Alfred McAlpine Homes North*[4] case, loss of overheads and profits were claimed under clause 26 of JCT 80 on three alternative bases: a calculation using the Emden formula, the overheads actually expended and not recovered during the extended period of the works, and an assessment of the overhead and profit that the contractor would have recovered on an alternative project which did not in fact take place. The arbitrator had awarded overheads and profits on the basis of the difference between the overheads expended and those recovered under the contract. The contractor was unusual in that it only performed one contract at a time and it was therefore easier to see the

1 [1982] 1 WLR 149 at 152E–H.
2 [1994] 41 Con LR 45.
3 [1988] 43 BLR 124. Although the judgment referred to the 'Hudson' formula it was in fact the 'Emden' formula which was applied.
4 [1995] 76 BLR 59.

difference in the recovery of overheads caused by the delay to the completion of the contract. However, the court held that even if it had not been such a company but had traded normally it would have been entitled to recover as a loss the shortfall in the contribution that the volume of work was expected to have made towards the fixed costs but which was not made because of a reduction in the volume and revenue. This is closely analogous to the calculation made under the Eichleay formula. The court held that any loss caused by the delay had to be proved as a matter of fact:

> 'If a contractor's overall business is not diminished during the period of delay so that whether, for example, as a result of an increase of work on the contract in question arising from variations etc or for other reasons, there will be a commensurate contribution towards the overheads which offsets any supposed loss, or if, as a result of other work, there is no reduction in overall turnover so that the cost of the fixed overheads continues to be met from other sources, there will be no loss attributable to the delay. Put another way, this aspect is brought out in the comparable proposition that the contractor has to show that there were no means of reducing the unrecovered cost of the fixed overheads in the circumstances in which he found himself as a result of the events giving rise to the delay.'[1]

Loss of profit

12.47 Claims for loss of profits are made on the similar basis to those for overheads; that because of the delay in completing the contract the contractor has lost the opportunity to earn profits from deploying his resources on other projects. In practice these claims are subject to similar problems of proof and analysis. The view taken by some quantity surveyors is that loss of profits cannot be claimed as part of the direct loss and expense incurred by the contractor. It is suggested by the authors that this view is erroneous as such a loss – if proved – must fall within the first head of *Hadley v Baxendale*.

Loss of productivity

12.48 It may be possible to show that the actual labour and plant costs have exceeded what was originally anticipated and planned. It may be difficult if not impossible to prove that the extra expenditure is attributable to the disruption caused by a matter for which the employer is responsible. It is therefore common to make a 'rolled up' or 'global' claim in respect of excess labour and plant costs. This has been the subject of a number of court decisions.

12.49 In *London Borough of Merton v Stanley Hugh Leach Ltd*,[2] the court was asked to consider a number of questions arising from an arbitration under the 1963 JCT Form of Contract, including whether a contractor could recover loss and expense 'when it is not possible for the contractor to state in respect in any alleged event the amount of loss and/or expense attributable'. The court held that such a claim could 'only be made in case where the loss or expense

---

1 [1995] 76 BLR 59 at 87.
2 [1985] 32 BLR 51.

attributable to each head of claim cannot in reality be separated and ... where apart from that practical impossibility the conditions are satisfied in relation to each head of claim'.

12.50 The presentation of such global claims has been viewed more critically since that decision. In *Wharf Properties v Eric Cummine Associates*,[1] the Privy Council had to consider whether such a claim should be allowed to continue in circumstances in which the plaintiff had not pleaded the causal link between the delays for which loss was claimed and the alleged breaches of contract. It was held that the *Leach* case was only authority for allowing a claim to be made where it was difficult or impossible to make an accurate apportionment of the extra costs between the various causes of the delay or disruption. Where the contractor is not able to separate the effects of disruption between a cause for which he is responsible and a cause for which he is entitled to be reimbursed, this may prove fatal to his claim for loss and expense. Although *Wharf Properties* was concerned with the way in which a claim had to be pleaded, similar principles must apply when a quantity surveyor is instructed to ascertain a claim for disruption.[2]

12.51 This point was considered most recently by His Honour Judge Humphrey Lloyd QC in *Bernhard's Rugby Landscapes Ltd v Stockley Park Consortium Ltd.*[3] The court had to consider an application to amend the statement of claim to include what were global delay claims in respect of variations which had been made under an engineering contract which was based on the ICE Conditions (5th edition). It was part of the plaintiff's case that the variations which had been made to the works had caused disruption and delays and had thereby increased his costs and that he was entitled to claim for the difference between the costs he would have incurred had there been no variations and his actual costs. The court found that this was a total cost claim and that the plaintiff had failed to indicate in its pleading the variations which it contended were crucial in causing the excess costs to be incurred. Leave to amend was therefore refused.

Interest/finance charges

12.52 It is now well established that contractors may recover as part of the direct loss and/or expense the interest charges they have had to pay on the other additional costs which are recoverable. The Court of Appeal in *Rees & Kirby Ltd v Swansea City Council*[4] extended the award of interest to include compound interest incurred by the contractor on such extra costs which should run until he was actually reimbursed. This case concerned a claim under the 1963 JCT Form of Contract. The court held that the contractor should expressly refer to financing costs in his application for loss and expense. This is not strictly

1 [1991] 52 BLR 1.
2 See the commentary on the *Wharf Properties* case at [1991] 52 BLR 6.
3 [1997] 82 BLR 39.
4 [1985] 30 BLR 1.

required under JCT 80 but to avoid uncertainty it would be wise for a contractor to do so.

The quantity surveyor's approach to loss and expense claims

12.53 It is possible to summarise briefly the way in which the quantity surveyor should approach a claim for loss and expense in the light of the principal cases discussed above:

(a) The first and most important point is that the quantity surveyor's task is to ascertain the loss and expense which the contractor has incurred. This means that the quantity surveyor must be satisfied on the evidence produced by the contractor that losses have actually been suffered or costs incurred by reason of the matters for which the contractor is entitled to claim under clause 26 of JCT 80 or the equivalent provisions of other forms of contract.

(b) It follows that the quantity surveyor should expect to see the contractor's records in order to substantiate his claim for delay and disruption and the loss or expense claimed. Under clause 26.1.3, the contractor is obliged to provide such details as are reasonably necessary for the quantity surveyor to ascertain the loss and expense claimed. If a quantity surveyor is not satisfied with the contents of the contractor's application, he should not hesitate to demand further details under this provision.

(c) Claims for loss and expense should be ascertained as soon as practicable because the contractor is entitled to be reimbursed in the interim certificates. As the contractor is entitled to claim compound interest on such costs until they are reimbursed, it is not in the client's interests for the ascertainment of loss and expense to be delayed. In order to reduce the interest that will run, it may be advisable for the quantity surveyor to recommend to the architect that a payment is made on account pending the final determination of such a claim.

(d) In carrying out his duty of ascertaining the claim for loss and expense, the quantity surveyor is required to deal fairly with the contractor and at the same time to protect his client's interests. However, there are limits in practice as to how far the quantity surveyor should maintain his impartiality in considering the contractor's claims. In many cases the process of ascertaining the claim will take the form of negotiation between the quantity surveyor and his opposite number in the contractor's organisation. In those circumstances, he should argue his client's case. However if the negotiations do not lead to an agreement, it is suggested that the quantity surveyor is obliged to consider the matter objectively when making his recommendation to the architect.[1]

---

1 See Powell-Smith and Sims, *Building Contract Claims* 2nd edn (Blackwell Science, 1988) at p 343.

FINAL ACCOUNT

12.54 It is the quantity surveyor's task under clause 30.6.1 of JCT 80, if so instructed by the architect, to receive all the documents which the contractor is required to produce within six months of Practical Completion and within three months thereafter to prepare a final account. Similar provision is made under clause 4.5 of IFC 84. There are slight differences in the terminology and procedure under the two contracts. Under JCT 80, the quantity surveyor (if so instructed) is to ascertain any loss and expense claimed and is to prepare a statement of all adjustments to be made to the contract sum in accordance with clause 30.6.2. Under IFC 84 clause 4.5, the quantity surveyor is (if so instructed) to prepare a statement of all final valuations of variations and provisional sums and the computations of the adjusted contract sum of which copies are to be sent forthwith to the contractor. The intervals allowed between the completion of these computations and the issue of the final certificate by the architect – subject to the completion of the contractor's obligations to make good any defects which occur during the Defects Liability Period – is two months under JCT 80 and 28 days under IFC 84.

In practice, the timetable provided in the contracts may break down because, for instance, the contractor fails to produce the requisite documents within the time allowed. Although such a failure would constitute a breach of contract by the contractor, it would not prevent the quantity surveyor from proceeding with the preparation of the final account after the documents are received, and in practical terms it is most likely that it will be the contractor who suffers meanwhile by losing the use of, or interest on, any monies that may be due to him. On the other hand, if a balance is due to the employer, he may be entitled to claim damages for the loss of interest.

In practice, the quantity surveyor is likely to meet the contractor while he is preparing the final account in order to discuss and hopefully resolve any differences. If any alterations to the variation account are required, these should be checked with the architect and the final account should be corrected and the contractor should be asked to sign a copy to indicate his agreement or to confirm the final figure by letter. A copy should be sent to the client with any necessary explanations. If there are any matters that the contractor does dispute, he has to commence proceedings or arbitration before or within 28 days after the final certificate is issued.

COST CONTROL

12.55 This is a crucial function for the quantity surveyor to perform during the course of the contract. Accurate estimates in advance of proposed variations may enable the client to ensure that the work is completed within budget. But there are limits to the quantity surveyor's ability to control costs under a building contract. In the unreported case of *Aubrey Jacobus & Partners v Gerrard*,[1] His Honour Judge Stabb QC observed:

> '... it is suggested that the quantity surveyor was under a duty to monitor or control the costs and advise the client. I am satisfied that no such duty exists. The architect is the team leader: he is primarily responsible for the design and for the cost of it. If called upon, the quantity surveyor is there to provide information as to cost but not in my view to monitor or control it by carrying out checks at regular intervals as was suggested.'

12.56 The quantity surveyor owes a duty to his client to exercise proper skill and care in making valuations and ascertaining claims for loss and expense as demonstrated in a number of older authorities. In *Tyrer v District Auditor for Monmouthshire*,[2] the plaintiff who had been employed as a quantity surveyor by Monmouthshire county council was surcharged for overpayments which he had approved to a contractor which had gone into liquidation. It was found that the surcharges were amply justified on the evidence. The district auditor had found that the plaintiff had negligently approved excessive quantities and prices in some of the contracts that the county council had made with the contractor and that in one particular contract he had made a simple mathematical error in an interim certificate which he had issued.

12.57 In an earlier case, *London School Board v Northcroft*,[3] the clients sued their quantity surveyor for alleged negligence in respect of clerical errors which had led to overpayments to the contractor of £118 and 15 guineas on contracts worth £12,000. It was admitted that the overpayments had been caused by the errors made by an experienced clerk who had been responsible for hundreds of calculations, who was not alleged to be incompetent and whose errors could only have been spotted by someone who had carried out all of the calculations. The court rejected the claims on the grounds that these two blunders did not prove that the quantity surveyor had been negligent. In the words of AL Smith J, 'I do not think a building owner ought to complain if he never meets with a worst fate than that the work costs more than £300 above what was originally contemplated'. One wonders whether a court would be so lenient now in respect of arithmetical errors by a quantity surveyor which led to overpayment being made to the contractor.

If a quantity surveyor is negligent in carrying out his duties under the contract so that the contractor does not receive a proper valuation of varied work or loss and expense, he may be liable for the costs of any claims which are then brought against his client for breach of the contract. The question of whether he also may be liable to the contractor or to any other party is considered below.

---

1 See *Jackson & Powell on Professional Negligence* (Sweet & Maxwell, 1997), p 206 footnote 44.

2 [1973] 230 EG 973.

3 [1889] reported in *Hudson's Building Contracts* 4th edn (1914) vol II p 147.

DUTIES TO THIRD PARTIES

12.58 There are no reported cases in which the quantity surveyor's liability to parties other than his client has been specifically considered. There are, however, a number of cases in which the courts have considered the scope of the duties owed by an architect or engineer to the contractor or subcontractor or to other third parties. It is necessary to look at these to see whether and if so what liabilities may arise between a quantity surveyor and another party in tort.

12.59 It is well established that architects and other building professionals owe a general duty of care not to cause personal injury to those who they could foresee could be injured by their negligence. This may apply in relation to the design of the building work, but it is difficult to envisage the circumstances in which the quantity surveyor carrying out his duties to his client under a building contract could be liable in negligence for personal injury to a third party. It is also well established that an architect or other building professional owes a duty to exercise reasonable care so as not to cause damage to another person's property, such as an adjacent building. Again, it is difficult to imagine the circumstances in which a quantity surveyor could be liable for damage of this kind.

Where a quantity surveyor is responsible for defects in work for which he is responsible under his contract of engagement he is not liable to subsequent owners for defects, because the loss – the cost of repair or diminution in value – is characterised as economic loss which cannot be recovered in tort except in special circumstances. The one major exception to this rule is where the quantity surveyor has been involved in work relating to the provision of a dwelling where he may be liable to subsequent occupiers under the Defective Premises Act 1972 if the building is not fit for habitation.

12.60 There remain three situations in which a quantity surveyor could be liable for economic loss caused to someone who is not his client. The first is under the complex structure theory. This may allow the cost of repairs to one part of a building to be recovered if it can be distinguished from another part of the structure. An example that has been given is of a central heating boiler which explodes causing damage not only to itself but to other parts of the building. The theory has been applied in only one reported case of *Jacobs v Moreton & Partners.*[1] This is considered at **10.17**.

A further exception to the rule against allowing recovery for economic loss is where expenditure is necessary to avoid liability to third parties. For example, the cost of propping up a building to prevent it collapsing and causing injury or damage to a neighbouring property. This exception was applied in the case of *Morse v Barratt (Leeds) Ltd.*[2]

---

1 [1994] 72 BLR 92.
2 [1993] 9 Const LJ 158.

The third and most important exception to the rule preventing the recovery of damages for economic loss for negligence is under the principles decided in *Hedley Byrne v Heller & Partners*.[1] This case established that where someone was asked to provide information or advice in circumstances in which he knew (or ought to know) that the person to whom such information or advice was given would be likely to and did rely upon such information or advice, he owed a duty to that person to exercise reasonable skill and care unless this had been negatived by a disclaimer of liability, as occurred in that case. This would seem to be the most likely basis upon which a quantity surveyor could be found liable to third parties such as contractors or subcontractors who may rely upon the information he provides in tender documentation or upon the proper performance of his duties under a construction contract in valuing variations and ascertaining claims for loss and expense.

12.61 In considering the possible liability of a quantity surveyor for economic loss, it is helpful to distinguish the duties that could arise in relation to the preparation of bills of quantities and other tender documents from those which might arise after the quantity surveyor's client has entered into a contract with the contractor. In the case of a fixed price contract in which the contractor is bound to perform the work indicated in the tender documents and therefore takes the risk if they are inaccurate, it is not difficult to foresee that a claim could arise in tort against the consultant who had prepared the documents negligently. The basis for such a claim is by applying the principle established in *Hedley Byrne v Heller* on the grounds that the consultant responsible for preparing the tender documents would in those circumstances be expected to appreciate that the contractor would be relying upon the information provided, which he might be unable to check for himself, and that the contractor would suffer loss if his tender was based on false or inaccurate information.

12.62 This principle has been applied in Canada in cases concerning inaccurate information provided for tenders in which claims for negligence have been brought successfully by contractors against the engineers responsible for their preparation. The leading case is *Edgeworth Construction Ltd v N D Lea & Associates*.[2] The plaintiff contractor had been successful in its bid for a contract to construct a section of highway. An express term in the contract provided that any representations in the tender documents were provided only for the information of bidders and were not warranted by the employer. The contractor alleged that it had lost money on the contract because of errors in the specifications and drawings which had been prepared by the defendant engineers. The action was struck out by the lower courts on the grounds that the engineers did not owe the contractor a duty of care and that its only remedy was under its contract with the employer.

The Supreme Court of Canada held that liability for a negligent misstatement arose where a person makes a representation where he knows that another

1 [1964] AC 465.
2 [1993] 66 BLR 56.

party will rely upon it. The engineers knew that the purpose of supplying the tender information was to allow the tenderers to prepare a price to be submitted for the contract. It was held that it was reasonable for the contractor to rely upon the information provided by the engineers in preparing its bid and that it had suffered loss as a result. While the representations made as to the design of the work also became the representations of the employer when the contract was made, they did not cease to be representations made by the engineers on which the contractor continued to rely. Neither the contractor nor the employer had assumed the risk of errors in the engineers' work. While the express term in the contract may have excluded the employer's liability for errors in the design, it did not purport to exclude the liability of the engineers. They could themselves have disclaimed responsibility for any errors in the design but had not done so. It was held that the contractor was in those circumstances entitled to bring a claim in tort against the engineers notwithstanding that the claim was in effect for economic loss.

The leading judgment of McLachlin J made a number of points which could apply equally to the position of a quantity surveyor who has drawn up bills of quantities or other tender information carelessly:

> 'One important policy consideration weighs against the engineering firm. If the engineering firm is correct, then contractors bidding on construction contracts will be obliged to do their own engineering. In the typically short period allowed for the filing of tenders – in this case about two weeks – the contractor would be obliged, at the very least, to conduct a thorough professional review of the accuracy of the engineering design and information, work which in this case took over two years. The task would be difficult, if not impossible. Moreover, each tendering contractor would be obliged to hire in its own engineers and repeat a process already undertaken by the owner. The result would be that the engineering for the job would be done not just once, by the engineers hired by the owner, but a number of times. This duplication of effort would doubtless be reflected in higher bid prices, and ultimately, a greater cost to the public which ultimately bears the cost of road construction. From the economic point of view, it makes more sense for one engineering firm to do the engineering work, which the contractors in turn are entitled to rely on, absent disclaimers or limitations on the part of the firm.'[1]

This decision was made on the preliminary issue of whether the engineers could owe the contractor a duty of care. There are various difficulties in applying this decision to a particular set of facts. No indication was given in the report of the case or in the judgments of what were the alleged errors in design which were held to constitute representations on which the contractor had relied. The decision appears to have ignored the history of contracting in that for many years contractors have been prepared to tender for contracts without the owner warranting that the specified design can be built. It also appears to ignore the fact that in most cases the contractors bidding for a contract have more expertise as to how a building is to be constructed than the designer retained by the client. Building and engineering contractors usually retain a large staff of

1 [1993] 66 BLR 56 at 69.

quantity surveyors and estimators and other professionals to study the proposed design and to prepare the pricing of a tender. If the architect or engineer was to be liable to the contractor because his design was not buildable, this could cause a conflict with his duty to his client. Finally, the judgments do not refer to the judgments of the Court of Appeal in the *Pacific Associates* case (considered in detail at **12.65**) in which the duties owed by a building professional to a contractor were reviewed. For these reasons, it would seem that the decision in the *Edgeworth* case may be of only limited assistance when the duty of a quantity surveyor to a prospective contractor in respect of tender information is to be considered.

Liability under a construction contract

12.63 In *Arenson v Arenson*,[1] which was a case concerning the liability of auditors for share valuations, it was suggested by Lord Salmon that an architect could be liable both to his client and to a contractor in respect of the performance of his tasks under the building contract. The liability to his client arose from the duties owed under the contract of engagement. It was suggested that the architect might also owe a duty to the contractor to exercise reasonable care in issuing certificates because of their proximity on the basis of *Hedley Byrne v Heller*:

> 'In *Sutcliffe v Thakrah*, the architect negligently certified that more money was due than was in fact due, and he was successfully sued for the damage which this had caused to his client. He might, however, have negligently certified that less money was payable than was in fact due and thereby starved the contractor of money. In a trade in which cash flow is especially important, this might have caused the contractor serious damage for which the architect could have been successfully sued.'

12.64 This point was considered under the 1963 JCT contract in the case of *Michael Salliss & Co Ltd v Calil and William F Newman & Associates*.[2] The contractor sued the employer, the architects and the quantity surveyors in relation to a claim for an extension of time. The decision only concerned the preliminary issue as to whether the architects owed the contractor a duty of care in tort in respect of the discharge of their duties under the contract. The judge, His Honour Judge James Fox Andrews QC held that the architects were liable to the contractor on the following grounds:

> 'it is self evident that a contractor who is party to a JCT contract looks to the architect/supervising officer to act fairly as between him and the building employer in matters such as certificates and extensions of time. Without a confident belief that that reliance will be justified, in an industry where cash flow is so important to the contractor, contracting could be a hazardous operation. If the architect unfairly promotes the building employer's interest by low certification or merely fails properly to exercise reasonable care and skill in his certification it is reasonable that the contractor should not only have the right as against the owner to have the

1 [1977] AC 405 at 438.
2 [1987] 13 Con LR 68.

> certificate reviewed in arbitration but also should have the right to recover damages against the unfair architect.'[1]

The court held that the architect owed no duty of care to the contractor in matters such as preparing plans and specifications or deciding whether he should have a survey carried out or should order a variation, because these were all matters in which he was acting exclusively for his client. But the court held that once an architect ordered a variation 'he has to act fairly in pricing it'. As we have discussed in para **12.11**, it is in fact the quantity surveyor who is exclusively responsible for pricing a variation after it has been instructed. In this respect the case is direct authority for the proposition that the quantity surveyor owes the contractor a duty to exercise reasonable care in valuing a variation as much as he owes such a duty to his client under his contract of engagement.

12.65 However, when the *Salliss* case was subsequently considered by the Court of Appeal in *Pacific Associates v Baxter*,[2] its authority was seriously doubted. It is necessary to consider this case in some detail as it is now the leading case on the question of whether a duty of care does arise between the contractor and the architect or engineer administrating the construction contract. The contract in that case was for dredging works under which the defendant engineers were to consider all applications made by the contractor for payment of additional sums caused by unforeseeable difficulties. The engineer had rejected the contractor's claims for additional payments and it brought a claim under the arbitration clause in the contract against the employer which was settled for £10 million. The contractor then brought a claim against the engineers in negligence to recover a further £45 million in respect of the additional costs which they had incurred on the basis that the engineer owed them a duty of care in considering their claim under the contract. A significant factor was that the contract expressly provided that the engineer would not personally be liable to the contractor in respect of the performance of his duties under the contract. The action had been struck out on the basis that it did not constitute a proper cause of action. That decision was upheld by the Court of Appeal.

The main issue in the case was whether it was appropriate to extend the principle established in *Hedley Byrne v Heller* to the relationship between the contractor and the engineer under the contract. Two matters were held to be decisive in determining that such a duty should not be extended to that case. The first was that the contract between the contractor and the employer included a comprehensive arbitration clause which enabled the contractor to challenge any decision made by the engineer with which it did not agree. The second factor was the exclusion of liability for the acts or omissions of the engineer which was held to constitute a sufficient disclaimer so as to negate any duty of care which might otherwise have been owed by the engineer to the contractor.

---

1 [1987] 13 Con LR 68 at 78.
2 [1990] 1 QB 993.

The first factor applies equally to the position of a contractor and a quantity surveyor under the JCT forms of contract which allow for any valuation or ascertainment to be challenged by the contractor in an arbitration. Lord Justice Ralph Gibson considered whether the engineer would have owed a duty of care not to cause economic loss to the contractor in certifying or in accepting or rejecting claims under the contract even if there had been no disclaimer. He held that the engineer's position under the contract was quite different to that of the bank providing the reference in *Hedley Byrne v Heller*. The engineer had not been requested by the contractor to provide any particular service. They had only become connected because of the contract made between the contractor and the employer. There was little or no risk of loss being caused to the contractor by the engineer's breach of the alleged duty because of the contractor's right to arbitrate under the contract. Nor was the engineer providing information or advice in respect of matters of which he had information which was not available to the contractor. For those reasons there was not the element of reliance which was necessary to establish liability under *Hedley Byrne v Heller*.

12.66 To summarise, it would seem possible that the quantity surveyor may owe a duty of care to a contractor or subcontractor for errors in his tender documents or in carrying out his duties under the contract in the following circumstances, drawing from the points made in the *Edgeworth* and *Pacific Associates* cases:

(a) where the contractor has no remedy against the employer because liability for such errors or for the failure by the quantity surveyor to perform his duties has been excluded under the contract. This point distinguishes the *Pacific Associates* case from the *Edgeworth* case;

(b) the quantity surveyor has not himself or by the terms of the tender or contract disclaimed responsibility to the contractor. In *Pacific Associates* the exclusion of personal liability under the terms of the contract between the contractor and the employer was a significant, if not, conclusive factor in the judgments given in the Court of Appeal, notwithstanding that the engineers were not a party to that contract. There was no such provision in the *Edgeworth* case;

(c) if a duty of care is established and the contractor also has contractual rights against the employer in respect of the matters alleged against the quantity surveyor, it may be possible to refute liability in negligence unless the contractor is unable to pursue such rights because of the employer's insolvency or failure.

12.67 There remains one further possible basis of liability for a quantity surveyor in tort to a contractor or even to a nominated subcontractor; that of inducing a breach of the contract by the employer or of wrongfully interfering with such a contract. For example, if the quantity surveyor deliberately undervalued the variations for which the contractor was entitled to be paid which might constitute a breach of the building contract. This possibility was raised in the case of *Lubenham v South Pembrokeshire District Council*.[1] The architect under contracts in the JCT 1963 Form had deducted liquidated damages against the sums payable under interim certificates to the contractor. The council was not entitled to make such a deduction under the contracts but it was found that the architect had honestly if mistakenly believed that it was. In the action brought by the contractor following the determination of the contracts, a claim was made against the architects for the sums which were properly due under the interim certificates on the grounds that they had wrongfully procured the council not to pay the sums due in breach of the contracts or had thereby wrongfully interfered with the contracts. The Court of Appeal was prepared to accept that an architect who had issued interim certificates from which deductions were made in breach of the contracts could be liable if he had deliberately misapplied the terms of the contracts with the intention of depriving the contractor of the larger sums to which he would otherwise be entitled. However such a claim could not succeed on the facts found by the trial judge, which were that the deductions had been made under an honest but mistaken interpretation of the contracts.

OTHER DUTIES PERFORMED BY A QUANTITY SURVEYOR

12.68 A number of the functions performed by quantity surveyors outside the usual course of a building contract have been mentioned in passing above and in the previous chapters. The role of the quantity surveyor has adapted to changes in the management and design of building and engineering projects. One role in particular with which quantity surveyors have become associated is that of project management. This has become so important that it is appropriate to consider this subject more fully in a separate chapter.

12.69 Another role which has developed with the growth of design and build contracting is the appointment of the client's quantity surveyor as the employer's agent under such contracts, while the other members of the professional team are often taken on by the contractor after the tender stage.

12.70 Outside the field of construction, quantity surveyors may be appointed to cover a variety of different tasks as indicated in the different fee scales published by RICS. For example, Scale No 46 relates to the loss assessment of damage to buildings by fire and Scale No 47 to the assessment of replacement costs of buildings for insurance, current cost accounting and other purposes.

12.71 One role which is likely to grow in importance is in the adjudication of disputes under non domestic building contracts, introduced by the Housing Grants, Construction and Regeneration Act 1996. The provisions made under this Act have already been summarised in Chapter 9. This topic is considered in

1 [1986] 33 BLR 39.

more detail in Chapter 14 together with the law and practice relating to arbitrations. The quantity surveyor's role in the preparation and defence of contractual claims has already been referred to briefly in Chapter 9. It is not proposed here to deal with this in more detail. The details of the duties and obligations undertaken by a quantity surveyor when undertaking a forensic role as an expert witness are covered in Chapter 7.

12.72 This leaves a variety of other specialist services which are undertaken by quantity surveyors. It is not appropriate to do more than identify these tasks here:

(a) *Grants, capital allowances and tax advice.* Quantity surveyors may be well-placed to advise their clients on the availability of development grants and other incentives as well as the tax consequences of construction. In particular, a quantity surveyor may advise on what items of expenditure in a project will qualify for capital allowances to be claimed against corporation tax and whether or not to elect for the transfer of property to be subject to VAT.

(b) *Insolvency Services.* A quantity surveyor is also well qualified to advise on the completion costs of projects in the event of insolvency and as to whether it is advisable to do so. Advice to insolvency practitioners and financial advisers may take the form of project appraisals and overviews, corporate rescues, receiverships, administrations and liquidations. In one case reported by RICS Insurance Services,[1] a quantity surveyor had been sued by the liquidators of a small subcontracting company for negligent advice as to whether he should adopt the contracts which were in progress and complete them. The quantity surveyor had to work quickly in examining each site and compiling details from the contractor's records which were incomplete. Their advice was that an overall profit of £30,000 could be made if the contracts were completed. Unfortunately this advice proved to be over optimistic and the contracts were completed at an overall loss of £100,000 because of late completion of work on some sites, escalating labour and material costs and the need for remedial work to be undertaken. The quantity surveyors were advised that there were some problems that they could have foreseen which would have made a loss inevitable and they agreed to compromise the claim.

(c) *Facilities management.* This may include the management of building, accommodation, premises and estate. Depending on the requirements of the client, this could involve:
   (i) long-term asset management and planning of capital expenditure;
   (ii) managing the operation of buildings, energy and space management, maintenance, communications and IT;
   (iii) the management of capital projects and staff movements;
   (iv) providing other support services.

---

1 In *Caveat Surveyor II* (RICS Insurance Services Ltd, 1989), p 46.

(d) *IT consultancy.*

(e) *QA consultancy.*

(f) *Development appraisals.*

(g) *Funding advice.*

(h) *Technical auditing.*

(i) *Schedules of condition and dilapidations.* Although these matters would normally come within the province of a building surveyor, the quantity surveyor's experience in pricing and costing work may be relevant and he may also be engaged to assist in these tasks.

Chapter 13

PROJECT MANAGEMENT

PROJECT MANAGER OR PROJECT COORDINATOR?

13.1 There are various different forms of project management, and it is necessary to set them out to avoid confusion. First, there is what is described as construction management, where the client engages a construction manager who may then select the consultants and the contractor and/or subcontractors who will each be retained under contracts with the client. The construction manager is responsible for the overall control of the design and construction throughout the project.

13.2 This should be distinguished from project management, in which the client appoints a project manager who is then responsible for appointing and contracting, with the members of the design team and also, in some cases, the contractors. The project manager is directly responsible to the client for the design and, where he engages the contractor, for the construction of the project. In that case the position is very similar to what is described as 'design and manage', in which a design manager is appointed who then contracts with the other consultants and the contractor and has full control over both the design and construction stages of a project.

13.3 These forms of contract have to be distinguished from project coordination, in which a project coordinator is appointed by the client to liaise with the consultants and the contractor who are all engaged directly by the client. Unfortunately, 'project coordination' in this sense is often confused with 'project management' as defined above. The distinction is crucial not only as to the duties to be performed but as to the contractual relationships which are involved. In the case of project management, the client may have no direct contract with the consultants and possibly the contractor except in the form of collateral warranties and the only direct contractual link is with the construction manager. This confusion is reflected in the 'Project Management Agreement and Conditions of Engagement' published by RICS. The same applies to the RICS Conditions of Engagement for Building Surveying Services which are published with Project Management as a possible Scope of Service to be attached to the Form of Agreement. These are both in fact intended to apply to 'project coordination' and not to project management in either of the forms defined above. A similar distinction was drawn by RICS Insurance Services Ltd. If the project manager appointed other consultants, this service was defined as project management. If the client appointed the other consultants the service was defined as project coordination.

13.4 As quantity surveyors may be appointed to carry out project management as well as project coordination, it is proposed to deal with both in this chapter after considering the RICS form of agreement and conditions of engagement. Finally, the term 'project manager' should not be confused with that of the person in the contractor's organisation who may (erroneously) hold the same title but carry out an entirely different role and who is more accurately described as the contract manager.

The RICS Project Management Agreement and Conditions of Engagement

13.5 A quantity surveyor is free to contract on whatever terms he thinks fit and the Memorandum of Agreement and Conditions of Engagement are not mandatory in any way. They do provide a useful and considered model form of agreement. In considering their terms in more detail, many of the points which may arise under such an appointment in practice will be covered so that this commentary will be relevant to any form of agreement which may be made between a project manager and his client. The current Memorandum of Agreement and Conditions of Engagement are the second edition which were published by RICS together with a Guidance Note in May 1992.

THE SERVICES TO BE PROVIDED BY THE PROJECT MANAGER

13.6 No express definition or list of services is provided in the Memorandum of Agreement. It is intended that a list of the services to be provided will be inserted in Appendix A. The Guidance Note sets out a schedule of possible services with definitions and explanations. Since these are fundamental to the agreement between the client and the project manager, the services listed in the Guidance Note are set out in detail below. The Scope of Service published for use with the RICS Conditions of Engagement and Form of Agreement for Building Surveying Services contains a similar but more concise list of services:

(a) *Site selection.* This is described in terms of liaising with the other consultants in respect of market appraisals, surveys, soil investigations, valuations and models.

(b) *Analysis.* This is described as advising on the need for research and viability studies and coordinating their preparation.

(c) *Agency, valuation, funding and relocation.* This refers to liaison with the client's agents in relation to sources and methods of funding and the acquisition or disposal of any property and on leasing, rating, maintenance, installation of services, insurance and pre-letting arrangements.

(d) *Legal services.* This describes coordinating with the clients' lawyers the preparation of the purchase, leasing and finance agreements and other matters concerning ownership and letting, and understanding and directing the consultants in accordance with all of the contracts.

(e) *Consultant appointments.* This includes a fairly comprehensive range of services, from advising the client as to the need for and recommending the appointment of other consultants; their terms of engagement, including their fees, professional indemnity insurance and any ancillary agreements, such as collateral warranties; advising on the limits of the architect's authority to issue instructions and on the need for a clerk of works or other supervisory staff to be appointed and monitoring the performance of the other consultants, clerk of works and contractors in the performance of their contracts with the client.

(f) *Brief, design and quality control.* This involves the formulation of the design of the project from coordinating with other professionals on the design brief, reporting on design proposals, preferred components, drawings and specifications; ensuring that the consultants review the 'buildability' and the technical design of their proposals with specialist contractors and establishing procedures to ensure that the work complies with the design and specification, to check the standard of workmanship and materials and advise on methods of quality assurance.

(g) *Reporting and meetings.* This refers to the tasks of convening and chairing of the principal project meetings.

(h) *Programming.* This involves preparing, with the other consultants, a master programme to identify the principal activities and the most critical dates and incorporating the contractor's programmes.

(i) *Capital budgeting.* This involves monitoring the preparation by the other consultants of budget costs and presenting feasibility studies to the client for approval and the preparation of a master cost plan.

(j) *Construction economics and financial management.* This heading covers a variety of different activities from advising the commissioning of cost studies of alternative designs and materials; checking that regular valuations and payment certificates are made by consultants under the building contract; obtaining the client's authority for variations; providing forecasts of the final costs and completion dates and arranging for the client to receive any necessary tax advice.

(k) *Cash flow.* This includes preparing, with other consultants, cash flow forecasts, statements of expenditure and checking and recommending payment of certificates.

(l) *Local authority and planning approvals.* This covers dealing, together with the other consultants, with all planning matters as well as health and fire safety approvals.

(m) *Contract procedures*. This includes advising the client, with the other consultants, on the most appropriate procurement methods for contractors and nominated subcontractors, the types of contract to be used and on the selection of tenderers and the tendering process and arranging the execution of the contracts and any collateral warranties. This heading includes matters which would normally be covered by a quantity surveyor prior to the letting of a building contract.

(n) *Contract management*. This covers checking that the consultants are performing their duties under their contracts as well as arranging for the client to place orders for long delivery materials and advising of any work which needs to be carried out under separate direct contracts.

(o) *Building management, commissioning and maintenance*.

(p) *Tenancies and fitting out*. This also includes preparing and carrying out a marketing campaign with the client and the other consultants as well as liaising with the client and solicitors over the terms of leases and monitoring any fitting out by tenants.

Fees for project management services

13.7 These are left to the parties to negotiate and in the Form of Agreement space is provided in Appendix C to insert any schedule of fees that may be agreed. These can be calculated on a percentage basis. Alternatively, provision is made for the payment of a lump sum fee. This may be adjusted in the case of delay to the completion of the project and in that case the anticipated completion date should be inserted in clause 10(c) of the Memorandum of Agreement.

13.8 In the event of the termination of the project manager's appointment or the postponement of the project by the client or by the project manager, provision is made for payment of a fair proportion of the fee and of any expenses reasonably incurred because of the termination or postponement.

13.9 The client may terminate the appointment at any time by giving written notice. The project manager may terminate his appointment when the project is delayed and he is prevented from carrying out his services for more than a period to be specified by the parties. Either side may terminate in the event of the other's breach or failure to remedy a breach of contract which is capable of remedy 30 days after written notice of such breach has been given or in the event of insolvency.

The project manager's obligations

13.10 The starting point is 'the Brief' which is defined as the written brief provided to the project manager prior to the agreement which describes 'the objectives of time, cost, quality and function of the project'. In practice, the project manager may initially discuss with the client what his objectives are so that these can be accurately stated in the Brief. It provides the basis for the project manager's strategy and the criteria by which his success or failure can be judged. The most important general obligations are set out in clause 3 of the Memorandum of Agreement: these are to communicate to the consultants the requirements of the client's Brief; to monitor the progress of design work by reference to the Brief; to monitor and regulate programme and progress; to monitor and use best endeavours to coordinate the efforts of those concerned with the project and to monitor the cost and financial rewards of the project by reference to the client's Brief.

13.11 The personal nature of the skills provided by the project manager is emphasised by the requirement in clause 11 of the Memorandum of Agreement for the project manager to appoint one identified individual as the principal person to undertake the direction and control of his duties and obligations under the agreement. That person may not be changed without the written consent of the client and his replacement has to be approved in writing.

13.12 The specific services which are to be provided by the project manager are set out in Appendix A to the Memorandum of Agreement. Clause 2 of the Memorandum of Agreement provides that the project manager 'shall act as the agent of the Client, and be responsible for the administration, management and communication coordination of the project.' A further Appendix is provided in which the limits of the project manager's authority as his client's agent are set out by stating the matters which require the client's written consent. Examples given in the Guidance Note include making variations to the design or specification of the work, confirming to the architect any instructions above a specific limit in value or which might delay completion of the project, consenting to the contractor or to any consultant assigning all or any part of their work and any delegation of the project manager's duties under the appointment. Some of these matters are also expressly covered by the Articles of Agreement. Clause 4.1 provides that the project manager shall not without the prior written consent of the client give any instruction which would have the effect of varying the project, increase the cost or the time taken to complete it, and clause 4.2 provides that the project manager shall promptly inform the client of any matter which he believes may have or will vary or increase the cost or alter the viability or increase the time taken to complete the project.

13.13 By clause 4 of the Conditions of Engagement, the project manager agrees to provide collateral warranties to any interested third party named by the client at any time until two years after practical completion to the effect that he has or will perform his duties under the agreement with reasonable skill, care and diligence.

13.14 Clause 16 of the Conditions of Engagement provides that copyright in all documents, calculations and data in any form provided by the project manager shall remain vested in him subject to the client's right to copy and use such documents for carrying out the project, repairs and renewals, advertising, lettings and promotion provided the client has paid all fees due to him.

Exclusions and limitations

13.15 Clauses 5 and 6.2 of the Memorandum of Agreement exclude the project manager's liability for:

(a) any forecasts of financial viability which he did not prepare;

(b) the consultants' designs or their technical coordination;

(c) any advice or recommendations provided by any other consultant or adviser appointed by the client;

(d) any loss, injury or damage caused by any defect in any material or any act, omission or insolvency of anyone save the project manager.

13.16 Clause 6.1 of the Memorandum of Agreement limits the project manager's liability to that 'as ought to be covered by the professional indemnity insurance referred to in clause 12 of the Memorandum of Agreement' and that any such liability is limited to the sum there specified as the sum insured. Clause 12 in turn refers to clause 15 of the Conditions of Engagement. This states that the project manager:

> 'shall effect a professional indemnity insurance for the figure stated in clause 12 of the Memorandum of Agreement for each and every claim and if necessary provide evidence of such insurance having been effected, and further shall maintain professional indemnity insurance so long as it remains available at reasonable rates in the market.'

What if the liability arises when the project manager has – in breach of clause 15 of the Conditions of Engagement – allowed his professional indemnity cover to lapse? Clause 6.1(a) refers to 'such liability *as ought to be covered*' [emphasis added] by the insurance referred to in clause 12. This must assume that the project manager complies with clause 15 and that there is such cover in existence. If there is no such cover, why should the project manager's liability be limited at all? Another point of construction is that the express terms do not provide what form of professional indemnity insurance should be effected. These terms pre-suppose (but do not state) that as a member of RICS, the project manager has taken out insurance no less comprehensive than that in the current RICS Professional Indemnity policy in compliance with the Compulsory Bye-Law and Regulations 1997. But as clause 15 does not provide for any specific time-limit, the limitation of liability is not subject to the same objection as the limitation clause in the RICS Terms and Conditions of Engagement for Appointment of Quantity Surveyors which may exclude liability altogether for claims arising more than six years after the quantity surveyor in question has retired.

13.17 It is acknowledged in clause 6.3 that these exclusions and limitations 'shall not be valid insofar as prohibited by statute'. This reflects the effect of the Unfair Contract Terms Act 1977 which renders ineffective any exclusion of liability for death or serious injury caused by negligence (including the breach of any contractual obligation to take or exercise reasonable skill in the performance of the contract) and in respect of any other loss and damage save insofar as the exclusion or limitation satisfies the requirement of reasonableness. This is that 'the term shall have been a fair and reasonable one to be included having regard to the circumstances which were, or ought reasonably to have been, known to or in the contemplation of the parties when the contract was made'.[1] This is considered more fully in paras **9.17** and **9.22**. Although the issue of reasonableness has to be considered on the facts of each particular case, the limitation of liability appears to satisfy that requirement providing the limit of the insurance cover obtained by the project manager is adequate. The limit of the sum insured is left for the parties to agree.

13.18 The exclusion of liability for the forecasts, designs, advice, recommendations of other consultants and for the acts, omissions or insolvency of anyone else does not appear to satisfy the requirement of reasonableness. The essence of the project manager's role is to monitor the performance of the other consultants and the contractors retained by the client. If the project manager should have spotted and reported the default of another consultant or contractor, why should he be exempted from liability for his own breach of contract? This would seem to frustrate one of the main objects of engaging a project manager which is to act as the eyes and ears of the unqualified and possibly inexperienced client. This point was considered in the case of *Chesham Properties Ltd v Bucknall Austin Project Management Services Ltd and Others*[2] which is considered fully below.

The client's obligations

13.19 Apart from paying the project manager's fees, the client's obligations are set out in clause 6 of the Conditions of Engagement. The most important of these are:

(a) providing the project manager with a written Brief;

(b) providing him any necessary information when required;

(c) giving written consent when required for the matters listed in the Appendix;

(d) appointing the other consultants on terms that they should provide any information required by the project manager;

(e) to notify the other consultants of the project manager's authority to act save for the matters listed in the Appendix.

Other matters

13.20 The Conditions of Engagement provide for any disputes not resolved by negotiation or mediation to be referred to arbitration by an arbitrator who is agreed or by one appointed by the Chartered Institute of Arbitrators.

13.21 When Part II of the Housing Grants, Construction and Regeneration Act 1996 is brought into force, various rights will be imported into this

1 Section 11(1) of the Unfair Contract Terms Act 1977.
2 [1996] 53 Con LR 1.

agreement or any other agreement made by a project manager with his client unless the project involves building a residence for the client. These have already been summarised in paras **9.38** and **9.39**. The most important of these is the right to have any dispute referred immediately to adjudication. This provision is discussed in more detail in paras **14.11–14.27**.

DUTIES AND LIABILITIES

13.22 Project management in either form has only been introduced quite recently into the UK and there are few reported cases in which the duties and responsibilities of a project manager have been considered. Guidance has to be sought from other cases concerning managers or agents. In the context of construction, there are some parallels with the duties of architects and engineers. Reference will be made to the relevant authorities as necessary in considering the scope of a project manager's duties and liabilities below. There appear to be various aspects to the role of the project manager which are quite different to that of a quantity surveyor which are separately considered and discussed below.

Coordination and management

13.23 The scope of a project manager's duties in relation to the co-ordination or management of a project have to be determined by reference to the express terms of his contract. As in any contract for the provision of services, the project manager will owe his client a contractual duty, imposed by s 13 of the Supply of Goods and Services Act 1982, to carry out his work with reasonable skill and care.

Monitoring the performance of others

13.24 This topic was considered recently in the case of *Chesham Properties Ltd v Bucknall Austin Project Management Services Ltd and Others*.[1] This concerned what was in fact a case of project coordination rather than project management as defined already above. The client brought a claim against the project manager, the architects, the structural engineers and the quantity surveyors who had all been engaged in respect of a development. The matters alleged against all of the defendants were that they had failed to advise the client that the extensions of time awarded to the contractor had been caused by the default of one or more of them and that, in the case of the project managers and quantity surveyors, they had negligently prepared progress reports and financial statements. The merits of these allegations were not considered in the judgment which was reported, which concerned an application to make extensive amendments to the pleadings and whether, assuming the allegations were true, the defendants owed the plaintiff the alleged duties. In ruling on the

1 [1996] 53 Con LR 1.

application, the court did consider the legal basis for some of the complaints in detail.

13.25 Most of the amendments for which leave was sought were in respect of claims which had accrued more than six years before and in order to succeed the plaintiffs had to show that the claims arose out of the same or substantially the same facts as alleged already in respect of a claim which had originally been included in the proceedings. One way in which the plaintiffs sought to side-step this restriction was to plead that the project manager's failures had been in breach of his fiduciary duty to his client as the limitation period would not apply to such a claim. A fiduciary duty was held to arise in circumstances in which an agent was exercising a power, such as making a contract or payment, on his client's behalf. Although the project managers did in limited respects have the power to act on their client's behalf, it was held that their main function and duty was to give professional advice. Since the basis of the plaintiffs' claim was that they (and the other consultants) had failed to discharge this duty properly, it was held that the existence and breach of a fiduciary duty did not apply. The court referred to and relied upon a dictum from the earlier case of *Clark Boyce v Mouat*:[1]

> 'A fiduciary duty concerns disclosure of material facts in a situation where the fiduciary has either a personal interest in the matter to which the facts are material or acts for another party who has such an interest. It cannot be prayed in aid to enlarge the scope of contractual duties.'

The court also considered the claim based in contract and in tort that the project managers had failed to monitor and report on the default or possible defaults of the other consultants. The project managers' 'proposal' which formed part of their contract had stated that they will 'implement and maintain all monitoring procedures including the performance of the contractor on-site, and all consultants, and ensure that any difficulties including contractual problems, which may prevent the successful outcome of the project are highlighted in good time and that corrective measures are taken whenever possible . . .'. This can be compared to the express provisions for monitoring the performance of contractors and consultants in the RICS Project Management Agreement and Conditions of Engagement.

The court had no hesitation in finding on the basis of the project managers' proposal and the circumstances in which they were engaged which were that there was a substantial construction project for which the professional team had already been appointed and a works contract was in existence for the first phase of the construction, that the project manager was under a duty to report to his client any deficiencies in the performance of the other consultants. It held that monitoring in those circumstances could not be confined to passive observation but that it must involve reporting to the client the performance being monitored by reference to the standards which should be achieved. The court held that even if such an obligation was not clear from the express terms

1 [1993] 1 AC 428 at 437.

of the contract, it would have been implied as a matter of law to give business efficacy to the contract.

Agency

13.26 Under the RICS form of agreement a project manager is expressly given authority to act on his client's behalf up to the limits set in the Appendix. As shown in the *Chesham* case, the exercise of a power to bind his client by making a contract or payment on his behalf will give rise to a fiduciary duty. This may be summarised as a duty of utmost good faith. For example, he should inform his client of any relevant matters known to the project manager or to disclose to his client that he has an interest, direct or otherwise, in the transaction.

13.27 Various questions may arise when a project manager acts outside his authority. In that case, if the project manager had ostensible authority to act on his client's behalf, his client will be bound by his agent's actions. Ostensible authority arises where the client, or someone acting on his behalf, represents, by his conduct or by his statement, that the project manager has authority in circumstances where he does not have the actual authority of his client. The client may also be liable where the project manager does not have authority, actual or ostensible, when he ratifies by his conduct or statement something that the agent did outside his authority but purported to do on his behalf. For example, by standing by when he knows that the project manager is acting outside his actual authority.

13.28 The converse may arise when a project manager acting within his authority contracts without making it clear that he is acting as an agent. In such circumstances, he may be held to be acting as principal in relation to the other contracting party and be liable personally on the contract made. This is illustrated by the case of *Sika Contracts Ltd v BL Gill & Closeglen Properties Ltd*[1] where an engineer contracted on his own notepaper without mentioning the name of his client or that he was acting as an agent. An action was brought against the owner and the engineer. The action against the owner was stayed when it became insolvent. The court rejected the engineer's argument that having written on his office notepaper and having recited his qualifications after his signature, he had made it clear to the contractor that he was accepting the quotation in his professional capacity as an engineer and not for himself personally. It was held that the fact the engineer had been acting professionally did not mean that he could not be contracting personally and it was held that he was fully liable for the sum due for the work carried out under the contract.

13.29 Finally, where the project manager contracts outside his authority, actual or ostensible, so that the other party cannot sue the client, he may be liable to that party in damages in an action for breach of his warranty of authority. This is based on the implicit representation made by someone purporting to act on behalf of another that he has his principal's authority to do

1 [1978] 9 BLR 11.

so. In effect, he is warranting to the other contracting party that he has authority and if he does not it follows that he may be sued for any loss caused by the breach of that warranty. This may extend to a situation where the agent did have actual authority but unbeknown to him that authority was determined, for example, by his principal's death or liquidation or bankruptcy. To establish liability, it is essential for the other contracting party to prove that it relied upon the warranty of authority. This action will not assist a contractor who actually knew that the project manager was acting outside his authority.

Chapter 14

ADJUDICATION AND ARBITRATION

INTRODUCTION

14.1 Adjudication and arbitration are both procedures for resolving disputes which are agreed by the parties under the contract between them. Adjudication was introduced in the construction industry in the late 1970s to deal with disputed claims of set-off made by contractors to justify non-payment of sums due to a subcontractor under a subcontract. Arbitration has much older origins and has always played an important part in the resolution of disputes in construction and engineering cases. Both procedures are consensual and private in nature. Both have been the subject of recent legislation in the form of the Arbitration Act 1996 and the Regulations which have effect[1] when Part II of the Housing Grants, Construction and Regeneration Act 1996 is brought into force in April or May 1998. As adjudication has been developed as an interim measure to deal with disputes prior to their final resolution by arbitration, it is appropriate to consider this subject first. An outline of the law and practice relating to arbitration will be provided in the second part of this chapter.

ADJUDICATION

The existing system of adjudication

14.2 The existing system of adjudication now provided under the JCT forms of subcontract was introduced in 1976 by amendments to the nominated and domestic forms of subcontract issued by the National Federation of Building Trades Employers and the Federation of Associations of Specialists and Subcontractors, known colloquially as the 'Green' and 'Blue' forms. This followed the decision of the House of Lords in *Gilbert-Ash (Northern) Ltd v Modern Engineering (Bristol)*[2] which confirmed the right of the employer or contractor at common law to set off cross claims for damages for alleged breaches of contract against interim payments which had been certified under the JCT forms of Building Contract. This had led to what was considered to be an abuse in that payments due to subcontractors could be withheld on such

1 The text is based up the draft Regulations which were laid before Parliament on 18 December 1997.

2 [1974] AC 689.

grounds and they then had to start litigation or arbitration to enforce payment thereby severely reducing their cash flow.

14.3 This reform was included in a package of provisions which were intended to curtail the exercise of the contractors' rights of set off against subcontractors. The contractor became obliged to give the subcontractor prior written notice of the amounts and grounds for which he intended to set off any sums against the payments due to the subcontractor not less than 17 days before payment to the subcontractor became due. The subcontractor could dispute the proposed set off by sending the contractor a written statement of his reasons and details of any counterclaim he wished to pursue. At the same time, the subcontractor was obliged to give the contractor notice of arbitration and to request the adjudicator, identified in the subcontract, to act by sending him the contractor's notice and the subcontractor's statement. Provision was made for the contractor to reply to the subcontractor's statement by sending the adjudicator a written statement briefly stating his defence to any counterclaim.

14.4 Strict time-limits were set down for the service of these documents and for a decision to be made by the adjudicator. The subcontractor had to send his statement within 14 days of receiving the contractor's notice of set off and the contractor had to send any further statement in defence of any counterclaim raised by the subcontractor within 14 days of receiving the subcontractor's statement. The adjudicator had to make a decision within seven days of receiving the contractor's statement or the expiry of the time allowed for making such a statement, whichever was earlier. He had to make his decision without any further statements (save those required to clarify or explain any ambiguity in those which had already been submitted) and without any hearing. He could only decide that the sum claimed in the set-off notice could remain in whole or in part with the contractor, or that it should be paid to the Trustee-Stakeholder appointed under the subcontract pending the outcome of the arbitration or that the money should wholly or partly be paid to the subcontractor. The adjudicator had absolute discretion without giving reasons to decide according to what he considered in all the circumstances of the dispute to be fair, reasonable and necessary. The contractor was bound to comply with the adjudicator's decision which was to be communicated immediately to both parties.

14.5 The timetable effectively provided that when a set-off was disputed, the dispute would be adjudicated within a maximum of seven days (plus the time taken to despatch and receive the statements and decision), after which the payment was due and payable to the subcontractor. The adjudicator's decision was subject to the outcome of the arbitration or subsequent agreement. The subcontract conditions provided for what was in effect a right of appeal to the arbitrator who could vary or cancel the adjudicator's decision if it appeared to him just and reasonable to do so at any time prior to making his final award. The arbitrator also had the power to decide who should pay the adjudicator's fees which initially had to be paid by the subcontractor.

14.6 These provisions were reproduced with minor revisions in the subcontract forms published for use with the 1980 JCT Standard Form of Building Contract, the NSC/4 form for a nominated subcontractor and the DOM/1 form for domestic subcontractors. Similar provisions are included in the latest generation of nominated subcontract forms published for use with Amendment 10 which introduced the new clause 35 of the JCT 80 main contract forms. The current subcontract forms now are NSC/A ('The Articles of Nominated Sub-Contract Agreement') and NSC/C. The provisions for set-off and adjudication are in clauses 4.26 to 4.37 of NSC/C.

14.7 The provisions restricting the contractor's right of set-off and for reference of any disputes to adjudication have been the subject of several reported decisions. Of particular interest are two decisions in which the adjudication provisions were expressly considered. The first of these is the decision of the Court of Appeal in *A Cameron v John Mowlem*.[1] This concerned a domestic subcontract in the DOM/1 form. Formal notice of set-off had been given by the contractor Mowlem indicating that £52,800 would be set off. This was disputed by the subcontractor who served a statement with a counterclaim for £77,564 and a notice of arbitration. An adjudicator was appointed who decided that the full amount of the set-off should be paid to the subcontractor. Mowlem failed to pay the full amount and the subcontractor sought to enforce the adjudicator's decision by applying for an order under s 26 of the Arbitration Act 1950 for an order to enforce as if it was an arbitrator's award. When this application failed, on the ground that an adjudicator's decision was not an award made in an arbitration, the subcontractor issued a writ and applied for summary judgment. This was in turn opposed by Mowlem who applied for the action to be stayed under s 4 of the Arbitration Act 1950. Summary judgment was given to the subcontractor and appeals were brought by the subcontractor against the dismissal of the application to enforce the adjudicator's decision and by the contractor, against the refusal of its application to stay the action.

The Court of Appeal held that because the decision of an adjudicator was only binding until the determination by the arbitrator, it did not constitute a valid arbitration award. In the words of Mann LJ:

> 'An adjudicator's decision is 'binding ... until' determination by an arbitrator. The decision has an ephemeral and subordinate character which in our view makes it impossible for the decision to be described as an award on an arbitration agreement.'

The Court of Appeal also allowed the contractor's appeal on the grounds that it was entitled to dispute the subcontractor's claim on the grounds that the subcontractor was not entitled to the amount claimed for its work. It held that the adjudicator only had jurisdiction to decide whether the contractor could make the set-off it claimed against any sum that might be due to the subcontractor. He could not decide whether the subcontractor was entitled to

1 [1990] 52 BLR 24.

the payment it claimed. In the event of disagreement, that dispute would have to be decided by arbitration. The adjudicator could not make the contractor pay any more than he was bound to pay the subcontractor under the subcontract. The court's decision turned on the distinction between a set-off which involves a claim that the subcontractor has breached his contract and has thereby caused the contractor to suffer loss and a defence (described as 'abatement') that the subcontractor was not entitled to be paid the amount claimed because, for example, the work was not performed in accordance with the subcontract. The contractor was entitled to resist paying the subcontractor on that ground even though the adjudicator had decided that it was not entitled to claim a set-off. If the subcontractor could not prove that it was entitled to the amount claimed irrespective of the set-off then the contractor was entitled not to pay him.

14.8 The case of *Drake & Scull Engineering Ltd v McLaughlin & Harvey plc*[1] also concerned a domestic subcontract on the DOM/1 form. Again notice of set-off had been given by the contractor and disputed by the subcontractor who gave notice of its disagreement and referred the dispute to adjudication and arbitration. The adjudicator ordered the contractor to pay £149,451 to the trustee stakeholder pending the outcome of the arbitration. When the contractor failed to comply with the decision, the subcontractor applied for a mandatory injunction to enforce the adjudicator's order. The judge hearing the application, His Honour Judge Peter Bowsher QC, did not refer to the case of *Cameron v Mowlem*. He appears to have construed the provision for the valuation of the subcontractor's work without considering the possibility that a claim might be resisted because of a dispute over the value rather than a set-off. However, he was prepared to enforce the adjudicator's decision over the disputed set-off by making a mandatory order pending determination by the arbitrator. He rejected the contractor's suggestions that the subcontractor should enforce the decision by applying to the arbitrator for him to vary or cancel the decision or for him to make an interim award. He held that it was for the contractor to apply to the arbitrator to cancel or vary the adjudicator's decision, and to make the subcontractor apply for an interim award would defeat the whole purpose of the provision which was to ensure that the money to be set off was paid to the subcontractor or to a stakeholder before the dispute got to an arbitrator.

14.9 The *Drake & Scull* case shows that where payment is disputed because of a set-off the correct way to enforce an adjudicator's decision for the money to be paid to the subcontractor is to go to court and seek an order by applying for summary judgment. Where the contractor fails to give notice of his intended counterclaim in accordance with the terms of the subcontract, the courts will refuse to either allow him to defend an action brought to enforce payment of the sum due to the subcontractor or to stay the enforcement of the judgment until his claims for set-off have been arbitrated. This is illustrated by the case of

1 [1992] 60 BLR 102.

Tubeworkers v Tilbury Construction[1] in which the parties had contracted under the Green form of nominated subcontract. The architect had issued an interim certificate which included £54,728 in respect of the subcontractor's work. The architect subsequently certified that the subcontractors had caused delay and the contractors then quantified their claim for a set-off of £97,069 and notified the subcontractor. The subcontractor issued a writ for the sum certified and obtained summary judgment. But the judge stayed execution pending the arbitration of the contractor's claim. On appeal, the stay of execution was lifted because it was held to be inconsistent with the subcontract which had provided that the subcontractor should be entitled to immediate payment of the sum certified. The Court of Appeal held that to grant a stay of execution would deprive the adjudicator of his power to decide whether a set-off should prevent immediate payment being made to the subcontractor.

14.10 The system of adjudication under the JCT subcontracts has provided a satisfactory means of resolving disputes promptly and economically without the need for or the expense of legal proceedings. But it is only, after all, an interim measure and the adjudicator's decision is not finally binding upon the parties. A triumph in the adjudication may be reversed by the arbitrator, and rightly so if it has been based on submissions which are subsequently disproved or are shown to be wrong in law. At its best it provides a rough and ready means of resolving a dispute while allowing the performance of the subcontract to continue. At its worst, the adjudicator's decision may be arbitrary and unjust leaving the wronged party with no recourse but to seek for it to be reversed in what can be an expensive and lengthy process of arbitration. Whatever its limitations, the general consensus in the industry was in favour of extending it to all construction contracts as recommended by Sir Michael Latham in his report *Constructing the Team* which was published in 1994.[2] He recommended that the adjudicators should be able to decide any disputes, that the adjudicator's award should be immediately enforceable, and that any appeal to the court or to an arbitrator should not take place until after practical completion and, except in exceptional circumstances, they should delay implementation of the award. Some of these recommendations were adopted in Part II of the Housing Grants, Construction and Regeneration Act 1996.

ADJUDICATION UNDER PART II OF THE HOUSING GRANTS, CONSTRUCTION AND REGENERATION ACT 1966

The statutory provisions

14.11 Section 108 of the 1996 Act provides for the right for any dispute under a construction contract to be referred to an adjudicator by either party. If the contract does not provide for adjudication in accordance with the

1 [1985] 30 BLR 67.
2 *Constructing the Team* (HMSO, 1994).

requirements set out subss (1) to (4), then the adjudication provisions set out in the Scheme for Construction Contracts will apply.[1] This will be described as 'the Scheme'. It is therefore appropriate to consider the provisions of s 108 before dealing with the Scheme.

14.12 Section 108 requires a construction contract to contain the following basic requirements failing which those in the Scheme will apply:

(a) each party has the right to refer any dispute (defined as including any difference) to adjudication under a procedure complying with s 108; this procedure:

   (i) must allow a party to give notice of his intention to refer a dispute to adjudication at any time;
   (ii) must provide a timetable with the object of securing the appointment of the adjudicator and the referral of the dispute to him within seven days of such notice;
   (iii) must require the adjudicator to reach a decision within 28 days or within such longer time as the parties to the dispute may agree;
   (iv) shall allow the adjudicator to extend the period of 28 days by up to 14 days with the consent of the party who referred the dispute;
   (v) must impose a duty on the adjudicator to act impartially; and
   (vi) must enable him to take the initiative in ascertaining the facts and the law;

(b) the adjudicator's decision is to be binding until the dispute is finally determined by legal proceedings, arbitration or agreement; and

(c) finally, that the adjudicator and any employee or agent of his is not to be liable for anything done or omitted in carrying out his functions, except where his act or omission is in bad faith.

14.13 There are a number of practical and significant differences between the system of adjudication imposed under the 1996 Act and the system incorporated by the provisions of the JCT subcontracts. The first is that it will apply to any contract made after Part II of the Act comes into force which is a contract for any work involved or connected with engineering or construction except one made with the occupier, or prospective occupier, of a dwelling house. The Act only applies to construction contracts that are in writing, but this term is defined by s 107 in the broadest possible terms to include not only contracts made by the exchange of correspondence or evidenced in writing, but those which incorporate written terms by reference. In the absence of such an agreement, the allegation in written submissions or pleadings in adjudication, arbitral or legal proceedings by a party of the existence of a contract not made in writing which is not denied, is deemed to constitute an agreement to the effect alleged. Certain categories of construction contracts are excluded from the Act by the Construction Contracts (England and Wales) Exclusion Order

---

1 See Part 1 of the Schedule to the Scheme for Construction Contracts (England and Wales) Regulations 1988.

1998. This excludes construction contracts made under statute, such as an agreement under s 106 of the Town and Country Planning Act 1990; contracts entered into under the private finance initiative, where part of the consideration due is determined by the standards of the performance of a service, and the extent of use or the right to operate any facility in the building or structure concerned and finance and development agreements. A finance agreement is defined as a construction contract under which the principal obligations include the formation or dissolution of a company, partnership or unincorporated association, or the creation or transfer of any securities or any right or interest in securities, the lending of money or the undertaking by anyone to be responsible as surety for the debt or default of any other person, including any bond and any contract of insurance. A development agreement is defined as a construction contract which includes the grant or disposal of a freehold or leasehold interest, for a period in excess of 12 months after the completion of any construction operation on the land in question. There are other exceptions such as the manufacture of components off site. The remedy can be exercised by any party to such a contract at any time and in relation to any dispute instead of only monetary claims. More fundamentally, the adjudicator's decision is to bind the parties to any dispute until it is varied or reversed as the result of litigation, arbitration or agreement. There is no requirement to commence an arbitration at the same time as referring the dispute to an adjudicator. Hand in hand with the interim binding nature of an adjudicator's decision are his express duties to act impartially and to investigate the facts and the law. This goes far beyond the rudimentary powers of the adjudicator called upon to decide whether the contractor may set off any claim against sums due to the subcontractor under the JCT subcontracts. The practical effect of this provision may be to transform the approach of the construction industry to disputes generally. The impact will largely depend upon the detailed provisions set out in the Scheme which will at least initially apply to a large proportion of the contracts made in the industry after Part II of the Act comes into force.

THE SCHEME FOR CONSTRUCTION CONTRACTS

14.14 The provisions of the Scheme relating to adjudication are set out in Part I of the Schedule to the Scheme for Construction Contracts (England and Wales) Regulations 1998 and are outlined below.

The notice of adjudication

14.15 The notice to refer any dispute to adjudication should be given to every other party to the contract. It should briefly set out the nature and description of the dispute, the parties involved and state the details of where and when it has arisen and the remedy which is sought together with details of all the parties to the contract. The person giving notice of adjudication is described as 'the referring party'.

The selection of the adjudicator

14.16 After notice of adjudication has been sent to the other parties, a request should be made to the person specified as adjudicator in the contract to act, or the body named in the contract to nominate an adjudicator, to do so. If no provision is made in the contract, or the contractual process for selecting an adjudicator breaks down, a nomination should be requested from one of the adjudicator-nominating organisations, such as RICS, who must communicate the selection within five days of receiving a request to do so. Although the request must be accompanied by a copy of the notice of adjudication, the request itself does not have to be made in writing. The person requested to act as adjudicator must indicate whether or not he is willing to act within two days of receiving the request. For the reason stated below the referring party should take every possible step he can to avoid any delay in the selection of an adjudicator.

The referral notice

14.17 Where an adjudicator has been selected, the referring party must 'refer the dispute in writing' to the adjudicator. No indication is given as to the form that this notice should take but it must be accompanied by copies of, or relevant extracts from, the construction contract and such other documents as the referring party intends to rely upon. At the same time, copies should be sent to the other parties. The referral notice must be sent to the adjudicator not later than seven days from the date of the notice of adjudication. It may be impossible to comply with this requirement if the adjudicator has to be selected by a nominating body because the time between sending and the receipt of a request to nominate by such a body (which then has five days to select someone), and between sending and the receipt of a request to act by an adjudicator (who then has two days to respond), are included in the calculation of the period of seven days or if there are delays because the person selected declines to act as adjudicator.

Multipartite and consolidated adjudications

14.18 The Scheme provides that an adjudicator may, with the parties' consent, adjudicate several disputes under the same contract at the same time and, with the consent of all of the relevant parties, adjudicate related disputes under different contracts.

Resignation, revocation and objections

14.19 An adjudicator may resign at any time by giving written notice to the parties. He is obliged to resign where the dispute is the same or substantially the same as a dispute which has already been referred to adjudication and in which a decision has been made. In that case, or where he resigns because the dispute varies significantly from the dispute in the referral notice and he is not competent to decide it, he may claim a reasonable amount for his fees and expenses as he may determine and the parties will be jointly and severally liable for any amount outstanding after any determination as to how payment ought to be apportioned. Where he resigns for other reasons no provision is made for payment of his fees and expenses. Following the resignation of an adjudicator the selection process recommences after the referring party has given a fresh notice of adjudication to the other parties. But the parties are obliged to provide the new adjudicator with copies of all of the documents provided to his predecessor, insofar as it is reasonably practicable. Any objection by a party to the appointment of a particular person as adjudicator shall not invalidate his appointment or any decision that he may make. The parties may, however, agree to revoke an adjudicator's appointment, when he shall be entitled to payment of a reasonable amount for his fees and expenses as he may determine, and they will be jointly and severally liable for any sum outstanding after any determination of how payment should be apportioned. But the parties shall not be liable for his fees and expenses if his appointment is revoked because of his default or misconduct.

The powers of the adjudicator

14.20 The adjudicator is expressly obliged to act impartially and in accordance with the terms of the contract and the applicable law and to avoid unnecessary expense. He is entitled to take the initiative in ascertaining the facts and the law necessary to determine the dispute and to decide on the procedure to be adopted. In particular, he is to have the following powers and the parties are to comply with any request or direction that he might make:

(a) to request any party to the contract to supply any documents he might reasonably require including if he so directs a written statement supporting or supplementing the referral notice or any document sent with it;

(b) to decide the language to be used and whether a translation of any document is required;

(c) to meet and question any of the parties and their representatives;

(d) to make site visits and inspections or to carry out any tests or experiments subject to obtaining any consent required from third parties;

(e) to obtain and consider such representations and submissions as he requires and to appoint experts, assessors or legal advisers provided he has notified the parties of his intention to do so;

(f) to direct the timetable for the adjudication including any deadlines and to limit the length of any written or oral submissions and to issue any other directions as to the conduct of the adjudication or dispute or action to be taken by any of the parties to the dispute;

(g) in the event of the default of any party the adjudicator may continue in that party's absence or without the document or statement requested, draw such adverse inferences as the failure may justify and make a decision on the information before him attaching such weight as he thinks fit to any evidence submitted late.

Representation

14.21 Subject to any agreement to the contrary, the parties are entitled to be assisted and represented by anyone they think fit, but in any oral evidence or representations they may only be represented by one representative, unless the adjudicator directs to the contrary.

Exchange of information and confidentiality

14.22 The adjudicator must consider any relevant information submitted to him by any of the parties and he shall make available to them any information taken into account in making his decision. Neither the adjudicator nor any party may disclose to anyone else any document or information which the party supplying it has indicated to be confidential except as required for the purpose of the adjudication.

The adjudicator's decision

14.23 This must be made no more than 28 days after the date of the referral notice or 42 days if the referring party consents, or within such further period as all the parties may agree and copies must be sent to all the parties. In the event of the adjudicator's failure to give a decision within the time limit, any of the parties may restart the adjudication by serving a fresh notice of dispute and a new adjudicator will be appointed.

The adjudicator must decide all the matters in dispute and he may:

(a) open up, revise or review any decision or certificate given by anyone referred to in the contract unless the contract provides that it is final and conclusive;
(b) decide that any of the parties to the dispute is liable to make a payment and when it is due and payable which in the case of a payment which has been withheld under a notice given under s 111 of the Act, will be either seven days from the date of the decision or the date on which the payment should have been made if no such notice had been given, whichever is the later;
(c) having regard to the terms of the contract, award interest (simple or compound) at such rates and for such periods as he may determine;
(d) order any of the parties to comply peremptorily with his decision or part of it; and
(e) if requested by one of the parties, he shall provide reasons for his decision.

The effects of the adjudicator's decision

14.24 Unless indicated to the contrary, the parties are to comply with the decision as soon as they receive it. It is to be binding until the dispute is finally determined by legal proceedings, arbitration or agreement. Unfortunately, the means by which a decision may be enforced is rather convoluted. The Scheme provides that the adjudication is to be treated as if it was an arbitration for the purpose of s 42 of the Arbitration Act 1996. The net effect is that a decision can only be enforced by an order of the court after a party has failed to comply with a peremptory order made by the adjudicator when the adjudicator (or a party with his permission) has applied for an order from the court to enforce the order. This could be a weak point in an otherwise robust procedure. But the court only has to be satisfied that the party in default has failed to comply within the time prescribed in the adjudicator's decision or, if no time was prescribed, within a reasonable time. It remains to be seen how this sanction will be applied by the courts.

The adjudicator's fees

14.25 Unless the fees or a method for determining them is agreed by the parties with the adjudicator, he is entitled to be paid such reasonable amount for fees and expenses as he may determine. The parties shall be liable to pay in such proportions as he may direct or they may agree, failing which they shall be jointly and severally liable for any sum which remains outstanding.

The role of the courts

14.26 A distinction has to be drawn for present purposes between the adjudication provisions made under s 108 of the Act and the procedure under the Scheme. It would appear that in the case of contracts which comply with the requirements of s 108, the enforcement of an adjudicator's decisions could be subject to a different regime than that applied to those covered by the Scheme. At present, it is not clear exactly how adjudicator's decisions could be enforced outside the Scheme. For example, it would seem possible that an adjudicator's decision might be enforced by taking proceedings for a summary judgment for the payment of a sum which the adjudicator has decided should be paid by one of the parties to the dispute. But if the construction contract contains an arbitration clause the other party could resist such an application by applying for the action to be stayed. On the present state of the authorities the court would be bound to stay the action, leaving the adjudicator's decision to be enforced by seeking an interim award from the arbitrator. If the contract does not contain an arbitration clause, then the application could be defended on the basis of a set-off or on other grounds which indicate that the other party may have a defence to the action. Without the introduction of special rules of procedure, it is difficult to see how adjudications under contracts which are not subject to the Scheme will be enforced.

The impact of adjudication on the surveying profession

14.27 The application of adjudication to construction contracts generally is likely to be of immense practical importance to quantity surveyors and to their clients. Quantity and building surveyors are well suited by their experience and training to work as adjudicators and it is likely that many will be attracted to take up appointments. As practically every dispute will involve adjudication at some stage the demand for adjudicators is likely to be high after Part II of the

Act and the Scheme come into force. Various courses for the training and accreditation of adjudicators have already been established.

ARBITRATION

14.28 Arbitration is widely used in the construction industry and this is reflected by the fact that the great majority of the standard forms of contract, including those published by RICS, incorporate arbitration clauses. It can be defined as the process by which the parties agree to refer a dispute between them to be decided by an agreed tribunal or a tribunal appointed by another body, such as the Chartered Institute of Arbitrators, or the President of RIBA or RICS.

Different rules apply to arbitrations depending upon when they were commenced. Arbitrations which started before 31 January 1997 are subject to the provisions of the Arbitration Acts 1950, 1975 and 1979. Arbitrations which commenced after 31 January 1997 are subject to the provisions of the Arbitration Act 1996. There are a number of significant differences between the rules governing 'old' arbitrations and those applying to 'new' arbitrations which will be highlighted in the topics considered below. In practice, old arbitrations in more complex matters were conducted in a similar way to litigation with the exchange of written pleadings, discovery of the parties' documents and the preparation and exchange of experts' reports and witness statements. In arbitrations the parties are respectively referred to as 'the Claimant' and 'the Respondent'.

Arbitration agreements

14.29 Agreements to arbitrate may be written or oral. Oral agreements are not subject to the 1950 Act and may be revoked at any time. Section 32 of the 1950 Act defines an arbitration agreement as a written agreement to submit present or future disagreements to arbitration. When both parties sign a written agreement containing an arbitration clause no difficulty arises over the existence of an arbitration agreement. But in practice the parties may contract without both signing such an agreement and the question of whether there is an arbitration agreement does arise. For example, the parties may exchange letters agreeing that work is to be carried out subject to the terms of a standard form of agreement, which contains an arbitration clause. This point has been the subject of a number of cases in which, until more recently, the courts have held that there was no arbitration agreement unless the arbitration clause had been expressly incorporated in the parties' agreement. In three cases decided in 1996,[1] the courts have taken a more liberal approach and have found that an

---

1 These were *Alfred McAlpine Construction Ltd v RMG Electrical* (unreported), *Roche Products Ltd v Freeman Process Systems* [1996] CILL 1171 and *Extrudakerb (Maltby Engineering) Ltd v Whitemountain Quarries Ltd* (1996) *The Times*, 10 July.

arbitration clause was incorporated where the agreement had referred specifically to a form of contract which included an arbitration clause.

14.30 This problem does not arise under the 1996 Act which states in s 6(2) that the reference in an agreement to a written form of arbitration clause or to a document containing an arbitration clause constitutes an arbitration agreement 'if the reference is such as to make that clause part of the agreement'.

14.31 Another common example when difficulty may arise is where the parties make an oral agreement for work to be carried out under the terms of a contract which contains an arbitration clause. Under the 1950 Act, such an agreement did not constitute a written arbitration agreement. Under s 5(3) of the 1996 Act the definition of a written agreement has been extended to include 'where the parties agree otherwise than in writing by reference to terms which are in writing' so that there will be a written arbitration agreement in that case.

Arbitration or certification

14.32 Where someone is appointed to determine an issue in order to prevent a dispute arising, where this takes the form of a valuation or certificate, this does not constitute an arbitration. However, where a dispute has arisen, it may be more difficult to distinguish between a valuation or certification and an arbitration when someone is appointed to use his own knowledge and expertise to decide the issue. It is then necessary to determine whether, in the circumstances, the parties intended that person to act as an expert or as an arbitrator.

The scope of the arbitration clause

14.33 The arbitrator only has power to deal with the matters specifically referred to in the arbitration clause. A problem which arose with old arbitrations is whether the arbitrator had any jurisdiction when one of the parties disputed the existence of the contract. This depended upon how widely the arbitration clause was drawn. It was possible for a clause to be wide enough to give the arbitrator power to decide whether the contract was void, for example, because of illegality, or whether it had been repudiated, and if so whether the repudiation had been accepted or whether the contract had been frustrated. But where the existence of the contract itself was disputed, the arbitrator would have no jurisdiction. Section 30 of the 1996 Act overcomes this problem by providing that the tribunal can rule on its own jurisdiction.

The arbitrator's powers

14.34 In *Northern Regional Health Authority v Derek Crouch Construction Co Ltd*,[1] the Court of Appeal considered the powers conferred upon the arbitrator under JCT 80 'to open up, review and revise any certificate, opinion,

---

1 [1984] QB 644.

decision ... as if no such certificate, opinion, decision, ... had been given'. The issue was whether the court had the same powers as an arbitrator. It was held that the court could only determine the validity of a certificate issued by the architect and could not, like an arbitrator, revise or re-open a certificate unless the machinery for an arbitration breaks down or is incapable of operating. The case has been followed by conflicting decisions on the scope of the court's powers under other forms of contract, such as the JCT Agreement for Minor Building Works. The procedural difficulties which have arisen from this case have not been fully resolved. Although provision has since been made for the High Court to exercise the same powers as the arbitrator this requires the consent of all of the parties.[1]

Joinder of parties and third party procedure

14.35 The arbitrator has no power to consider claims made by parties who are not parties to the arbitration agreement nor can he (without the parties' agreement) hear two disputes involving separate arbitrations concurrently, even though the same issues of fact or law may arise. Where the arbitration was between parties who were both in the UK (known as 'domestic arbitrations'), the court did have discretion to refuse to stay legal proceedings under s 4 of the 1950 Act where: (a) injustice might be caused to the litigating party because of the need to join another party in the litigation who was not a party to the same arbitration agreement; and (b) where the granting of a stay might lead to different tribunals possibly making inconsistent decisions on the same facts, as well as causing additional expense. The leading case is *Taunton-Collins v Cromie*[2] where the employer sued his architect for negligent design and supervision. The architect blamed the contractor; when the employer sought to join the contractor as co-defendant, the Court of Appeal refused to stay the proceedings brought against the contractor under the arbitration clause in the building contract, because of the risk of inconsistent findings and to avoid a multiplicity of proceedings.

14.36 One unfortunate effect of the 1996 Act is that under s 9, which applies to all arbitrations including domestic arbitrations, the court no longer has any discretion to refuse to stay legal proceedings which are brought where there is a valid and enforceable arbitration clause. This provision has recently been interpreted so widely that a stay will be granted even where there is no real defence to the claim made in an action, on the grounds that the arbitrators are to have exclusive jurisdiction whenever there is a dispute.[3]

14.37 The joinder of arbitrations of related disputes between parties under different contracts is covered by express provisions in the JCT family of main and subcontracts. These confer power for the same arbitrator to hear related

---

1 See s 100 of the Courts and Legal Services Act 1990.

2 [1964] 1 WLR 633.

3 *Halki Shipping Corporation v Sopex Oils Ltd ('The Halki')* [1997] 1 WLR 1268, see para **14.41** below.

disputes under different contracts. In such cases the arbitrator is to have the same powers as the court to hear related disputes and to issue directions and necessary awards to join in one or more co-defendants or third parties. Similar provisions are made for joinder under the ICE Arbitrations Procedure and in the FCEC form of subcontract.

Commencing arbitration

14.38 This is done by the party referring the dispute serving written notice on the other party requiring him to appoint an arbitrator, or to agree to the appointment of an arbitrator, or, where the arbitration agreement specifies the arbitrator, by serving a notice requiring the other party to submit the dispute to the person named. In each case the notice must identify the disputes in respect of which the arbitrator is to be appointed. Under the 1996 Act, where the arbitrator is to be appointed by a third party, an arbitration may be commenced by serving a request on the third party for an arbitrator to be appointed without notifying the other party.[1]

Extension of time for commencing arbitration

14.39 The parties may agree that an arbitration is to be commenced before the end of a period which expires before the end of the limitation period. In such a case the court has jurisdiction under s 27 of the 1950 Act to extend the time for commencement of arbitration. However, where a contract provides that a state of affairs shall become conclusive if arbitration (or litigation) is not commenced within a time limit, such as under clause 30.9.3 of JCT 80, this is not treated as a time limit for commencing proceedings and the court has no power to extend the time for commencing an arbitration.[2] Under s 27 of the 1950 Act, the court may exercise the power to extend time if it considers that undue hardship would be caused. The 1996 Act contains a similar power in s 12, but it may only be exercised if either the circumstances were outside the reasonable contemplation of the parties when they agreed the provision and it would be just to extend the time, or where the conduct of one party would make it unjust to hold the other to the strict terms of the provision.

The appointment of an arbitrator by the court

14.40 In the event of the agreed machinery for appointing an arbitrator breaking down, an arbitrator may be appointed by the court under s 10 of the Arbitration Act 1950. Under ss 16 to 19 of the 1996 Act, the court continues to have power to appoint arbitrators in the event of the breakdown of agreed procedures, but provisions are also made for procedures which will apply if the parties fail to agree how the arbitrators are to be appointed or for a sole arbitrator to act where each party is to appoint an arbitrator and one party fails to appoint one. Under both the 1950 and 1996 Acts, an Official Referee may

---

1 See s 14(5).

2 *Crown Estate Commissioners v John Mowlem & Co* [1994] 70 BLR 1.

accept appointment as an arbitrator if the parties so agree and he can be made available.

Stay of legal proceedings

14.41 This is the primary means by which an arbitration agreement can be enforced if one party starts legal proceedings. Reference has already been made to the different regimes which apply depending upon whether or not the arbitration is subject to the 1996 Act. In either case, the party seeking to apply for a stay must not take any positive step in the proceedings or he will lose his chance to rely upon the arbitration clause. Under s 4 of the Arbitration Act 1950, the court had a discretion whether or not to stay the proceedings. The court would not normally allow an action to be stayed where there appeared to be no defence to the claim and it could refuse to stay an action where this could cause difficulties in proceeding against other parties who were not subject to an arbitration clause or who could not be compelled to accept the appointment of the same arbitrator. Under s 9 of the 1996 Act which now applies to all applications to stay – except where an arbitration was started before 31 January 1997 – the court has no power to refuse an application for a stay unless the arbitration agreement is null and void, inoperative or incapable of being performed. In *Halki Shipping Corporation v Sopex Oils Ltd ('The Halki')*[1] a case in the Commercial Court relating to a claim, for demurrage under a charterparty (similar to liquidated damages for delay), it was held that although there was no defencc to a substantial part of the claim, the court was bound to stay the proceedings. The court accepted the submission that any other construction of s 9 might remove the arbitrators' power to make an award where there was no defence to the claim. Although the decision followed an earlier Court of Appeal case, in which Saville LJ (one of the architects of the 1996 Act) had commented that there could be a dispute over the result in last year's boat race, it seems likely that this restrictive interpretation of the court's jurisdiction will be subject to challenge before very long.

14.42 It is not difficult to think of circumstances in which the enforcement of arbitration clauses in this way may create unnecessary expense and inconvenience to claimants, if not injustice. Take as an example the facts in the *Taunton-Cromie v Collins* case,[2] where the building owner wished to sue the architect and the contractor in respect of defects. Although an architect who is appointed under the RIBA Appointment will be bound by the arbitration clause in that agreement, he will not be bound to agree to a dispute being referred to the arbitrator appointed under the building contract. Where proceedings have already been commenced by the owner against one of the parties and the other then relies on an arbitration clause, it will then be difficult, if not impossible, for the owner to compel the party against whom he has litigated to agree to restart the process by arbitration. In either event, the owner

1 [1997] 1 WLR 1268.
2 [1964] 1 WLR 633.

faces the doubled expense of running litigation and arbitration against the parties who are responsible for the same defects.

The conduct of the arbitration

14.43 The position under the 1950 Act was that the parties were free to agree the procedure and powers that were conferred upon the arbitrator in the arbitration agreement. Section 12 provided that, in the absence of an agreement to the contrary, the arbitrator would have power to hear and obtain evidence in the same way as the court, he would be master of the procedure in conducting the reference and that, in any event, the court would have the same powers as it would in an action in relation to matters such as ordering security for costs, the examination of witnesses, to preserve or sell any goods which were the subject of the dispute or to detain, preserve or allow inspection of any property or thing which was the subject of the dispute or to make interim injunctions or to appoint a receiver.

14.44 Under the 1996 Act, the arbitrator has, unless the parties otherwise agree, the same powers as the court in relation to the examination of witnesses, to order one (or both) of the parties to provide security for costs and for the preservation, inspection or detention of any property which is the subject of the proceedings. The power to order security for costs immediately gives rise to a practical problem where the party against whom security is sought has received an offer of settlement which is made on terms that its existence can be revealed after the issues have been decided. In such circumstances, the offer may have the same effect as a payment into court and when the party to whom the offer has been made fails to recover more in the arbitration, he may be ordered to pay his opponent's costs that were incurred after the offer was made. This form of offer is known as a 'sealed offer'. When resisting an application for security for costs, the party in receipt of the sealed offer may wish to reveal it to the arbitrator, as he would be entitled to do if the application was made to the court, in order to show that his opponent accepts that he has a good case and that he should not thereby be prevented from pursuing it. If the sealed offer is revealed to the arbitrator, it may prejudice the other party's position when the arbitrator deals with the dispute. This can only be avoided if the parties agree for the application to be heard by the court.

14.45 In the old arbitrations, the arbitrator could, if one of the parties failed to comply with his directions, apply to the court for an order to enable him to continue the proceedings in the absence of the defaulting party. Under s 13A of the Arbitration Act 1950, the arbitrator was given the power (in the absence of any contrary agreement) to make an award dismissing the claim in the event of inordinate and inexcusable delay by the claimant which gave rise to a substantial risk that it would not be possible to have a fair resolution of the issues, or had or was likely to cause serious prejudice to the respondent. Section 41 of the 1996 Act confers greater powers (unless the parties agree to the contrary) on the arbitrator in the event of default. For example, the arbitrator may, if a party fails to comply with a peremptory order, debar the party in default from relying upon any allegation or material which was the subject of the order or draw such adverse inferences from the non-compliance as the circumstances justify.

14.46 The JCT forms of agreement all incorporate the JCT Arbitration Rules 1988. These provide for a preliminary meeting to decide how the reference should be conducted. The parties may agree or, if not, the arbitrator may decide that the arbitration should be conducted without a hearing or for a full or short procedure to apply with a hearing. In each case, strict time-limits are imposed for the service of pleadings and for the disposal of the arbitration. Pleadings must have all relevant documents attached to them. The arbitrator has power to disregard pleadings which are not served in time unless proper reason is shown and may make an award dismissing a claim if the claimant fails to serve its pleading in time. The arbitrator is given power to order one of the parties to give security for costs, to give directions for the preservation or disposal of any property which is the subject of the dispute and to order the production of any relevant documents. It can be seen that the Rules anticipated many of the reforms made by the 1996 Act.

Interim and final awards

14.47 Under both regimes, interim awards can be made where this is appropriate to dispose of specific issues or claims. Such awards will be final and binding in relation to the matters decided and may be enforced, if leave is granted by the court, in the same way as a judgment.

Form and content of awards

14.48 Under the old regime there were no statutory requirements as to the form of the award and an oral award could be made and enforced. Section 52 of the 1996 Act requires (unless the parties agree otherwise) that the award should be made in writing and signed by all the arbitrators or those assenting to it (in the case where more than one arbitrator has been appointed), that the award should state the reasons unless it is an agreed award or the parties have agreed to dispense with reasons and that it should state 'the seat of the arbitration' and the date.

Costs

14.49 Unless otherwise agreed, the arbitrator may make an award in respect of the costs of the parties and in respect of his own fees and the expenses of the arbitration. In awarding costs, the arbitrator must follow recognised judicial principles. This is emphasised in s 61(2) of the 1996 Act which provides that the principle that the costs should follow the event (ie the costs should be awarded against the unsuccessful party) should be applied unless it appears to be inappropriate in the circumstances. The arbitrator may tax the costs himself or they may be determined by the court. The arbitrator's own fees and expenses may also be subject to taxation, if disputed by either of the parties.

Appeals

14.50 The right to challenge an award was restricted to questions of law by the Arbitration Act 1979 and was subject to leave being granted by the court, for which application had to be made within 28 days of the award being published. The courts restricted granting leave to cases which were obviously wrong on the face of the award or cases which involved the construction of standard terms where a strong prima facie case had to be shown. These have now been incorporated in s 69 of the 1996 Act together with the further requirement that the point of law was raised in the arbitration. The application for leave is considered on the papers without a hearing unless the court considers that this is required. The requirement for leave can be dispensed with by prior agreement as, for example, in clause 41.6 of JCT 80. The parties may agree to exclude the right to appeal but in the case of a domestic arbitration this cannot be agreed before the arbitration has commenced. By s 69(1), an agreement to dispense with reasons for the award is deemed to be such an exclusion agreement.

Removal of the arbitrator, setting aside and remission of the award

14.51 Under the 1950 Act, an arbitrator could be removed or the award could be set aside or remitted by the court to the arbitrator for reconsideration in the case of misconduct which included a failure to observe the rules of natural justice such as hearing evidence in the absence of one of the parties, bias or failure to follow the procedure agreed by the parties. The 1996 Act no longer refers to misconduct and provides that the court may vary or set aside an award if a party challenges it on the grounds that the arbitrator had no jurisdiction or because of a serious irregularity in respect of the arbitrator, the proceedings or the award. Serious irregularity is defined in s 68(2) by reference to failures to follow or comply with the duties to act fairly and impartially or in accordance with the agreed procedure and other specific matters which the court considers have or will cause substantial injustice to the applicant.

Conclusion: the effects of the Arbitration Act 1996

14.52 It is too early to comment upon the effects that the 1996 Act will have on the practice and conduct of arbitrations. The most immediate effect of the implementation of the Act has been upon the stay of legal proceedings under s 9 as discussed above. The Act adopts a non-interventionist approach, leaving the parties free to agree as to the powers and procedure to be adopted except for the mandatory provisions listed in Sch 1 to the Act. The Act also confers greater power on the arbitrator to decide the appropriate way to determine the dispute, for example by adopting a 'documents only' procedure as long as he complies with his general duty set out in s 33 to act fairly and impartially and 'to adopt procedures suitable to the circumstances of the particular case, avoiding unnecessary delay and expense, so as to provide a fair means for the resolution of the matters falling to be determined'.

PART III

APPENDICES

PART III

APPENDICES

Appendix I

PRECEDENT STATEMENT OF CLAIM AGAINST SURVEYOR

ORB 1

IN THE HIGH COURT OF JUSTICE

QUEEN'S BENCH DIVISION

[DISTRICT REGISTRY]

OFFICIAL REFEREES BUSINESS

BETWEEN:

[ ]

Plaintiff

and

[ ] Defendant

STATEMENT OF CLAIM

1. At all material times hereto:

   .1 The Plaintiff was the prospective purchaser of [ ], 'the property').

   .2 The Defendant was a firm of surveyors and valuers, carrying on business from premises at [ ] and holding itself out as competent to undertake inspections and valuations for mortgage purposes.

2. On or about day of [ ] the Plaintiff engaged the Defendant for reward to inspect the property and provide a mortgage valuation thereupon.

3.1 It was an implied term of the Defendant's retainer as aforesaid that it would exercise all due care and skill in and about inspecting and reporting upon the property.

3.2 Further or in the alternative, the Defendant owed the Plaintiff a duty of care in like terms.

4.1 On day of [ ] the Defendant, by its servant or agent one [ ] inspected the property.

4.2 On day of [ ] the said [ ] provided a report ('the report') upon and valuation of the property to the Plaintiff.

5. The report advised and/or represented

.1 The property was free from serious structural defects.

.2 The property was not in need of any essential repair work.

.3 The property was in the condition found at the date of the report reasonably valued at £90,000.

6. In reliance upon the report and advice and representations set out above the Plaintiff exchanged contracts to purchase the property on day of [ ], completing the said purchase on day of [ ].

7.1 The inspection and report were negligently undertaken and completed, by reason whereof the Defendant is in breach of the express/implied terms and/or duty of care set out above.

7.2 Particulars of breach of contract/negligence

Negligently and/or in breach of contract the Defendant:

.1 Failed to heed, alternatively to warn of the evidence of roof spread indicative of structural failure of main roof timbers to the property.

.2 Failed to heed, alternatively to warn of the existence of cracks to the rear gable wall, indicative of roof thrust acting on the said wall by reason of the failure of the roof structure.

.3 Failed to heed, alternatively to warn as to the opening of joints in structural roof timbers.

.4 Failed properly to inspect the property.

.5 Failed to provide a proper appraisal of the state and condition of the property.

.6 Wrongly advised in the terms summarised in and under paragraph 5 above.

.7 In the premises, over valued the property.

8.1 In consequence of the matters hereinabove complained of the Plaintiff has suffered loss and damage.

8.2. Particulars

.1 Diminution in value: the Plaintiff is entitled to an award of damages representing the difference between the price paid for the property in reliance upon the Defendant's report and its true value, taking into account the defects hereinabove summarised.

.2 Further, the Plaintiff will be obliged to find alternative accommodation during the execution of remedial works to the roof which will cost £[ ] and cause the Plaintiff anxiety, inconvenience and distress.

AND the Plaintiff claims:-

1. Damages
2. Interest pursuant to Section 35A of the Supreme Court Act 1981
3. Costs

Appendix II

PRECEDENT DEFENCE AGAINST CLAIM

ORB 1

IN THE HIGH COURT OF JUSTICE

QUEEN'S BENCH DIVISION

[DISTRICT REGISTRY]

OFFICIAL REFEREES BUSINESS

BETWEEN:

[ ]

Plaintiff

and

[ ] Defendant

DEFENCE

1.1 References herein to numbered paragraphs are references to the numbered paragraphs of the Statement of Claim.

1.2 Paragraph 1 is admitted.

2.1 Subject to the matters pleaded below, paragraph 2 is admitted.

2.2 The Defendant agreed to inspect the property and report thereupon in accordance with the specification for residential mortgage valuation of the Royal Institution of Chartered Surveyors, to the full terms whereof the Defendant will make reference at the trial hereof.

3.1 The Defendant agreed inter alia:

.1 To 'carry out such inspections and investigations as [were] in the [Defendants] professional judgment, appropriate and possible' in the circumstances particular to the inspection of the property.

.2 To 'have regard to the apparent state of repair and condition of the property but [would] not carry out a building survey nor inspect those parts of the property which [were] covered, unexposed or inaccessible. Such parts will be assumed to be in good repair and condition'.

3.2 Subject as aforesaid, paragraphs 3.1 and 3.2 are admitted.

4. Paragraphs 4.1 and 4.2 are admitted.

5.1 Paragraph 5 is admitted.

5.2 The report further advised:

.1 The Defendant had been unable to gain access to the roof space and was unable to comment upon the state and condition of the roof timbers.

.2 In view of cracking observed to part of the exterior of the property the Plaintiff ought to obtain a report from a structural engineer prior to purchase.

6. Subject to production of documents or title and save that no admissions are made as to any matter of reliance, paragraph 6 is admitted.

7.1 It is denied the Defendant was negligent and/or in breach of contract whether as contended for and/or particularised under paragraph 7 or at all.

7.2 Each particular set out under paragraph 7.2 is traversed.

8.1 No admissions are made as to any matter of loss and damage whether as contended for and/or particularised under paragraph 8 or at all.

8.2 Yet further, it is denied that such loss and damage as the Plaintiff may establish he has suffered was caused by the alleged or any negligence/ breach of contract by the Defendant.

8.3 Further or in the alternative, such loss and damage as the Plaintiff establishes he has suffered were caused or contributed to by the Plaintiff's own negligence in

.1 Failing to follow the recommendation that the property be inspected by a Structural Engineer prior to purchase.

.2 Failing to request further investigations into the state and condition of the roof in the light of the Defendant's warning that access to the roof space had not been possible to obtain.

.3 Failing to heed the warning as to evidence of cracking to part of the exterior of the property.

9.1 The Plaintiff's claim to interest is noted and denied.

9.2 Save as hereinbefore expressly admitted or not admitted the Defendant denies each and every allegation contained in the Statement of Claim as if the same were herein set out and traversed seriatim.

Appendix III

SPECIFICATION FOR RESIDENTIAL MORTGAGE VALUATION

RICS/ISVA SPECIFICATION FOR THE VALUATION AND INSPECTION OF RESIDENTIAL PROPERTY FOR MORTGAGE PURPOSES ON BEHALF OF BUILDING SOCIETIES, BANKS AND OTHER LENDERS

This Specification applies to inspections carried out on or after 1 January 1998 and, in respect of such inspections, supersedes previous published Guidance. The Council of Mortgage Lenders was consulted during the production of this Specification.

1. THE VALUER'S ROLES

1.1 The roles of the Valuer, who must have knowledge of and experience in the valuation of the residential property in the particular locality, are:

1.1.1 to advise the Lender as to the Open Market Value but usually excluding development value (see Sections 4.3 and 4.4 hereof) at the date of inspection;

1.1.2 to advise the Lender as to the nature of the property (see Section 4 below) and any factors likely materially to affect its value; and

1.1.3 if required by the Lender, to provide an assessment of the property's estimated current reinstatement cost in its present form (unless otherwise stated) for insurance purposes including garage, outbuildings, site clearance and professional fees, excluding VAT (except on fees).

1.2 The Valuer is not to make a recommendation as to the amount or percentage of mortgage advance or the length of the mortgage term. Nor is it the valuer's responsibility to give advice as to the suitability of the property 'for second mortgage purposes'.

2. THE VALUER'S INSPECTION

Subject to the Valuer's judgement, a visual inspection is to be undertaken of so much of the exterior and interior of the property as is accessible to the Valuer without undue difficulty. Accordingly, it is to include all that part of the property which is visible whilst standing at ground level within the boundaries of the site and adjacent public/communal areas and whilst standing at the various floor levels, as follows:

2.1 Main Building—External

Roof coverings, chimneys, parapets, gutters, walls, windows, doors, pipes, wood or metalwork, paintwork, damp proof courses, air bricks and ground levels.

2.2 Main Building—Internal

2.2.1 Parts not readily accessible or visible are not inspected and furniture and effects are not moved or floor coverings lifted.

2.2.2 Subject to reasonable accessibility, the roof space is inspected only to the extent visible from the access hatch, without entering it.

2.2.3 Celings, walls, load bearers and floor surfaces are inspected except where covered or obscured. Readings are to be taken with a moisture meter for rising dampness.

2.2.4 Cellars are inspected to the extent that they are reasonably accessible, but under floor voids are *not* inspected.

2.3 Services

The Valuer is to identify whether or not there are gas, electricity, central heating, plumbing and drainage services. Testing of services is *not* undertaken.

2.4 Outbuildings

Garages and other buildings of substantial permanent construction, and any structure(s) attached to the dwelling, are to be inspected.

2.5 Site

The inspection is to include the general state of boundaries, structures, drives, paths, retaining walls and the proximity of trees only to the extent that they are likely materially to affect the property's value.

2.6 Neighbouring properties

The nature, use and apparent state of repair of neighbouring properties in the immediate vicinity is to be considered only to the extent that they may materially affect the value of the subject property.

2.7 Flats, maisonettes or similar units forming part of a larger building or group of related buildings

The above provisions apply, but here 'Main Building' means the building containing the proposed security but not including other main buildings physically attached to it.

2.7.1 *Main Building—External*

The exterior of the proposed security and sufficient of the remainder of the Main Building to ascertain its general state of repair.

2.7.2 *Main Building—Internal*

The interior of the proposed security, the communal entrance areas within the Main Building from which the proposed security takes access and the communal area on the floor(s) of the proposed security. The roof space will only be inspected (as defined in paragraph 2.2.2 above) where access is directly available from within the proposed security.

2.7.3 *Outbuildings*

Garaging, car parking, other buildings (excluding sports complexes) of permanent construction and any other structures attached to the Main Building or which serve the Main Building or which serve the proposed security.

2.8 No enquiries regarding contamination are made, but if a problem is suspected, the Valuer is to report accordingly.

3. THE VALUER'S REPORT

3.1 Subject to covering the matters referred to in Section 1 above, reporting is to be confined strictly to answering questions raised by the Lender.

3.2 If it is suspected that hidden defects exist which could have a material effect on the value of the property, the Valuer is to so advise and recommend more extensive investigation by the intending Borrower prior to entering into a legal commitment to purchase or, in the case of a re-mortgage, as a pre-condition of the mortgage advance. It may be appropriate in exceptional circumstances to defer making a valuation until the results of the further investigations are known.

3.3 If it is not reasonably possible to carry out any substantial part of the inspection (see Section 2 above) this is to be stated.

3.4 Any obvious evidence of serious disrepair to the property or obvious potential hazard to it is to be reported, as should any other matters likely materially to affect the value.

3.5 Where the Valuer relies on information provided, this is to be indicated in the Report, together with the source of that information.

3.6 The Lender is to be informed of the existence of any apparently recent significant alterations and extensions, so as to alert the Lender's legal adviser to any enquiries to be made.

3.7 Where the proposed security is part of a building comprising flats or maisonettes, the Valuer's Report is to identify any apparent deficiencies in the management and/or maintenance arrangements observed during the inspection which materially affect the value, and will provide the current amount or assumed amount of the service charges payable, on an annual basis.

3.8 Where the apparent sharing of drives, paths, or other areas might affect the value of the subject property, the Valuer is to inform the Lender.

3.9 The form of construction is to be reported and, where non-traditional, the Valuer is to advise accordingly, stating the type of construction and the source of this information if it is not apparent from the inspection.

3.10 Where the Valuer decides to report a necessity for works to be carried out to a property as a condition of any advance and the valuer identifies the property as being:

3.10.1 of architectural or historic interest, or listed as such; or

3.10.2 in a conservation area; or

3.10.3 of unusual construction,

the Valuer is to advise that a person with appropriate specialist knowledge be asked to give advice as to the appropriate works unless, exceptionally, the Valuer believes he/she is competent to give advice which if adopted would not be detrimental to the property's architectural or historic integrity, its future structural condition or conservation of the building fabric.

3.11 In the case of new properties or conversions where the Valuer is obliged to base the valuation upon drawings and a specification, this fact is to be stated in the Report and the reference numbers and dates of such documents recorded.

4. THE VALUATION

4.1 Unless it is made apparent by an express statement in the Report, the Valuer is to make the following assumptions and will have been under no duty to have verified these assumptions:

4.1.1 that vacant possession is provided;

4.1.2 that all required, valid planning permissions and statutory approvals for the buildings and for their use, including any extensions or alterations, have been obtained and complied with;

4.1.3 that no deleterious or hazardous materials or techniques have been used, that there is no contamination in or from the ground, and it is not landfilled ground;

4.1.4 that the property is not subject to any unusual or especially onerous restrictions, encumbrances or outgoings and that good title can be shown;

4.1.5 that the property and its value are unaffected by any matters which would be revealed by a Local Search (or their equivalent in Scotland and Northern Ireland) and replies to the usual enquiries, or by a Statutory Notice and that neither the property, nor its condition, its use, or its intended use, is or will be unlawful;

4.1.6 that an inspection of those parts which have not been inspected, or a survey inspection, would not reveal material defects or cause the Valuer to alter the valuation materially;

4.1.7 that the property is connected to and there is the right to use the reported main services on normal terms;

4.1.8 that sewers, main services and the roads giving access to the property have been adopted, and that any lease provides rights of access and egress over all communal estate roadways, pathways, corridors, stairways and to use communal grounds, parking areas and other facilities;

4.1.9 that in the case of a new property, the construction of which has not been completed, the construction will be satisfactorily completed;

4.1.10 that in the case of a newly constructed property, the builder is a registered member of the NHBC, the Zurich Municipal Mutual, or equivalent and will construct the property to obtain its cover; and

4.1.11 that where the proposed security is part of a building comprising flats or maisonettes, unless instructed or otherwise aware to the contrary:

(a) the costs of repairs and maintenance to the buildings and grounds are shared equitably between those flats and maisonettes;
(b) there are suitable, enforceable covenants between all leaseholds, or through the landlord and upon the freeholder/any feuholder;
(c) there are no onerous liabilities outstanding; and
(d) there are no substantial defects or other matters requiring expenditure (in excess of the current amount or assumed amount of service charge payable on an annual basis) expected to result in charges to the leaseholder of the subject property during the next five years equivalent to 10% or more of the Open Market Value being reported; and

4.1.12 that, because the dwelling is leasehold and because the Valuer has no further and better knowledge or information:

(a) the unexpired term of the lease is 70 years, and no action is being taken by any eligible party with a view to acquiring the freehold or to extending the lease term;
(b) there are no covenants exceptionally onerous upon the leaseholder;
(c) the lease cannot be determined except on the grounds of a serious breach of covenant in the existing lease agreement;
(d) if there are separate freeholders, head and/or other sub-head leaseholders, the terms and conditions of all the leases are in the same form and contain the same terms and conditions;
(e) the lease terms are mutually enforceable against all parties concerned;
(f) there are no breaches of covenant or disputes between the various interests concerned;
(g) the leases of all the properties in the building/development are materially the same;
(h) the ground rent stated or assumed is not subject to review and is payable throughout the unexpired lease term;
(i) in the case of blocks of flats or maisonettes of over six dwellings, the freeholder manages the property directly or it is managed by a professional, properly bonded managing agent;
(j) where the subject property forms part of a mixed residential or commercially used block or development, there will be no significant changes in the existing use pattern therein;
(k) where the property forms part of a development containing separate blocks of dwellings, the lease terms of the subject property apply only to the subject block, and there will be no requirement to contribute towards costs relating to other parts of the development, other than in respect of common roads, paths, communal grounds and services;
(l) where the property forms part of a larger development the ownership of which has since been divided, all necessary rights and reservations have been reserved;
(m) there are no unusual restrictions on assignment or subletting of the subject property for residential purposes;
(n) there are no outstanding claims or litigation concerning the lease of the subject property or any others within the same development;
(o) where the subject property benefits from additional facilities within the development, the lease makes adequate provision for the lessee to continue to enjoy them without exceptional restriction, and for the facilities to be maintained adequately, and that there are no charges over and above the service charge for such use and maintenance; and

(p) in respect of insurance:

(i) the property will be insured under all risks cover, which includes subsidence, landslip and heave, for the current reinstatement cost;
(ii) the cover assumed is available on normal terms;
(iii) there are no outstanding claims or disputes;
(iv) where individuals in a block make separate insurance arrangements, the leases make provision for mutual enforceability of insurance and repairing obligations; and
(v) the landlord obliged to insure is required to rebuild the property with such alterations as may be necessary to comply with then current building regulations and planning requirements.

4.2 Among the relevant factors to be taken into account in the valuation are:

4.2.1 the tenure of the interest to be offered as security and, if known, the terms of any tenancies to which that interest is subject;

4.2.2 the age, type accommodation, siting, amenities, fixtures and features of the property and other significant environmental factors within the locality; and

4.2.3 the apparent general state of and liability for repair, the construction and apparent major defects, liability to subsidence, flooding, and/or other risks. Particular care is needed with non-traditional construction.

4.3 Unless otherwise instructed, any value for development which has or requires planning permission is to be excluded from the 'open market valuation' and the Valuer is not to include any element of value attributable to furnishings, removable fittings and sales incentives of any description when arriving at an opinion of the value. Portable and temporary structures are to be excluded also.

4.4 The definition of 'Open Market Value' is the Valuer's opinion of the best price at which the sale of an interest in property would have been completed unconditionally for cash consideration at the date of the valuation assuming:

4.4.1 a willing seller;

4.4.2 that, prior to the date of valuation, there had been a reasonable period (having regard to the nature of the property and the state of the market) for the proper marketing of the interest, for the agreement of price and terms and for the completion of the sale;

4.4.3 that the state of the market, level of values and other circumstances were, on any earlier assumed date of exchange of contracts, the same as on the date of valuation;

4.4.4 that no account is taken of any additional bid by a prospective purchaser with a special interest; and

4.4.5 that both parties to the transaction had acted knowledgeably, prudently and without compulsion.

5. ESTIMATE FOR INSURANCE PURPOSES

In assessing the current reinstatement cost (see paragraph 1.1.3 above) the Valuer should have regard where relevant to the ABI/BCIS House Rebuilding Cost Index.

6. THE VALUER'S RECORD OF INSPECTION AND VALUATION

6.1 The Valuer is to make and retain legible notes as to his/her findings and, particularly, the limits of the inspection and the circumstances in which it was carried out.

6.2 The Valuer is to keep a record of the comparable transactions and/or valuations to which he/she has had regard in arriving at his/her valuation.

7. THE VARIATION OF INSTRUCTIONS

The Service is to be in accordance with this Specification unless variations are notified to or agreed with the Valuer in writing.

MODEL CONDITIONS OF ENGAGEMENT BETWEEN THE LENDER AND THE VALUER

1. The Valuer will carry out for the Lender's current fee an inspection of the proposed security, and report, in accordance with the extant RICS/ISVA Specification for the Valuation and Inspection of Residential Property for Mortgage Purposes on Behalf of Building Societies, Banks and Other Lenders, and other relevant material in the RICS *Appraisal and Valuation Manual*, subject to any variations specified by the Lender in the issue of instructions.

2. The purpose of the report and valuation for mortgage is to enable the Lending Institution to assess the security offered by the property for the proposed loan and, where applicable, to enable the Director to fulfil the requirements of Section 13 of the Building Societies Act 1986.

3. The report and valuation will be presented on the Lender's prescribed form or on any other type of form as may be agreed.

4. Before the Valuer proceeds, the Lender will take all reasonable steps to inform the Borrower as to the limitations of the inspection report and valuation, and will suggest that the Borrower commissions a more detailed inspection and Report before entering into a legal commitment.

5. Unless the parties otherwise agree in writing, all disputes arising out of this agreement shall be finally settled under English Law and the parties irrevocably submit to the jurisdiction of the English Courts, save that where the subject property is in Scotland, Scots Law shall apply and the Scottish Courts shall have jurisdiction.

Appendix IV

THE RICS/ISVA HOMEBUYER SURVEY & VALUATION: REPORT FORM

THE SURVEY

PLEASE READ THIS PAGE WITH EXTRA CARE

- OBJECTIVE
- CONTENT
- ACTION
- OVERALL OPINION

A: INTRODUCTION

Please note that this Report is solely for your use and your professional advisers', and no liability to anyone else is accepted. Should you not act upon specific, reasonable advice contained in the Report, no responsibility is accepted for the consequences. [Standard Terms of Engagement, Clause 6]

The Report has been prepared in line with the *Description of the HOMEBUYER Service* already provided (an additional copy is attached). If any addition to the standard Service was agreed before the Inspection, this is confirmed at the foot of the last page.

Objective

The principal objective of the Report and Valuation is to assist you to:

- make a reasoned and informed judgement on whether or not to proceed with the purchase
- assess whether or not the Property is a reasonable purchase at the agreed price
- be clear what decisions and actions should be taken before contracts are exchanged.

Content

The general condition and particular features of the Property are covered, but the Report focuses on the matters which the Surveyor judges to be urgent or significant.

Urgent matters are defects judged to be an actual or developing threat either to the fabric of the building or to personal safety; it will be advisable to have these put right as soon as possible after purchase (in some cases even before). *Significant matters* are those which, typically, in negotiations over price would be reflected in the amount finally agreed.

Matters assessed as *not urgent* or *not significant* are outside the scope of the HOMEBUYER Service, and are generally not reported. However, other matters (such as legal and safety considerations) are reported where the Surveyor judges this to be helpful and constructive.

ACTION

If – after reading and considering all the information and advice in the Report – you decide to proceed with the purchase, then there are probably some things on which you should take action at once. Each such item is highlighted in the Report with the word ACTION and is also listed in Section F: Summary together with advice on what to do next.

OVERALL OPINION

Below are the Surveyor's conclusions, in brief, on whether or not this Property is a reasonable purchase at the agreed price, and on particular features which affect its present value and may affect its future resale. The opinion takes no account of factors outside the scope of the HOMEBUYER Service.

It is hoped that this overall view will help you to keep in perspective the detailed facts and advice which follow. You are asked to bear in mind particularly that it can be misleading to treat individual matters in isolation. So that you may use this Report to best advantage in reaching your decision on whether or not to proceed with the purchase of this Property, *you are most strongly advised to read and consider its contents as a whole.*

THE SURVEY

B: THE PROPERTY & LOCATION

PLEASE READ THESE NOTES

This section covers the important general background information on the Property and its location, including amenities and features of the vicinity as well as any environmental and other wider considerations. It also includes the state of occupation and the weather at the time of the Inspection.

Please note that, throughout the Report, the principal features and parts of a property are given in the left-hand margin thus: – often followed by a list of supplementary items, such as:

B1
THE PROPERTY
- Type and age

B1
THE PROPERTY
- Type and age
- Construction
- Accommodation
- Garage and grounds

B2
THE LOCATION

B3
CIRCUMSTANCES OF THE INSPECTION

THE SURVEY

C: THE BUILDING

Please read these notes

Movement, timber defects and dampness are, in their various forms, the three greatest potential threats to the structure of a building. Where evidence is found of any of these conditions, advice is given on what action should be taken. (Where a problem is judged to be serious, it might prove necessary for a separate, detailed examination to be undertaken – perhaps by specialists. For example, the foundations might have to be laid open to analyse the cause of some structural movement, or the full extent of timber rot might require further investigation.)

C1
MOVEMENT

C2
TIMBER DEFECTS

C3
DAMPNESS

- Damp-proof course
- Rising and penetrating damp
- Condensation

C4
INSULATION

THE SURVEY

PLEASE READ THESE NOTES

C: THE BUILDING *(continued)*

C5
THE EXTERIOR

- Roof structure and covering
- Chimneys
- Rainwater fittings
- Main walls
- External joinery
- External decoration
- Other

The roofs, chimneys and other external surfaces of the building are examined from ground level, where necessary from adjoining public property and with the help of binoculars. The roof structure is examined from inside the roof space where accessible (insulation material, stored goods and other contents are not moved or lifted). The efficiency of rainwater fittings (gutters and downpipes) can only be assessed properly during the Inspection if there is heavy rain.

THE SURVEY

PLEASE READ THESE NOTES

C: THE BUILDING *(continued)*

C6

THE INTERIOR

- Roof space
- Ceilings
- Floors
- Internal walls and partitions
- Fireplaces etc.
- Internal joinery
- Internal decoration
- Other

Floor surfaces and under-floor spaces are examined so far as they are accessible (furniture, floor coverings and other contents are not moved or lifted). If a part or area normally examined was found to be not accessible, this is reported; if a problem is suspected, advice is given on what action should be taken. It is not possible to assess the internal condition of any chimney, boiler or other flues. (In some cases, when furniture and pictures are removed internal decorations may prove to be damaged or faded.)

THE SURVEY

PLEASE READ THESE NOTES

D: THE SERVICES & SITE

The efficiency, compliance with regulations and adequacy of design of services can only be assessed by tests conducted by suitably qualified specialists. Although surveyors are not specialists in these particular areas, an informed opinion can be given on the basis of the accessible evidence. Where possible, drainage inspection-chambers are examined (except in the case of flats), but drains are not tested during the Inspection. However, in all cases advice is given if there is cause to suspect a problem. Leisure facilities and non-permanent outbuildings are noted but not examined.

D1
THE SERVICES

- Electricity
- Gas
- Water
- Heating
- Other

D2
DRAINAGE

D3
THE SITE

- Garage and outbuildings
- Grounds and boundaries

THE SURVEY

PLEASE READ THESE NOTES

E: LEGAL & OTHER MATTERS

Your Legal Advisers are responsible for checking relevant documents relating to the Property (these might include servicing records and any guarantees, reports and specifications on previous repair works) as well as for carrying out all the standard searches and inquiries. However, if any specific matters are identified which the Legal Advisers should investigate on your behalf, these are reported in this section. *You are asked to pay particular attention to the* ACTION *paragraph at E4 below.*

E1
TENURE

E2
REGULATIONS etc.

E3
GUARANTEES etc.

E4
OTHER MATTERS

THE SURVEY

PLEASE READ THESE NOTES

F: SUMMARY

Assuming that you decide to proceed with the purchase of this Property, there may be some things on which you should take action *before you exchange contracts* – such as obtaining competitive quotations for urgent repairs. (If any further investigation of some urgent matter is recommended, this will involve a second visit to the Property, perhaps by an appropriate specialist who will submit a separate report.)

F1
ACTION

- Copy of Report to Legal Advisers
- Urgent repair
- Further investigation

F2
MAINTENANCE CONSIDERATIONS

F3
OTHER CONSIDERATIONS

THE SURVEY

PLEASE READ THESE NOTES

G: VALUATION

In arriving at the opinion of the Property's Open Market Value as defined in Section D2 of the *Description of the HOMEBUYER Service* (attached), a set of standard assumptions* is adopted, subject to any change stated below. Legal Advisers, and others who undertake property conveyancing, should be familiar with the assumptions and are responsible for checking those concerning legal matters. *The opinion of the Open Market Value given below could be affected by the outcome of the inquiries by your Legal Advisers [Section E] and/or any further investigation and quotations for urgent repairs [Section F]. The valuation assumes that your Legal Advisers will obtain satisfactory replies to their inquiries relating to the assumptions made in this Report.*

G1
OPEN MARKET VALUE

G2
INSURANCE COVER
[REINSTATEMENT COST]

- This Report is provided in accordance with the terms of the *Description of the HOMEBUYER Service* previously supplied, subject to any agreed addition noted below. (An additional copy is attached herewith.)
- The Report is solely for your use and your professional advisers', and no liability to anyone else is accepted. Should you not act upon specific, reasonable advice contained in this Report, no responsibility is accepted for the consequences.
- I hereby certify that the Property has been inspected by me and that I have prepared this Report, including the opinion of Open Market Value.

SIGNATURE

SURVEYOR'S NAME AND PROFESSIONAL QUALIFICATIONS

NAME AND ADDRESS OF SURVEYOR'S ORGANISATION

DATE OF REPORT

AGREED ADDITION (IF ANY) TO THE *DESCRIPTION OF THE SERVICE*

* Full details of these assumptions are available from the Surveyor. The most important are, in brief:

concerning the materials, construction, services, fixtures and fittings, etc., that:

- No significant defects or cause to alter the valuation would be revealed by an inspection of those parts which have not been inspected;
- No harardous or damaging materials or building techniques have been used in the Property; there is no contamination in or from the ground; and the ground is not land-filled;
- The Property is connected to, and there is the right to use, the reported main services; and
- The valuation takes no account of furnishings, removable fittings and sales incentives of any description.

concerning legal matters, that:

- The Property is sold "with vacant possession" (i.e. only you will be entitled to occupy it when it is sold);
- No laws are broken by the condition of the Property or by its present or intended use;
- The Property is not subject to any particular troublesome or unusual restrictions; it is not affected by any problems which would be revealed by the usual legal inquiries; and all necessary planning permissions and building regulations consents (including consents for alterations) have been obtained and complied with; and
- The Property has the right to use the main services on normal terms; and the sewers, main services and roads giving access to the Property have been "adopted" (i.e. are under local authority, not private, control).

Description of the HOMEBUYER Service

A The Service

A1 The HOMEBUYER Service comprises:

- an Inspection of the Property (Section B below)
- a concise Report based on the Inspection (Section C)
- the Valuation, which is part of the Report (Section D)

A2 The Surveyor's main objective in the HOMEBUYER Service is to give Clients considering buying a particular Property the professional advice which will assist them:

- to make a reasoned and informed judgement on whether or not to proceed with the purchase
- to assess whether or not the Property is a reasonable purchase at the agreed price
- to be clear what decisions and actions should be taken before contracts are exchanged.

A3 The HOMEBUYER Service therefore covers the general condition of the Property and particular features which affect its present value and may affect its future resale. The Report focuses on what the Surveyor judges to be urgent or significant matters. *Significant matters are those which, typically, in negotiations over price would be reflected in the amount finally agreed.*

B The Inspection

B1 The Inspection is a general surface examination of those parts of the Property which are accessible: in other words, *visible and readily available for examination from ground and floor levels, without risk of causing damage to the Property or injury to the Surveyor*. Due care is therefore exercised throughout the Inspection regarding safety, practicality and the constraints of being a visitor to the Property (which may be occupied). So furniture, floor coverings and other contents are not moved or lifted; and no part is forced or laid open to make it accessible.

B2 The services are inspected (except, in the case of flats, for drainage, lifts and security systems), but the Surveyor does not test or assess the efficiency of electrical, gas, plumbing, heating or drainage installations, or compliance with current regulations, or the internal condition of any chimney, boiler or other flue. Also, the Surveyor does not research the presence (or possible consequences) of contamination by any harmful substance. However, if a problem is suspected in any of these areas, advice is given on what action should be taken.

B3 Where necessary, parts of the Inspection are made from adjoining public property. Such equipment as a dampmeter, binoculars and torch may be used. A ladder is used for hatches and also for flat roofs not more than three metres above ground level. Leisure facilities and non-permanent outbuildings (such as pools and timber sheds) are noted but not examined. In the case of flats, exterior surfaces of the building containing the Property, as well as its access areas, are examined in order to assess their general condition; roof spaces are inspected if there is a hatch within the flat.

C The Report

C1 The Report provides the Surveyor's opinion of those matters which are urgent or significant and need action or evaluation by the Client before contracts are exchanged. It incudes some or all of the following:

- *urgent repairs* (e.g. gas leak; defective chimney stacks) – for which the Client should obtain quotations where appropriate
- *significant matters requiring further investigation* where essential (e.g. suspected subsidence) – for which the Client should obtain (and may have to pay for) reports and quotations from suitable contractors
- *significant but not urgent repairs and renewals* (e.g. new covering for flat roof before long)
- *other significant considerations* (e.g. some potential source of inconvenience) which the Surveyor wishes to draw to the attention of the Client
- *legal matters* (e.g. a possible right of way) which the Client should instruct the Legal Advisers to include in their inquiries.

C2 Matters assessed as not urgent or not significant are outside the scope of the HOMEBUYER Service and are generally not reported; however, other matters (such as safety) are reported where the Surveyor judges this to be helpful and constructive. If a part or area normally examined is found to be not accessible during the Inspection, this is reported; if a problem is suspected, advice is given on what action should be taken.

C3 The Report is in a standard format arranged in the following sequence: *Introduction & Overall Opinion*; *The Property & Location*; *The Building*; *The Services & Site*; *Legal and & Other Matters*; *Summary*; *Valuation*. In the case of leaseholds, the Report is accompanied by a standard appendix called *Leasehold Properties*.

D The Valuation and Reinstatement Cost

D1 The last section of the Report contains the Surveyor's opinion both of the Open Market Value of the Property and of the Reinstatement Cost, as defined below.

D2 "Open Market Value" *is the best price at which the sale of an interest in property would have been completed unconditionally for cash consideration on the date of valuation.* In arriving at the opinion of the Open Market Value, the Surveyor also makes various standard assumptions covering, for example: vacant possession; tenure and other legal considerations; contamination and hazardous materials; the condition of uninspected parts; the right to use mains services; and the exclusion of curtains, carpets, etc., from the valuation. (If required, details are available from the Surveyor.) Any additional assumption, or any found not to apply, is reported.

D3 "Reinstatement Cost" *is an estimate for insurance purposes of the current cost of rebuilding the Property in its present form,* unless otherwise stated. This includes the cost of rebuilding the garage and permanent outbuildings, site clearance and professional fees, but excludes VAT (except on fees).

LEASEHOLD PROPERTIES

Appendix to the HOMEBUYER Report

PLEASE NOTE: *This Appendix is an integral part of the HOMEBUYER Report for all Leasehold Properties.*

Everybody planning to buy a Leasehold property (most flats and maisonettes and a few other properties are Leasehold) is advised to pay particular attention to the terms of the Lease.

Your Legal Advisers, who are responsible for checking the Lease for you, do not normally see the Property – so it is only the Surveyor who has the opportunity to note any specific features which may have legal implications.

Any such matters are reported in Section E: Legal & Other Matters (which you are advised to pass a copy of the Report immediately to your Legal Advisers).

In arriving at the opinion of the Open Market Value of the Property (Section G: Valuation), unless otherwise stated the Surveyor assumes that all the terms of the Lease which might have an effect on the value of the Property are standard ones*, and that only a small ground rent is payable. This should not be relied upon, however, without being checked by your Legal Advisers.

You are advised to ask your Legal Advisers to supply the answers to the following questions:

a) Are the other flats occupied by owners or tenants?

b) Is there a Management Company and/or Managing Agent correctly set up to deal with the running and maintenance of the block containing the Property?

c) Does a suitable annual maintenance and replacement fund exist, with suitable reserves, to deal with general cleaning, maintenance and repair of the common parts, and repairs to the main structure, centralised heating installation, lifts, etc?

d) What is the ground rent; what sum was last paid as a maintenance/service charge, and what period did it cover; and are the maintenance/service charge accounts satisfactory and up-to-date?

e) Is there evidence of regular maintenance of services; and are there satisfactory current certificates for the testing/servicing/maintenance of the following common services: (1) the lifts; (2) the fire escapes and fire alarms; (3) the security system(s); (4) any common water/heating system; and (5) other communal facilities?

f) Are there any existing or foreseeable management problems or disputes, or any known outstanding repairs or programmed works, which would affect the level of the service/maintenance charge payable?

g) Is the liability clearly set out – as between the Leaseholders, the Freeholder and the Management Company – for repairs to the Property and to the common parts and the main structure; is the liability shared equally between Leaseholders; and is there suitable machinery for settling any disputes which may arise in this area?

h) Is it the Management Company or each individual Leaseholder who is responsible for the building insurance, and is there a block insurance policy?

i) Are there any unusual restrictions on the sale of the Property?

---

* Full details of these assumptions are available from the Surveyor. The most important are, in brief:

- If there are more than six properties in the building, the Property is managed either directly by the freeholder or by a professional managing agent;
- If there is more than one block in the development, the Lease terms apply (except for upkeep of common roads, paths, grounds and services) only to the block containing the Property;
- There are rights of access and exit over all communal roadways, corridors, stairways, etc., and to use communal grounds, parking areas and other facilities;
- Where there is more than one Leaseholder, all the Leases are the same in all important respects;
- The Lease has no particularly troublesome or unusual restrictions;
- There is no current dispute over the Lease or any outstanding claim or lawsuit concerning it;
- The unexpired term of the Lease is 70 years;
- The Property is fully insured.

STANDARD TERMS OF ENGAGEMENT

PLEASE NOTE: *These Standard Terms of Engagement form part of the contract between the Surveyor and the Client.*

A modified form of the Homebuyer Survey & Valuation Service applies in Scotland.

PART 1:
GENERAL

1 **The Service**. The standard HOMEBUYER Survey & Valuation Service ("the Service") which is described in Part 2 of these Terms ("the Description") applies unless an addition to the Service is agreed in writing before the Inspection. (An example of such an addition is reporting upon parts which are not normally inspected, such as the opening of all windows.)

2 **The Surveyor** who provides the Service will be a Chartered Surveyor, or a Fellow or Associate of the Incorporated Society of Valuers and Auctioneers, who is competent to survey, value and report upon the Property which is the subject of these Terms.

3 **Before the Inspection**. The Client will inform the Surveyor of the agreed price for the Property and of any particular concerns (such as plans for extension) which he or she may have about the Property.

4 **Terms of payment**. The Client agrees to pay the fee and any other charges agreed in writing.

5 **Cancellation**. The Client will be entitled to cancel this contract by notifying the Surveyor's office at any time before the day of the Inspection. The Surveyor will be entitled not to proceed with the provision of the Service (and will so report promptly to the Client) if, after arriving at the Property, he or she concludes:

a) that it is of a type of construction of which he or she has sufficient specialist knowledge to be able to provide the Service satisfactorily; or

b) that it would be in the typical Client's best interests to be provided with a Building Survey, plus valuation, rather than the HOMEBUYER Service.

In case of cancellation, the Surveyor will refund any money paid by the Client for the Service, except for expenses reasonably incurred. In the case of cancellation by the Surveyor, the reason will be explained to the Client.

6 **Liability**. The Report provided is solely for the use of the Client and the Client's professional advisers, and no liability to anyone else is accepted. Should the Client not act upon specific, reasonable advice contained in the Report, no responsibility is accepted for the consequences.

PART 2:
DESCRIPTION OF THE HOMEBUYER SERVICE
overleaf

Description of the HOMEBUYER Service

A The Service

A1 The HOMEBUYER Service comprises:

- an Inspection of the Property (Section B below)
- a concise Report based on the Inspection (Section C)
- the Valuation, which is part of the Report (Section D)

A2 The Surveyor's main objective in the HOMEBUYER Service is to give Clients considering buying a particular Property the professional advice which will assist them:

- to make a reasoned and informed judgement on whether or not to proceed with the purchase
- to assess whether or not the Property is a reasonable purchase at the agreed price
- to be clear what decisions and actions should be taken before contracts are exchanged.

A3 The HOMEBUYER Service therefore covers the general condition of the Property and particular features which affect its present value and may affect its future resale. The Report focuses on what the Surveyor judges to be urgent or significant matters. *Significant matters are those which, typically, in negotiations over price would be reflected in the amount finally agreed.*

B The Inspection

B1 The Inspection is a general surface examination of those parts of the Property which are accessible: in other words, *visible and readily available for examination from ground and floor levels, without risk of causing damage to the Property or injury to the Surveyor*. Due care is therefore exercised throughout the Inspection regarding safety, practicality and the constraints of being a visitor to the Property (which may be occupied). So furniture, floor coverings and other contents are not moved or lifted; and no part is forced or laid open to make it accessible.

B2 The services are inspected (except, in the case of flats, for drainage, lifts and security systems), but the Surveyor does not test or assess the efficiency of electrical, gas, plumbing, heating or drainage installations, or compliance with current regulations, or the internal condition of any chimney, boiler or other flue. Also, the Surveyor does not research the presence (or possible consequences) of contamination by any harmful substance. However, if a problem is suspected in any of these areas, advice is given on what action should be taken.

B3 Where necessary, parts of the Inspection are made from adjoining public property. Such equipment as a dampmeter, binoculars and torch may be used. A ladder is used for hatches and also for flat roofs not more than three metres above ground level. Leisure facilities and non-permanent outbuildings (such as pools and timber sheds) are noted but not examined. In the case of flats, exterior surfaces of the building containing the Property, as well as its access areas, are examined in order to assess their general condition; roof spaces are inspected if there is a hatch within the flat.

C The Report

C1 The Report provides the Surveyor's opinion of those matters which are urgent or significant and need action or evaluation by the Client before contracts are exchanged. It incudes some or all of the following:

- *urgent repairs* (e.g. gas leak; defective chimney stacks) – for which the Client should obtain quotations where appropriate
- *significant matters requiring further investigation* where essential (e.g. suspected subsidence) – for which the Client should obtain (and may have to pay for) reports and quotations from suitable contractors
- *significant but not urgent repairs and renewals* (e.g. new covering for flat roof before long)
- *other significant considerations* (e.g. some potential source of inconvenience) which the Surveyor wishes to draw to the attention of the Client
- *legal matters* (e.g. a possible right of way) which the Client should instruct the Legal Advisers to include in their inquiries.

C2 Matters assessed as not urgent or not significant are outside the scope of the HOMEBUYER Service and are generally not reported; however, other matters (such as safety) are reported where the Surveyor judges this to be helpful and constructive. If a part or area normally examined is found to be not accessible during the Inspection, this is reported; if a problem is suspected, advice is given on what action should be taken.

C3 The Report is in a standard format arranged in the following sequence: *Introduction & Overall Opinion*; *The Property & Location*; *The Building*; *The Services & Site*; *Legal and & Other Matters*; *Summary*; *Valuation*. In the case of leaseholds, the Report is accompanied by a standard appendix called *Leasehold Properties*.

D The Valuation and Reinstatement Cost

D1 The last section of the Report contains the Surveyor's opinion both of the Open Market Value of the Property and of the Reinstatement Cost, as defined below.

D2 "Open Market Value" *is the best price at which the sale of an interest in property would have been completed unconditionally for cash consideration on the date of valuation.* In arriving at the opinion of the Open Market Value, the Surveyor also makes various standard assumptions covering, for example: vacant possession; tenure and other legal considerations; contamination and hazardous materials; the condition of uninspected parts; the right to use mains services; and the exclusion of curtains, carpets, etc., from the valuation. (If required, details are available from the Surveyor.) Any additional assumption, or any found not to apply, is reported.

D3 "Reinstatement Cost" *is an estimate for insurance purposes of the current cost of rebuilding the Property in its present form*, unless otherwise stated. This includes the cost of rebuilding the garage and permanent outbuildings, site clearance and professional fees, but excludes VAT (except on fees).

CHOOSING BETWEEN SURVEYS

BACKGROUND INFORMATION AND ADVICE
from the Royal Institution of Chartered Surveyors and The Incorporated Society of Valuers and Auctioneers

Why do I need my own Survey?

The best way to reach an informed decision on such an important investment as a home is to have a professional survey and valuation of the property which interests you. Before you decide to go ahead and commit yourself legally, you can minimise the risks by asking a qualified surveyor to answer these questions for you:

- ***Is the agreed price reasonable?***
- ***Are there any drawbacks I don't know about?***
- ***If so, what do I need to do about them?***

Commissioning your own survey is the simple, economical way to avoid unpleasant – and perhaps costly – surprises after moving in. In some cases, the surveyor's report may enable you to renegotiate the price.

I already have a Mortgage Valuation report . . .

Even if you are seeking a mortgage – and may be paying for a Mortgage Valuation report – it is still advisable and prudent to arrange a survey by your own surveyor. The Consumers' Association *Which?* magazine and the Council of Mortgage Lenders both give this advice.

The reason is simple: the Mortgage Valuation report is prepared for the lender – *not for you, the borrower.* It answers only the lender's questions concerning the appropriate security for your loan. *You cannot rely on it to answer the questions which concern your personal interests.*

What choice of surveys do I have?

RICS and ISVA members also offer two forms of survey which are specifically designed to help homebuyers:

A Building Survey

(formally called a structural survey)

A Building Survey is *suitable for all residential properties and provides a full picture of their construction and condition.* It is likely to be needed if the property is, for example, of unusual construction, is dilapidated or has been extensively altered – or where a major conversion or renovation is planned. It is usually tailored to the client's individual requirements. The report incudes extensive technical information on construction and materials as well as details of the whole range of defects, major to minor.

The HOMEBUYER Survey & Valuation

(usually called 'The HOMEBUYER Service')

By contrast, The HOMEBUYER Service is *in a standard format and is designed specifically as an economy service.* It therefore differs materially from a Building Survey in two major respects.

♦ **It is intended only for particular types of home:** houses, flats and bungalows which are:

- conventional in type and construction
- apparently in reasonable condition.

♦ **It focuses on essentials:** defects and problems which are urgent or significant and thus have an effect on the value of the property – although it also includes much other valuable information.

The HOMEBUYER, unlike a Building Survey, provides not only a survey but also a valuation as an integral part of the Service.

What else should I know about the HOMEBUYER Service?

The Service – the inspection, the report and the valuation – are all explained in detail in the accompanying *Description of the HOMEBUYER Service*, but the highlights are:

♦ **This is an economy package.** Because of the practical limits on the type of property and on the scope of its coverage, *the HOMEBUYER Service is priced mid-range* – more expensive than a Mortgage Valuation, but less than a Building Survey.

♦ **The Surveyor's main objective in providing the Service** is to assist the prospective home-buyer to:

- make a reasoned and informed judgement on whether or not to proceed with the purchase
- assess whether or not the property is a reasonable purchase at the agreed price
- be clear what decisions and actions should be taken before contracts are exchanged.

CHOOSING BETWEEN SURVEYS

The surveyor also gives his or her professional opinion on the particular features of the property which affect its present value and may affect its future resale.

♦ **The concise report** covers the building inside and outside, the services and the site. It focuses on the defects and other problems which in the judgement of the surveyor are urgent or significant, but it also covers:

- the general condition and particular features of the property
- particular points which should be referred to the client's legal advisers
- other relevant considerations concerning, for example, safety, the location, the environment, or perhaps insurance.

Matters which are judged to be not urgent or not significant are in general *not* included in the report, but the surveyor will mention matters judged to be both helpful and constructive.

♦ **Where the client has a particular concern** – perhaps whether the property is suitable for a disabled person – the surveyor will keep this in mind during the inspection. Or, a specific addition to the Service – perhaps to the standard inspection – may be agreed between client and surveyor.

Where necessary, the surveyor may also be able to provide some extra service which is outside the scope of the standard package – perhaps providing a schedule of minor defects (for later discussion with a contractor), or arranging for the testing of mains services by suitably qualified specialists.

♦ **Where the client should take some action** before deciding to proceed with the purchase, this is signalled clearly in the text of the report and included in the summary of action and other key considerations.

The main features of the HOMEBUYER Service are compared below with those of a Building Survey:

	HOMEBUYER Survey & Valuation	**Building Survey**
Type of property	Conventional houses, flats, bungalows, etc., in apparently reasonable condition	Any residential or other property, in any condition
Type of service	Economy package in standard form	Custom-made to client's individual needs
Objects of service	To assist client to: (i) make an informed judgement on whether or not to proceed; (ii) decide whether or not property is a reasonable purchase at agreed price; and (iii) assess urgent and significant matters before exchanging contracts	To provide client with: (i) assessment of construction/ condition of property; and (ii) technical advice on problems and on remedial works
Special features	Focus on urgent and significant matters	Details of construction/materials/ defects
Valuation	Integral part of HOMEBUYER Service	Provided as agreed extra
Form of Report	Compact, fixed RICS/ISVA format	Usually much longer, in surveyor's format

Appendix V

THE RICS/ISVA HOMEBUYER SURVEY & VALUATION: HSV PRACTICE NOTES

PRACTICE STATEMENT 11

PS 11.1 REQUIREMENTS

Those who accept instructions to provide reports in accordance with the RICS/ISVA Homebuyer Survey & Valuation (HSV) Service ('the Service') must:

(a) satisfy PS 5.1.1 (qualification requirements) and be competent to undertake the surveys;
(b) fulfil the commissions in compliance with this Practice Statement, the Standard Terms of Engagement ('the Terms') including the Description of the Homebuyer Service ('the Description'), reproduced as Annex A to this Practice Statement, adopting without amendment the reporting headings and standard material reproduced in Annex B to this Practice Statement, and the Practice Notes in PSA 12; and
(c) add to the Service, as allowed for in Clause 1 of the Terms, only where a Client requires some addition to it and, subject to PS 11.6 below, such addition is capable of being reported upon within the HSV reporting format and does not alter materially the concept of the Service.

PS 11.2 APPLICATION

This Service must not be applied to property which is not used primarily for residential purposes or to a unit in a building not primarily used for residential purposes.

PS 11.3 RELATIONSHIP TO THE REST OF THE MANUAL

Other material in this Manual has no application to work pursuant to this Service, except:

(a) PS 4.2 (the definition and commentary on OMV);
(b) PS 6.2 (material considerations);
(c) paragraph 4.1 (valuation assumptions) of Annex A to Practice Statement 9;
(d) PSA 3.2 (radon) and PSA 3.7 (high voltage electrical supply apparatus); and
(e) GNA2 (recommendation for works in respect of listed buildings, etc.).

PS 11.4 BEFORE THE SERVICE IS PROVIDED

Before a legal commitment to provide the Service is entered into in respect of a specific property, the prospective Client must be provided with:

(a) the complete Terms in Annex A to this Practice Statement;
(b) a statement in writing of the other terms upon which the Surveyor is prepared to provide the Service, including the fee and any other charges reasonably incurred which would be payable, or the bases thereof, with a statement that these may have to be revised by agreement if the Client requires any addition to the Service as specified in the Description, or if it is found on arrival at the property that it is substantially different from what has been described to the Surveyor;
(c) if the Surveyor is not prepared to accept instructions to provide the Service in respect of particular types of dwelling, a statement to that effect in which those types are noted; and
(d) where the model descriptive material in Annex C to this Practice Statement is not used, a brief description of a residential building survey.

PS 11.5 ADDITIONS TO THE SERVICE

The Surveyor must confirm in writing, either before or at the time of provision of his Report, any agreed addition to the Service. As stated in PS 11.1(c), such additions must be capable of being reported upon within the HSV reporting format and not alter materially the concept of the Service. Such additions are likely to be more extensive inspection or investigation to address a particular concern of the Client.

PS 11.6 EXTRA SERVICES

This Service is designed for lay clients interested in obtaining an 'economy' professional service in which non-significant defects are in general not reported and where there is therefore an element of risk that defects will not be discovered which would be reported if testing and/or a fuller inspection had been undertaken. It is not permitted to report within the format minor defects which do not fall to be reported by virtue of paragraphs C1 and C2 of the Description. If a Client requires concurrently information or advice which is outside the concept of the Service (e.g. a list of 'non-significant' defects, tests of services, sales/marketing advice), this is a different, extra service which must be provided outside the Terms and the HSV reporting format.

PS11.7 COMPETENCE AND RESPONSIBILITIES

Particular attention is drawn to PS 11.1(a) above. This implies the possession of sufficient knowledge of the area in which the subject property is situated. It also demands adequate competence in the survey of the sorts of dwelling for which the Service is suitable. Subject to PS 11.4(c), the level of expertise required of the Surveyor is the same as for a building survey, albeit that the inspections may be more limited – as is the degree of detail and extent of reporting in respect of condition. These factors do not imply that the Surveyor can avoid expressing opinions and advice relating to condition which can be formed on the basis of the defined level of inspection. Reports should include caveats and recommendations for further investigation only when the Surveyor feels unable to reach necessary conclusions with reasonable confidence. In such cases it may be appropriate to provide the valuation on a special assumption as to the outcome of such further recommended investigation, or to defer providing the valuation until the results of such further investigation are available.

PS 11.8 APPLICATION TO SCOTLAND

PS 11.1–PS 11.7 and Annexes A–C to this Practice Statement apply to properties in Scotland subject to the amendments noted in Annex D to this Practice Statement.

Note to PS 11 for information: The RICS/ISVA Homebuyer Survey and Valuation Service may be provided only on the forms purchased from, or pursuant to a licence granted by, RICS Books.

> The text of the Annexes to PS 11 is not reproduced herein because they are published separately:
> Annex A: Standard Terms of Engagement*
> (published as *HSV: Standard Terms of Engagement*)
> Annex B: Reporting Headings and Standard Material
> (published as *HSV: Boxed Set of Reports* and *HSV: Leasehold Properties*)
> Annex C: Model Descriptive Material
> (published as *HSV: Choosing Between Surveys*)
> Annex D: Scottish Edition
> (available from March 1998)
> *However, three sections of Part 2 of the Terms are included:
> Section A: The Service (this page, below)
> Section B: The Inspection (annotated, pages 33–4)
> Section C: The Report (page 8)

PS 11 ANNEX A PART 2

A The Service

Description of the Homebuyer Service

A1 The Homebuyer Service comprises:

- an **Inspection** of the Property (Section B below)
- a concise **Report** based on the Inspection (Section C)
- the **Valuation** which is part of the Report (Section D).

A2 The Surveyor's main objective in the Homebuyer Service is to give Clients considering buying a particular Property the professional advice which will assist them:

- to make a reasoned and informed judgement on whether or not to proceed with the purchase
- to assess whether or not the Property is a reasonable purchase at the agreed price
- to be clear what decisions and actions should be taken before contracts are exchanged.

A3 The Homebuyer Service therefore covers the general condition of the Property and particular features which affect its present value and may affect its future resale. The Report focuses on what the Surveyor judges to be urgent or significant matters. *Significant matters are those which, typically, in negotiations over price would be reflected in the amount finally agreed.*

C The Report

C1 The Report provides the Surveyor's opinion of those matters which are urgent or significant and need action or evaluation by the Client before contracts are exchanged. It includes some or all of the following:

- *urgent repairs* (e.g. gas leak, defective chimney stacks) – for which the Client should obtain quotations where appropriate
- *significant matters requiring further investigation* where essential (e.g. suspected subsidence) – for which the Client should obtain (and may have to pay for) reports and quotations from suitable contractors
- *significant but not urgent repairs and renewals* (e.g. new covering for flat roof before long)
- *other significant considerations* (e.g. some potential source of inconvenience) which the Surveyor wishes to draw to the attention of the Client
- *legal matters* (e.g. a possible right of way) which the Client should instruct the Legal Advisers to include in their inquiries.

C2 Matters assessed as not urgent or not significant are outside the scope of the Homebuyer Service and are generally not reported. However, other matters (such as safety) are reported where the Surveyor judges this to be helpful and constructive. If a part or area normally examined is found to be not accessible during the Inspection, this is reported; if a problem is suspected, advice is given on what action should be taken.

C3 The Report is in a standard format arranged in the following sequence: *Introduction & Overall Opinion; The Property & Location; The Building; The Services & Site; Legal & Other Matters; Summary; Valuation.* In the case of leaseholds, the Report is accompanied by a standard appendix called *Leasehold Properties.*

HSV PRACTICE NOTES* (PRACTICE STATEMENTS APPENDIX 12)

INTRODUCTION

These Practice Notes are concerned solely with what and how matters are to be reported in the Homebuyer Report. Although the Description defines what is or is not to be inspected as part of the Service (please see Annex A to this Appendix), this has nothing to do with *how* the Surveyor inspects a property.

The Surveyor has, of course, a duty of care and diligence and, if the Inspection reveals a cause for concern, nothing in the Description restricts or prevents the Surveyor from commenting on any such matter in addition to those covered therein.

*NB: The following abbreviations and short forms are used in these Notes:

DHS Description of the Homebuyer Service ('the Description')
HSV The Homebuyer Survey & Valuation Service ('the Service')
PN Practice Notes ('the Notes')
PS Practice Statement
STE Standard Terms of Engagement ('the Terms')

The focus of the Homebuyer Service and of the Report is on what are defined as 'urgent matters' and 'significant matters'. *It is taken as read in these Notes that the first consideration in recording items in the Report is to say what, if anything, is 'urgent' and/or 'significant'.*

These Notes concentrate on what other information it is (in a few cases, is not) appropriate to give under each heading and what, if any, action is to be advised.

The decision on whether or not to include particular items in the Report – that is, to determine which items are 'urgent' and/or 'significant', and which others are to be included for any of the other reasons specified in the Description and in these Notes (please see in particular Part 2.2d of these Notes) – can only be made by the Surveyor. He makes these decisions on the basis of his training, experience and knowledge, and he must be prepared to stand by them.

The basic principles on which the original House Buyers Report & Valuation was introduced in 1981 have not changed; rather, they are re-emphasised in the 1997 Homebuyer Survey & Valuation.

HSV SERVICE ESSENTIALS

The Surveyor is expected conscientiously to observe the spirit as well as the letter of PS 11 and of PSA 12 (these Practice Notes) in fulfilling each and every HSV commission. The essential elements are:

Re Practice Statement 11 (PS 11)

(a) overall, providing the HSV Service only:

- in compliance with PS 11; and
- observing the mandatory elements in PSA 12.

(b) in particular (interpreting specific elements of PS 11) providing the HSV Service only:

- where the Surveyor is competent to do so; and
- within the agreed Standard Terms of Engagement, incorporating the standard Description of the Service, except where additions fall within the concept and parameters of the Service and are agreed in advance.

Re the Description of the Homebuyer Service (DHS) and the Report

(i) the satisfactory fulfilment of each of the professional objectives specified in paragraphs A2 and A3 of the DHS, including the provision of an Overall Opinion and, as and where appropriate, ACTION paragraphs;
(ii) the consistent application of the 'focus on what the Surveyor judges to be urgent or significant matters' as defined in paragraph A3 and expanded upon in paragraphs C1 and C2 of the DHS;
(iii) observance of the contents of the DHS;
(iv) use without variation of the contents of Annex B to PS 11: 'the reporting headings and standard material' – in other words, inclusion of the complete pre-printed content of the Report form; and
(v) conciseness in reporting.

PART 1: PURPOSE AND SCOPE OF THE HOMEBUYER SERVICE

1.1 The commitments

The Homebuyer Service is founded on a set of commitments made to the Client in the Standard Terms (particularly in the Description), some of these being reinforced in the Report in Section A: Introduction.

These commitments – most of which undertake to give advice, opinion and judgement rather than simple facts – are listed below. They spell out clearly and unambiguously not only what the Service will provide but also what it will not.

NB: References to paragraphs in the Description are given in the left-hand column; key phrases are in *italic*; terms marked (defined) are explained in Part 1.2 of these Notes.

The Service

A2 The Surveyor's main objective in the Homebuyer Service is to give Clients ... *the professional advice which will assist them*:

- to make a reasoned and informed judgement on *whether or not to proceed* with the purchase.
- to assess whether or not the Property is a *reasonable purchase* at the agreed price.
- to be clear about what *decisions and actions* should be taken before contracts are exchanged.

A3 The Homebuyer Service therefore covers the *general condition* of the Property and *particular features* which affect its present value and may affect its future resale.

STEI The standard Service applies unless an *addition to the Service* (defined) is agreed in writing.

The Inspection

B1 The Inspection is a *general surface examination* of those parts of the Property which are *accessible* ... (defined).

The Report

A3 *The Report focuses on what the Surveyor judges to be urgent or significant matters* (defined).

C1 The Report provides the *Surveyor's opinion* of those matters which are urgent or significant and *need action or evaluation* by the Client before contracts are exchanged.

C1 The Report includes some or all of the following:

- urgent repairs
- significant matters requiring further investigation
- significant but not urgent repairs and renewals
- other significant considerations
- legal matters.

C3 Overall Opinion

If a problem is suspected concerning any of the following, this is reported and advice is given on what action should be taken:

B2 • any of the services, or flues, or contamination

C2 • a part or area normally examined which is found to be not accessible during the Inspection.

C2 Matters *assessed* as not urgent or not significant are outside the scope of the Homebuyer Service and are *generally not reported*, but other matters (such as safety) are reported where the Surveyor *judges this to be helpful and constructive*.

The Valuation

D1 The ... *Surveyor's opinion* of the Open Market Value of the Property and of the Reinstatement Cost ... (defined).

D2 [Standard assumptions are made.] Any additional assumption, or any found not to apply, is reported.

Exactly how and where in the Report the Surveyor meets these commitments is detailed in Parts 2 and 3 of these Notes.

1.2 The definitions

These are the six terms which carry particular, defined meanings whenever they are used in the Homebuyer Report. They are used as defined throughout these Notes.

Urgent

Urgent matters are defects judged to be an actual or developing threat either to the fabric of the building or to personal safety. *[Section A: Introduction]*

A 'developing threat' is one where the first sign of defect is visible and the Surveyor judges that this is certain or likely to develop into an actual threat unless remedial action is taken.

Urgent matters do not have to be – and frequently are not – *significant*.

Please see also Parts 2.1, 3.1 and 3.2 of these Notes.

Significant

Significant matters are those which, typically, in negotiations over price would be reflected in the amount finally agreed. *[DHS–A3]*

The definition of 'significant' is crucial. It is essential to use this word in the Report solely as defined. (It is prudent to avoid completely the use of other terms such as major, important, serious, substantial and material.)

The word 'typically' qualifies the rest of the definition. The Surveyor uses his judgement – based on his training, experience and local knowledge – in order to interpret its application to each element of the definition, as it relates to the circumstances of the Property and the market conditions prevailing at the date of the

Report. A 'typical' negotiation may be taken as one in which the hypothetical parties are average for the type of property and have no unusual attitudes or requirements.

The legal advice which the Institution has received on the use of 'significant' is:

> 'It is essential for both the Surveyor and the Client to have a clear understanding of the matters that may affect the price to be paid, and the use of a single term will undoubtedly focus their minds on all such matters.
>
> The word '*significant*' is immediately recognisable by the Client but still retains an important element of subjective impression on the part of the Surveyor.'

Please see also Parts 3.1 and 3.2 of these Notes.

Accessible

> ... in other words: **visible and readily available for examination from ground and floor levels, without risk of causing damage to the Property or injury to the Surveyor.** *[DHS–B1]*
>
> Due care is therefore exercised throughout the Inspection regarding safety, practicality and the constraints of being a visitor to the Property (which may be occupied). So furniture, floor coverings and other contents are not moved or lifted; and no part is forced or laid open to make it accessible. *[DHS–B1]*
>
> Where necessary, parts of the Inspection are made from adjoining public property. Such equipment as a damp-meter, binoculars and torch may be used. A ladder is used for hatches and also for flat roofs not more than three metres above ground level. *[DHS–B3]*

The other limitations on the Inspection relate to competence or economy rather than to accessibility. Please see also Annex A to these Notes.

Addition to the Service

> **... agreed in writing before the Inspection. (An example of such an addition is reporting upon parts which are not normally inspected, such as the opening of all windows.)** *[STE Clause 1]*

For further definition and examples of 'additions' (and of 'extra services'), please see also Part 2.2f and Annex D to these Notes.

Open Market Value

> is **the best price at which the sale of an interest in property would have been completed unconditionally for cash consideration on the date of valuation.** *[DHS–D2]*

This is the standard definition: PS 4.2 applies. Please see also Part 3.5 of these Notes.

Reinstatement Cost

> is **an estimate for insurance purposes of the current cost of rebuilding the Property in its present form**, unless otherwise stated. This includes the cost of rebuilding the garage and permanent outbuildings, site clearance and professional fees, but excludes VAT (except on fees). *[DHS–D3]*

PART 2: INSPECTION AND REFLECTION

2.1 Primary duty

Within the parameters of the standard Inspection (Description, Part B), **the primary duty of the Surveyor is to identify**:

- *Urgent Matters* – non-significant as well as significant; and
- *Significant Matters* (please see definitions at Part 1.2 of these Notes).

These are spelt out for the Client in paragraph C1 of the Description (examples are as given therein):

(a) *urgent repairs* ... (e.g. gas leak; defective chimney-stack)
(b) *significant matters requiring further investigation* ... (e.g. suspected subsidence)
(c) *significant but not urgent repairs and renewals* ... (e.g. new covering for flat roof before long)
(d) *other significant considerations* ... (e.g. some potential source of inconvenience)
(e) *legal matters* ... (e.g. a possible right of way)

All matters under (a)–(d) are recorded in Sections B–D of the Report and are itemised in Section F: Summary.

All the above are matters which 'need action or evaluation by the Client before contracts are exchanged' *[DHS–C1]*. They are itemised below in accordance with where they appear in Section F: Summary.

(Matters under (e) above are recorded in Section E: Legal & Other Matters; please see Part 2.2e of these Notes.)

F1 ACTION ■ Urgent repair [2.1(a) above]

Any 'defect judged to be an actual or developing threat either to the fabric of the building or to personal safety' *[Section A – Introduction]* constitutes an 'urgent repair'. Please see also the note on this definition at Part 1.2 of these Notes, and Part 3.2.

Included under this heading are:

- all those 'essential repairs' which are normally covered in a Mortgage Valuation report (e.g. structural; timber defects; damp; water leak but *not* dripping tap; electrical installation upgrading);
- any other repairs, not necessarily significant, but judged to be necessary, or highly desirable, in order to bring the Property up to habitable condition (e.g. renewal of exterior cladding; renewal of defective plasterwork; extensive internal redecoration);
- safety matters which are *not* also significant (e.g. serious wear in fixed floor covering; visible broken power-point); and
- urgent and/or significant defects concerning the site (e.g. repair of defective drainage).

F1 ACTION ■ Further investigation [2.1(b) above]

- any further investigation judged to be necessary (e.g. movement; contamination); please see also Part 2.3a of these Notes.

F2 Maintenance Considerations [2.1(c) above]

- significant but not urgent repairs and renewals – covering any predictable major maintenance matters (e.g. general external redecoration); and
- a number of non-significant defects which in aggregate amount to a significant figure.

In such as case, the minor defects concerned do not need to be detailed in the Report. A general statement as to their nature suffices, and this is to be given at 'Other' in C5 and/or C6. Please see also Part 3.3d of these Notes.

F3 Other Considerations [2.1(d) above]

- significant considerations other than ACTION and future maintenance (e.g. apparent breach of building regulations; insurance);
- any inherent problem concerning the site, the location or the environment which the home-owner can do nothing about (e.g. dangerous access; pollution); and
- forewarning of any potential significant problem (e.g. future airport extension planned).

2.2 Further duties

Based on the standard Inspection, **the Surveyor's further duties are to establish:**

(a) the **basic facts** concerning the Property, its location and its environment
The Surveyor's 'sufficient knowledge' [*PS 11.7*] of the locality is critically important here. All this information is to be assembled in Section B of the Report.

(b) the **general condition** of the accessible elements of the Property
Where, subject to matters coming under Part 2.2d of these Notes, it is established that there is no visible evidence of an urgent or significant defect/problem in an element, any minor defects it may have are not reported. The only requirement is to establish the *general* condition of the element.

(c) the **particular features** of the Property
These are the key features which, in the opinion of the Surveyor, 'affect its present value and may affect its future resale' *[DHS–A3]*.

(d) the **other, non-urgent and non-significant considerations** which should be reported 'where the Surveyor judges this to be helpful and constructive' *[DHS–C2]*
Such matters as are within the concept of the Service and which it will be helpful and constructive to bring to the attention of the Client include:

- *reassurance* on any matter which the Surveyor judges might otherwise cause unnecessary concern to the typical Client (e.g. hairline cracks; old damp patches; isolated minor attack of wet rot);
- *possible upgrading* of sub-standard features (e.g. central heating; kitchen; bathroom);
- *maintenance tips* helping Client to avoid/reduce future problems (e.g. cleaning concealed gutters); and
- *a single, very concise example (in brackets)* of a minor defect in any specific element which is in fair or poor condition but contains no apparent urgent or significant defect. Examples are:

'The . . . is in fair condition; there is some disrepair (for example, . . .) but this is not significant.'

'The ... is in poor condition, but the extent of the disrepair (which includes ...) is not significant.'
All non-significant matters eligible for reporting can be reported only in Sections C and D. Please see also Part 2.3c of these Notes.

(e) the **matters with probable legal implications** which the Client should be advised to refer to his Legal Advisers for inquiry/response
All such matters are assembled at Section E of the Report. Any one of these may turn out to be urgent or significant or neither; at the time of compiling the Report, they are assumed to be urgent. Please see also Part 3.3e of these Notes.

(f) any **addition to the Service** which has been agreed
Matters defined in PS 11.5 as 'additions' to the standard Service are only to be included in the Report where the Surveyor is so instructed.
Services which are 'outside the concept of the Homebuyer Service' and are defined in PS 11.6 as 'different, extra services' are *not* to be included in the Report. Annex D to these Notes gives several examples of appropriate *additions* to the HSV, and of *extra services*.
It is up to the individual Surveyor to decide which, if any, additions and/or extra services he is prepared to offer, and to inform Clients accordingly – in the same way as with any limits he may place on types of property *[PS 11.4(c)]*. He may quote on an *ad hoc* basis, or offer a short menu of charges, or even in some circumstances make no extra charge for a simple addition.
The legal advice which the Institution has received on 'additions' is:

> 'The value of including additions to the Service is that the Client is told that the specified additions are not included in the Service. The inclusion of additions also helps with any assessment of the fairness or reasonableness of the limited service being provided, and should strengthen the argument that the Client had no inducement to agree to the more limited service provided under the standard Service.'

2.3 Conclusions

After reflective thought, **the Surveyor formulates his conclusions concerning:**

(a) the need, if any, for **further investigation**

> 'Reports should include caveats and recommendations for further investigation only when the Surveyor feels unable to reach necessary conclusions with reasonable confidence.' *[PS 11.7]*

The Surveyor will normally be able to make the basic decision that repair work – however large or small – is undoubtedly required. In such cases, his recommendation should be for an urgent repair.
It is an unnecessary complication to recommend for further investigation (e.g. by a contractor preparing a quotation) any matter which can satisfactorily be presented in the Report as an urgent repair. (On occasion, it may also cause the Client unnecessary expense.)

(b) the **action** which the Client should be advised to take before exchanging contracts
At the stage of formulating conclusions before starting to compile the Report, it is prudent to highlight in the site notes each ACTION item. This same process also, of course, identifies every item which is to be included in FI-ACTION. Please see also Parts 3.2 and 3.4 of these Notes.

(c) the items which, although noted during the Inspection, are **not to be reported**

It is also prudent to mark appropriately in the site notes any item which is not to be included in the Report.

> 'It is not permitted to report within the format minor defects which do not fall to be reported by virtue of paragraphs C1 and C2 of the Description.' *[PS 11.6]*

The contents of paragraph C1 have already been covered in Part 2.1 of these Notes (and, for legal matters, in Part 2.2e). The relevant part of paragraph C2 is:

> 'Matters assessed as not urgent or not significant are outside the scope of the Homebuyer Service and are generally not reported. However, other matters (such as safety) are reported where the Surveyor judges this to be helpful and constructive.'

The various types of non-urgent and non-significant matters covered by this commitment are specified in Part 2.2d of these Notes.
The legal advice received by the Institution on the inclusion of 'minor defects' is:

> 'We confirm our view that where a surveyor includes some minor defects within the Homebuyer Report, a Court would be entitled to find that he had assumed a more onerous duty to report on all minor defects, and he would therefore be at risk of a finding of negligence if he missed one such defect or a series of minor defects.'

Where a Client wants a list of minor defects, the Surveyor is free to provide this if he so wishes, but not within the Homebuyer Service. The provision of such a list is 'outside the concept of the Service', and is 'a different, extra service which must be provided outside the Terms and the HSV reporting format' *[PS 11.6]*. Please see Annex D to these Notes.

(d) the **Open Market Value** (OMV) and the Reinstatement Cost of the Property
In arriving at his opinion of OMV, the Surveyor should consider whether there is any special assumption which needs to be made; if so, this should be noted for inclusion in the Report. Please see also Part 3.5 of these Notes.
(e) the **agreed price** and whether or not this is reasonable
(f) the **future resale** of the Property and what particular features may affect this
The Notes relating to this pair of conclusions are at Part 3.6 of these Notes.

PART 3: REPORTING

The Report must fulfil all the commitments made to the Client in the Description and in Section A: Introduction. The Surveyor's attention is drawn particularly to Part 1.1 of these Notes, which lists all of these commitments.

3.1 Urgent and/or significant

The key features of the Report are designed to facilitate the fulfilment of the commitments to the Client, and all of them – significant matters; urgent matters and ACTION; and the Overall Opinion – relate to the objective given in paragraph A2 of the Description. Here the Surveyor is committed to giving Clients 'the professional advice which will assist them' in three ways:

- *to make a reasoned and informed judgement on whether or not to proceed with the purchase*

This is of course something which the Surveyor cannot do on behalf of the Client. He is seldom privy to the Client's priorities – and even if he were, he should not allow them to influence his judgement. He offers only his evaluation, on a detached and professional basis, of what he judges to be the key factors; that is, the matters judged to be urgent and/or significant.

He will further assist the Client greatly by keeping all his comments short and to the point, so that his Report is concise in fact as well as in theory. This is to avoid confusing and distracting the Client with jargon or unhelpful and unconstructive detail.

- *to assess whether or not the Property is a reasonable purchase at the agreed price*

The Surveyor provides his overall opinion of the Property, and of whether the agreed price is reasonable, at the start of the Report. Please see Part 3.6 of these Notes.

- *to be clear what decisions and actions should be taken before contracts are exchanged*

This point is echoed in paragraph C1 of the Description:

> 'The Report provides the Surveyor's opinion of those matters which are urgent or significant and need action or evaluation by the Client before contracts are exchanged.'

The Surveyor identifies all urgent defects/problems (whether or not also significant) and all significant defects/problems and features (positive as well as negative). He comments on each of these in the appropriate place in the body of the Report, and also includes each in headline form in the check-list in the Summary. Those which do not require action nevertheless need to be evaluated by the Client. Please see also Part 3.2 following of these Notes.

He also tags as ACTION those matters which require the Client to do something immediately, itemising all these under FI-ACTION.

In sum, the treatment of all urgent and/or significant matters in the Report is as follows:

1. **All matters identified as urgent** (whether or not also significant) are:
   - highlighted in the text of the Report with the ACTION tag; and
   - itemised briefly in the Summary at F1 only.
2. **All other matters identified as significant** are:
   - reported at the appropriate location in Sections B–C–D–E; and
   - itemised briefly in the Summary at F2 or F3 as appropriate.

3.2 ACTION

The most important reference to ACTION is in Section A: Introduction:

> **ACTION.** If – after reading and considering all the information and advice in the Report – you decide to proceed with the purchase, then there are probably some things on which you should take action at once. Each such item is highlighted in the Report with the word ACTION and is also listed in Section F: Summary together with advice on what to do next.

The Introduction also contains the following definition and advice:

> *Urgent matters* are defects judged to be an actual or developing threat either to the fabric of the building or to personal safety; it will be advisable to have these put right as soon as possible after purchase (in some cases even before).

For reporting purposes, all urgent matters are ACTION – and vice versa. They are either urgent repairs or matters for further investigation (please see Part 2.3a of these Notes). The rules governing ACTION paragraphs are:

1. The Surveyor is to tag *only* those matters which in his judgement require action by the Client before exchange of contracts.
2. The advice (not instruction) is to be given, after the description of the defect/problem, in a separate paragraph which is to commence with the word ACTION in capital letters and is to contain *only* this advice. (In cases where two or more items in a sub-section are urgent, it may be helpful to have only one ACTION paragraph covering them all.)
3. The paragraph is to be framed in terms of what the Client is to do – *not* in terms of the repair, etc., which is needed. Thus:

APPROPRIATE	INAPPROPRIATE
ACTION. You are advised to obtain quotations for replacing the chimney-stack. Please see Section F1.	Action. The chimney-stack is dangerous and must be replaced urgently.
ACTION. You are advised to arrange for a qualified contractor to test the electrical installation and quote for necessary work. Please see Section F1.	Action. The electrical installation is showing signs of age and needs to be upgraded.

4. Every ACTION item is to be listed in the Summary at F1: ACTION; please see Part 3.4 of these Notes, and also the sample paragraph at Annex E to these Notes.
5. The quotation from Section A: Introduction above concludes with the words: 'together with advice on what to do next'. In order to avoid unnecessary repetition, all general advice concerning how to take the recommended action is to be confined to a single but comprehensive statement at Section F1. (This is the reason for 'Please see Section F1' in the examples above.)

The legal advice received by the Institution relating to the treatment of ACTION matters in the HSV Report is:

> 'In our experience most claims arise from structural instability, roof or timber infestation problems. Of these, perhaps 75% are cases where the surveyor saw or noted some symptoms but then *failed to assess properly* their significance. Of these, in perhaps half of the cases the Surveyor gave advice in the report about the defects. However, *the advice was not clear* about the steps which the Client should take, and that advice *did not appear* in the summary/recommendations section.'

3.3 Sections B–C–D–E etc.

NB: Details on the contents of Section B, C and D and their subsections are given in Annex B to these Notes, in the form of an itemised list with introductory notes.

(a) COVER + SECTION A: Introduction + Overall Opinion

The Cover is to carry the following information:

- Property address (including postcode if available);
- Client name and address (the Client is the person to whom the Report is addressed; if the instructions come from the Legal Advisers, the Report is to be addressed to the Client, care of them);
- Inspection date; and
- Surveying organisation name and address.

The Overall Opinion at Section A cannot be written until the rest of the Report has been compiled. Please see Part 3.6 of these Notes.

(b) SECTION B: The Property & Location

At B1 (The Property), only the briefest description is required of the type and construction, the latter being confined to roof, walls and floors.

Listed Buildings etc.: No enquiries need be made to determine whether a building is Listed or located within a Conservation Area. However, if the Surveyor is aware that the Property is so classified, he must report this at B1 and refer there to further comment at Section E4 (Other matters): on this further comment, please see Part 3.3e following of these Notes.

All comment on the location and environment is to be confined to B2 (The Location) and is not to encroach on D3 (The Site).

Please see also Part 2.2a as well as Annex B and Annex C to these Notes.

(c) SECTION C: The Building

(i) C1–3 (Movement/Timber defects/Dampness): where a serious condition is revealed by symptoms in different parts of the building, these are to be brought together after the Inspection for reporting at the appropriate sub-section here.

Isolated cases of wet rot attack or damp are, if urgent, to be included in C2 or C3 (and therefore requiring an ACTION paragraph); if not urgent or significant, they are to be reported at the appropriate sub-headings in C5 or C6.

(ii) C5–6 (Exterior/Interior): in each of these sub-sections, the final item in the itemised parts/features list is 'Other'.
In the case of flats, these locations will always be used to report on the relevant common areas.
In other cases, they will be used only for exceptional items which do not sit comfortably under any of the other sub-headings (for example, 'minor defects in aggregate' – please see the passage on Section F2 at Part 2.1 of these Notes).

(d) SECTION D: The Services & Site
Concerning 'Other' in the itemised parts/features list at D1 (The Services), in the case of flats this location will be used for the common services.

(e) SECTION E: Legal & Other Matters

As explained to the Client in the Introduction to Section E in the Report form, the Legal Advisers are responsible for checking relevant documents. The Surveyor's role is to act as their eyes on the site.

The sub-headings at E1–4 are therefore only for the Surveyor to identify apparent and specific items with probable legal implications which the Client should ask his Legal Advisers to pursue (either in their necessary standard searches and inquiries or, where appropriate, with the vendor's advisers).

Examples of items which may arise under the four subsections are:

E1: Tenure (e.g. apparent tenancies; shared drives/boundaries; all leasehold matters)

E2: Regulations etc. (e.g. Listed Building, etc.; planning permission for an extension or loft conversion; roads; rights of way; drains/sewers liability; easements, servitudes, wayleaves)

E3: Guarantees etc. (e.g. central heating servicing record; possible advantage of taking over existing insurance)

E4: Other matters including legal (e.g. shared drive/boundary; flying freehold) but also any non-legal matter which does not sit comfortably anywhere else in the Report (e.g. Council Tax Band [if known]; leisure facilities; agreed addition).

If the Surveyor has cause to suspect that the Property is not freehold as assumed, he should consider advising that, if this should turn out to be so, the valuation and any action recommended will need to be reviewed.

Leasehold properties: The question to be addressed here is: Does the management company appear to be meeting its obligations and doing its job satisfactorily?

The Client is to be referred to the Appendix to the Report entitled 'Leasehold Properties', which is to be attached to all Reports on such properties.

The only exception to this rule is that of leasehold houses, where in most cases a paragraph along the following lines will be suitable:

(i) the Property is understood to be leasehold but the standard Appendix on leasehold properties (as promised in paragraph C3 of the Description) is not attached because in this case the lease is not likely to be common to other building owners and therefore may not involve the usual complications of management companies, service charges, etc.;

(ii) the Legal Advisers should be asked to confirm this assumption; if it is so, they should be asked also to confirm the level of rent, the unexpired term of the lease, and that the lease contains no unusual or troublesome clauses; and

(iii) the Client may also wish them to investigate the possibility of purchasing the freehold (which might be complicated).

The matter should also be referred to in the OMV statement at G1.

Listed Buildings etc.: If the Surveyor knows or suspects that the Property is Listed or located in a Conservation Area (please see Part 3.3b of these Notes), he should advise at E4 that:

(i) the Client should discuss the various implications of ownership with his Legal Advisers; and

(ii) if and when repair work is required, the Client should seek advice from someone with appropriate specialist knowledge.

If an urgent repair or further investigation is indicated, this should be recommended in the normal way, but accompanied by the advice given above.

If, exceptionally, the Surveyor is himself competent to give such advice, this would need to be treated as an 'extra service' – please see Part 2.2f and Annex D to these Notes. GNA 2 in the *Appraisal and Valuation Manual* is also relevant.

E4 – Other Matters: ACTION. The Client should be advised, in an ACTION paragraph here that – if he is minded to proceed – he should immediately pass a copy of the Report to his Legal Advisers and ask them to confirm that they will check:

- not only each of the items raised in this Section
- but also the standard assumptions concerning legal matters made in arriving at the opinion of the Open Market Value.

3.4 Section F: Summary

The principal function of the Summary is to provide:

- a checklist of all the urgent and/or significant matters reported in Sections B–D; and
- advice on how to take any action recommended.

The Summary therefore:

- does NOT contain any items which have not already been reported upon;
- does NOT contain additional description of any kind; and
- does NOT contain any opinion of the Property, its value, or the agreed price.

It is most important that the checklist of urgent and/or significant matters should:

- contain every ACTION item reported in Sections B–D (care must be taken to ensure that no item is overlooked); and
- be concise, give the sub-section reference, and be consistent in style.

F1: ACTION

(a) The Client is to be advised first that – if he intends to proceed – he should:

- immediately send a copy of the Report to his Legal Advisers; and
- draw their attention particularly to the ACTION paragraph at Section E4.

(b) Each ACTION paragraph in Sections C and D is to be listed here, giving the sub-section reference and a very brief description in headline form, e.g.

APPROPRIATE LISTING	INAPPROPRIATE LISTING
C1: investigation of cracking at rear	The SW corner foundations need to be opened up.
C5: chimney-stack replacement	The chimney-stack is in urgent need of replacement.
D1: electrical installation	The electrical installation needs to be upgraded.

This list may include matters for further investigation together with urgent repairs: one list, arranged in the reporting sequence, is simpler than two.

(c) The summary list should be preceded by a paragraph to the effect that:

- the Client is advised to commission a suitable contractor to provide a quotation for each of the items in the following list, as soon as possible (together with the Surveyor's advice, as seems appropriate, on how best to do this); and
- any recommendation requiring work to be done should be treated as urgent after purchase.

(d) The summary list should be followed by a paragraph to the effect that:

- the quotations received and/or the findings of the Legal Advisers' inquiries might give the Surveyor cause to amend the valuation and/or some particular advice contained in the Report; and
- the Client may therefore wish to contact the Surveyor as soon as he receives the relevant quotations/reports.

The Surveyor may also choose to emphasise the disclaimer given in Clause 6 of the Standard Terms of Engagement.

(e) The Surveyor will of course add any further comment or advice required by the special circumstances of a particular survey.

Examples of paragraphs for Section F1 are given at Annex E to these Notes.

F2: Maintenance Considerations

These are future maintenance matters – not for ACTION but nevertheless significant. Examples are given at Part 2.1 of these Notes.

Any recommendation made in Sections C or D for significant future repairs and renewals (including 'minor defects in aggregate') is to be noted here in headline form as in F1.

F3: Other Considerations

These are significant, or potentially significant, matters other than ACTION or future maintenance which have been raised earlier (e.g. concerns such as marketing, insurance or environmental factors). They are to be noted here in headline form as in F1. Examples are given at Part 2.1 of these Notes.

Occasionally it may be appropriate to advise that some particular action (perhaps keeping briefed on plans for a nearby major public project) should be taken after purchase. Because the matter is not urgent in the defined sense, such advice given in the text should be noted under this F3 heading, rather than being tagged ACTION and included in F1 above.

3.5 Section G: Valuation

G1: Open Market Value

> The Surveyor makes various standard assumptions ... Any additional assumption, or any found not to apply, is reported. *[DHS–D2]*
> In arriving at the opinion of the OMV ... , a set of standard assumptions is adopted, subject to any change stated below. *[Introduction to Section G]*

As noted in Part 2.3d of these Notes, the Surveyor is to report any special assumptions made in arriving at his opinion of the Open Market Value (OMV).

Excluding those concerning legal matters (on which the Legal Advisers should comment), the assumptions and exclusions noted both in the Description and in the footnote to Section G (and which many Clients will therefore be aware of) are:

- contamination and hazardous materials;
- condition of uninspected parts;
- exclusion of curtains, carpets, etc.; and
- right to use the mains services reported.

As noted in PS 11.3, the other *Appraisal and Valuation Manual* material which applies is:

- PS 4.2 (the definition and commentary on OMV); and
- Annex A to PS 9, paragraph 4.1 (valuation assumptions).

The standard reporting material states that full details of the valuation assumptions are available from the Surveyor. Permission is hereby given to reproduce or photocopy paragraph 4.1 of Annex A to PS 9 for the purpose of meeting requests for this detail.
The Surveyor's statement in the Report of his opinion of the OMV is to include the following:

(i) whether the Property is valued as freehold or as leasehold;
(ii) the date of the valuation;
(iii) any change to the assumptions (as noted above);
(iv) that the value is that of the Property in its present condition; and
(v) the amount (to be given in words as well as in figures).

Please see the sample paragraph at Annex E to these Notes.
In cases where 'the Surveyor feels unable to reach necessary conclusions with reasonable confidence' and includes in the Report a caveat or recommendation for further investigation, 'it may be appropriate to provide the valuation on a special assumption as to the outcome of such further recommended investigation, or to defer providing the valuation until the results of such further investigation are available.' *[PS 11.7]*
Where significant repairs are recommended, the Surveyor may wish to assist the Client further by providing also a 'when repaired' valuation.

G2: **Insurance Cover** [Reinstatement Cost]

The Surveyor's statement of his opinion of the Reinstatement Cost is to include the substance of the following:

(i) that the current cost of reinstating the Property in its present form is estimated for insurance purposes to be approximately ... (the amount to be given in words as well as in figures);
(ii) that the estimated external area of the accommodation is approximately ... (the area to be given in square metres);

and, in the case of flats, maisonettes and other such Leasehold properties:

(iii) that the estimate is made on the assumption that the Property is insured under a satisfactory policy covering the whole building.

The Surveyor is to have regard to the ABI/BCIS House Rebuilding Cost Index (Association of British Insurers/Building Cost Information Service).

3.6 Section A: Overall Opinion

The commitment to the Client on the Overall Opinion is made in Section A: Introduction in these terms:

> Below are the Surveyor's conclusions, in brief, on whether or not this Property is a reasonable purchase at the agreed price, and on particular features which affect its present value and may affect its future resale. The opinion takes no account of factors outside the scope of the Homebuyer Service.
>
> It is hoped that this overall view will help you to keep in perspective the detailed facts and advice which follow. You are asked to bear in mind particularly that it can be misleading to treat individual matters in isolation. So that you may use this Report to best advantage in reaching your decision on whether or not to proceed with the purchase of this Property, **you are most strongly advised to read and consider its contents as a whole**.

The Overall Opinion is the single most important element of all in the HSV Report to help the Client to reach his most important decision of all: whether or not to proceed with the purchase. It has two principal functions, as stated in the passage above:

- to provide the Client with the Surveyor's professional opinion on:
  - whether or not the Property is a reasonable purchase at the agreed price *[DHS–A2·2]*
  - the future resale of the Property
- to highlight the particular features which affect its present value and may affect its future resale. *[DHS–A3]*

The Overall Opinion is therefore:

- NOT a summary list of urgent or significant defects;
- NOT a description of the Property; and
- NOT the Surveyor's opinion of whether or not he himself would buy the Property.

Whereas the Summary is a checklist of ACTION, etc., combined with advice on what to do next, the Overall Opinion serves a completely different purpose.

It serves the same indispensable function as the large-type panel introducing a newspaper article. In other terms, it provides Clients with a brief, simple and clear signpost to help them to orient themselves as they prepare to embark on the Report. It is the only place in the Report for key general observations (including a concise description of the overall condition of the Property).

In short, the Overall Opinion at the beginning of the Report sets Clients off on the right road, looking in the appropriate direction. The Summary at the end provides them with the wherewithal to take the next steps.

The response to the question: 'Is this Property a reasonable purchase at the agreed price?' is likely to fall clearly within one of four basic groups:

UNQUALIFIED YES – QUALIFIED YES – NO – CANNOT SAY UNTIL . . .

A satisfactory opinion on price and resale cannot be given without reference to the effect on these of the Property's key features – positive or negative – and key defects, if any. It is *not* appropriate to mention all the matters classified as urgent or significant; the Surveyor should mention *only* those matters to which he feels the greatest weight should be attached, particularly in terms of future resale. (In themselves, the general condition and standard of maintenance of the Property may or may not be significant.)

So the four factors which must always be taken into account are:

AGREED PRICE – KEY FEATURE(S) – KEY DISREPAIR – RESALE

If the Surveyor has reason to believe that furnishings and/or removable fittings may have been included in the agreed price, he may consider it helpful to remind the Client that these have not been included in his opinion of the Open Market Value.

Occasionally, an additional factor may be included: the opinion that there may be legitimate grounds for renegotiating the price.

It is helpful to keep the Overall Opinion as concise as possible, excluding all extraneous detail. The space provided on the pre-printed form will be ample for all but the most exceptional circumstances.

Examples of Overall Opinions for various situations are given in Annex E to these Notes.

3.7 Other Matters

(a) Report: preparation sequence

The contents of the Report are arranged in the sequence which is understood to be the most acceptable to the average client.

For practitioners using the pre-printed form, this causes a minor problem in compiling the Report because in two cases the sequence of presentation does not match the sequence of preparation.

The first case is the Overall Opinion which comes first, at Section A, but cannot be composed until last; the second is Section C1–4 (Movement etc.), which cannot be composed until after the remainder of Section C plus Section D have been considered.

However, the problem is solved very simply by preparing Sections A and C1–4 out of sequence and then repositioning these two sheets when the printed Report is collated thus:

(NB: the page numbers given on the left below are those of the pre-printed report form.)

REPORT SEQUENCE	PREPARATION SEQUENCE
[1] A: Overall Opinion	–
[2]: B: Property & Location	B: Property & Location
[3] C1–4: Movement etc.	–
[4] C5: Exterior	C5: Exterior
[5] C6: Interior	C6: Interior
[6] D: Services & Site	D: Services & Site
–	[p.3] **C1–4: Movement etc.**
[7] E: Legal & Other	E: Legal & Other
[8] F: Summary	F: Summary
[9] G: Valuation	G: Valuation
–	[p.1] **A: Overall Opinion**

Within each section, the sequence of the standard reporting material – including the itemised parts/features listed under some sub-sections – is to be followed without variation. Additional items are to be added only where it is necessary to do so.

(b) Pre-printed report form design

In the pre-printed form, the itemised parts/features which appear under some of the sub-headings in the margin are solely for the benefit of the Client. Their purpose is to indicate only the broad scope of the particular element; they are quite inadequate for the purpose of taking site notes.

In the pre-printed form, the marginal lists of sub-headings are located at the top of the page and uniformly spaced, thus allowing maximum flexibility in the text area to accommodate the great variety of conditions encountered in different properties.

Only in very exceptional circumstances should there be a need for a continuation sheet.

(c) Property address

Space is provided for the Property address to be printed in short form – e.g. 23 Green Road – at the head of each page of the pre-printed form.

(d) Certification Panel (This is the panel, following Section G, which the Surveyor signs.)

Where an addition to the standard Service has been agreed, the Surveyor is to note the nature of the addition (in abridged form if necessary) in the space provided on the pre-printed form.

PART 4: SUMMARY

The practitioner offering the Homebuyer Service must observe the following:

1. **Compliance** with PS 11 and the mandatory elements of PSA 12 (see HSV Service Essentials)
2. The **commitments** made to the Client in the STE (see Part 1.1), including the use of specified terms in the senses defined (see Part 1.2)
3. The **primary duty** to identify and report urgent matters and significant matters (see Parts 2.1 + 3.1)
4. The **further duties** of establishing, within the limits of the standard inspection (see Annex A + Annex C):

   4.1 the basic facts, the general condition and the particular features of the Property (see Part 2.2a–b–c)
   4.2 the other, non-urgent and non-significant matters which should be reported if helpful and constructive (see Part 2.2d)
   4.3 matters with probable legal implications (see Part 2.2e)
   4.4 additions to the Service (but only in conformity with PS 11.1(c) and PS 11.5) and 'extra services' (see Part 2.2f + Annex D)

5. **Further investigation:** the circumstances appropriate to recommending a further investigation (see Part 2.3a)
6. **ACTION:** the signalling of urgent matters with the ACTION tag (see Part 2.3b + 3.2 + Annex E)
7. **Minor defects:** the conditions covering the reporting of only certain categories of minor defects (and see 4.2 of these Notes) (see Part 2.3c)
8. **Movement etc.:** the reporting of all relevant matters concerning movement, timber defects and dampness at sub-sections C1–2–3 (see Part 3.3c)

9. **Sections B–C–D:** the matters for reporting, both invariably and as particular circumstances require (see Part 3.3b–c–d + Annex B)
10. The conditions covering the **content and presentation** of:

    10.1 Cover information (see Part 3.3a)
    10.2 E: Legal (see Part 3.3e)
    10.3 F: the Summary (see Part 3.4 + Annex E)
    10.4 G: the opinion of the OMV (see Part 3.5 + Annex E)
    10.5 A: the Overall Opinion (see Part 3.6 + Annex E)

THE INSPECTION [DHS SECTION B]

Important: No wording in the DHS prevents the Surveyor from examining or commenting on any other matter if the Inspection reveals a cause for concern which, in his judgement, needs to be pursued.

Concerning 'following the trail', the relevant passage is from *Roberts v. J. Hampson & Co.*, in which Kennedy J. stated:

> 'As it seems to me, the position that the law adopts is simple. If a surveyor misses a defect because its signs are hidden, that is a risk that his client must accept. But if there is specific ground for suspicion and the trail of suspicion leads behind furniture or under carpets, the surveyor must take reasonable steps to follow the trail until he has all the information which it is reasonable for him to have before making his valuation.'

The 'reasonable steps' may include recommending further investigation, and the Description does not preclude the giving of such advice (but see PS 11.7).

The full text of the Description, Part B – The Inspection is reproduced below with explanatory notes where appropriate.

> **B1** The Inspection is a general surface examination of those parts of the Property which are accessible: in other words, *visible and readily available for examination from ground and floor levels* [1], *without risk of causing damage to the Property or injury to the Surveyor* [2]. Due care is therefore exercised throughout the Inspection regarding safety, practicality and the constraints of being a visitor to the Property (which may be occupied). So furniture, floorcoverings and other contents are not moved or lifted [3]; and no part is forced or laid open to make it accessible.

NOTES ON B1

1 This includes examination from staircases and within accessible roof voids and sub-floor areas. Individual timbers are not examined. Where sub-floor access is simply a trap, the inspection is restricted to the timbers and over-site visible from the trap on an 'inverted head-and-shoulders' basis.
2 The RICS publication 'Surveying Safely' applies.
3 This point is also made in the Introductions to Sections C5 and C6. Loose corners of carpets which can be lifted without use of tools may of course be lifted.

> **B2** The services are inspected (except, in the case of flats, for drainage, lifts and security systems), but the Surveyor does not test or assess the efficiency of electrical, gas, plumbing, heating or drainage installations, or compliance with

current regulations [4], or the internal condition of any chimney, boiler or other flue. Also, the Surveyor does not research the presence (or possible consequences) of contamination by any harmful substance. However, if a problem is suspected in any of these areas, advice is given on what action should be taken [5].

NOTES ON B2

4 Despite the standard valuation assumption that main services are connected (paragraph 4.1.7 of Annex A to PS 9), this is to be checked where possible. Note also that services are not to be turned on or off.

5 Where relevant, the Surveyor is to report appropriately.

B3 Where necessary, parts of the Inspection are made from adjoining public property [6]. Such equipment as [7] a damp-meter, binoculars and torch may be used. A ladder is used for hatches and also for flat roofs not more than three metres above ground level [8]. Leisure facilities and non-permanent outbuildings (such as pools and timber sheds) are noted but not examined. In the case of flats, exterior surfaces of the building containing the Property, as well as its access areas [9], are examined in order to assess their general condition; roof spaces are inspected if there is a hatch within the flat.

NOTES ON B3

6 Seeking permission to enter private property is at the Surveyor's discretion.

7 The list of equipment is not comprehensive. The Surveyor may, but is not obliged to, use other equipment at his discretion (e.g. tape, compass, meter-box key, inspection-cover lifter, spirit-level). The use of cameras, while encouraged, is discretionary. There is no objection to the use of machines for recording site notes.

8 Any further extent to which the ladder is used is – within the 'due care' provision at B1 above – at the discretion of the Surveyor.

9 **FLATS:** This definition means exactly what it says. It therefore excludes, for example, the roof space and roof of the building (unless, of course, either is directly accessible from the subject property).

REPORT SECTIONS B–C–D

On the following pages are checklists for each of the sub-sections in the Sections directly related to the Inspection, i.e. B (The Property & Location), C (The Building) and D (The Services & Site). They are arranged in the sequence in which the Report needs to be compiled:

(a) B1–2–3
(b) C5–6
(c) D1–2–3
(d) C1–2–3–4.

This is because the last four sub-sections cover general conditions, rather than specific areas or elements, of the Property:

Movement – Timber defects – Dampness – Insulation

They cannot therefore be compiled until all the evidence from the Inspection – both internal and external – has been assembled and assessed. Please see also Part 3.7a of these Notes.

All the items in the itemised parts/features lists (i.e. those preceded by the symbol ■) and all the items in CAPITAL LETTERS in the checklist should be mentioned, if only to say (in order to avoid any uncertainty) that there are none, e.g.

> Chimneys. The house has none.

All the items in lower-case (small) letters and all those followed by a question-mark only require comment if there is something to say which is urgent or significant or comes under the heading of 'helpful and constructive' (please see Part 2.2(d) of these Notes).

It is necessary to report under the appropriate sub-heading any suspected problem, and also to advise any appropriate action, concerning:

- any of the services; flues; contamination *[DHS–B2]*
- any part or area which the Surveyor would normally expect to examine but which he finds to be not accessible during the Inspection *[DHS–C2]* (please see also note (b) at sub-section B3 in this Annex).

It is important to make positive statements where there are no defects or problems, and to give brief reassuring comments where the typical Client might be alarmed e.g.

> The damp patch at the junction of the ceiling and two walls in the main bedroom is an old one; it will therefore not cause problems when the room is redecorated.

FLATS: All Notes in this Annex concerning flats are introduced thus: **FLATS:**

Matters coming under the general heading of 'common parts and services' are to be reported under the following sub-headings:

• common parts:		
• main external communal parts accessing the Property:	C5–Exterior	■ Other
• proximate grounds:	D3–The Site	–
• interior access areas:	C6–Interior	■ Other
• common services:	D1–The Services	■ Other

SECTION B: THE PROPERTY & LOCATION

B1 THE PROPERTY

■ **Type**
CONCISE DESCRIPTION/NO. OF STOREYS
FLATS: CONVERTED/PURPOSE-BUILT
No. of UNITS IN BLOCK
No. of FLOORS/FLOOR LEVEL

and age (approx. year built)
+ ORIENTATION

■ **Construction** (any detail at C5/6)
ROOF/WALLS/FLOORS only
Major alteration?/extension?/conversion?
Exceptional feature?
Flats: ROOF/WALLS only of BLOCK

- **Accommodation** – current use of rooms

- **Garage** (all detail at D3)
  Concise description; if none, state
  + Parking: on/off Site
  Difficulties?/restrictions?

  and grounds
  Garden/approx. extent
  Outbuildings (all detail at D3)
  Permanent/non-permanent
  + Leisure facilities?

B2 THE LOCATION

(a) Situation
Exceptional features?
FLATS: No. of Blocks in Development
(b) Access
Roads/Paths?
Difficulties?/restrictions?/traffic volume?
(c) Type of area
(d) Amenities
(e) Environmental etc.

Main features affecting use/enjoyment of Property:

(i) Physical factors?
e.g. flooding risk/contamination/exposed etc.
(ii) Character of neighbourhood?
e.g. signs of improvement/deterioration etc.
(iii) Sources of inconvenience?
e.g. crowds/noise/smell/pollution etc.
(iv) Special circumstances?
e.g. conservation area etc.

B3 CIRCUMSTANCES OF THE INSPECTION

(a) Weather

(i) at time of inspection
(ii) in preceding period?

(b) Limitations (Major only, where relevant)
Exceptional circumstances?
Occupied?/furnished?/floor coverings?
Roof space/under-floor space
(only if inaccessible or restricted to head/shoulders)
(c) **FLATS:** Extent of external inspection

SECTION C: THE BUILDING

C5 THE EXTERIOR

- **Roof structure**
  EXTERNAL AND INTERNAL
  TYPE/CONSTRUCTION: STABILITY
  CONDITION: STRUCTURE
  TIMBERS – general only
  Roof lights?/dormers?
  Underfelt?

  and covering
  TYPE/CONDITION
  Flashings + soakers?
  Ridges + hips?
  Valleys + outlets?

- **Chimneys**
  STACKS: CONDITION
  Pointing?/flashings?/pots?/finishes?

- **Rainwater fittings**
  TYPE
  GUTTERS/DOWNPIPES: CONDITION
  Concealed downpipes?/parapet gutters?
  External plumbing?

- **Main walls**
  WALLS: TYPE/THICKNESS (metric)
  CONDITION/EXTERNAL FINISHES
  Parapets?/party upstand walls?
  Bays?/balconies?/porches?
  FLATS: Walls of building containing Property
  GENERAL CONDITION of relevant area

- **External joinery**
  WINDOWS: TYPE(S)/GENERAL CONDITION
  DOORS: TYPE(S)/GENERAL CONDITION
  OTHER EXTERNAL JOINERY: GENERAL CONDITION

- **External decoration**
  EXTERIOR: TYPE(S)/OVERALL CONDITION
  Exceptional decoration procedures?

- **Other**
  NB: Use this for anything external requiring reporting which does not sit comfortably earlier in C5 (e.g. minor defects in aggregate)
  FLATS: MAIN COMMUNAL
  areas accessing subject property (walkways, staircases, etc.)

C6 THE INTERIOR

- **Roof space**
  CONDITION

Use/misuse?/flooring?/lighting?
FLATS: ONLY IF ACCESS within subject property

- **Ceilings**
  TYPE/CONDITION
  Plaster/other finishes

- **Floors**
  TYPE/CONDITION
  FINISHES/CONDITION
  SUB-FLOOR SPACE – if any accessible
  SUB-FLOOR VENTILATION – here if not at C3

- **Internal walls and partitions**
  TYPE/CONDITION
  Plaster/other principal finishes
  Existing structural alteration?

- **Fireplaces etc.**
  CHIMNEY BREASTS: CONDITION
  FIREPLACES: TYPE/CONDITION
  Structural support?
  Disused flues: ventilation?

- **Internal joinery**
  KITCHEN FITTINGS: GENERAL CONDITION
  DOORS/stairs
  BUILT-IN FITMENTS: GENERAL CONDITION

- **Internal decoration**
  INTERIOR DECORATIONS: OVERALL CONDITION
  Exceptional decoration procedures?

- **Other**
  NB: Use this for anything internal requiring reporting which does not sit comfortably earlier in C6 (e.g. minor defects in aggregate)
  Cellar: use/structure/condition
  ventilation?/lighting?/damp?
  Conservatory etc.: structure/condition

  FLATS: INTERNAL ACCESS AREAS: GENERAL CONDITION

SECTION D: THE SERVICES & SITE

D1 THE SERVICES

- **Electricity**
  MAINS SUPPLY?/CONNECTED?/OFF?/meter location?
  INSTALLATION: Unsatisfactory feature?
  NB: If not connected and if this has an effect on valuation, state at G1

- **Gas**
  MAINS SUPPLY?/CONNECTED?/OFF?/meter location?
  INSTALLATION: Unsatisfactory feature?
  NB: If not connected and if this has an effect on valuation, state at G1

- **Water**
  WATER: SOURCE OF SUPPLY?
  Stopcock location?/meter?
  PLUMBING: KITCHEN/SANITARY FITTINGS
  GENERAL CONDITION/Unsatisfactory feature?

- **Heating**
  WATER: TYPE/EXTENT/Unsatisfactory feature?
  SPACE: TYPE/EXTENT/Unsatisfactory feature?
  Boiler/balanced flues

- **Other**
  Safety: fire alarm?/fire escape?
  Security: entry?/intruder?/CCTV?
  Cable: available?
  Exceptional feature?

  FLATS: Existence/type of:
  COMMON SERVICES
  FIRE PRECAUTIONS
  SECURITY
  Refuse chutes/waste bin system
  LIFTS: passenger/goods/capacity/floors served/ service hoists

D2 DRAINAGE

RAINWATER: SYSTEM/GENERAL CONDITION
FOUL: SYSTEM/GENERAL CONDITION
Shared drainage?

D3 THE SITE

- **Garage**
  GARAGE: TYPE/CONDITION

  and outbuildings
  PERMANENT OUTBUILDINGS: TYPE/CONDITION

- **Grounds**
  Retaining walls
  Drives/paths
  Terrace/patio/steps
  Trees unless covered at C1

  and boundaries
  Boundary walls/fences/gates

SECTIONS C1–2–3–4: MOVEMENT ETC.

IMPORTANT

(a) These four sub-sections cannot be compiled until all the evidence – internal and external – has been assembled and assessed.
(b) **A positive statement of conclusions is to be made in each case.**

(c) Re C2–C3–C4: isolated cases which are not urgent or significant are to be treated under the appropriate sub-heading in C5 (Exterior) or C6 (Interior) – but see Part 3.3c(i) of these Notes.
(d) Repetition of points made in sub-sections C1–4 is to be avoided in C5/6 – although reference back may be helpful on occasion.
(e) **FLATS:**

1. *Re* C1–C2–C3: the condition both of the subject property and of the building containing it is to be reported;
2. Common parts: any problems are to be reported at Section E1 as matters for referral to the Legal Advisers;
3. Subject property: specific problems are to be reported in an ACTION paragraph at the appropriate sub-heading in C5 or C6.

C1 MOVEMENT – NB notes above

CRACKING: SETTLEMENT/SUBSIDENCE
CONDITION
Trees: any problematic?
If evidence of movement, consider distinction between:
foundational/above ground//long-standing/recent//
stable/progressive (if progressive, cause?)

C2 TIMBER DEFECTS – NB notes above

ROT/WOODWORM: CONDITION

C3 DAMPNESS – NB notes above

- **Damp-proof course**
  TYPE (Concealed?)/CONDITION
  GROUND LEVEL (*re* DPC/internal floor levels/adjoining property)
- **Rising and penetrating damp**
  DAMP: probable cause?/future risk?
  LEAKS to fabric/plumbing/rainwater goods:
  Treat all as Urgent Repairs in ACTION paragraph
  Evidence from old damp?
- **Condensation**
  VENTILATION: air bricks/sub-floor
  Sub-floor ventilation: likely consequences of inadequate SFV
  VENTILATION: ROOF SPACE
  Other areas of concern?
  FLAT ROOF (if any): VENTILATION REQUIREMENTS

C4 INSULATION – NB notes above

INSULATION: ROOF/CAVITY WALL
Double-glazing?
Plumbing/heating
Soundproofing?
All above: type/unsatisfactory feature?

IF MAIN WALLS SINGLE-SKIN: SHORTCOMINGS *re* damp/ventilation/insulation
SAP Rating? (if known)

CONTAMINATION ETC.

CONTAMINATION: GENERAL

The Surveyor's duty in respect of contamination is stated in the Description:

> The Surveyor does not research the presence (or possible consequences) of contamination by any harmful substance. However, if a problem is suspected ... advice is given on what action should be taken. *[DHS–B2]*

HAZARDOUS MATERIALS: ASBESTOS

If asbestos is found:

1. Note location and give general warning about the danger; and
2a. If immediate replacement is not considered to be necessary, this is to be stated, together with brief advice on the implications of disturbing the status quo; or
2b. If removal or oversealing is judged to be advisable, then the ACTION to be recommended is a further investigation by a specialist – with brief advice on how to find one, and noting the necessity of observing current Health & Safety regulations.

HIGH VOLTAGE ELECTRICAL SUPPLY EQUIPMENT

If the Property has, for example, a proximate sub-station or overhead power cables:

1. Consider the advice given in the *Appraisal and Valuation Manual* at PS 6.2.4(d) and PSA 3.7; and
2. Report at Section B2 and treat as Section F3 item (i.e. potentially significant, but no action and not a maintenance matter).

RADON

If the Property is situated in one of the areas designated by the NRPB (National Radiological Protection Board):

1. Consider the warning and recommendation given at PSA 3.2; and
2. Report at Section B2 and treat at Section F3 as a matter for inquiry by the Client after purchase (via the Environmental Health or Building Control Department of the local council).

ADDITIONS TO THE HSV SERVICE

Additions to the standard HSV Service, as specified in the Terms, Part 1: General, Clause 1, are to be included only if they:

1. are required by the Client *[PS 11.1(c)]*;
2. are agreed between the Client and the Surveyor before the Inspection *[PS 11.5 + STE 1]*;
3. are 'capable of being reported upon within the HSV reporting format' *[PS 11.1(c)]*; and

4. do 'not alter materially the concept of the Service' *[PS 11.1(c)]*

EXTRA SERVICES

Other services which do not meet the criteria for acceptable additions as specified at points 3 and 4 above – i.e. 'information or advice which is outside the concept of the Service' *[PS 11.6]* but which fall short of being in effect a Building Survey – are to be:

(a) 'provided outside the Terms and the HSV reporting format' *[PS 11.6]* (i.e. separately agreed and reported); and
(b) called not additions but 'extra services' *[PS 11.6]*.

Examples of both Additions and Extra Services are:

	ADDITIONS **to the standard HSV Service**	**EXTRA SERVICES** **outside the standard HSV Service**
DEFINING FEATURES	• are required by the Client and provided for in the STE	• are required by the Client but not provided for in the STE
	• are agreed before the Inspection	–
	• do not materially alter the concept of the Service	• are outside the concept and the Terms of the HSV Service
	• can be reported concisely within HSV reporting format	• must be reported in a separate document and charged separately
EXAMPLES	• inspection of part(s)/areas(s) not normally examined, e.g. – concealed roof surfaces, valley/parapet gutters – opening *all* windows – substantial outbuildings	• a list of 'non-significant' defects • arranging for testing of services • separate 'summary' of construction/ materials (i.e. an augmented version of HBSV Section B7, 1993 Edition)
	• general comment on plan for limited extension to property	• detailed comment on plan for extension to property
	• more extensive inspection of a flat's common parts/services	• scrutiny of site plan/boundaries (perhaps at the instigation of the Client's Legal Advisers)
	• more detailed information than normal on amenities/environmental matters	• scrutiny/advice on quotations/ reports • providing ERP/ERRP in addition to OMV • advice on sales/marketing

ACTION, VALUATION AND OVERALL OPINION: EXAMPLES

SAMPLE PARAGRAPH: ACTION

D1: The Services

Electricity. Connected to the mains supply; the meters and fuses are in a cupboard in the kitchen. Much of the installation appears to have been rewired in recent years, but there are some signs of poor alteration work.

ACTION. You are advised to ask a qualified electrical contractor to test and report on the whole installation, and to quote for necessary repairs and upgrading. Please see also our further comments at Section F1.

SAMPLE PARAGRAPHS: F1 – ACTION

Copy of Report to Legal Advisers. If, after reading and considering this Report, you intend to proceed with the purchase, you are advised to send a copy as soon as possible to your Legal Advisers. Please draw to their attention the whole of Section E and in particular the paragraph headed ACTION at Section E4.

Urgent repair. We recommend that you should treat the following matters – all discussed earlier in the Report – as urgent repairs, to be remedied as soon as possible after purchase.

C1: investigation of cracking at rear

C5: chimney-stack replacement

D1: electrical installation

You are most strongly advised to obtain competitive quotations from reputable contractors before you exchange contracts. As soon as you receive the quotations and report for the work specified above, and also the responses from your Legal Advisers, we will be pleased to advise whether or not they would cause us to change the advice or valuation which we give in this Report.

We must advise you, however, that if you should decide to exchange contracts without obtaining this information, you would have to accept the risk that adverse factors might come to light in the future.

SAMPLE PARAGRAPH: SECTION G – VALUATION

Open Market Value. In our opinion, the Open Market Value on *[state date]* of the freehold interest in this property, as inspected, was £100,000 (one hundred thousand pounds).

SAMPLE PARAGRAPHS: SECTION A – OVERALL OPINION

IMPORTANT. The sample paragraphs below are offered only as examples of appropriate comment on a variety of possible situations. *Their coverage is not comprehensive, and they are not intended to be copied verbatim.*

Surveyors form their own judgements on the price and the marketability of a property and of course express their opinion in their own carefully weighed words. The need is simply that the Surveyor should give his overall opinion on price and resale, with appropriate brief reference to the presence (or absence) of key features and disrepair.

Please read Part 3.6 of these Notes in conjunction with this Annex.

Below are examples of Overall Opinions which might be appropriate to the four basic groups noted in Part 3.6 of these Notes (unqualified yes – qualified yes – no – cannot say until . . .). As can be seen from the following table, there are many possible combinations of the most likely and distinctive conditions of the four elements of the opinion also noted in Part 3.6 of these Notes and repeated below (the neutral situation in each case being in *italic*):

1. Agreed price — *reasonable* – higher than reasonable
2. Key features(s) — positive – *none* – negative – very negative
3. Key disrepair — *none* – some – substantial
4. Resale prospects — good – *average* – problematic – very poor

A: **Unqualified Yes** The price is reasonable/there are no significant defects/drawbacks

Example A

We are pleased to advise you that in our opinion this Property is, on the whole, a reasonable proposition for purchase at the agreed price. We found no evidence of any significant defects or shortcomings, and we cannot foresee any special difficulty arising on resale.

B: **Qualified Yes** Because of price and/or other major factor; e.g.

Example B1 Reasonable price but significant defects

This Property is considered to be a reasonable proposition for purchase provided that you are prepared to accept the cost and inconvenience of dealing with the various repair/improvement works reported. These deficiencies are quite common in properties of this age and type. Provided that the necessary works are carried out to a satisfactory standard, we can see no reason why there should be any special difficulties on resale.

Example B2 Reasonable price but exceptional drawback

This Property suffers from the exceptional disadvantage that *[state nature of drawback concisely]*, and the agreed price reflects this. However, we must advise you that in our opinion it is likely to have an adverse effect on resale. We therefore urge you to consider with the utmost care whether you wish to proceed with the purchase.

Example B3 Overpriced and substantial disadvantages

This Property is considered to be a reasonable proposition for purchase provided that you are prepared to accept the cost and inconvenience of dealing with the various repair/improvement works reported. However, the agreed price is in our opinion too high, and you may wish to renegotiate it on the basis of the cost of the necessary repairs.

There is the further consideration that even if the works are carried out to a satisfactory standard, the particular disadvantage of *[insert concise description]* will remain. You may therefore find resale difficult even if market conditions are favourable at the time.

C: **No** Because of some basic flaw discovered during the Inspection

Example C

In our opinion this Property is not a reasonable purchase at the agreed price. This is because *[give reason concisely]*. We very much regret, therefore, that we must advise you that it would be most unwise to proceed.

D: **Cannot Say Until ...** e.g. necessary to await reports/quotations

Example D

This Property is in need of extensive remedial/modernisation works and we recommend that, if you wish to proceed, you should obtain further advice and quotations as discussed in the Report and listed in Section F.

Although our overall opinion on the Open Market Value of the Property would normally be given here, in this particular case it is not possible to do so because of the very substantial nature and extent of the proposed works. However, we will be pleased to give our opinion as soon as this additional information becomes available.

Index

References are to paragraph numbers.